SAP® R/3® System Administration

 PRESS

SAP PRESS and SAP Technical Support Guides are issued by
Bernhard Hochlehnert, SAP AG

SAP PRESS is a joint initiative of SAP and Galileo Press. The know-how offered by SAP specialists combined with the expertise of the publishing house
Galileo Press offers the reader expert books in the field. SAP PRESS features
first-hand information and expert advice, and provides useful skills for professional decision-making.

SAP PRESS offers a variety of books on technical and business related topics
for the SAP user. For further information, please visit our website:
www.sap-press.com.

Liane Will
SAP APO System Administration
Principles for effective APO System Management
2003, 240 pp., ISBN 1-59229-012-4

A. Rickayzen, J. Dart, C. Brennecke, M. Schneider
Practical Workflow for SAP
2002, 504 pp., ISBN 1-59229-006-X

Frédéric Heinemann, Christian Rau
Web Programming with the SAP Web Application Server
The complete guide for ABAP and web developers
2003, 528 pp., ISBN 1-59229-013-2

Horst Keller, Joachim Jacobitz
ABAP Objects. The Official Reference
2003, 1094 pp., 2 Volumes and CD Set
ISBN 1-59229-011-6

Helmut Stefani
Archiving Your SAP Data
A comprehensive guide to plan and execute archiving projects
2003, 360 pp., ISBN 1-59229-008-6

Sigrid Hagemann, Liane Will

SAP® R/3®
System Administration

Translation Lemoine International, Inc.,
Salt Lake City, UT
Copy Editor Nancy Etscovitz, UCG, Inc.,
Boston, MA
Cover Design department, Cologne, Germany
Printed in the Netherlands

ISBN 1-59229-014-0

Contents

3   Service and Support   73

4   Installation Concepts   95

5 Setting Up the System Landscape 123

6 Software Logistics 147

7   Client Administration   179

8   R/3 Users and Authorizations   211

9   Background Processing   257

10   Update   281

14 Maintaining Instances 379

15 System Monitoring 405

16 Monitoring Architecture 441

Foreword to the series of books

At SAP, our first priority is to ensure that the SAP software solutions in your enterprise run successfully and at a minimal cost. This "Lowest Cost of Ownership" is achieved with fast and efficient implementation, together with optimal and dependable operation. SAP Active Global Support is actively and consistently there to help you, with the new SAP Solution Management strategy. Throughout the entire lifecycle of a solution, SAP offers customers all necessary services, first-class support, a suitable infrastructure, and the relevant know-how. The new strategy is backed up by three powerful support programs: *Safeguarding*, or, in other words, risk management; *Solution Management Optimization*, which aims to optimize the customer's IT solution; and *Empowering*, which ensures a targeted, effective transfer of knowledge from SAP to the customer.

The imparting of knowledge is also one of the key aims of this book-part of the line of *SAP Technical Support Guides*. This series gives you a detailed overview of technical aspects and concepts for managing SAP software solutions. The topics dealt with in these books range from a technical implementation project to running a software system and the relevant database system.

Whether you are new to SAP system management or wish to gain further qualifications, you will benefit from the wealth of practical experience and firsthand information contained in these books. With this line of books, SAP also endeavors to help prepare you for qualification as a "Certified Technical Consultant". Please note, however: These books cannot replace, nor do they attempt to replace, personal experience gained from working with the various SAP solutions! Rather, the authors offer suggestions to help in your day-to-day work with the software. Innovation in SAP solutions always brings with it new challenges and solutions for system management. The demands made on the customer's own or external support organizations also increase. The expertise and knowledge of these organizations can be a great help in avoiding problems when using the software. Therefore, one of the core tasks of this series of books is to teach problem-solving skills.

Even in this Internet age, books prove to be an ideal medium for imparting knowledge in a compact form. Furthermore, their content complements the new service and support platform, the SAP Solution Manager, and other new services offered by SAP. The series provides background knowledge on the operation and functioning of new SAP solutions and contributes to customer satisfaction.

Gerhard Oswald
Member of the executive board of SAP AG

Dr. Uwe Hommel
Senior Vice President at SAP AG
SAP Active Global Support

Rot, October 2003

Foreword

Almost exactly three years have passed since the first edition of Liane Will's book on R/3 administration, which has become something of a classic. That's a long time in the world of information technology. This book builds on the structure of its predecessor; however, it is more than just a new edition, because of its numerous new developments and enhancements.

If you're an SAP R/3 system administrator who has already traveled on the evolutionary path of Basis administration from SAP R/3 4.0 to the EnjoySAP changes in SAP R/3 4.5, you'll notice that SAP R/3 4.6C has significantly enhanced many approaches-in the Transport Management System and in monitoring, for example. Nevertheless, the design of Basis systems 4.6C and 6.x (SAP Web Application Server) does not essentially differ regarding classic administrative topics, which make up the contents of this book.

If you still want to pursue the topic of Basis administration unencumbered, I'd be pleased if this book helps you to become familiar with this truly complex area and sail around some critical crags.

All the specifications, statements, menu paths, and screenshots in this book are based on SAP R/3 4.6C and SAP Web Application Server 6.20 and 6.30. Unfortunately, I cannot guarantee that what you see in this book won't appear differently in later releases. Therefore, I ask that you factor this into your work. This book would not exist without the support of Roland Mayr, who spent endless hours proofreading it, and contributed many valuable tips from his experience in the administration of complex landscapes, and Karen Hagemann, whose illustrations clarify contexts and backgrounds. Of course, I also wish to thank Liane Will and Florian Zimniak for nudging me forward and for their patience. In addition, I want to mention Günter Lemoine for the translation, and Nancy Etscovitz for editing the book in English.

Sigrid Hagemann
SAP Systems Integration AG

Alsbach-Hähnlein, October 2003

Introduction

With over 60,000 installations of SAP software in more than 120 countries, SAP has achieved a market penetration without equal in business management. SAP R/3 has become something of a standard in business software.

The Basis technology of SAP R/3 is part of this development. It is also used in other components of SAP's palette of solutions and is the core of SAP Web Application Server; it forms the technological foundation of the new SAP platform—SAP NetWeaver.

For the purpose of simplification, this book refers to the SAP R/3 system from the system administrator's viewpoint, even when the function being discussed can be used in the same or similar form in SAP Business Warehouse (SAP BW) or SAP Advanced Planner & Optimizer (SAP APO).

The book is not intended as a replacement for the documentation available from SAP—it does not offer a complete functional description of tools. Rather, it describes practical processes and behaviors in the context of administrative tasks, and incorporates these descriptions within the design, thereby promoting a better understanding of how these tools can best be used.

The peculiarities of administration that result from the addition of a Java environment to SAP Web Application Server are referenced, but not explored in detail.

Chapter 1, "Technical Realization of Client/Server Architecture in SAP R/3", discusses the basics of SAP R/3 architecture. It explains the technical realization of client/server architecture in SAP R/3 and introduces important SAP R/3 terms.

Chapter 2, "Getting Started", familiarizes the reader with general operating processes such as starting and stopping the system and logging on. This chapter also introduces the first important functions in an SAP R/3 system.

Chapter 3, "Service and Support", focuses on the offerings of SAP Service Marketplace and SAPNet R/3 Frontend, perhaps better known as the *Online Service System* (OSS). This chapter also highlights an important topic: linking a customer system with SAProuter.

On the threshold between SAP R/3 4.6C and the SAP Web Application Server—the basis for all mySAP solutions—installation concepts and procedures have changed. **Chapter 4** introduces these "Installation Concepts". Although the theory of each installation concept is similar, the technical implementation of each installation is different. This chapter also discusses the daily work required after an installation.

Chapter 5, "Setting Up the System Landscape", and **Chapter 6**, "Software Logistics", describe the architecture and use of the Transport Management System (TMS). The setup of a system landscape and the central administration of transport settings are the primary topics discussed in Chapter 5. Chapter 6 deals with transports of software logistics; the TMS is required to process the logistics. This chapter also describes the Change and Transport System (CTS) as the application used in every installation to import support packages and add-ons.

Chapter 7 discusses a foundational pillar of the application—"Client Administration". From the viewpoint of Basis administration, this chapter examines client maintenance, particularly various options for copying and transporting, and settings for changeability.

Chapter 8, "SAP R/3 Users and Authorizations", defines SAP R/3 users and the authorization concept in detail. Beyond the basics—such as the authorization object, individual authorizations, and roles—this chapter explains concepts such as Central User Administration (CUA) and working with directory services.

In addition to dialog processing, SAP R/3 offers the option of planning and executing jobs in the background. **Chapter 9** focuses on this "Background Processing".

Data is usually changed with asynchronous *updating*. In **Chapter 10**, Update, the tasks of the SAP R/3 system administrator are discussed in the context of changed data, particularly the monitoring of updates and procedures in the event of errors.

Chapter 11, "Output Configuration and Administration", looks at options for output/print configuration and the administration of print/output requests.

Growing volumes of data demand more administrative effort. Because a great deal of data becomes obsolete so quickly and is no longer necessary for direct access, in **Chapter 12**, "Data Archiving", the reader learns how to use and store data from the SAP R/3 database.

Chapter 13, "Data Distribution and Transfer", describes the Remote Function Call (RFC) as an important basis for communication. RFC is also used as a Basis technique to realize distributed business processes with Application Link Enabling (ALE). This chapter also explains the basics of the batch input procedure to transfer data into an SAP R/3 system quickly.

Chapter 14, "Maintaining Instances", discusses the administration and maintenance of parameters in SAP R/3. It shows how using definitions of types of operation can help the administrator tailor the R/3 system to meet the changing requirements of users. This chapter also describes *load distribution*—balancing the load between instances with the help of *logon groups*.

Chapter 15, "System Monitoring", introduces the tools a system administrator can use to monitor a system and analyze errors. It also deepens the reader's understanding of familiar tools. This chapter concludes with an overview of an SAP R/3 system administrator's routine tasks.

Chapter 16, "Monitoring Architecture", discusses the structure, configuration, and possible uses of monitoring architecture as an important component of the Computing Center Management System (CCMS) within all SAP Basis systems.

Included in the **appendices** are: a list all the review questions (and their answers) in a comprehensive form; a compilation of all the important transaction codes; a list of the most important R/3 parameters; charts of menu structures; a glossary of all the important terms in the SAP R/3 environment, and a bibliography.

You can navigate to most actions or tasks via following a menu path or entering a transaction code. The text notes the choice: ▶**Event maintenance**, for example. Each chapter has a section on paths and transaction codes; it explains the conventions used in the chapter:

Event maintenance: SAP Menu · Tools · CCMS · Jobs · Maintain Event (SM62)

Sources of additional information are provided in sections on *Quicklinks* and *SAP Service Marketplace Notes*. You will find these links in SAP Service Marketplace on the Internet at *http://service.sap.com*.

System properties differ on various operating-system platforms. Accordingly, UNIX always includes all UNIX derivatives for which a given component has been released. Windows NT refers to the current release of the Microsoft operating system used for SAP solutions. You will find a complete release matrix of the permissible combinations of operating system, database, and SAP components at SAP Service Marketplace under the Quicklink */platforms*.

Typography conventions

1 Technical Realization of Client/Server Architecture in SAP R/3

SAP Basis technology, long known simply as SAP R/3 Basis, has proven itself to be a reliable platform, because of its high-performance architecture. The SAP Web Application Server (Web AS) is therefore not only the Basis component of the current SAP R/3 Enterprise; it is also the technological basis in similarly structured SAP solution components such as SAP APO, SAP BW, and SAP CRM.

The underlying technology for all mySAP solutions is based on familiar, multilevel, client/server architecture. As we will see in the following sections, adhering to this concept enables us to develop a reliable and flexibly scalable foundation for the operation of complex systems.

The following section begins from the viewpoint of the SAP system administrator and deals with those areas that the administrator must address in order to guarantee that the application runs seamlessly. In later sections, we will discuss the various aspects of system administration, and the role that the architecture plays in these considerations.

1.1 Client/Server Architecture in SAP R/3

Three-tier client/server technology differentiates between the following layers:

▶ Presentation

▶ Application

▶ Database

In terms of hardware, the technical realization can occur somewhere between these two extremes: "all components on one computer" or "one computer for each instance of a layer." According to your plans for the use of the system, availability requirements, and performance, you can define an optimal variant.

The operation of all three layers of client/server architecture on one computer is appropriate only for demonstrations or tests.

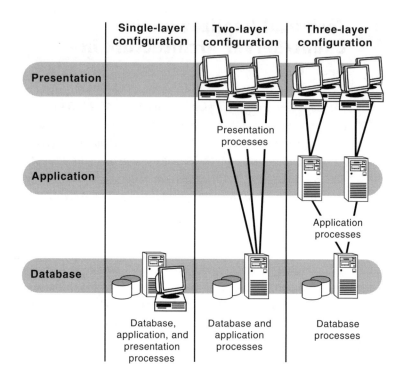

Single-layer configuration	Two-layer configuration	Three-layer configuration

Presentation

Presentation
processes

Application

Application
processes

Database

Database, application, and presentation processes	Database and application processes	Database processes

Figure 1.1 Configuration Variations

Two-layer configuration

Smaller SAP R/3 systems are often operated in a central configuration with a separate presentation layer (see Figure 1.1). Both the database and the application run together on the same machine; PCs or other workstation computers are used for the front-end systems.

Three-layer configuration

If a two-layer configuration no longer meets users' requirements, the database and application servers are separated from each other. The software architecture of SAP R/3 permits distribution of the application layer to several *instances* that can be operated on separate computers. This technology produces a high degree of scalability; the database is the only component that cannot run on separate computers. Benchmarks have been able to simulate several thousand SAP R/3 users in parallel in a three-layer configuration. From the system administrator's point of view, however, each additional computer increases the administrative efforts required for the system landscape.

In the early phases of implementing SAP R/3, you should select what type of architecture and hardware you want to use. As part of the follow-up specifications, the system administrator must then adjust the system to meet the requirements of SAP R/3 users. Once the SAP R/3 system has gone into productive operation, if the selected architecture does not meet the requirements, or cannot be adjusted enough to meet them, the cost increases and additional organizational efforts are usually required.

The software and technical decisions that we make are determined by the type of architecture that we want to implement as system administrator. We address these considerations in the following section.

The *presentation layer* is of primary interest to typical SAP R/3 users, who use the system for their work. On the SAP R/3 side, the *SAP graphical user interface (SAP GUI)* usually operates behind the scenes in this layer. The SAP GUI accepts user entries and communicates with the application layer, where queries are processed. In the reverse role, the SAP GUI accepts data from the application layer and formats it into a user-friendly form. Most SAP R/3 sessions are executed using SAP GUI. The technical realization of the SAP GUI is a process in the operating-system layer of the front-end.

Presentation

The *application layer* in SAP R/3 takes user requests from the presentation layer. In the *application layer* the actual calculations, evaluations, and so on are executed. The data required for these tasks is requested from the database layer. New, incoming data is processed and sent on to the database. The application layer is the central switchboard of an SAP R/3 system. Accordingly, the application layer is one of the central areas that can be controlled by an SAP R/3 administrator. The actual tools for the administration of an SAP R/3 system are almost completely integrated into SAP R/3.

Application layer

An SAP R/3 *instance* is a group of processes that use a common area of memory, are controlled by a dispatcher process, and access the same database. The application layer of an SAP R/3 system can consist of one or more instances. The term *application server* is used as a synonym for the term *instance*. The system administrator also has to configure the number and type of processes for an instance in order to optimize performance with the smallest possible amount of resources.

Instance

A *relational database management system* (RDBMS) is used in the last layer—the database. The data exchange between the application processes and the RDBMS happens via the SQL interface. In almost all cases, the data of an SAP R/3 system is contained in exactly one database on exactly one computer. Nonetheless, you can also implement options such as using parallel databases or one database for several SAP systems (see Chapter 4).

Database

The administration of an SAP R/3 system therefore includes the following typical database administration tasks:

▶ Software installation and maintenance

▶ Configuration

▶ Flow control and optimization

▶ Management of disk space

▶ Database backups and restoration of data in the event of errors

▶ Reorganization of data pools (tablespaces, tables, and so on)

The standard delivery of SAP R/3 software includes tools integrated into SAP R/3 itself and special tools used with the database server.

If the database and application layer are split across at least two computers, it is called a *distributed SAP R/3 system*.

SID With the exception of using MCOD systems (*multicomponent, one database*), the name of the database simultaneously defines the name of the complete SAP R/3 system. The name must consist of three characters (letters or letter and numbers); the first letter must be uppercase (capital). The abbreviation "SID" is usually used as a placeholder for the name of the SAP R/3 system: it stands for *system identifier*. Sometimes "SAPSID" is used: it stands for *SAP system identifier*.

Network Familiar network technology is used between the layers distributed across various computers, sometimes within the levels, and as the connection between the SAP R/3 system and the outside world. TCP/IP is used as the transport protocol. The amount of data transferred between a frontend in the presentation layer and an application server is so small that a WAN connection between the presentation computers and the application servers can be used without any problems. This is not the case regarding the communication between the database server and the application server.

SNA (*systems network architecture*) protocol LU6.2 from IBM can link an SAP R/3 system to mainframes.

1.2   Internet Connection

Current technology uses three variations to connect SAP components to the Internet. The *Internet Transaction Server* (ITS) and *Internet Communication Manager* (ICM) can support dialog processing. The *Business Connector* establishes the automated exchange of business data with HTTP and XML between partner systems.

1.2.1 Internet Transaction Server (ITS)

The *Internet Transaction Server* (ITS) performs the following tasks:

▶ Automatically converts SAP screens to enable the use of the SAP GUI for HTML.

▶ Provides a Web presentation of business processes via screen-based Internet Application Components (IACs) that use a predefined HTML presentation of selected transactions.

▶ Provides a Web presentation of business processes via flow-file-based IACs. The flow files handle flow control; formatting for the Internet is an additional task.

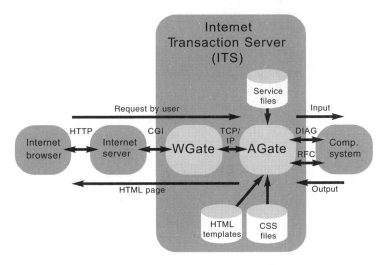

Figure 1.2 Log Conversion with an ITS

The ITS uses the following components to perform these tasks:

▶ *WGate*: to support the HTTP server interface, to forward queries to the AGate, and to transfer HTML pages transmitted by the AGate.

▶ *AGate*: a primary component responsible for session management, depicting R/3 images in HTML, administration of SAP R/3 connections, and generating HTML documents.

The ITS communicates with SAP R/3 over the DIAG interface or with RFC (see Chapter 13).

SAP plans to integrate the functions of the ITS into a later release of the SAP Web Application Server (SAP Web AS).

1.2.2 Internet Communication Manager (ICM)

The *Internet Communication Manager* (ICM) is an additional process. It runs at the operating-system level and processes HTTP, HTTPS, and SMTP queries within the SAP Web AS. Therefore, it establishes direct communications between SAP systems and the outside world.

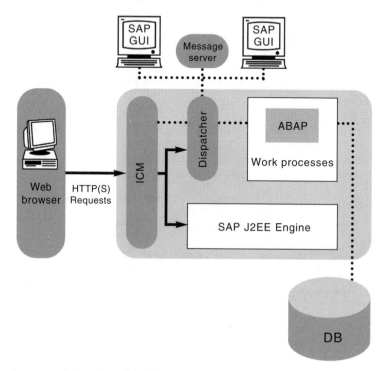

Figure 1.3 Integration of the ICM

As of Release 6.10 of SAP Basis, ICM can transfer Web-compliant content created with the SAP Web Application Builder directly to the browser front-ends that have requested it.

1.2.3 Business Connector

With the *Business Connector* (BC), two SAP systems, or one SAP system and a non-SAP system, can exchange messages in XML data format over the standard HTTP Internet protocol. You can choose between synchronous or asynchronous exchange.

Even if a business partner does not use any SAP technology, a connection over the Business Connector is still possible because of the open data format.

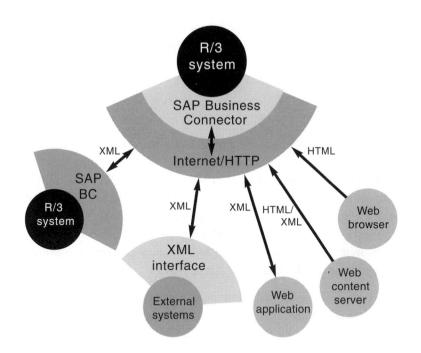

Figure 1.4 Connections with the Business Connector

1.3 Presentation Layer

The *presentation layer* of SAP R/3 is the interface to a user. Depending on the variety of user profiles—which can range from an SAP R/3 system administrator to a manager, and all the way to the executive board—the user interface must fulfill the most varied requirements:

▶ Simple and ergonometric use

▶ Options for personalization

▶ Simple management

▶ Flexible access—regardless of location

▶ Multilingual features

▶ Portability between various hardware and operating systems, but with the same scope of functions and screen appearance

The SAP GUI meets these requirements with various technological methods.

The SAP GUI creates a single system/single task work environment. When running SAP GUI, users enter the name of the SAP R/3 system that they want to log on to as a parameter. On Windows operating systems, an

SAP GUI

appropriate icon can be stored to call this program. The SAP GUI is controlled with a mouse and menus. To complete their work tasks, users navigate through menus and work sequentially. If users need to execute work tasks in parallel, they can start another SAP GUI or open a new window (*session*) in an SAP GUI that is already running. In terms of technical flows, a new session generally corresponds to an additional SAP GUI window.

SAPLOGON Typically, users who want to access more than one SAP system do not want to be forced to place an icon for each system on their desktop. The **SAPLOGON** program offers options to define all the SAP GUI connections that users might want with an easily modified configuration file, or with a direct adjustment of **SAPLOGON**. When they want to start an SAP GUI connection, users simply select the appropriate system entry from a list of all known connections. See Chapter 2 for a description of the configuration and use of **SAPLOGON** to distribute load.

The design of the SAP GUI follows the guidelines of the *Windows Style Guide*. It also reflects the findings on the ergonomics of user interfaces summarized in the EG 90/270 and ISO 9241 standards.

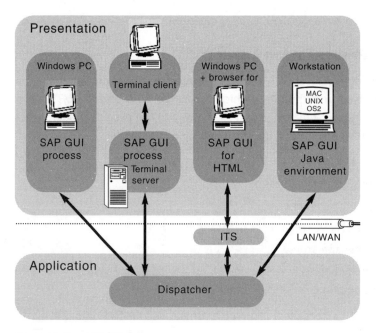

Figure 1.5 Front-End Variations

SAP offers different versions of the SAP GUI to support various front-end hardware (see Figure 1.5):

- ▶ SAP GUI for the Windows Environment
  Supported platforms include:

  - ▶ Windows 98, Windows NT4, Windows 2000, and Windows XP

  - ▶ Older versions of Windows over a terminal server

- ▶ SAP GUI for the Java Environment
  Supported platforms include:

  - ▶ Windows 98, Windows NT4, and Windows XP

  - ▶ MacOS 9

  - ▶ MacOS X

  - ▶ Linux, HP-UX, Solaris, AIX, and Tru64

  - ▶ OS/2

- ▶ SAP GUI for the HTML Environment
  The front-ends require only a Web browser; an ITS is necessary to convert the presentation into HTML (see Section 1.4.1).

The front-end software is designed to be backward-compatible, so you can always use the current version. At a minimum, the release level of the SAP GUI must correspond to the Basis release of the SAP system.

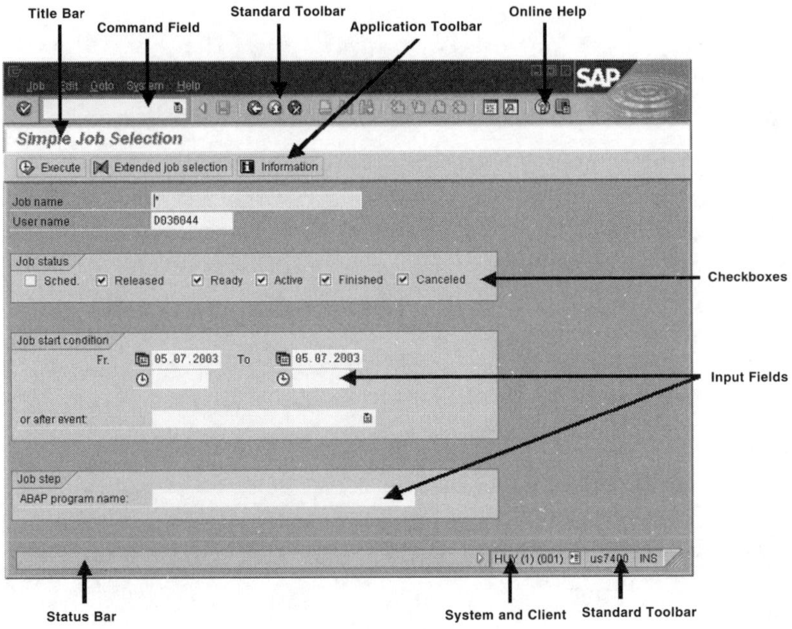

Figure 1.6 SAP GUI

A *SAP GUI* window is divided into various areas. Each window has a title bar that contains the name of the window. "Simple Job Selection" is displayed in the title bar in Figure 1.6.

Menu bar The *menu bar* appears at the top edge of the screen. Every menu bar integrates the menu System and Help functions. The menu System contains important functions such as starting or deleting a session, editing, help, and system status. The Help menu enables you to activate SAP R/3 documentation and a context-sensitive Help function at any time.

Standard toolbar Frequently used functions can be symbolized with standard icons. The icon at the right edge of this toolbar give users access to functions to customize color, font, and font size within the SAP GUI. Table 1.1 lists and describes the most important icons. In addition to the icons, context-dependent buttons might also be available.

Icon	Function Key	Description
	Ctrl + S	Save
	F3	Back
	⇧ + F3	Exit
	F12	Cancel
	↵	Enter
	Ctrl + P	Print
	Ctrl + F	Search
	Ctrl + Bild ↑	First page of a list
	Bild ↑	Previous page of a list
	Bild ↓	Next page of a list

Table 1.1 Important Icons in SAP R/3

Icon	Function Key	Description
	[Ctrl] + [Bild ↓]	Last page of a list
	[F1]	Help
	[F8]	Refresh
		Copy
		Create
		Delete
		Display
		Generate
		Change
		Check
		Execute
		Sort ascending
		Sort descending

Table 1.1 Important Icons in SAP R/3 (cont.)

After you log on to the system, a list of personal favorites and your user menu are displayed first so that you can choose a function. The user menu is configured as part of role definition (see Chapter 8) and reflects a selection of transactions that you need for your daily work.

The entire set of transactions that you can access over menu paths is made available by changing the display with **Menu · SAP Menu**. You can store frequently used transactions and links to Web sites or documents in the Favorites list. For example, Figure 1.7 shows a Favorites list supplemented with an Internet link to SAP Service Marketplace.

Favorites list and user menu

Transaction code The standard toolbar includes a *command field*. Because the functions available in SAP R/3 are very complex, the SAP R/3 menu tree is also complex and not strictly hierarchical. Accordingly, all workflows within SAP R/3 are assigned a short description, a *transaction code*. You can enter the transaction code as a direct command; if you do so, you go directly to the selected function without having to navigate through the menus. You can also enter a transaction code by adding /n or /o. When you enter /n, the current workstep ends and the action assigned to the transaction code is executed in the current window. When you enter /o, the new action is executed in a new window, called a *session*. At first glance, this procedure might seem archaic, but experience has shown that it has its supporters, particularly among experienced users of SAP R/3.

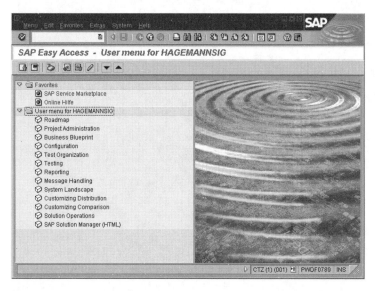

Figure 1.7 User Menu and Favorites List

Status bar The last line in a SAP GUI window is the *status bar*. It contains important information on the SAP R/3 system that the user has logged on to; it might also contain information, notifications, or error messages on a workflow.

The actual work area of an SAP R/3 user appears between the upper area and the last line of an SAP GUI window. How the window is divided and which functions appear in this area of the window will depend on the user's tasks.

Multilingual features The *multilingual features* of the SAP GUI are provided by storing text elements separately from the display. Users can choose a language when they log on to an SAP R/3 system, or by using a fixed setting in the SAP R/3 system. The only caveat is that the language must have been installed previously, which means that the text elements for the language were imported in the SAP R/3 database. By default, every system contains English and German. More than 20 different languages can be installed currently; Basis Release 6.10 supports Unicode.

1.4 Application Layer

This section focuses on the structure of the application layer. It describes the SAP R/3 processes in this layer and the interfaces to the presentation and database layers. It informs SAP R/3 system administrators which flows and settings they can and must administer, monitor, and optimize.

When viewed collectively, all SAP R/3 processes in the application layer form a logical unit. The application layer of an SAP R/3 system offers the following services:

▶ Dialog service (D)

▶ Update service (Update, V)

▶ V2 update service (Update2, V2)

▶ Enqueue service (Enqueue, E)

▶ Batch service (Batch, B)

▶ Message service (M)

▶ Gateway service (G)

▶ Spool service (S)

The services can be distributed to individual instances (see Section 1.3), depending on various factors. The number and characteristics of processes on each instance is defined with a profile that is analyzed when the application server starts.

The name of an instance contains the name of the SAP R/3 system and the letters that represent the services. A central SAP R/3 system with exactly one instance would be named <SID>_DVEBMGS<instance number>_<host name>, where <SID> is the unique, three-character name of the system in the system landscape and <instance number> is the last two digits of the TCP/IP port used for network connections. However, this method of naming is only a naming convention-a convention that is not checked technically. When installing a dialog server, the instance is usually installed with the name <SID>_D<instance number>_<host name>, even when the instance offers additional services. The instance number can be between 00 and 96: numbers 97 to (and including) 99 are reserved for special purposes.

Message Server Within the application layer, there is exactly one message server per instance. This service supports communication between the various instances of an SAP R/3 system. It controls, and if need be assigns, free process resources in the application layer. The instance on which the message server runs is usually called the *central instance* of the SAP R/3 system. The central instance performs special tasks that we'll discuss in the following sections. All other instances are dialog instances, even if they offer additional services.

Dispatcher and work processes *Work processes* perform dialog, enqueue, update, batch, and output services. *Dispatcher processes*, which exist once on each instance, coordinate work processes. Dispatcher processes recognize the communication requirements of the work processes and pass them on as appropriate. Work processes and the dispatcher always involve one and the same program that is started with parameters, which depend on each function. The administrator must configure which particular process and how many processes make up a service for each instance, depending on the requirements of the application and the capabilities of the hardware. The dispatcher starts and manages these processes. A dispatcher failure leads to a failure of the entire instance. The dispatcher works in the interface between the presentation and application layers. All requests that come from the presentation layer (the SAP GUI) are accepted by the dispatcher and are assigned to a work process available in the instance (see Figure 1.8).

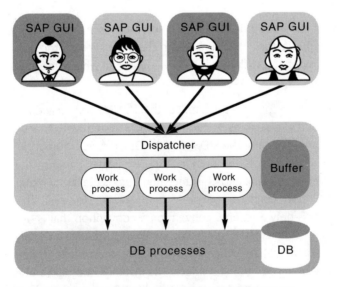

Figure 1.8 The Role of the Dispatcher in an SAP R/3 Instance

If we examine the structure of a work process more closely, we can distinguish between the task handler, screen processor, ABAP processor, and SQL interface, all of which work together by using special areas of main memory. The task handler coordinates activities within a work process. Depending on the task required, the task handler transfers processing to the screen processor, the ABAP processor (programs written in ABAP, the proprietary SAP programming language), or the SQL interface when data is to be exchanged with the database or changed.

Work processes are differentiated according to their work tasks; dialog processes execute the requirements of running user sessions. Each SAP R/3 instance must make at least two dialog processes available to manage the required flows internal to SAP R/3. The dispatcher does not assign a dialog process to exactly one user (SAP GUI). Instead, the dispatcher for the instance assigns the execution of each dialog step to a free dialog process. The user data required for execution, such as authorizations, are stored as the user context in the areas of main memory that are also available to the work processes. A user's dialog steps correspond to screen changes. A dialog process is generally busy only during the processing of a dialog step by one user. This mechanism allows a dialog process to serve multiple users.

Dialog service

Batch work processes or *background processes* execute work processes in the background. It makes sense to execute particularly tedious work tasks in the background, particularly when they don't require any dialog input. The user can define the programs to be executed as a partial step of a job and then schedule them for a particular time, or in response to a specific event. An instance with at least one appropriate work process must support the batch service.

Batch service

The *update service* executes asynchronous changes in the database. This service is used when the time at which the data is changed is not particularly critical—when it does not require immediate, synchronous execution. An SAP R/3 user cannot determine when the update service is used, or whether it is used at all. That decision is made during the development of a business application. Consider order entry as an example. Individual orders should be entered as quickly as possible in dialog. The actual update, however, occurs somewhat later in the background. The user does not have to wait for the procedure to end. At least one update service must exist on one instance in the system.

Update service

The update service is subdivided for performance reasons. A separate *V2 update service* is available for less-critical portions of an update. This service can execute a portion of the updates collectively. Configuration of a

V2 update service

V2 update service is not mandatory. If none exists, the update service continues to perform its tasks.

Output service Output requests are transferred to the *output service*, also known as the *spool service*, which stores the requests temporarily in the *TemSe (temporary sequential object)* until they are actually output. The SAP R/3 system administrator must decide if TemSe objects should be maintained within the database (and thus with the use of the RDBMS security mechanisms), or in the file system (with management by the operating system).

At least one spool process must be available in a system. Each instance can have as many spool processes as needed.

Spool processes coordinate all output processes, such as print and fax requests. Depending on the configuration, the output requests can be transferred directly to the output device or processed by the spool system within the operating system. The output is monitored in each case. Any messages pertaining to the execution of the requests are available in the SAP R/3 system logs.

Enqueue service The *enqueue service* plays a special role among the services. Just like the message server, the enqueue service operates throughout the system: only one instance can offer this service in the entire system. Typically, one process makes the enqueue service. If the system operates with a particularly heavy load, multiple enqueue processes are allowed, but they must exist on the same instance, because enqueue information is stored in the computer's main memory (shared memory). Accordingly, the term *enqueue server* is used as a synonym for both the instance that offers the service and for the service itself.

SAP R/3 transaction If possible, the enqueue server and the message server should run on the same instance because they work closely together. The enqueue server manages the logical object locks initiated by SAP R/3 transactions. An *SAP R/3 transaction* consists of a series of consistent business, functional, and logically related worksteps. It typically has several screen changes (dialog steps) that can be carried out by various processes. To the database, a screen change is a database transaction and is closed after the dialog step. The RDBMS can coordinate only this transaction with its own enqueue procedures. For SAP R/3, however, an entire SAP R/3 transaction must be able to be executed or rolled back completely, which is why *logical units of work* were introduced in SAP R/3. SAP R/3 supports the ACID maxim (see below for definition of ACID) for logical units of work (LUWs) as they are defined for transactions within the RDBMS. The following rules apply to an LUW:

► **Atomic**
LUWs form a unit: either the entire LUW or none of it is executed.

► **Consistent**
LUWs transfer one consistent state of the database to a new consistent state: a logically correct state is reached after an LUW is closed.

► **Isolated**
LUWs are isolated from each other; they can run in parallel. If several LUWs attempt to process the same source, they can only do so if they run sequentially.

► **Durable**
The result of LUWs that close successfully is enduring. For example, if system errors occur, the results of LUWs do not change, that is, the errors are not reflected in, nor do they impact, the LUWs.

The enqueue server is needed to meet these requirements. Enqueue requests from an SAP R/3 transaction are transferred to the message server, which allows the enqueue server to execute these requests. To avoid additional load on the network, we recommend that you install the enqueue server and the message server on the same instance. The enqueue server manages these locks in its own area of main memory. A failure of the enqueue server therefore means the loss of all SAP R/3 locks, which would result in an automatic rollback of all the affected LUWs. If the enqueue server fails, the dispatcher immediately attempts to start a new enqueue work process on that instance.

Each SAP R/3 instance also requires a gateway service to carry out work tasks that go beyond the local instance (in the broadest sense). These tasks include:

Gateway service

► Communication between various SAP R/3 systems
► RFC (Remote Function Call)
► CPI-C (Common Programming Interface for Communications)
► Connecting external systems, such as MAPI servers, EDI systems, external fax devices, and telex services

The gateway process exists exactly once for each instance. It is activated automatically at the start of an instance, without any special configuration needed by the administrator.

Table 1.2 lists the rules that apply to the number of SAP R/3 processes in the application layer.

Service	System-wide	Per instance
Dialog	>=2	>=2
Update	>=1	>=0
Enqueue	1	0 or 1
Batch	>=1	>=0
Message	1	0 or 1
Gateway	>=1	1
Spool	>=1	>=0

Table 1.2 Rules for the Type and Number of SAP R/3 Processes in the Application Layer

The message server is always informed about the available instances and services. It is the system-wide controlling unit. If the message server fails, the SAP R/3 system can no longer operate. The dispatcher is the controlling unit within an instance. If the dispatcher fails, the affected instance can no longer operate. However, if the work processes fail, the dispatcher can start new work processes. Every work process can take over any task. The dispatcher uses default settings, which the SAP R/3 administrator must create in order to determine the task of a given work process. Before an administrator can deal with these tasks, he or she must know the requirements of the particular SAP R/3 system. The requirements should have been clarified during the technical implementation of the SAP R/3 system. Therefore, later phases of an implementation would only require system enhancements, or the refinement of a defined configuration.

Performance tuning in the application layer is one of the primary tasks of an SAP R/3 system administrator. The administrator's responsibilities include decisions about the type and number of instances and their processes, the size of each main memory area, and other characteristics and settings. The options for configuring an SAP R/3 system, especially in the application layer, are very complex. For central systems (when the application layer consists of only one instance), the administrator must configure the number of processes and the size of their main memory area. Main memory areas are used to buffer frequently used tables, the factory calendar, ABAP runtime objects, and the user context, among other objects. For distributed systems (when several instances exist within an SAP R/3 system), and in an extreme case, the administrator can define instances that offer only one service, such as an update, batch, or spool server. The rationale behind such decisions usually arises from performance or management considerations. See Chapter 14 for more information.

1.5 Database Layer

A central RDBMS realizes the database layer of an SAP R/3 system. This section examines the database layer in SAP R/3 in more detail. It shows the reader how the RDBMS is used for SAP R/3 purposes and what administrative activities can be expected.

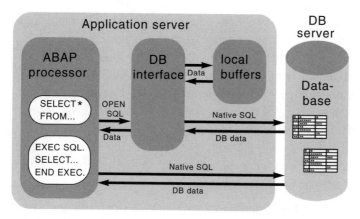

Figure 1.9 Database Interface

Figure 1.9 shows the interfaces between the RDBMS and the work processes. Communication between the application and the database layers occurs exclusively over SQL. Despite the SQL standard, however, every RDBMS that can be used with SAP R/3 offers its own SQL dialect that goes beyond the standard. To remain as independent as possible from these kinds of manufacturer- and release-specific enhancements and adjustments, SAP R/3 work processes typically use only the Open SQL interface. ABAP Open SQL corresponds to the entry level in the SQL2 standard. Within the database interface integrated into the work processes, the *Open SQL* is converted, if necessary, into the *Native SQL* of the RDBMS in use. You can also use the special SQL language scope of the RDBMS, which is used within ABAP programs. However, because the applications thereby become manufacturer-specific, they are encapsulated in the corresponding modules of the SAP R/3 application components. The use of such applications is to be kept at the absolute minimum required. Nevertheless, specific applications, such as database monitors, are permitted to use these programs. Native SQL statements are encapsulated within ABAP programs with the following statements:

Native and Open SQL

```
EXEC SQL.
    <Native SQL statement>
ENDEXEC.
```

Table types Actual data storage occurs in the RDBMS tables. All application data is mapped 1:1 in *transparent tables*. In theory, other SQL- or manufacturer-specific tools can access this data. Purely administrative and technical data of the SAP R/3 system can also be stored in other types of tables. The RDBMS still considers all of these types of data storage as tables. SAP R/3 sometimes combines several smaller tables into one table in the RDBMS— these table containers are known as *table pools*. The tables in a table pool are visible only to SAP R/3. The greatest advantage of table pools is a reduction in the total number of tables for the RDBMS. Individual tables are identified by their unique names and record key within the table pool. Tables in a table pool are called *pool tables*. Because of the structure and type of storage of pool tables, accessing their data without SAP R/3 tools is significantly more complicated. Table ATAB is an example of a typical table pool. It contains several SAP R/3 control tables. The control tables themselves are rather small and their content is relatively static, so that buffering the entire table pool is both possible and sensible.

Cluster The way in which *table clusters* and their logical *cluster tables* are used is similar. Cluster tables do not exist as independent tables in the RDBMS. Several cluster tables constitute a table cluster—usually referred to as a *cluster*. In this case, several rows of a cluster table are summarized under a common key for a data record in a cluster. Unlike a table pool, where one data record in the pool table is assigned to a data record in the table pool, here, a data record is formed into a cluster from several data records in the cluster table. The data records are simply strung together and supplemented with the cluster key. This technique is employed primarily for documentation.

Overall, an SAP R/3 4.6B system at the database layer consists of about 21,600 tables and 25,000 database indices, or about 23,700 tables for SAP R/3. All ABAP programs that realize the business functions of SAP R/3 are also stored in the database.

The database and RDBMS play a central role in the operation of an SAP R/3 system. The database manages all data entered by users, including SAP R/3 administrative data. The administration of this data—particularly its storage—is therefore important. These activities are also part of SAP R/3 system administration. In larger systems, database administration can constitute the full-time work of a single individual or even of a group.

However, many RDBMS-specific quirks characterize database administration. This book deals with only universally valid procedures. For more specific questions, see the books on the special aspects of RDBMS administration in this series.

Visit SAP Service Marketplace under the Quicklink */platforms* for a list of currently released combinations of RDBMS and operating systems.

1.6 Network

Network services come into play between the individual layers of client/server architecture. TCP/IP is always the basis for communication among the components of an SAP R/3 system and between an SAP R/3 system and other systems.

SAP R/3 offers various services to simplify communications. It uses its own CPI-C (*common programming interface for communication*) interface between ABAP programs, which guarantees both the consistency and standardization of the communications interface. CPI-C meets the requirements of the System Application Architecture (SAA) standard that was first defined by IBM in 1987. The SAA standard includes the following processes:

CPI-C

1. Setup of the communications link

2. Control of communications

3. Exchange of information

4. Shutdown of the communication link

The SAP Gateway is in charge of converting CPI-C queries. The CPI-C interface is always used when SAP R/3 systems communicate with each other, when SAP R/3 systems communicate with SAP R/2 systems, or when either SAP system (i.e., R/3 or R/2) communicates with external systems. The message server itself handles any short messages.

The *SAP Gateway* handles the exchange of large quantities of data; it is specifically responsible for this task and uses TCP/IP and LU6.2 to execute it. The CPI-C language is an integrated component of ABAP, the programming language specific to SAP R/3. It is available within the scope of the starter set and additional functions for data conversion. To save users the trouble of writing their own CPI-C communications routines, SAP R/3 offers the RFC (*Remote Function Call*) interface. RFC contains its own protocol to execute both internal and external function modules, both of which are managed in the function library specific to SAP R/3. A special

SAP Gateway

parameter, *destination*, can trigger execution of a function module on any specific target computer within an SAP R/3 system or in other SAP R/3 or R/2 systems. RFC supports asynchronous and synchronous communication (see Chapter 13).

Synchronous communication has a disadvantage: the call of the remote program can occur only when the partner is active. If the receiver is very slow, delays can arise on the sender side. An abrupt failure of the receiver can require a recovery of both systems.

Asynchronous communication, however, can guarantee the consistency of transactions. To do so, the keyword IN BACKGROUND TASK is appended to the RFC call. If the processing in the target system must be triggered manually, or if the target system is temporarily unable to meet the requirements, the data is stored in a queue. The administrative mechanism involved is *Q-API*, the *queue application programming interface*.

OLE   *Object Linking and Embedding* (OLE) resides above RFC. OLE connects PC programs to the SAP R/3 system. OLE commands within ABAP programs are handled as RFCs on the SAP GUI and the PC software. This feature enables the exchange of data with Microsoft Word or Excel.

For the administrator, the first requirement here is the presence of the technical preconditions, such as stable network connections. Security measures, such as the erection of firewalls, must also be provided. In practice, however, the technical service handles these tasks. In larger systems, we recommend assigning these tasks to a network administrator who defines and monitors the required SAP R/3 connections.

1.7   Operating System

In the previous sections, we discussed the structure of the individual layers of client/server architecture in SAP R/3 and network connections between SAP R/3 systems. In this section, we'll examine how to embed the SAP R/3 system in various operating systems. The interplay between the SAP R/3 kernel and the operating system on an application server is of particular interest.

The software of the SAP GUI and of its associated components is installed as usual in any directory of the front-end, or is made available remotely. It is then maintained manually or automatically with every new update to SAP R/3. In the database layer, embedding the SAP R/3 system in the operating system depends to a great extent on the RDBMS and is not valid universally. Because the primary task of the SAP R/3 system administrator is fine-tuning the SAP R/3 application layer, the SAP kernel, this section will focus primarily on that topic.

1.7.1 Directory Structure

Just as individual SAP R/3 processes form a unit in an instance that belongs to an SAP R/3 system, so do the various branches of the various instances form the SAP R/3 directory tree, regardless of whether the individual instances reside on Windows NT or UNIX systems. Figure 1.10 shows the universally valid structure of the directory tree.

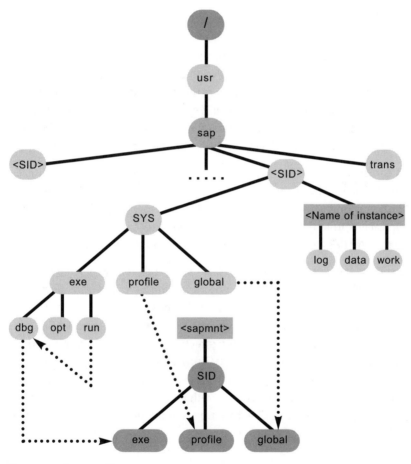

Figure 1.10 Directory Tree

The system identifier (<SID>) identifies the unique name of the SAP R/3 system; it usually includes the name of the database. SIDs always consist of three characters (letters or numbers). Beneath that level, the directory tree branches into directories named *SYS* and the name of the instance, such as DVEBMGS00 for a central instance with the number 00. For Windows NT, the two Windows NT shares, *sapmnt* and *saploc*, are stored in the root directory, \usr\sap. In UNIX, links handle this only for the */sapmnt* directory. The *SYS* directory consists of the following subdirectories:

▶ **profile**
Profile of the instance

▶ **global**
Data and logs relevant throughout the SAP R/3 system

▶ **exe**
Executable programs

The *exe* directory is subdivided into subdirectories *dbg*, *opt*, and *run*. It contains the executable programs of the SAP R/3 runtime environment; each of the programs is executed in the *run* subdirectory. For historical reasons, the *run* directory in the UNIX system is mapped with a link to the *dbg* directory. This directory contains optimized SAP R/3 programs and programs ready for debugging, as indicated by the *dbg* extension.

In earlier releases of SAP R/3, UNIX systems also contained the optimized SAP R/3 kernel in the *opt* directory; the SAP R/3 kernel, which was ready for debugging, was contained in the *dbg* directory. In problem cases, the typical link from the *run* directory to the *opt* directory could be converted to the SAP R/3 kernel that can be debugged, which means that it is slower.

Logically, beneath the nodes */usr/sap/<SID>*, a directory for each instance of the SAP R/3 system exists: it consists of directories *log, data,* and *work*. The *log* directory contains the system log of the SAP R/3 instance. The *work* directory contains trace and error information on the SAP R/3 processes of the instance. The *data* directory contains data produced by memory management of the SAP R/3 processes. Physically, these directories are localized on the application server of each instance. They are logically visible on the central instance with NFS Mount. In the same manner, each */usr/sap/<SID>/SYS* directory tree is appended to the directory tree of the central instance.

1.7.2   Users

Special users are required at the operating-system level for SAP R/3 users. During installation of SAP R/3, the required work environment is created for these users: it consists of authorizations, default settings, and, depending upon the RDBMS, database users.

The operating-system users <sid>adm and <RDBMS><sid> must be cre- ated for an SAP R/3 system on UNIX platforms. Here, <sid> stands for the system ID (in lowercase letters) of the SAP R/3 system, and <RDBMS> stands for the three-character abbreviation that describes the database:

► sqd (SAP DB)
► db2 (DB2)
► inf (Informix)
► ora (Oracle)

At the operating-system level, users are generally distinguished by their respective work areas, and therefore, by their authorizations. For administrative purposes, in SAP R/3, the operating-system user <sid>adm is used. Administrative tasks in the RDBMS environment belong to the task area of <RDBMS><sid>; however, other users can certainly handle such tasks as well.

In Windows NT systems all the tasks described are realized by the <sid>adm user. Background services operate under the ID of the SAP-Service <SID> user.

On the database side, the SAPR3 user is available for the SAP R/3 system. These database tables in an R/3 system belong to this user. Any other database users that exist do not have access rights to these tables.

1.8 Tips

► Menu paths
If you're searching for the menu path to a transaction, you can use transaction **search_sap_menu** for the standard menu, or **search_user_ menu** for entries in your user menu.

► Transaction
If you're searching for transactions with a keyword or with wildcards, you can use ►**Data Browser** of table TSTCT.

1.9 Transactions and Menu Paths

Data Browser: SAP Menu · Tools · ABAP · Workbench · Overview Data Browser (SE16)

1.10 Additional Documentation

Quicklinks

▶ SAP Service Marketplace, alias *netweaver*

▶ SAP Service Marketplace, alias *platforms*

▶ SAP Service Marketplace, alias *sapgui*

▶ SAP Service Marketplace, alias *sap-its*

▶ SAP Service Marketplace, alias *releasestrategy*

SAP Service Marketplace Notes

The following table provides an overview of the most important notes in SAP Service Marketplace that pertain to basic questions about SAP R/3 architecture.

Contents	Note
ITS Maintenance Strategy	197746
SAP GUI Resources	26417
SAP GUI Maintenance Strategy	147519
SAP GUI Limitations for Java	454939

Table 1.3 SAP Notes on SAP R/3 Client/Server Architecture

1.11 Questions

1. Which services does the application layer offer?

   a. Communications service

   b. Dialog service

   c. Spool service

   d. Update service

   e. Message service

   f. Transport service

   g. Gateway service

   h. Network service

   i. Enqueue service

   j. Batch service

   k. Change service

2. **Which of the following recommendations is correct?**

   a. The dispatcher and dialog process should not run in the same instance.

   b. The enqueue and message servers work closely together and therefore, should run on one instance.

   c. The batch service and update service work closely together and therefore, should never run on different instances.

3. **What's the purpose of the gateway service?**

   a. Communication between SAP R/3 processes

   b. Communication between SAP R/3 systems and instances of another SAP R/3 system

   c. Communication with the spooler of the operating system

   d. Connections to external programs, such as MAPI, EDI, and telex service

   e. Communication with SAP R/3 systems

4. **How many message servers are active in an SAP R/3 system?**

   a. 0

   b. 1

   c. 2

5. **How many updates can be active per instance?**

   a. 1

   b. 2

   c. The SAP R/3 system regulates the number automatically, depending on the need.

   d. As many as requested, depending on the available resources. The administrator must set the number of tasks in advance.

2 Getting Started

This chapter introduces you to the initial administrative tasks and operating procedures. The basic tools introduced here are integral to the equipment that is required by every system administrator.

2.1 Starting the Database and SAP R/3 Instances

Starting the SAP R/3 system is a process that is made up of several steps, for which the operating system user <sid>adm is responsible. Unless it is already running, you first start a special program called **saposcol** (*SAP operating system collector*). The saposcol program collects statistical information on the computer's load and operating system (see Chapter 15). Only one **saposcol** runs for each SAP server, even if several SAP R/3 systems or instances operate on the same computer. Once you have activated saposcol, the actual startup procedure of the SAP R/3 system begins. The first step here is to prepare the database so that it's ready for operation—an essential element of the SAP R/3 system. The next step activates the central instance of the SAP R/3 system. Additional instances can be started only after the message and enqueue servers are running. This step completes the process that's usually described as starting the SAP R/3 system. The frontends required to access the SAP R/3 system can be started separately and at any time. Starting the frontends is not part of starting the SAP R/3 system itself. The individual steps required to start SAP R/3 are usually performed automatically at one go; the procedure and the means available to start SAP R/3 depend on the operating system in use.

On Windows NT, management of all accessible R/3 systems is integrated as a snap-in into the *Microsoft Management Console* (MMC). The MMC uses a tree structure. The SAP R/3 snap-in consists of a root node, *SAP R/3 System*; the various SAP R/3 systems and their instances are displayed beneath the root as subnodes. Information on processes, current status, and open alerts are also displayed. When you use expert mode, the display also includes additional and more detailed data. Checking an R/3 system or an instance and selecting **Start** actually starts the components.

Windows NT

SAP Service Manager was used in older SAP R/3 releases to start the system under Windows. Although, today, the use of MMC is recommended, you can still use SAP Service Manager. When you trigger the startup function, SAP Service Manager first verifies if the relational database management system (RDBMS) with the SAP R/3 database is already running. If it isn't, it starts automatically. Next, the SAP R/3 processes on the central instance are started. Information on the current status of the two most important processes—the message server and the dispatcher—is displayed via a traffic light. It is important to remember that the dispatcher is the superordinate process for all other work processes. Accordingly, if the dispatcher is already running, you must wait until the dispatcher starts the remaining work processes. Only then is the SAP R/3 system ready for operation. The traffic light in SAP Service Manager uses a color code to indicate the status of each process:

Grey	Process is not running.
Yellow	Process is being started.
Green	Process is running.
Red	Process terminated after an error.

UNIX   Shell scripts realize the startup of an SAP R/3 system on UNIX. The SAP R/3 administrator, <sid>adm, can use the alias **startsap**, which refers to the actual shell script, **startsap_<hostname>_<instance_number>**, for starting the system in that user's home directory.

The flow of the startup procedure is almost identical to that of Windows. Calling startsap [all] starts the following program and systems (unless they are already running) in this order:

1. The **saposcol** collector

2. The RDBMS with the SAP R/3 database

3. The SAP R/3 system

In addition, startsap offers the following options:

▶ startsap db
The script is executed only up to the start of the database.

▶ startsap r3
The script assumes that the database is already running.

Additional   To start additional instances in a distributed SAP R/3 installation, you use
instances   the same tools that you used to start the central instance. However, when several instances are involved, the message server and the RDBMS are not started. The tools are configured accordingly.

If no SAP R/3 instance is running on the database server, the database can be activated either with tools specific to the RDBMS or with `startsap db`.

The startup procedure also stores logs (in text format) at the file-system level in the home directory of user <sid>adm. If problems arise during startup, the logs can provide valuable information, such as error messages or descriptions of problems. Logs are analyzed manually; however, in a Windows environment, you can also work from within the MMC to view the logs via the context menu of the instance. The following logs are created during the startup procedure:

Logs

▶ *startdb.log*

▶ *startsap_<computer_name>_<instance_number>.log*

The *startdb.log* log contains all the required information on the startup of each database system. The *startsap_<computer_name>_<instance_number>.log* logs the startup procedure of the SAP R/3 system. The following startup log of system "SKP" on UNIX computer "prdsapr3" clearly illustrates the individual startup phases of the SAP R/3 instance.

Listing 2.1 SAP R/3 Startup Log: startsap_prdsapr3_00.log

```
Trace of system startup/check of R/3 System SKP on Sun Oct
6 15:02:25 UTC 2002
Called command: /usr/sap/SKP/skpadm/startsap_prdsapr3_00
r3
Starting SAP-Collector Daemon
------------------------------
saposcol already running
Checking SAP R/3 SKP Database
------------------------------
Database is running
Starting SAP R/3 Instance
------------------------------
SAP-R/3-Startup Program V1.7 (92/10/21)
-----------------------------------------
Starting at 2002/10/06 15:02:29
Startup Profile: Startup Profile: "/usr/sap/SKP/SYS/
profile/START_DVEBMGS00_prdsapr3"
Execute Pre-Startup Commands
------------------------------
(24389) Local: /usr/sap/SKP/SYS/exe/run/sapmscsa -n
pf=/usr/sap/SKP/SYS/profile/SKP_DVEBMGS00_prdsapr3
/usr/sap/SKP/SYS/exe/run/sapmscsa: make new mode. SCSA
```

```
currently non existent.
sapcscsa: SCSA defined. sapscsaId == 1283 == 00000503
sapcscsa: SCSA attached at address ffffffff7ee00000
sapcscsa: SCSA initialized.
rslgwrl(21): Searching for overlap point in pre-existing
SysLog file...
/usr/sap/SKP/SYS/exe/run/sapmscsa: finished.
(24389) Local: rm -f ms.sapSKP_DVEBMGS00
(24389) Local: ln -s -f /usr/sap/SKP/SYS/exe/run/msg_
server ms.sapSKP_DVEBMGS00
(24389) Local: rm -f dw.sapSKP_DVEBMGS00
(24389) Local: ln -s -f /usr/sap/SKP/SYS/exe/run/disp+work
dw.sapSKP_DVEBMGS00
(24389) Local: rm -f co.sapSKP_DVEBMGS00
(24389) Local: ln -s -f /usr/sap/SKP/SYS/exe/run/rslgcoll
co.sapSKP_DVEBMGS00
(24389) Local: rm -f se.sapSKP_DVEBMGS00
(24389) Local: ln -s -f /usr/sap/SKP/SYS/exe/run/rslgsend
se.sapSKP_DVEBMGS00
Starting Programs
-----------------

(24410) Starting: local ms.sapSKP_DVEBMGS00
pf=/usr/sap/SKP/SYS/profile/SKP_DVEBMGS00_prdsapr3
(24411) Starting: local dw.sapSKP_DVEBMGS00
pf=/usr/sap/SKP/SYS/profile/SKP_DVEBMGS00_prdsapr3
(24412) Starting: local co.sapSKP_DVEBMGS00 -F
pf=/usr/sap/SKP/SYS/profile/SKP_DVEBMGS00_prdsapr3
(24413) Starting: local se.sapSKP_DVEBMGS00 -F
pf=/usr/sap/SKP/SYS/profile/SKP_DVEBMGS00_prdsapr3
(24389) Waiting for Child Processes to terminate.
Instance on host prdsapr3 started
```

As the log indicates, after checking to determine if the **saposcol** collector is already running, the database is checked to determine if it's ready for operation. In the sample log, the database is ready for operation. The processes of the SAP R/3 kernel are started next. You can see that the startup procedure references start profile START_DVEBMGS00_prdsapr3.

The properties of an SAP R/3 instance, such as the type and number of processes, the size of main memory reserved for SAP R/3, and additional options, are controlled with profiles, which is typical of many software products. SAP R/3 systems use three profiles:

- System profile: DEFAULT.PFL
- Start profile: START_<instance><instance_number>_<computer_name>
- Instance profile: <SID>_<instance><instance_number>_<computer_name>

All profiles are stored in the profile directory (see Chapter 1) defined during installation of SAP R/3. All instances can read the directory with share or mount technology.

The DEFAULT.PFL profile exists uniquely in an SAP R/3 system: it contains system-wide settings. These settings include the name of the system, the database computer, and the name of the enqueue server. Each SAP R/3 instance to be started reads this profile first. The information in the profile is important throughout the system.

DEFAULT.PFL

However, the START_<instance><instance_number>_<computer_name> and <SID>_<instance><instance_number>_<computer_name> profiles are specific to an instance. Default names are assigned during the installation of an instance; the names are created from the processes running on the instance. For example, the name of the central instance (see Chapter 1), "DVEBMGS," indicates that the following processes are started:

Start profile of an instance

- Dialog
- Update
- Enqueue
- Batch
- Message
- Gateway
- Spool

Please note that all additional instances receive the name "D" during installation, even if they are primarily used for batch processing or as spool servers.

Let's examine the profile START_DVEBMGS00_prdsapr3. The first segment of the profile name shows that we're dealing with the start profile of an instance. The underscore separates the type of profile from the name of the instance. The next segment, "DVEBMGS," represents the services running on the instance and is also the name of the instance. In this case, we know that we're dealing with a central instance, because it has a message service. The numbers "00" represent the last two numbers of the

TCP/IP port that the dispatcher uses on this computer. The next underscore separates the name of the instance from the name of the computer, "prdsapr3," on which the instance is running. The start profile of an instance determines how, where, and under what name individual SAP R/3 services and processes are to start. For example, the following excerpt from a start profile starts the message server and the dispatcher in instance "DVEBMGS00_prdsapr3."

Listing 2.2 Excerpt from the Start Profile of an Instance

```
Directory  /usr/sap/SKP/SYS/profile
Name: START_DVEBMGS00_prdsapr3
#.************************************************************
#.*        Start profile START_DVEBMGS00_PRDSAPR3
#.*        Version              = 000003
#.*        Generated by user  = HAGEMANN
#.*        Date of generation   = 10/23/2002,
#.*        15:04:19
#.************************************************************
SAPSYSTEMNAME = SKP
INSTANCE_NAME = DVEBMGS00
#
# Start SCSA administration
#
Execute_00 = local $(DIR_EXECUTABLE)/sapmscsa -n
 pf=$(DIR_PROFILE)/SKP_DVEBMGS00_prdsapr3
#
# start message server
#
_MS = ms.sapSKP_DVEBMGS00
Execute_01 = local rm -f $(_MS)
Execute_02 = local ln -s -f $(DIR_EXECUTABLE)/msg_server
$(_MS)
Start_Program_01 = local $(_MS) pf=$(DIR_PROFILE)/SKP_
DVEBMGS00_prdsapr3
#
# start application server
#
_DW = dw.sapSKP_DVEBMGS00
Execute_03 = local rm -f $(_DW)
Execute_04 = local ln -s -f $(DIR_EXECUTABLE)/disp+work
$(_DW)
```

```
Start_Program_02 = local $(_DW)
pf=$(DIR_PROFILE)/SKP_DVEBMGS00_prdsapr3
. . . . . . .
```

The operations listed with `Execute_<number>` prepare for the execution of the actual commands, which are started with `Start_Program_<number>`. The keyword `local` or alternatively, the specification of a server name at the same location, define the computer on which the command should run.

The runtime environment of the instance is configured in the *instance profile*. Configuration primarily refers to the definition of the resources used, a description of the services provided by the instance, and a specification of where other services, such as the database, can be found. The instance profile uses the following naming convention:

Instance profile

```
<SID>_<instance><instance_number>_<computer_name>
```

The example uses profile SKP_DVEBMGS00_prdsapr3. This profile defines how many work processes of a given type are to be started. The following excerpt from this profile starts seven dialog processes (parameter: *rdisp/wp_no_dia=7*). The definition of the size of the main memory area of the SAP R/3 system is an important element of the instance profile. However, the tasks of the instance profile also include settings such as logon parameters and log size.

Listing 2.3 Excerpt from an Instance Profile

```
#.***********************************************************
#.*       Instance profile SKP_DVEBMGS00_PRDSAPR3
#.*       Version              = 000003
#.*       Generated by user  = HAGEMANN
#.*       Date of generation   = 10/23/2002,
#.*       15:04:18
#.***********************************************************
# Instance Profile (CI, 1156 MB RAM)
# Fri Jul 5 11:51:17 2002
SAPSYSTEMNAME = SKP
INSTANCE_NAME = DVEBMGS00
SAPSYSTEM = 00
rdisp/wp_no_dia=7
rdisp/wp_no_vb=2
rdisp/wp_no_vb2=1
rdisp/wp_no_enq=1
```

```
rdisp/wp_no_btc=3
rdisp/wp_no_spo=1
em/initial_size_MB=800
rdisp/PG_SHM=0
rdisp/ROLL_SHM=0
rdisp/ROLL_MAXFS=64000
rdisp/PG_MAXFS=65024
abap/buffersize=320000
.......
```

During the installation of an SAP R/3 system, the required profiles are created with standard values, based upon user entries. During productive operations, it is important to tailor the settings to the actual requirements—particularly in the early stages. Chapter 14 addresses the details of how to do so and outlines which parameters are available. At this point, we'll simply assume that the profiles exist.

Evaluating profiles The source code of the SAP kernel already sets standard (default) values for most system parameters. Nevertheless, you must specify the special properties of the system environment being used, such as the computer name, the system name, and the distribution of resources, in the profiles. The profiles themselves are read during the startup of an instance. In order for any changes to an instance profile to take effect, you must often restart the relevant instance. For any changes to a system profile to take effect, you must restart all instances.

The values defined in the system profile DEFAULT.PFL overwrite the standard settings in the source code. The values provided in an instance profile overwrite the parameter values of DEFAULT.PFL for the instance (see Figure 2.1).

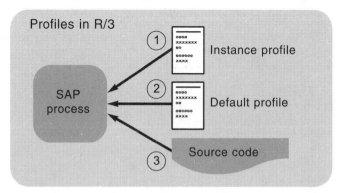

Figure 2.1 Evaluation Hierarchy of Parameter Definition

2.2 Stopping SAP R/3 Instances and the Database

The sequence used to stop an SAP R/3 system is the opposite of the sequence that is used to start it: you first stop the dialog instances, then the SAP R/3 central instance, and finally the database. In Windows systems, you use the R/3 Manager snap-in for the MMC or a menu entry in SAP Service Manager to stop SAP R/3 instances. The database must be stopped explicitly; the RDBMS in use determines which procedure you must use for that purpose.

The **stopsap** shell script is used in UNIX systems. You can use it as follows: stopsap

▶ `stopsap [all]`
   To stop SAP R/3 instances and the database.

▶ `stopsap r3`
   To stop the instances of an SAP R/3 system.

▶ `stopsap db`
   To stop the database when the SAP R/3 system is already shut down.

The stop procedure is logged, just as is the startup process. The following log files are stored in the home directory of user <sid>adm: *stopsap_<computer_name>_<instance_number>.log* and *stopdb.log*.

But for now, we'll assume that the central instance of the SAP R/3 system is running.

2.3 Starting the Frontend

During the installation of the software in the presentation layer, the system prompts you for information about the SAP R/3 target system; this information is used to create icons to call a frontend. The command that actually calls the SAP GUI works behind-the-scenes of the icon and has the following structure:

`sapgui /H/<computer_name>/S/sapdp<instance_number>`

To enable the frontend to connect to an SAP R/3 instance, the computer name and instance number of the instance must be transferred. You can, of course, create an icon on the desktop of frontend PCs in order to have the SAP GUI call each and every instance of every SAP R/3 system. Doing so, however, means that a number of similar icons will soon clutter the desktop. Use of the **SAPLOGON** program is much more effective. **SAPLOGON** allows the definition of all possible connections, and you can name the connections at will. The user simply selects the appropriate connection from a list of names, and the correct SAP GUI is generated. The data for **SAPLOGON** is created only once and is stored in the following files:

- ▶ *saplogon.ini*
- ▶ *sapmsg.ini*
- ▶ *saproute.ini*

You can also transfer these files to other front-end computers. Doing so significantly reduces the effort that would be necessary in entering all the possible connections manually. The use of load distribution for all the instances of an SAP R/3 system is even more convenient. To do so, you simply enter the name of the message server of each available SAP R/3 system in the *sapmsg.ini* file as follows:

```
<SID>=<computer_name_of_the_message_server>
```

The TCP/IP port for communications between the frontend and the message server is stored in the *services* file (UNIX: */etc/services*, Windows: *%SYSTEMROOT%\system32\drivers\etc\services*). The message server owns information on all the instances within an SAP R/3 system. The administrator can create groups from among all the instances, such as groups for specific work areas like materials management or financial accounting. **SAPLOGON** users would then select the instance group that is relevant to them. The message server selects the instance with the least load, based on the statistical information that the message server has. A SAP GUI is started on that instance. This procedure is called *load distribution* based on logon groups. For more information, see Chapter 14.

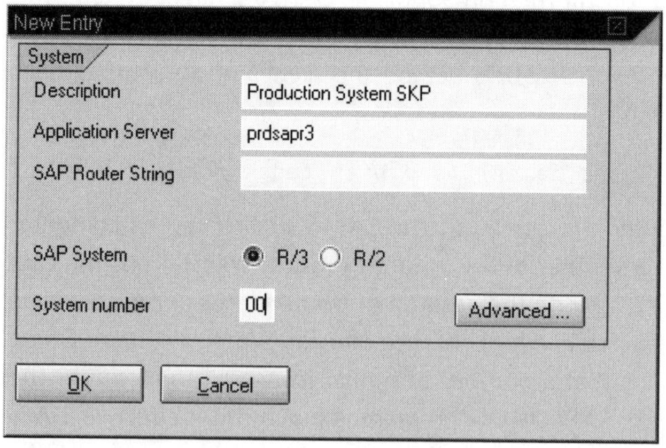

Figure 2.2 Creating a New Entry in SAPLOGON

Figure 2.2 shows the addition of **SAPLOGON** entries for our sample production system, "SKP," on computer (application server) "prdsapr3," with system number "00." You could also call a SAP GUI on SKP directly, as follows:

```
sapgui /H/prdsapr3/S/sapdp00
```

2.4 General Administrative Tasks

Once the SAP R/3 system has been started and access to it enabled via a frontend, you can perform all administrative tasks within the system. Before we proceed to the following chapters, in which we will explore the details of these administrative tasks, we'd like to introduce some basic functions in SAP R/3.

2.4.1 Status

From any menu entry of the SAP R/3 system, you can display the most important system information with **System · Status**. The display shows SAP R/3 system data (release, installation number, license validity, and the name of the database server and the RDBMS in use), the current user name, the active transaction (based upon the transaction code), and the program (screen) being executed (see Figure 2.3).

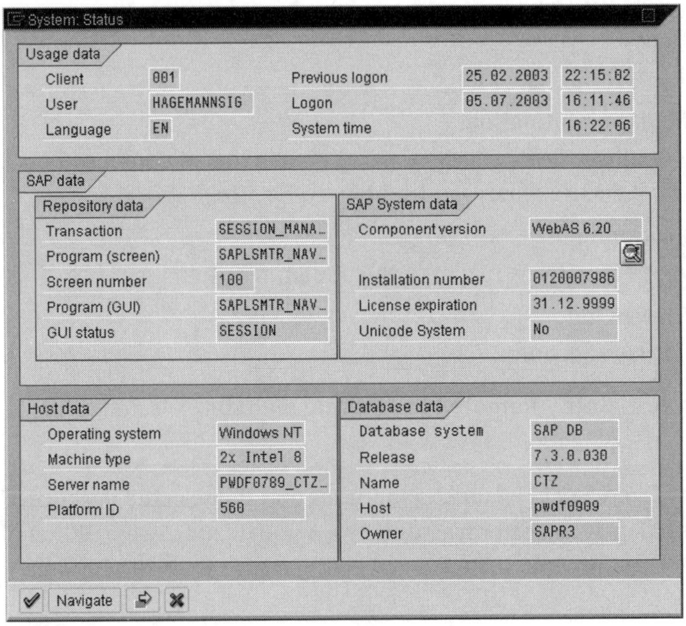

Figure 2.3 System Status

2.4.2 System Monitoring

System monitoring is an essential task of the system administrator. A number of monitors are available to perform this task; they will be discussed in detail later. Let us start, however, with a brief look at an overview of all the instances and processes running in the application layer. Select ▶ **Server list** to display a list of all instances running and their services (see Figure 2.4).

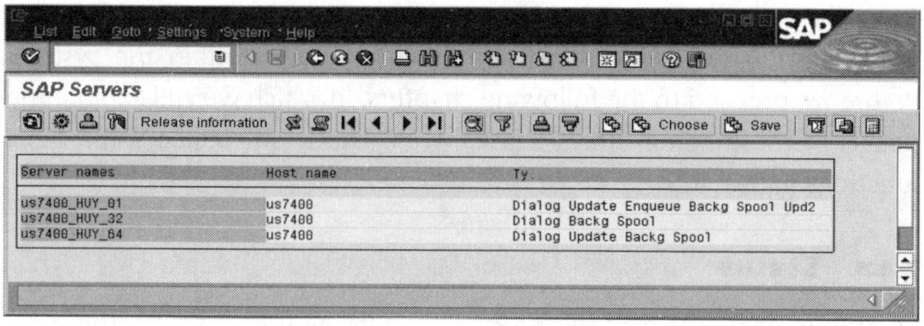

Figure 2.4 List of All Instances and Their Services

After you select an instance, you can branch to a number of overviews, including the following:

▶ **Goto · Processes**
Process overview (see Figure 2.5)

▶ **Goto · User**
The user currently logged on

▶ **Goto · Release information**
Description of the SAP R/3 kernel data (version, patch number, generation data, database library, and supported environment)

▶ **Goto · Environment**
Environment of user <sid>adm at the operating-system level

▶ **Goto · System log**
System log (see Section 2.4.3)

You can also use **Goto · Remote Logon** to log on to the selected instance directly.

The **Process Overview** in Figure 2.5 indicates that the selected instance is currently running 11 dialog processes (DIA), 3 update processes (UPD and UP2), 1 enqueue process (ENQ), 3 background processes (BGD), and 1 spool process (SPO).

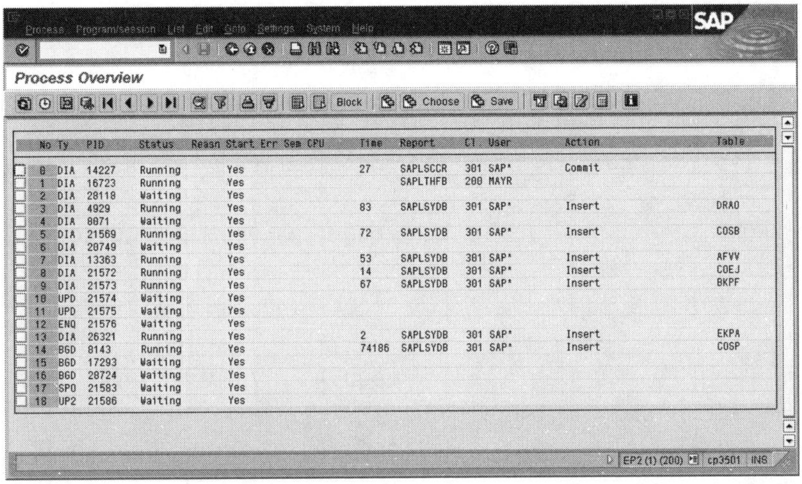

Figure 2.5 Process Overview of an Instance

In this example, the instance is busy with a client copy. The administrator can use the process overview to estimate the current activities and the resulting load on an instance. The process overview plays a special role in system monitoring. The system administrator has numerous display options, which Chapter 15 explores in detail. In an emergency, the administrator can terminate work processes (**Process · Cancel with core** or **without core**) from within the process overview. Terminating a work process has no significant effect on the ability of the instance to perform its functions: open transactions would be rolled back. The dispatcher for the instance would recognize the terminated work process and immediately attempt to start a new work process of the same type. The process overview does not display the processes of the dispatcher itself or of the message server. The ▶ **User overview** provides similar options, albeit options that are tailored to users.

At the operating-system level, the administrator, as operating-system user <sid>adm, can use a tool with a similar range of functions:

```
dpmon  pf=<instance_profile>
```

This tool provides a character-based overview of the processes running on an instance, as shown in the following listing. The initial screen provides a brief, statistical summary of the previous I/O load.

Listing 2.4 Output of dpmon

```
Dispatcher Queue Statistics
===============================
+------+--------+--------+--------+--------+--------+
| Typ  |   now  |  high  |   max  | writes |  reads |
+------+--------+--------+--------+--------+--------+
| NOWP |     0  |    18  |  2000  | 2349360| 2349360|
+------+--------+--------+--------+--------+--------+
| DIA  |     0  |    49  |  2000  | 1428784| 1428784|
+------+--------+--------+--------+--------+--------+
| UPD  |     0  |     2  |  2000  |   7587 |   7587 |
+------+--------+--------+--------+--------+--------+
| ENQ  |     0  |     0  |  2000  |      0 |      0 |
+------+--------+--------+--------+--------+--------+
| BTC  |     0  |     3  |  2000  |  15464 |  15464 |
+------+--------+--------+--------+--------+--------+
| SPO  |     0  |     1  |  2000  |  25638 |  25638 |
+------+--------+--------+--------+--------+--------+
| UP2  |     0  |     1  |  2000  |    612 |    612 |
+------+--------+--------+--------+--------+--------+
max_rq_id             9351
wake_evt_udp_now      0
wake events           total3102978,   udp2954229
(95%),   shm148749 (  4%)
since last update     total     0,  udp     0 (  0%),
shm     0 (  0%)
    q - quit
    m - menu
```

Users can use m to select from the following available monitors:

```
Dispatcher Monitor Menu
-----------------------
d - dispatcher queue statistic
p - work-process-admin-table
l - work-process-admin-table (long)
t - trace level/components for wp
w - wp_ca blocks
a - appc_ca blocks
m - mbuf status
v - tm_ad dump
q - quit
```

Option 1 essentially corresponds to the process overview in the SAP R/3 system. The following listing was taken from a UNIX system. When it was produced, dialog processes 0, 2, and 3, in addition to four background work processes, were running. Processes can be terminated from within **dpmon**, just as they can from within the process overview of the SAP R/3 system.

Listing 2.5 Process List

```
Work Process Table (long)
=========================
```

No	Ty. Program	Pid	Cl	Status User	Cause Action	Start	Err	Sem	CPU	Table	Time
0	DIA	28577		Run	yes		0	0	37		
	SAPLEDI1		001	SCHAAK	Insert					EDI40	
1	DIA	28578		Wait	yes		0	0	0		
2	DIA	28579		Run	yes		0	0	9		
			001	SCHAAK	Sequential Read					DD01L	
3	DIA	28580		Run	yes		0	0	33		
	SAPLEDIN		001	SCHAAK							
4	DIA	28581		Run	yes		0	0	8		
			001	SCHAAK							
5	DIA	28582		Wait	yes		0	0	0		
6	DIA	28583		Wait	yes		0	0	0		
7	DIA	28584		Wait	yes		0	0	0		
. . . .											
20	DIA	28597		Wait	yes		0	0	0		
21	UPD	28598		Wait	yes		0	0	0		
22	UPD	28599		Wait	yes		0	0	0		
23	UPD	28600		Wait	yes		0	0	0		
24	ENQ	28601		Wait	yes		0	0	0		
25	BTC	7176		Run	yes		0	0	158		
	/SAPAPO/		001	SCHAAK						DB-PROC "S	
26	BTC	6590		Run	yes		0	0	439		
	/SAPAPO/		001	SCHAAK	Direct Read					/SAPAPO/MA	
27	BTC	10238		Run	yes		0	0	7		
			001	SCHAAK	Delete					RSDELPART	
28	BTC	6823		Run	yes		0	0	17		
			001	SCHAAK						DB-PROC "S	
29	SPO	28606		Wait	yes		0	0	0		

```
30 SPO    28607 Wait          yes      0   0   0
31 BTC    28608 Wait          yes      0   0   0
32 UP2    28609 Wait          yes      0   0   0
     s - stop work process
     k - kill work process (with core)
     r - enable restart flag (only possible in wp-status
         "ended")
     q - quit
     m - menu
```

Users can also employ other means specific to the operating system to obtain information about SAP R/3 processes. Windows systems offer the *Task Manager* along with the monitoring options of the MMC. However, the SAP R/3 system itself can provide information much more comprehensively than can these tools; it contains detailed information on its own processes.

The following excerpt (see Listing 2.6) was created with ps -ef in a UNIX environment hosting a distributed instance running the Oracle RDBMS. For clarification purposes, we have manually limited and sorted the contents of the process overview to include only SAP R/3 and Oracle processes. The first process in the overview is the **saposcol** program. The following process, **sapstart,** was activated by execution of the startsap shell script and start individual SAP R/3 processes on the central instance ("01") and the dialog instance ("64"). The **co.sap<SID>_<instance>** process collects and writes the data for the central system log of an SAP R/3 system. The analog process, **se.sap<SID>_<instance>**, functions as the sender of information for the system log. These processes are activated directly from the start script, which is evident given that the process number (column **PID**) of the **sapstart** program is identical to the parent process number (column **PPID**) of the other processes. The message server is identified by **ms**. All the work processes of an instance are abbreviated as **dw,** which stands for **disp+work**, dispatcher and work processes. You can recognize the dispatcher among the work processes by the agreement of the parent process number and the process number of the start script: only the dispatcher is started directly from the start script. All other work processes are started by the dispatcher, so that their parent process numbers agree, logically, with the process number of the dispatcher. The message server and the dispatcher are formatted in bold print in the following listing.

Listing 2.6 Process Overview with Tools of the Operating System

```
  UID    PID      PPID    COMMAND
 root   29710       1     saposcol
orahuy  13047       1     /oracle/HUY/817_64/bin/tnslsnr
huyadm  19080       1     /usr/sap/HUY/SYS/exe/run/sapstart
     pf=/usr/sap/HUY/SYS/profile/START_DVEBMGS01_us7400
huyadm  24273       1     /usr/sap/HUY/SYS/exe/run/sapstart
     pf=/usr/sap/HUY/SYS/profile/START_D64_us7400
huyadm  19113     19080   co.sapHUY_DVEBMGS01
     pf=/usr/sap/HUY/SYS/profile/HUY_DVEBMGS01_us7400
huyadm  19114     19080   se.sapHUY_DVEBMGS01
     pf=/usr/sap/HUY/SYS/profile/HUY_DVEBMGS01_us7400
huyadm  19111     19080   ms.sapHUY_DVEBMGS01
     pf=/usr/sap/HUY/SYS/profile/HUY_DVEBMGS01_us7400
huyadm  19112     19080   dw.sapHUY_DVEBMGS01
     pf=/usr/sap/HUY/SYS/profile/HUY_DVEBMGS01_us7400
huyadm   5063     19112   dw.sapHUY_DVEBMGS01
     pf=/usr/sap/HUY/SYS/profile/HUY_DVEBMGS01_us7400
huyadm  19117     19112   dw.sapHUY_DVEBMGS01
     pf=/usr/sap/HUY/SYS/profile/HUY_DVEBMGS01_us7400
huyadm  19120     19112   dw.sapHUY_DVEBMGS01
     pf=/usr/sap/HUY/SYS/profile/HUY_DVEBMGS01_us7400
huyadm  19121     19112   dw.sapHUY_DVEBMGS01
     pf=/usr/sap/HUY/SYS/profile/HUY_DVEBMGS01_us7400
huyadm  19128     19112   dw.sapHUY_DVEBMGS01
     pf=/usr/sap/HUY/SYS/profile/HUY_DVEBMGS01_us7400
huyadm  19131     19112   dw.sapHUY_DVEBMGS01
     pf=/usr/sap/HUY/SYS/profile/HUY_DVEBMGS01_us7400
huyadm  19191     19112   dw.sapHUY_DVEBMGS01
     pf=/usr/sap/HUY/SYS/profile/HUY_DVEBMGS01_us7400
.......
huyadm  24290     24273   dw.sapHUY_D64
     pf=/usr/sap/HUY/SYS/profile/HUY_D64_us7400
huyadm  24292     24290   dw.sapHUY_D64
     pf=/usr/sap/HUY/SYS/profile/HUY_D64_us7400
huyadm  24293     24290   dw.sapHUY_D64
     pf=/usr/sap/HUY/SYS/profile/HUY_D64_us7400
huyadm  24294     24290   dw.sapHUY_D64
     pf=/usr/sap/HUY/SYS/profile/HUY_D64_us7400
huyadm  24295     24290   dw.sapHUY_D64
     pf=/usr/sap/HUY/SYS/profile/HUY_D64_us7400
```

```
huyadm  24296    24290    dw.sapHUY_D64
      pf=/usr/sap/HUY/SYS/profile/HUY_D64_us7400
huyadm  19115    19112    gwrd
      pf=/usr/sap/HUY/SYS/profile/HUY_DVEBMGS01_us7400
huyadm  24291    24290    gwrd
      pf=/usr/sap/HUY/SYS/profile/HUY_D64_us7400
orahuy  5067     1        oracleHUY
orahuy  7305     1        oracleHUY
orahuy  7307     1        oracleHUY

. . . . . . .

orahuy  7237     1        ora_arc0_HUY
orahuy  7231     1        ora_ckpt_HUY
orahuy  7227     1        ora_dbw0_HUY
orahuy  7229     1        ora_lgwr_HUY
orahuy  7225     1        ora_pmon_HUY
orahuy  7235     1        ora_reco_HUY
orahuy  7233     1        ora_smon_HUY
```

Gateway processes are identified as **gwrd**. The dispatcher of each instance also starts the gateway processes. The command names of the processes, as they appear at the operating-system level, are defined in the start profile of the instance (see Listing 2.2). This tool does not provide additional details, such as the current task of a process within SAP R/3. Only SAP R/3 tools can supply that information.

2.4.3 System Log

The system log of an SAP R/3 system, or of an instance, records all the essential events that occur during operations. Accordingly, monitoring the log is an ongoing task for the system administrator. Select ▶ System log in the SAP R/3 system for information on messages that appear in the system log. If an error in the SAP R/3 system occurs, the system log is the starting place for more exact analysis, as this chapter has already indicated. Chapter 15 contains a detailed description for dealing with this log.

2.4.4 System Messages

A system administrator will sometimes find it helpful to send messages to all or selected SAP R/3 users. For example, such a situation occurs when planned maintenance will limit the operation of the system. This basic function is available to you with ▶ Create system messages. You can select all users of the entire SAP R/3 system, all users of a specific instance, or all users of a specific client as recipients of a system message. You can also set a validity period for a message, so that only users who are working at the affected instance at the specified time receive the message. The system message is delivered with the user's next dialog step: a session-independent window opens and the message is displayed. Sending a system message is especially useful, for example, when a special instance must be stopped. In such cases, we recommend that users be forewarned (see Figure 2.6).

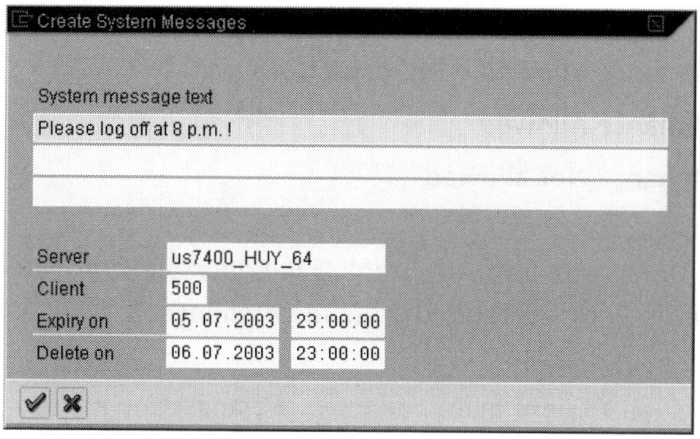

Figure 2.6 Creating a System Message

2.4.5 Lists

All screen displays that don't require any user input are called *lists*. Lists can be printed, stored by the SAP R/3 system in local files in the presentation, or sent to other users. From any display, select **System · List** for the list functions. You can also trigger specific actions in the command field:

▶ %sc permits searching for a character string in the list and the subsequent positioning. %sc+ searches for the same pattern.

▶ %pc can be used to save a list as a local file on the frontend.

▶ %sl saves a list in SAP Office.

Within system administration, lists are used with statistics, logs, and analyses. The system administrator must analyze lists frequently, so knowing how to deal with them is essential.

2.4.6 Table Maintenance

You can use the table maintenance integrated into SAP R/3 to modify some administrative tables in SAP R/3. For example, table T000 contains a list of all the clients in an SAP R/3 system. If a new client is created, you must first create a new entry in this table. You use table maintenance to do so and can use various tools offered by SAP R/3:

▶ The ▶**Data Browser** within the ABAP Workbench
The ability of a table to be maintained with the Data Browser must be anchored in the properties of the table. Up to SAP R/3 4.6C, you can set the flag that allows table maintenance with ▶**ABAP Dictionary: Start · Change · Attributes**. In the SAP Web Application Server, use ▶**ABAP Dictionary: Start · Change · Delivery and maintenance** to choose between the following three variations:

- ▶ **Display/maintenance Allowed with restrictions**
- ▶ **Display/maintenance Allowed**
- ▶ **Display/maintenance Not allowed**

▶ Extended table maintenance
You can navigate to this tool from any SAP R/3 window: **System · Services · Table maintenance · Extended table maintenance**

▶ Special, object-dependent transactions
Examples here include ▶**Client maintenance** or ▶**Transaction maintenance**; you can use the latter to record entries in table TSTC.

Extended table maintenance has completely replaced the standard table maintenance used in earlier releases of SAP R/3. Extended table maintenance can be used for a table only when the appropriate maintenance dialog has been defined for the table. The appearance of table maintenance depends upon the maintenance dialog created for a specific table. All the tables delivered by SAP that might require modifications are already delivered with a predefined dialog for table maintenance, including table T000.

To add an entry to table T000, proceed as follows (see Figure 2.7):

1. Call ▶**Table maintenance.**
2. Enter the table to be modified (here: T000).
3. Select **Maintain.**
4. Select **New Entries**.

If you select **Customizing** (see Figure 2.7), you will see an overview of the activities within the Implementation Guide (IMG: see Chapter 6) which require maintenance of the selected table. You can branch to these activities directly.

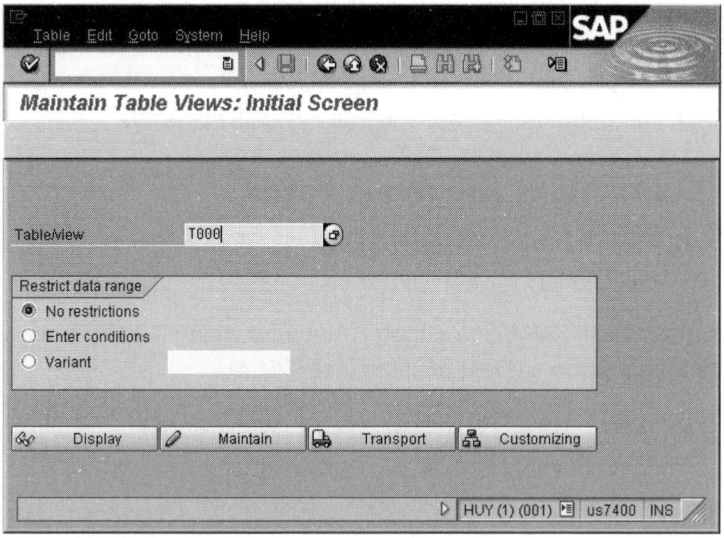

Figure 2.7 Enhanced Table Maintenance

Table maintenance within the ABAP Workbench, however, does not depend on the contents and the purpose of the table. It is primarily used to display the contents of tables.

You can log modifications to the contents of tables made with tools in SAP R/3. You simply need to activate that option for the table in the Dictionary of the SAP R/3 system.

2.5 Tips

▶ **Startup problems**

If the system won't start, it's best to isolate the source of the problem by first starting the database with database tools only. If the database starts, you can then start the SAP R/3 system with MMC or a script.

In addition to the special log files in the home directory of user <sid>adm, consult the developer traces (see Chapter 15) and the application area of the Event Viewer in Windows systems.

Checking the profile files themselves can be particularly helpful after modifying parameters.

▶ **Communication problems after adding an application server**

If a new application server has been added to an existing system landscape, I recommend that you check the completeness of the entries in the services file (see Section 2.3) on all servers and in the presentation layer.

▶ **Problem analysis without access to the SAP R/3 system**
Routines at the operating-system level, such as **dpmon**, are particularly helpful when you cannot log on to an SAP R/3 system (even one that's running), and therefore, cannot use internal analytical tools.

2.6   Transactions and Menu Paths

ABAP Dictionary: Start: SAP Menu • Tools • ABAP Workbench • Development ABAP Dictionary (SE11)

Client maintenance: SAP Menu • Tools • Administration • Administration • Client administration • Client maintenance (SCC4)

Create system messages: SAP Menu • Tools • Administration • Administration • System messages (SM02)

Data Browser: SAP Menu • Tools • ABAP Workbench • Overview • Data Browser (SE16)

Process overview: SAP Menu • Tools • Administration • Monitor • System monitoring • Process overview (SM50)

Server list: SAP Menu • Tools • Administration • Monitor • System monitoring • Servers (SM51)

System log: SAP Menu • Tools • Administration • Monitor • System log (SM21)

Table maintenance: System • Services • Table maintenance • Enhanced table maintenance (SM31)

Transaction maintenance: not accessible with the standard SAP menu (SM93)

User overview: SAP Menu • Tools • Administration • Monitor • System monitoring • User overview (SM04)

2.7   Additional Documentation

SAP Service Marketplace Notes

The following table provides an overview of the most important notes in SAP Service Marketplace that deal with the topics addressed in this chapter.

Content	Note
Table Maintenance in SAP R/3	28504
Using the dispatcher monitor: **dpmon**	42074
Test tool for the message server: **lgtst**	64015
Using the SAP Gateway Monitor: **gwmon**	64016

Table 2.1 Notes on General Administration

2.8 Questions

1. Which profiles are used to configure the SAP R/3 system?

   a. R/3 profile

   b. Instance profile

   c. Application server profile

   d. *DEFAULT.PFL*

   e. Start profile

   f. Stop profile

2. Your SAP R/3 system will not start. Where can you find information on the cause of the problem?

   a. *startdb.log*

   b. *startsap_<computer_name>_<instance_number>.log*

   c. *startsap.log*

   d. Developer traces

   e. System log

   f. SQL trace

3. Which of the following statements is correct?

   a. The **SAPLOGON** program enables you to define accesses to various SAP R/3 systems.

   b. If you use **SAPLOGON**, you no longer need an SAP GUI.

   c. The names of the entries in **SAPLOGON** must be identical to the SID of the SAP R/3 system.

3 Service and Support

For service and support, system administrators have access to several tools that simplify work—and sometimes, these tools even make service and support possible.

In addition to the comprehensive information offering that SAP makes available on the Internet at *www.sap.com*, certain factors that influence system operation and customization are critical to the system administrator. SAP Service Marketplace, the Online Service System (OSS, see Section 3.2), and sapserv[x], the service computer, offer support at various levels.

Some services are available over a specific connection between SAP and the customer environment; other services are accessible over the Internet.

3.1 Remote Connection

Despite the simple access options provided by Internet-based service offerings, setting up a direct and secure connection between customer systems and SAP service systems is still required. This connection enables service personnel to access a customer system directly. The staff can then analyze and address any problems that may arise with minimal effort and in real time.

Access to customer systems must meet the highest security requirements and guarantee the customers' ability to monitor access completely. A combination of organizational and technical measures is therefore required to realize these goals.

Maximum security

3.1.1 General Comments

Connections between a local network and the outside world always raise security risks. Access to the local network and its computers may be granted only to authorized persons and applications. A firewall, sometimes even more than one, is usually erected to ensure that access is secure. SAP offers an *Application Level Gateway* with **SAProuter** as an enhancement in the application layer to provide security for communications between remote SAP systems or between an SAP system and the outside world. You can use **SAProuter** to monitor and log all incoming and outgoing connections to the local SAP system. Therefore, it is sufficient to provide a connection between the server running SAProuter and the WAN. All other computers, particularly the SAP R/3 application server and the database server, do not require a separate access. Therefore, the

SAProuter

required administrative work on the network is concentrated in a central location. **SAProuter** is installed on the computer that functions as the interface between the local network and the outside world.

The computer running **SAProuter** must be accessible over an officially assigned IP address. In common parlance, the computer that runs **SAProuter** is also called SAProuter, although **SAProuter** is only one of many functions available on that computer. The costs and benefits of various methods determine the type of connection between the local and remote systems that a customer prefers. The options include the following:

▶ ISDN

▶ Dedicated lines

▶ Internet

The type and scope of the intended use of the connection are critical in selecting and dimensioning it.

SAP organizes the connection to customers in a similar manner (see Figure 3.1) The SAP firewall systems and the **SAProuters** in use operate on dedicated computers. All customers who want to set up a connection to the SAP service must first provide the IP addresses of their SAP R/3 server and **SAProuter** computers and request registration of the systems from SAP. In return, SAP stores the customers' IP addresses at SAP and from there activates the access. Table 3.1 lists the **SAProuters** that SAP operates throughout the world.

Computer	Location
sapserv1	Internet connection (VPN)
sapserv2	Internet connection (SNC)
sapserv3	Walldorf (Germany)
sapserv4	Foster City, California (USA)
sapserv5	Tokyo, Japan
sapserv6	Sydney, Australia
sapserv7	Singapore

Table 3.1 SAProuters Available from SAP

Given the increasing number of SAP installations, the number of **SAProuters** will continue to increase. Figure 3.1 shows the general procedure for handling connections between customer systems and SAP.

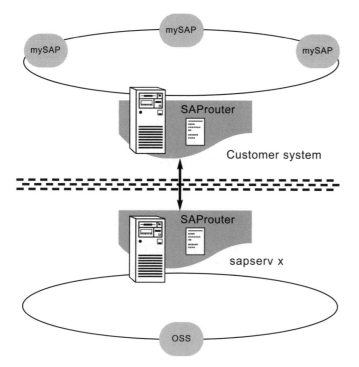

Figure 3.1 Principal Connections over SAProuter

A connection presumes that a physical connection can be established between the **SAProuter** at the customer site and the **SAProuter** (sapserv x) operated by SAP. You can use the operating-system command, `ping`, to test the connection before taking any further steps.

3.1.2   **SAProuter**

A standard installation of SAP R/3 stores the **SAProuter** executable in the kernel directory (see Chapter 1). You can find the current version of **SAProuter** at SAP Service Marketplace under Quicklink */patches*. It is advisable that you create a specific directory for **SAProuter** and its log and configuration files. You can copy the programs from the default directory into the directory that you've created. For easy identification, the directory is often named */usr/sap/saprouter* or *<LW>:\usr\sap\ saprouter*.

To determine which connections to permit or deny, **SAProuter** analyzes a *route permission table* as the basis for access control. This table, with the default name *saprouttab*, is actually not a table. It's really a text file that typically exists in the same directory as **SAProuter**. Entries in saprouttab use the following syntax:

Route permission table

```
[P|S|D] <source_system> <target_system> [<service>
<password>]
```

Switches P, S, and D stand for:

▶ **Permit**
The connection described in the following is explicitly permitted.

▶ **Secure**
Only connections that use the SAP protocol are permitted. The SAP protocol is an attachment to the TCP/IP protocol. Only SAP components use it.

▶ **Deny**
The connection described in the following is explicitly denied.

Entering a password can make access to your system landscape even more secure. You can also use wildcards (*) in statements.

Permitted entries in saprouttab include the following:

```
D  194.3.*.* host1
```

Denies access from all computers on network 194.3.*.* to local computer "host1", regardless of the service requested.

The following entry permits the computer with IP address 195.7.8.102 access to **ServiceX** on "host2" with password "Schrat":

```
P  195.7.8.102  host2FServiceX  Schrat
```

If several entries appear in the routing table, the first correct entry is used. Depending on your needs, it's entirely possible to use several routing tables and to start **SAProuter** with a specific saprouttab.

You start **SAProuter** with saprouter -r and stop it with saprouter -s.

Table 3.2 lists and describes the most important options for working with this program.

Option	Description
-r	Start **SAProuter** with the default route permission table, saprouttab.
-s	Stop **SAProuter**.
-n	Reread the route permission table without restarting **SAProuter**. Any changes affect only new connections.

Table 3.2 Options for SAProuter

Option	Description
-1/ -L	Output routing information with less or more detail.
-t	Change the trace level 1 -> 2 -> 3 -> 1.
-d	Write detailed connection information to file *dev_rout*. New information is appended to an existing file.
-T <file>	Change the name of the log file to <file>.
-p	Soft shutdown of **SAProuter**. **SAProuter** quits when all connections are closed.
-R <saprouttab>	Assigns any routing table that differs from the default.
-c <id>	Terminates a special connection, <id>, that has already been determined with the option -1.
-K	Start **SAProuter** in a Secure Network Communications (SNC) configuration. The argument of the option is the SNC name of the **SAProuter** server.
-G	Start option to specify a log file.
-V	Start option to specify a trace level.
-S	Start option to specify a different port (3299 is the default port).

Table 3.2 Options for SAProuter (cont.)

3.1.3 Setting Up a Connection

Before you can use a connection between a local SAP R/3 system and OSS, you must maintain the technical settings. You can use ▶OSS to do so. You must first set the **SAProuter** (as recommended by SAP): use menu option **SAProuter at SAP**.

The data on the local **SAProuter** must be entered on the customer's side. Technically, you can implement two **SAProuters**, one after the other, in which case you must enter both. You must use a SAP GUI in order to work with the OSS. Specify where this program can be found on the frontend with an entry in the lower portion of the screen (see Figure 3.2).

After you save these entries, you can use the Logon to SAPNet button to start a connection to ▶OSS. Internally, the connection at the local **SAProuter** is activated and a SAP GUI for the OSS is started.

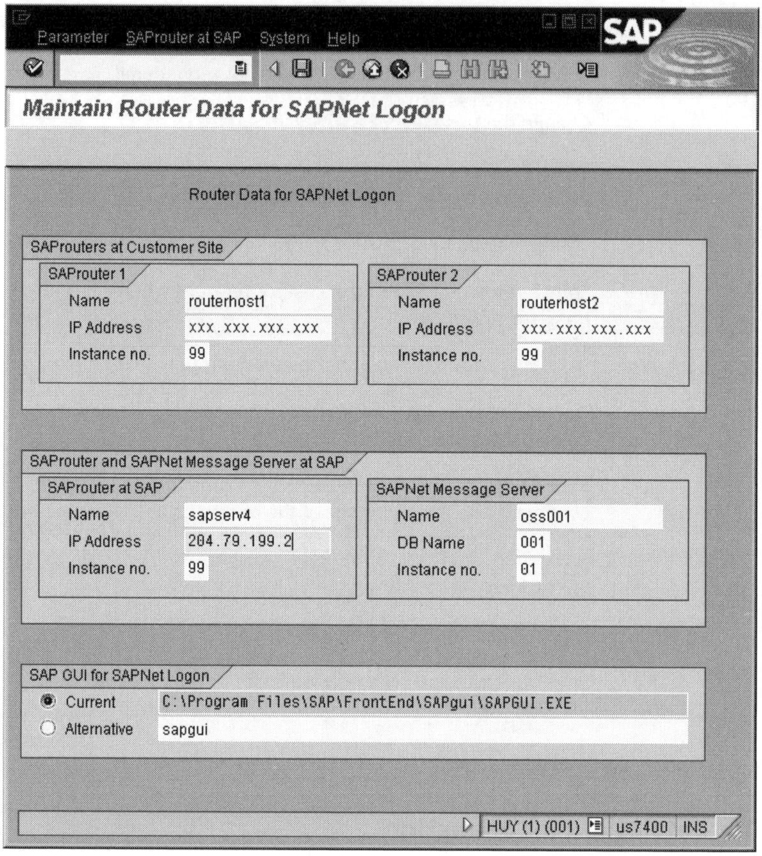

Figure 3.2 Configuration of Router Data

Router string

The **SAProuter** connection between two communicating end points is set with a *router string*, which consists of substrings in the following form:

```
/H/<Host/IP address>/S/<service/port_number>/W/password
```

Specification of the service and password is optional: the default service is defined with port 3299.

Calling the SAP GUI to access the OSS occurs implicitly as follows:

```
Sapgui /H/<first_local_SAProuter>[/H/<second_local_
SAProuter>] /H/<router_at_SAP>/H/<OSS>/S/<instance_
number_of__OSS>
```

If the route between local systems and SAP is activated in the saprouttab being used, the OSS connection can be called directly, without calling a logon in your SAP system.

3.2 SAP Services

SAP offers comprehensive service and information options on the following platforms:

▶ **SAPNet R/3 Frontend**
This special SAP R/3 system was previously called the *Online Service System* (OSS) and is available to every registered SAP customer over a dedicated connection (see Section 3.1). To simplify things, the following description also uses *OSS* as an acronym for the SAPNet R/3 Frontend.

▶ **SAP Service Marketplace**
SAP Service Marketplace is the SAP Internet service portal. It is available along with additional information on the services in the OSS under the heading **Support.**

Both types of access offer SAP customers almost exactly the same services. However, the functions of the OSS will be further limited in the future; new offerings will be integrated only into SAP Service Marketplace.

Table 3.3 lists the essential services that you can use; Section 3.4 addresses these services in more detail.

Service	Menu path in SAPNet R/3 Frontend	Quicklink in SAP Service Marketplace
Problem management	Messages	message
Notes database	Gen. Functions SAP notes	notes
Administration of service connections	**Service · Service connection**	serviceconnection
Registration of developers and objects (SSCR)	**Registration · SSCR Registration**	sscr
Registration of naming environments	Unavailable	namespaces
Requesting a license key	**Registration · System Request license key**	licensekeys
Requesting a migration key	Unavailable	migration-keys
Downloading support packages	**Service · SAP Patch Service**	patches
User administration	**Administration · User administration**	user-admin

Table 3.3 Essential Services

SAPNet R/3 Frontend and SAP Service Marketplace are different ways of accessing the same database, therefore, customer messages, in particular, can be created with one method and analyzed with the other.

SAPNet User Specially created SAPNet users are required to use the services of OSS and SAP Service Marketplace; a SAPNet user with full administrative rights is defined for each customer number. This user can then create additional users for the customer number and assign the required authorizations. These functions are available in SAPNet R/3 Frontend via ▶ **OSS · Administration · User administration** or in SAP Service Marketplace in Quicklink */user-admin*. By specifying a customer number, you can also request an additional user in the initial page of SAP Service Marketplace; however, because the new user is created without any authorizations, your SAPNet user administrator must modify it on the customer side.

The IDs created in this manner are always in the form S<10-digit_number>, so the term *S user* is common.

3.3 Essential Services

3.3.1 Problem Management

You can create customer messages with SAPNet R/3 Frontend and SAP Service Marketplace and send them to the SAP Hotline. The messages are automatically forwarded to the SAP service personnel, processed, and then answered with a recommended solution. You can view, edit, and close the solutions with OSS or SAP Service Marketplace.

The SAP service system administers all customer messages. Each message receives a unique number when it is created. For instance, you can use the number to search for and view closed messages. SAP regards the message data and general data on an SAP R/3 installation as very important, because the data created by a customer number during the initial customer registration is automatically referred to when a message is created. The user entering the message must also specify the current release number of SAP R/3 and the role of the relevant system (test or production, for example). Then, that user can assign the particular issue to a problem area and define the scope of the message more precisely. The priority given to a message should reflect its urgency. The highest priority should only be used when production systems are inoperative. Every message is assigned a status based on the level of processing it warrants. An overview shows the progress of processing for messages. Depending on its processing status, a message can be assigned to one of the following categories:

Message status

- To be sent to SAP
- New at SAP
- In process by SAP
- Inquiry from SAP
- Solution proposed by SAP
- Confirmed today

Figure 3.3 shows the screen for entering a message in OSS.

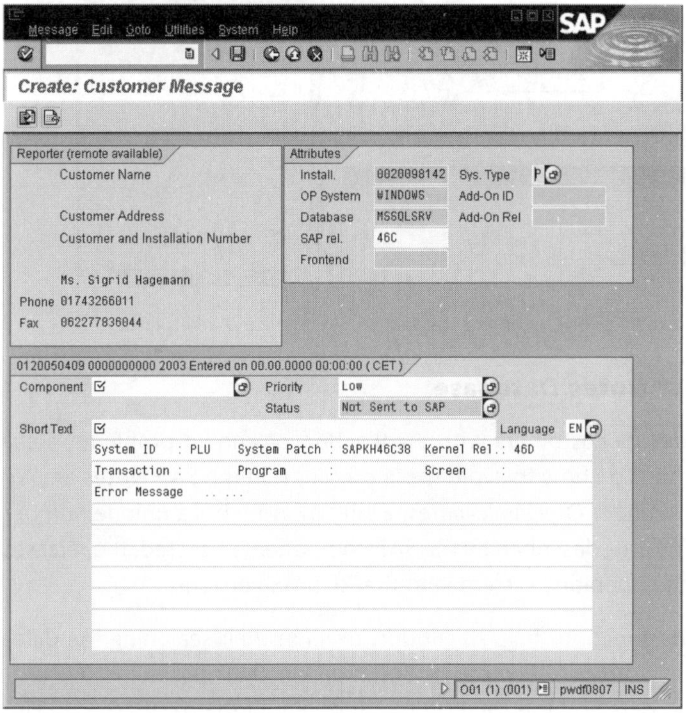

Figure 3.3 Creating a Customer Message with OSS

You can use Quicklink */message* to create a new message in SAP Service Marketplace: the Message Wizard prompts you for all the required information. Your logon data specifies the details about the customer, and these details are automatically inserted into the message.

Acknowledgement

You can find acknowledgements of registered problems in the OSS in the submenu **Inquiry from SAP** or **Solution proposed by SAP**. In SAP Service Marketplace, you can these documented acknowledgements via */message* **Search for messages** (see Figure 3.4).

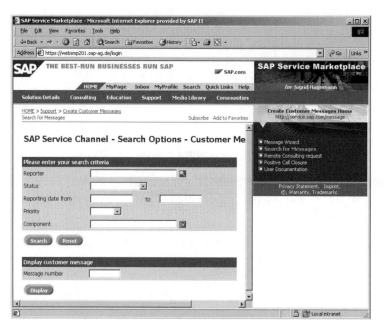

Figure 3.4 Searching for Customer Messages in SAP Service Marketplace

3.3.2 SAP Notes Database

SAP provides its customers with a collection of known problems, solutions, and hints on how to avoid these problems in the **SAP Notes** area of the OSS and under Quicklink */notes*. Each SAP note has a unique number and a validity area described by the SAP components affected, the releases involved, the operating system, and the RDBMS version.

Various filter functions help to support users in their searching the database via keyword for concrete information on their problems. Accordingly, many users find the solution to a problem in the database (see Figure 3.5).

3.3.3 Service Connections

When SAP works on a problem, it often requires a more exact analysis of the situation in your particular SAP R/3 system. To enable employees of SAP and its partner companies to log on to your system, the connection to your system must be explicitly activated by an authorized *S user* from within the OSS or SAP Service Marketplace (see Figure 3.6). The stored customer data serves as the foundation for setting up a connection; therefore, the data must be continuously maintained—it is a prerequisite for setting up a service connection.

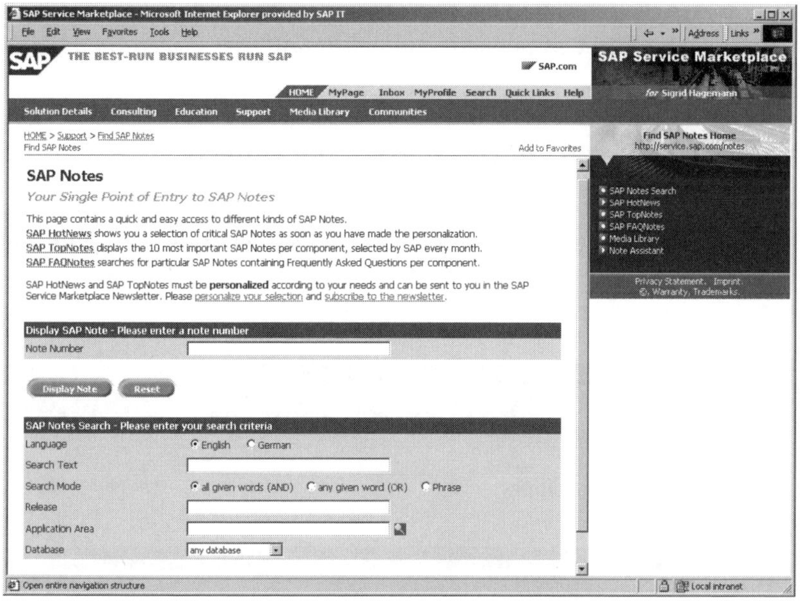

Figure 3.5 Searching for SAP Notes in SAP Service Marketplace

To open a service connection for a specified period, use the menu path
▶OSS · **Service** · **Service connection** · **Select system** · **Edit** · **Open** or
Quicklink */serviceconnection* in SAP Service Marketplace.

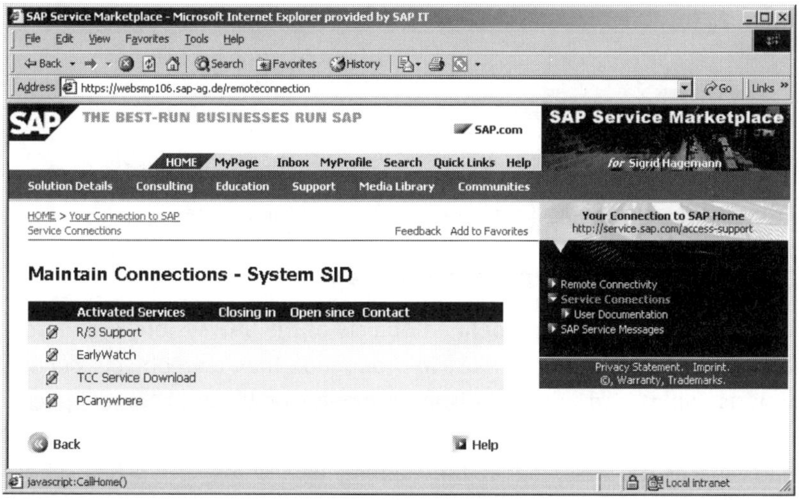

Figure 3.6 Illustration of a Service Connection in SAP Service Marketplace

For security reasons, special means of opening a connection, which are
activated individually, are used for different service activities.

You can use the integrated log book to trace when and under what ID a service connection was opened, and which SAP user logged on to your system.

3.3.4 Registration of Developers and Objects

You register developers and objects as part of SAP Software Change Registration (see Chapter 6) in OSS with ▶OSS · Registration · SSCR Registration, and in SAP Service Marketplace under Quicklink /sscr (see Figure 3.7).

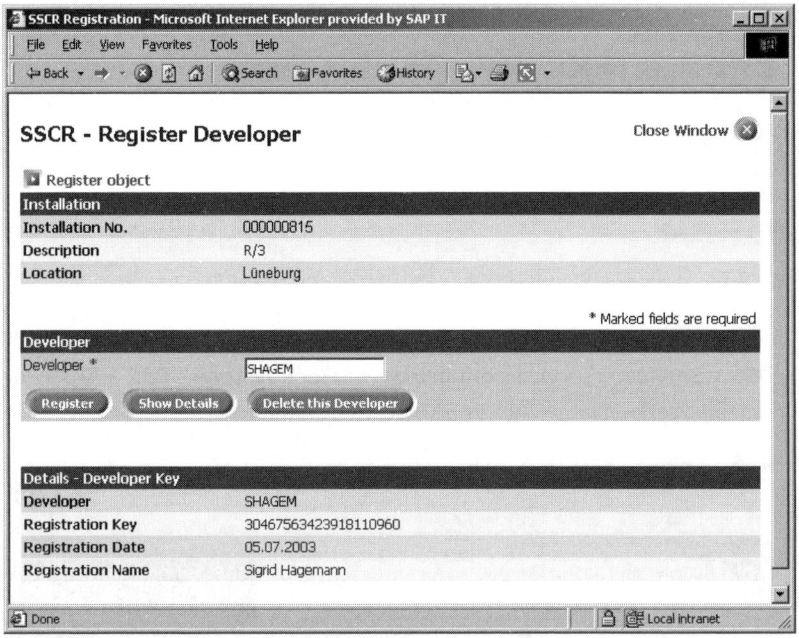

Figure 3.7 Registration of a Developer in SAP Service Marketplace

3.3.5 Registration of Namespaces

Customers can use the predefined objects of the SAP system and, if necessary, create, transport, and use in production their own objects, such as reports, tables, and so on. To distinguish between these customer-specific objects and the original SAP objects during an upgrade, special namespaces are reserved in the naming environment. Objects whose name begins with a Y or Z are recognized as customer objects.

These conventions might prove insufficient for developments of SAP partner firms or large-scale, customer-specific development projects. In these cases, you can use SAP Service Marketplace under Quicklink /namespaces to request a specific *namespace* (see Chapter 6). The new objects will then be recognized, because their names begin with the namespace ID. To ensure that the owners or other authorized persons can change the objects, the namespace must be equipped with a developer license.

After SAP has released the namespace, you can generate the developer license online.

Only SAP Service Marketplace supports working with namespaces: the corresponding selection in the OSS is no longer active.

3.3.6 License Key

If a new installation, reconfiguration, or move requires a new license key, you can request one online. In OSS, use ▶ **OSS · Registration · System · Registration · Request license key**; in SAP Service Marketplace, use Quicklink */licensekeys* (see Figure 3.8).

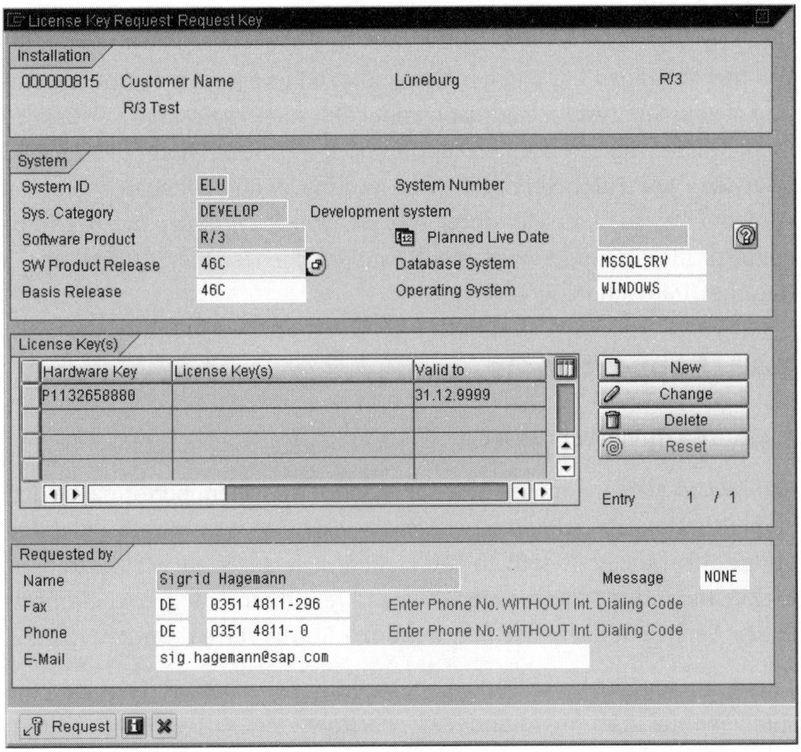

Figure 3.8 Requesting a License Key

Chapter 4 describes the activation of a license key.

3.3.7 Migration Key

You need a special migration key to perform a heterogeneous system copy. *Heterogeneous* means a system copy in which the RDBMS or operating system is changed. You can generate the key in SAP Service Marketplace under */migration-keys* by specifying the following source and target parameters:

▶ System ID

▶ SAP R/3 release

▶ Operating system

▶ Database system

▶ Host name of the database server

You must enter the key generated in the manner when prompted by the migration program.

3.3.8 Support Packages and Software Download

You can download the patches that you need to ensure a smooth operation of your SAP system landscape under Quicklink */patches* in SAP Service Marketplace. You can also find support packages (see Chapter 6) via ▶ **OSS** · **Service** · **SAP Patch Service**, as well as discover additional technological components, such as **SAProuter** (see Section 3.2), *binary patches* (programs of the runtime environment), and patches for the SAP GUI or ITS (Internet Transaction Server).

3.4 Support Tools

3.4.1 EarlyWatch Alert

EarlyWatch Alert is a free service for monitoring system performance and administration. You should schedule it weekly. The system data generated during this process is sent to SAP, where it is analyzed with automatic checks and returned to the customer as a report. You can find the reports in SAP Service Marketplace in the **Inbox** · **Status trace** drop-down box.

To prepare for EarlyWatch or GoingLive sessions, you must download the supplemental tools found under */supporttools*.

3.4.2 Note Assistant

The standard delivery of SAP R/3 includes *Note Assistant* as of Basis Release 6.10. This tool supports the system administrator during implementation of a solution in SAP notes. Previously, the implementation of these solutions required that a user manually change the source code, or wait for the next support package.

You can load the selected SAP Notes that you want from the OSS or SAP Service Marketplace, and implement the code changes automatically via Note Assistant. Note Assistant will also automatically check if the current status of the system (support packages, already-implemented notes, and modifications) permits the proposed change. If changes described in other SAP Notes are a precondition for the planned code change, these changes are also loaded and inserted into the SAP Notes queue (see Figure 3.9).

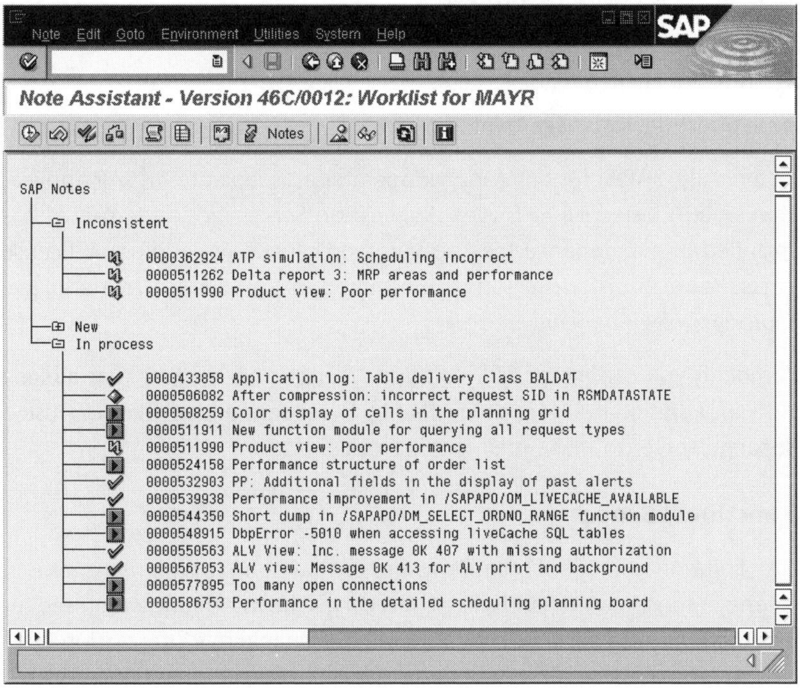

Figure 3.9 Operation Queue of Note Assistant

The changes are recorded in a request (see Chapter 6) and can therefore be transported to subsequent systems. Use ▶**Note Assistant** to administer the queue and download changes. If implementation requires adjustments of parameters in addition to the required changes in the source code, you must include these modifications manually, even when using Note Assistant.

Using Note Assistant does not require an SSCR key. Changes made with Note Assistant can often be undone.

You can use a transport to download the functions of Note Assistant into earlier Basis releases.

3.5 SAP Solution Manager: Overview

SAP Solution Manager offers a central platform to implement and operate a solution landscape. The following describes the use of SAP Solution Manager in system management.

SAP Solution Manager provides tools and functions for the following areas:

▶ Business process management

▶ Management of mySAP technology

▶ Software change management

▶ Support desk management

Technically, SAP Solution Manager operates as a separate mySAP application system based on SAP Web Application Server; however, use of it is included in maintenance fees, so you won't incur any additional license costs. You can order the software required in SAP Service Marketplace: Quicklink */solutionmanager*.

Although you can install SAP Solution Manager on a server that already runs an additional SAP system, it's highly recommended that you use a separate server to make maintenance easier.

Functional Scope

SAP Solution Manager functions as the central node for the management of one or more system landscapes. It receives the information required for its functions from each individual system. To enable this information flow, you must maintain RFC connections (see Chapter 13) to all the system landscapes and their respective R/3 systems that are managed. All the required data of the SAP systems will be called or transferred over the RFC interfaces. The following selections are available to each system landscape:

▶ Scope
  The relationships between the individual systems of a landscape are defined here. The definition includes the selected core business processes that typically run across a system in a system landscape. Technically, key figures are maintained for both hardware and software.

▶ **Implementation**

In this area, SAP Solution Manager offers the *Solution Management Roadmap* to support the implementation of a new business process and SAP systems. The Solution Management Roadmap is structured according to the phases of project implementation.

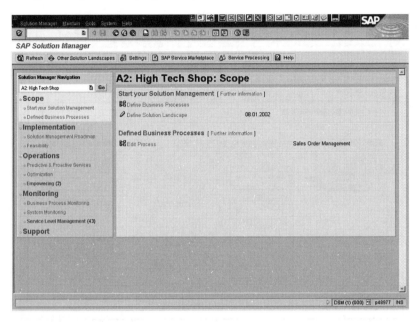

Figure 3.10 Maintaining the Key Figures of a System Landscape

▶ **Operations**

The operations portal is the platform for executing and administering all the services offered by SAP Active Global Support. The services include not only GoingLive Check or EarlyWatch, but also *Self Services* and *Solution Management Optimization Services* (SMO). You can obtain these services directly from SAP Solution Manager via SAP Service Marketplace. You can execute Self Services on your own, although doing so does presume a certain level of knowledge. Consultants or online support perform other services on site or remotely. Best Practice documents on selected topics of solution management are a valuable source of information.

▶ **Monitoring**

Unlike most products that monitor software operations, the monitoring area in SAP Solution Manager uses a business-process approach, which makes it easy to diagnose the affects that problems in system operations can have on business processes. SAP Solution Manager supports various views of a system landscape.

Business Process Monitoring

The business-oriented view (*Business Process Monitoring*) displays the flow and processing steps within a business process across the systems involved (see Figure 3.11).

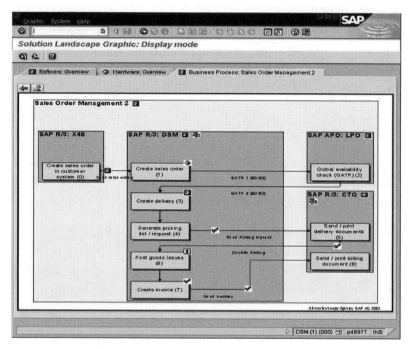

Figure 3.11 View of the Steps in a Core Business Process

Red markings indicate interruptions in the business process. Alert monitors and analysis functions are assigned to each business process. You can branch automatically to the alert monitors and then to the analysis functions by double-clicking on a selected business step. The depiction of business processes and the assignment of alert monitors and analysis functions makes it much easier for you to keep an overview of core business processes. You can address problems according to their affects on the business.

System Monitoring

The technically-oriented view (*System Monitoring*) displays all systems and their connections (see Figure 3.12). Red, yellow, and green icons in the initial screen indicate the general condition of a system. You can select a system and automatically branch to its monitoring architecture. These monitors are built on the foundation of the alert monitors defined in each system (see Chapter 16). In principle, monitoring in

SAP Solution Manager displays a special view of the alert monitors defined in the system.

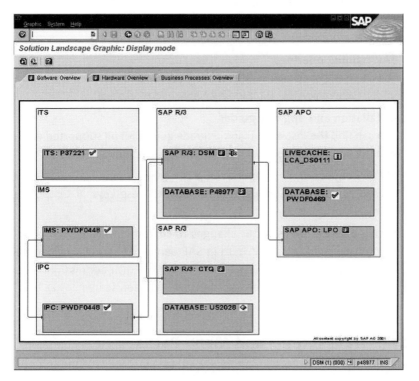

Figure 3.12 Monitoring the System Landscape

The area of *Solution Management and Reporting* holds particular interest for manufacturers of software solutions. You can define *service level reporting* for a system landscape, based on automatic and regular runs of the EarlyWatch Alert service. Data collected about the system is used to create a report that provides information on the relevant key figures, such as data growth, historical development of response times, workload, hardware load, and availability. You can use this feature to produce regular reports on the system landscape rather comfortably.

Service Level Reporting

▶ **Support Portal**
The *Support Portal* enables a view of the actions in the service channel, such as preparations for service or services themselves. It also offers an overview of all the problem messages opened for the system. You can view and process the messages directly from SAP Solution Manager. In addition, you can set up a user-specific view of and access to SAP Service Marketplace, which is the central node for support tools and services.

3.6　Tips

▶ **Online documentation on the Internet**
You can find complete online documents on mySAP solutions and SAP for various industries at *help.sap.com*. No ID is required.

▶ **SAP training offerings**
You can find the complete SAP training catalog and even register online under Quicklink */education* in SAP Service Marketplace.

▶ **Installation and upgrade guides**
You can find the installation and upgrade guides for all supported components in SAP Service Marketplace under Quicklink */instguides*.

▶ **SSCR: Requesting developer or object keys**
A valid license must be installed to request these keys. A temporary license is insufficient.

▶ **E-mail notification of status changes to customer messages**
If you used the Message Wizard in SAP Service Marketplace to create customer messages and have maintained the e-mail address, you will be notified by e-mail when your message has been solved or has been set to customer action.

3.7　Transactions and Menu Paths

Note Assistant: no standard menu entry (SNOTE)

OSS: System • Services • SAP Service (OSS1)

3.8　Additional Documentation

Quicklinks

▶ SAP Service Marketplace: alias *saprouter*
▶ SAP Service Marketplace: alias *remoteconnection*
▶ SAP Service Marketplace: alias *internetconnection*
▶ SAP Service Marketplace: alias *supporttools*
▶ SAP Service Marketplace: alias *solutionmanager*
▶ SAP Service Marketplace: alias *dbosmigration*

SAP Service Marketplace Notes

The following table provides an overview of important notes in SAP Service Marketplace that address service and support topics:

Content	Note
Guide to OSS1	33135
Network suppliers for a connection to SAPNet R/3 Frontend	33953
Schedule connection to SAP extranet, OSS, and SAPNet	137342
Collective note on service connections	35010
OSS logon	17285
SAProuter documentation	30289
Schedule VPN connection to the SAP network	486688
Customer messages in SAPNet R/3 Frontend	74131
Customer Message Wizard	307037
User administration in SAPNet R/3 Frontend	103926
Activating SAP EarlyWatch Alert	207223
Service tools for ST-A/PI applications	69455 and 91488

Table 3.4 SAP Notes on Service and Support Topics

3.9 Questions

1. What is SAProuter used for?

   a. It replaces a firewall.

   b. It controls the setup of remote connections to the application server of an SAP R/3 system.

   c. It sets up connections between the frontends and the application servers of an SAP R/3 system in the local network.

2. Which file is used as a default to maintain the routing data of SAProuter?

   a. saprouttab

   b. *DEFAULT.PFL*

   c. *autoexec.bat*

3. Which preconditions must be met in order for SAP to set up a service connection to a customer's SAP R/3 system?

   a. The SAP R/3 system must be registered in the OSS.

   b. The connection data of the application server and **SAProuter** must be maintained on the customer side.

   c. The customer must open the connection.

4 Installation Concepts

The individual phases of an installation reflect the architecture of the SAP R/3 system. The installation first creates the RDBMS and the database, then the individual instances (beginning with the central instance), and finally the frontends. This chapter describes the prerequisites and basic procedures that make up an SAP R/3 installation. This chapter does not discuss the technical details, which you can find in the installation manuals. Instead, it focuses on the background issues that can affect your installation, so that you can better understand the procedures.

4.1 Preparations

Before you can begin the actual installation, you must decide on the hardware and software that you want to use. The following text briefly summarizes the critical questions that you must ask. The most important considerations include estimating the expected initial size and future growth of the SAP R/3 system, and mapping the requirements in an appropriate system landscape: *sizing* for short. The following parameters play an important role in determining the size of an SAP R/3 system:

Sizing

▶ Total number of users and the number of concurrent active users

▶ Solutions used and the number of users per solution

▶ The volume of data to be entered and how long it is to be stored

▶ Requirements for background processing

▶ Exchanging data over interfaces

▶ Number and size of output/print requests

SAP offers a *Quick Sizing Tool* on its Internet site for rough sizing estimates based on customer entries. The most important factors are the planned number of users per application component and the estimated activity (low, medium, or high) in the SAP R/3 system.

The next step selects the appropriate hardware, operating system, RDBMS software, peripherals, and so on. The planning phase should not be taken lightly: you can only correct decisions that are incorrect with higher costs and greater effort.

Hardware requirements

SAP Service Marketplace lists the permitted combinations of operating system and database for running an SAP R/3 system at *http://service.sap.com/platforms*. An installation can be either homogeneous (all physical components using the same operating system) or heterogeneous:

▶ Using various UNIX derivates for the database and application servers

▶ Using a UNIX server for the database and Windows servers for application instances

The installation and administration of heterogeneous environments requires more effort in both planning and operations. Because of license technicalities, SAP does not support mixed homogeneous installations (with the development system running on Windows and the consolidation and production systems running on UNIX, for example).

We'll assume that these points have been sufficiently clarified and that the necessary hardware and SAP R/3 software are available.

Before you begin an installation, the first step is checking the prerequisites against the checklist in the installation package. The checklist contains the most important requirements for every RDBMS and operating system. Using SAP R/3 4.6C requires 25 GB of disk space (at least) for the central instance that runs the SAP R/3 database. Disk size varies somewhat, based on the various operating systems and the RDBMS. When you calculate the required disk space, you must also factor in the swap space. The recommended size of the swap space depends on the operating system and SAP kernel (32- or 64-bit) being used. Note the following requirements for each component (database and application server):

▶ **Windows NT**
The swap space should be four times as large as the computer's RAM: at least 4 GB and a maximum usable size of 10 GB.

▶ **32-bit kernel UNIX**
The swap space should be three times as large as the computer's RAM plus 500 MB: at least 3 GB and a maximum usable size of 20 GB.

▶ **64-bit Kernel UNIX**
The swap space should be at least 20 GB, regardless of the computer's memory.

The minimal memory size for a UNIX system is 256 MB and 512 MB for Windows NT systems. Using the SAP J2EE engine requires an additional 64 to 512 MB of RAM.

A dedicated application server requires about 800 MB of disk space exclusively for the working area of the SAP R/3 software. If the central transport directory, for example, is also to be created on a given computer, even more space must be available. Experience has shown that the following releases require more memory (Mem) and a more powerful CPU because of increased demands on performance. Table 4.1 displays the average increase for the database and application servers in the most recent releases of SAP R/3.

		Target release			
		4.0B	4.5B	4.6C	R/3 Enterprise
Source release	3.1I	Mem_{DB}: +10 % Mem_{APP}: +30 % CPU_{DB}: +10 % CPU_{APP}: +30 %	Mem_{DB}: +10 % Mem_{APP}: +56 % CPU_{DB}: +10 % CPU_{APP}: +56 %	Mem_{DB}: + 10 % Mem_{APP}: +100 % CPU_{DB}: + 10 % CPU_{APP}: + 72 %	Mem_{DB}: + 10 % Mem_{APP}: +115 % CPU_{DB}: + 10 % CPU_{APP}: + 80 %
	4.0B	–	Mem_{DB}: + 0 % Mem_{APP}: +20 % CPU_{DB}: + 0 % CPU_{APP}: +20 %	Mem_{DB}: + 0 % Mem_{APP}: +56 % CPU_{DB}: + 0 % CPU_{APP}: +32 %	Mem_{DB}: + 0 % Mem_{APP}: +64 % CPU_{DB}: + 0 % CPU_{APP}: +40 %
	4.5B	–	–	Mem_{DB}: + 0 % Mem_{APP}: +30 % CPU_{DB}: + 0 % CPU_{APP}: +10 %	Mem_{DB}: + 0 % Mem_{APP}: +37 % CPU_{DB}: + 0 % CPU_{APP}: +16 %
	4.6C	–	–	–	Mem_{DB}: +0 % Mem_{APP}: +5 % CPU_{DB}: +0 % CPU_{APP}: +5 %

Table 4.1 Average Additional Resource Requirements

The requirements for the system's front-end PCs depend on the following factors:

▶ SAP GUI version

▶ Scope of front-end functions

▶ Activation of resource-saving SAP GUI settings

▶ Level of usage of non-SAP applications (such as Microsoft Office, mail programs, and so on)

At a minimum, 64 MB of memory is recommended (by the OSS notes related to this question); however, 128 MB of memory is advisable.

There are also requirements regarding the software, such as an appropriate version of the operating system, NFS, language support (*locales*), and TCP/IP. In the SAP R/3 environment, Windows NT and Windows 2000 systems must be set for "English (International)." The software prerequi-

Software requirements

sites also vary depending on individual operating systems and the RDBMS, and particularly between SAP R/3 releases. Accordingly, you should double-check the requirements against the checklist very carefully.

Disk design After the prerequisites have been checked, the next step is to plan the distribution of the data across the individual disk drives. The most important consideration here is security against data loss, followed by methods to optimize performance. In particular, you should obey some basic rules about the properties of the production system (see Figure 4.1):

▶ Regardless of the RDBMS software, the data and log areas must be stored on different disks. The philosophy behind this approach is that the failure of one disk cannot affect the data and the log areas simultaneously. If the drives are addressed via several controllers, you must also distribute the data and log areas over different controllers.

▶ The log area must always be mirrored so that a drive failure affects only half the mirror.

▶ If you want to store data onto a disk of the server which is running the database of the SAP R/3 system, the backup disk must be different from the one that is running the database.

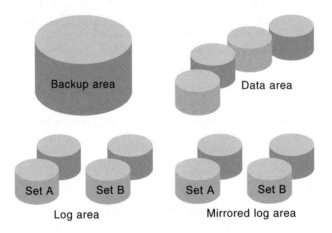

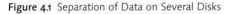

Figure 4.1 Separation of Data on Several Disks

Ignoring these rules can easily lead to security risks and degraded performance. The reasons for the rules lie primarily in the RDBMS architecture, which cannot be discussed in more detail in this book.

At least three disk drives are required for a minimal installation of an SAP R/3 system intended for testing.

The use of RAID systems has proven itself in the SAP R/3 environment. The essential features of this technology include security against failure and read/write performance.

RAID — Redundant arrays of independent disks

RAID-Level	Properties	Redundancy	Disk space efficiency	Reading [Random/ sequential]	Writing [Random/ sequential]
No RAID	Single disk drives	None	1	0/0	0/0
0	Striping without parity	None	1	++/+++	++/++
1	Mirroring and duplexing	Very high to extremely high	0.5	+/0	-/+
5	Block striping with distributed parity	High	(n-1)/n with n disks	++/+	--/0
01/10	Mirroring and striping without parity	Very high to extremely high	0.5	+++/+++	++/++

Table 4.2 RAID Level Used for Operation of SAP R/3

A RAID1, RAID01, or RAID10 system can be used to establish high security and good performance, as long as you keep in mind the physical separation of the individual data areas as described above. You can also use a RAID5 system for the SAP R/3 database in order to use the available disk space more efficiently. Because it lacks redundancy, RAID0 is unsuitable for operating an SAP R/3 system.

If it has been correctly installed, the SAP R/3 system will continue to run if a disk within a redundant RAID configuration should fail during operations. In most disk subsystems that are used for the SAP R/3 system, the defective disk can be exchanged and reintegrated while the system continues to run. During synchronization, however, you should expect decreased performance.

Disk failure

SAP Service Marketplace offers valuable SAP Notes on short-term changes to and guidelines for the installation procedure. You can also find the current SAP Note numbers that pertain to the installation in the installation manuals. Even experienced installers should be familiar with these SAP Notes before beginning with an installation.

Up to Basis Release 4.6D (see Chapter 1), installation of mySAP components is done with **R3setup**; **SAPinst** is used as of Basis Release 6.10.

You must perform some manual preparations with the support of tools before installing system components. The actual tasks depend on the operating system in use:

▶ UNIX

   ▶ Creation of file systems and raw devices

   ▶ Configuration of the UNIX kernel parameters and the swap space

▶ Windows NT

   ▶ Installation of Microsoft Management Console (MMC)

   ▶ Configuration of virtual memory and the file cache

The installation programs require their own installation directory with about 50 to 150 MB of free disk space to store command and log files.

LDAP integration If an LDAP (Lightweight Directory Access Protocol) directory is already used in the installation environment to administer system-wide data, you can configure the SAP R/3 system being installed to address the LDAP to store and evaluate data. The LDAP is the basis for collaboration between the SAP R/3 system and the LDAP directory. The interface is used to define communications between partners and to set the rules for data storage and access.

Information stored in the LDAP directory can be analyzed with the following mechanisms:

▶ **Microsoft Management Console (MMC)**
   Examines data such as the status and parameterization of the application servers.

▶ **LDAP Connector**
   The LDAP Connector is an ABAP interface that SAP applications can use to access information in the LDAP directory.

▶ **SAPLOGON**
   Instead of using manual configuration of the accessible systems for **SAPLOGON** by specifying technical details (system ID, name of the message server, instance number, and router string), you can set the **SAPLOGON** parameters in the configuration file sapmsg.ini so that the required information can be called via the LDAP directory.

The LDAP directory must first be prepared to store data from the SAP R/3 system. You can do so manually or use **R3setup** with the Active Directory service of Windows 2000. **R3setup** and **SAPinst** handle the special settings in the SAP R/3 system for communication with the LDAP directory as part of the installation of the SAP R/3 central instance.

4.2 Architecture of the R3setup Installation Tool

The installation procedure with **R3setup** (see Figure 4.2) can benefit from the advantages of client/server technology. You can call and work with the **R3setup** program locally, or over any computer with a TCP/IP connection to the target computer by using the **InstGUI. InstGUI** is a Tcl/Tk script available for X Windows (UNIX) and various Windows desktops. In addition to the InstGUI program, there is the actual installation program, **R3setup**, which exists on the server side. Installation can occur in dialog (by direct local call or controlled by an **InstGUI**) or as a background process executed by transferring all the parameters.

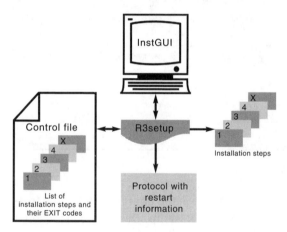

Figure 4.2 Installation with R3setup

If you use an **InstGUI**, confirmation of individual installation steps are sent to the frontend.

If errors occur, you can solve the problems and then continue with the installation from the point of termination.

The great advantage of this architecture is its uniform display of the **InstGUI** seen by a user, which is independent of the type of OS or database used. The architecture ensures that the different requirements of UNIX, Windows NT, and the RDBMS in the installation procedure are handled by R3setup. Because tasks are split between the frontend (**InstGUI**) and the server (**R3setup**), the installer is no longer bound to the future SAP R/3 server. Once **R3setup** starts on the target computer, the installer can log on to it from any computer. If the network connection between **InstGUI** and **R3setup** goes down during the installation or if the **InstGUI** is stopped, the **R3setup** process continues to run unobserved. The connection can be reestablished at any time.

Handling the InstGUI When starting **InstGUI** on any computer, the TCP/IP port for communication with **R3setup** (to be started later) is first determined. The required command line to start **R3setup** is displayed on the target computer (see Figure 4.3).

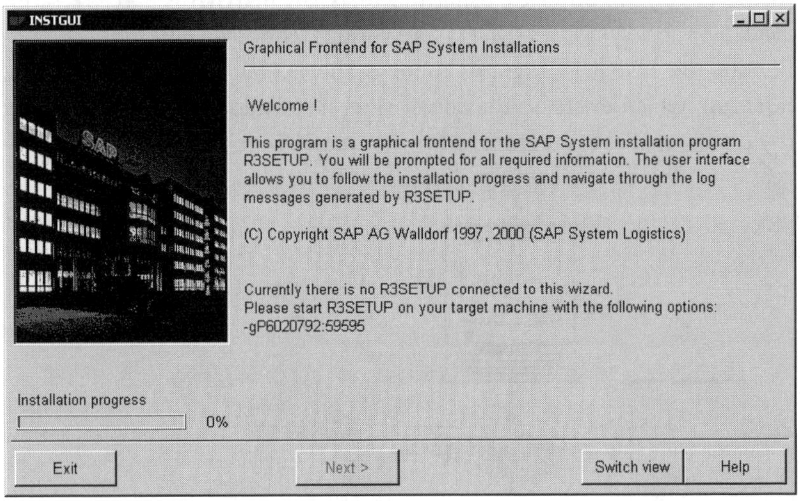

Figure 4.3 Starting the InstGUI

If **R3setup** is started with these options on the target computer, the **Inst-GUI** has established the connection to **R3setup**. Once the connection is successful, the screen changes (see Figure 4.4).

Within **InstGUI**, you can change between two views with **Switch view** (again, see Figure 4.4):

▶ **Step view**
An **InstGUI** window displays the installation step being executed and enables you to make any entries required. Click on **Help** to access specific help for **R3setup**: the Help files are stored in the installation directory.

▶ **Log view**
R3setup writes a run-specific log file that you can view directly from the **InstGUI**. The log contains the current installation step and all the warnings or errors that have occurred so far (see Figure 4.5).

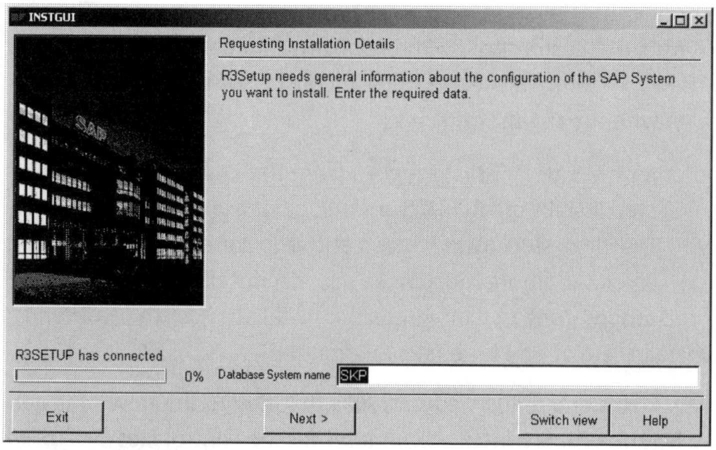

Figure 4.4 Successful Connection of InstGUI to R3setup

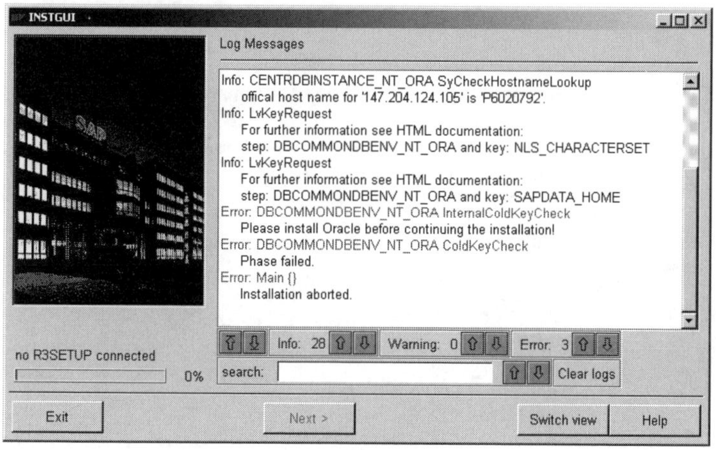

Figure 4.5 Log View of an Error Message Displayed in the InstGUI

4.3   Installation Steps

The setup of an operational SAP R/3 system requires installation of the following components:

▶ RDBMS software and the database instance

▶ Central instance

▶ Additional dialog instances (if needed)

▶ Instances operating as a standalone gateway to other SAP R/3 and R/2 systems (if needed)

▶ Frontends

Every component installation with **R3setup** runs in two phases. The first phase prompts the customer-specific configuration data required for the future SAP R/3 system. The second phase consists of the actual processing—ideally, without any user entries.

The setup of a new SAP R/3 system goes from the backend to the frontend. The first step installs the RDBMS and the database on the future database server. The next step installs the central instance on the selected application server. Additional instances can be installed afterward. The **R3setup** procedure does not integrate the installation of the frontends; you can install them at any time (see Section 4.5).

Control files **R3setup** evaluates and adjusts control files that define the flow of installation (see Figure 4.2). Predefined templates for the control files are stored in the installation directory during installation of **R3setup**. The controls files are editable text files; their names reflect the type of installation (see Table 4.3).

Control file	Content	Comments
CNTRDB.R3S	Installation of the central instance and a database instance on one server	No longer available for SAP R/3 4.6C on UNIX
CENTRAL.R3S	Installation of the central instance	
DATABASE.R3S	Installation of the database instance	
DIALOG.R3S	Installation of an additional application instance	
GATEWAY.R3S	Installation of a gateway instance	
CDINST.R3S	Installation of **R3setup**	Not available on UNIX systems

Table 4.3 List of Standard Control Files for R3setup

The control files consist of individual sections: each section begins with a descriptive name in brackets and describes a *step* within the installation.

Phase 1—Input The essential part of a section consists of the key word and value pairs. **R3setup** prompts system-specific values during the input phase. It then checks the entries and writes them to the control file.

Required entries include the following:

▶ Name of the SAP R/3 system

▶ Name of the database instance—identical to the name of the SAP R/3 system, except for Multiple Components on One Database (MCOD) systems (see Section 4.4.2)

▶ Number of the R/3 instance

▶ Server for the transport directory

▶ Directories for temporary storage of database export files

▶ File structure for the database

▶ Level of parallelization when loading the database

Additional entries are also required, depending on the RDBMS and operating system in use.

The [EXE] area of the control file lists the numbered installation steps in the order of execution as a flow plan.

The following section of the control file *CENTRDB.R3S* for the installation of a central and database instance shows an excerpt of the flow plan for the installation along with the steps executed there (see Listing 4.1).

Listing 4.1 Excerpt from Control File CENTRDB.R3S

```
[EXE]
10=CENTRDBINSTANCE_NT_ORA
20=DBCOMMONDBENV_NT_ORA
30=DBSAPDATAPATH_NT_IND
40=CALCRAM_IND_IND
50=CDSERVER46CSR2_NT_ORA
60=OSGROUPSAPLOCALADMIN_NT_IND
70=OSGROUPSAPLOCAL_NT_IND
. . . . . . .
610=DBCREATEDB_NT_ORA
620=DBPOSTBUILD_NT_ORA
630=DBCREATEROLLSEGSTART_NT_ORA
640=DBCREATETSP_NT_ORA
650=DBCREATEROLLSEG_NT_ORA
660=ORADBUSR_NT_ORA
. . . . . . .
890=RFCRSWBOINI_IND_IND
900=RFCRADDBDIF_IND_IND
```

```
910=R3CIFILEPERMISSIONS_NT_IND
920=QUERIESFINISHED_NT_IND
[CENTRDBINSTANCE_NT_ORA]
CLASS=CNTCommonParameters
CONFIRMATION=SAPSYSTEMNAME SAPSYSNR SAPLOC SAPNTDOMAIN
SAPTRANSHOST DB_SID
INSTALLATIONTYPE=CI
MSGID=RI_GIST_CENTRALINSTANCE_IND_IND
SAPLOC=(RI_GIKY_NA_COM_SAPLOC, entry { { label RI_GIKY_NA_
COM_SAPMNT_LABEL }{ regexp ^[A-Z][:]?$ } } )
SAPNTDOMAIN=(RI_GIKY_NA_COM_SAPNTDOMAIN, entry { { label
"Domain of all SAP Users and Groups" } } )
SAPSYSNR=00 (RI_GIKY_NA_COM_SAPSYNR,entry { { label RI_
GIKY_NA_COM_SAPSYNR_LABEL } { regexp ^(([0-8][0-9])|(9[0-
6]))$ } } )
SAPSYSTEMNAME=C11 (RI_GIKY_NA_COM_SAPSYSTEMNAME,entry { {
label RI_GIKY_NA_COM_SAPSYSTEMNAME_LABEL } { regexp ^[A-
Z][A-Z0-9][A-Z0-9]$ } } )
SAPTRANSHOST=(RI_GIKY_NA_COM_SAPTRANSHOST, entry { { label
RI_GIKY_NA_COM_SAPTRANSHOST_LABEL } } )
[DBCOMMONDBENV_NT_ORA]
CLASS=COraDbIniDefKey
CONFIRMATION=NLS_CHARACTERSET SAPDATA_HOME DB_HOME_NAME
DB_HOME_NAME=(RI_GIKY_NA_COM_ORANT_DBHOMENAME)
INST_MODE=OLD (RI_GIKY_NA_QT_INSTMODE,radiobox { { label
"Install for Multi Schema?" } { OLD "No (old style)" } {
NEW "Yes (new style)" } })
MSGID=RI_GIST_DBCOMMONDBENV_IND_IND
NLS_CHARACTERSET=WE8DEC
SAPUSERPASSWD=(RI_GIKY_NA_COM_SAPUSERPASSWD)
SVRMGR=@DB_HOME@\bin\svrmgr30.exe
[DBCREATEDB_NT_ORA]
CLASS=COraCreateDb
LIST=Z_ORACREATETSP
MSGID=RI_GIST_DBCREATEDB_IND_IND
STEP_ENV=DB_ENV
STEP_USER=@SAPNTDOMAIN@\@LOWER_SAPSYSTEMNAME@adm
STEP_USERPASSWORD=@OSUSERSIDADMPASSWD_NT_IND=PASSWORD@
```

Depending on the component to be installed, **R3setup** is started with the
required control file as a parameter. **R3setup** inserts all the values entered

by the installer into the control file. Accordingly, the prompts ultimately produce a text file that contains all the necessary data for a customer-specific installation. **R3setup** can now process the control file in phase 2-without additional dialog. For example, you might want to perform several installations, such as the identical installation of application servers that differ only in the name of the host. In this case, you can simply modify the control file written by **R3setup** and then reuse it.

If you prepared for the installation carefully, it's unlikely that errors will occur. The tasks required of the installer in phase 2 will be limited to changing the installation CDs and installing the RDBMS software.

Phase 2—Processing

R3setup begins with a check of the preparations on the target computer, including a look at authorization checks, monitoring available disk space, and verifying if the database software was installed correctly (with Windows NT). Figure 4.5 shows you an example whereby a user forgot to install the database.

In this case, **R3setup** aborts and writes the following entry for the failed step in the control file for a later restart.

```
STATUS=ERROR
```

Every execution of **R3setup** creates a specific log file named *<installation_type>.log*. To simplify the analysis of errors, one entry for each finished step is written to the file. The example in Listing 4.2 shows a problem in step DBCOMMONDBENV_NT_ORA.

Listing 4.2 Error Entry in Log File CENTRDB.log

```
ERROR 2002-11-03 14:21:07 DBCOMMONDBENV_NT_ORA Internal-
ColdKeyCheck:0
    Please install Oracle before continuing the
    installation!
ERROR 2002-11-03 14:21:07 DBCOMMONDBENV_NT_ORA ColdKey-
Check:0
    Phase failed.
ERROR 2002-11-03 14:21:07 InstController Action:0
    Step DBCOMMONDBENV_NT_ORA could not be performed.
ERROR 2002-11-03 14:21:08 Main :0
    Installation failed.
ERROR 2002-11-03 14:21:08 Main :0
    Installation aborted.
```

Once you fix the problem, you can simply restart **R3setup**; it will pick up where the error occurred.

The entire SAP R/3 installation packet consists of several CDs; therefore, you'll probably have to change CDs manually during the installation. However, if you have sufficient disk space, you can copy the CDs to a hard drive and inform **R3setup** of the path in phase 1.

Installation of the RDBMS When and how you install the RDBMS software depends on the database and the operating system in use. Execution of **R3setup** integrates only the installation of the SAP DB. The installation guides for other supported RDBMS software describe the process for these products.

The most tedious step of the installation process consists of importing data in the SAP R/3 database. Depending on how well your computer performs, this step can take several hours.

The installation steps performed by **R3setup** are mostly transparent to the installer, unless unexpected errors require correction. The following table (Table 4.4) contains an overview of the most important steps during the installation of a central instance running on UNIX with an Oracle database. This overview gives you a good idea of the complexity of the tasks involved. Depending on the operating system and the RDBMS in use, the sequence of phases and the tools used might differ. However, the type and number of phases remain identical. An asterisk (*) indicates those phases that run automatically and typically do not require operator intervention.

Phase	Content
Checking against the checklist	
Manual preparation	Adjusting the UNIX kernel parameters Setting up the file systems Configuration of the swap space
	Creation of the required data directories according to the installation manual: ▶ Installation directory ▶ Database directories ▶ Directories for the SAP R/3 instance
Installation of **R3setup**	Startup of shell script: *insttool.sh*

Table 4.4 Installation Phases for a Central Instance with a Database

Phase	Content
Queries of specific parameters	Name of the SAP R/3 system Instance number Transport directory Name of the database Language settings Memory settings CD mount Directory for copies of the CDs
Check*	Disk space Existence of directories
Communication*	Service entries for dispatcher, gateway, and message server Existing service entries are not changed
Users and groups*	Creating users and groups at the UNIX level for the database and the SAP R/3 system Existing users and groups are not changed
Directories*	Creating the required directories and setting access rights Existing directories and access rights are not changed
Unpacking the SAP R/3 software*	Distributing the software across the appropriate directories
Default profile*	Creating system profile DEFAULT.PFL
Setting users' work environment*	Definition of profile files for ora<sid> and <sid>adm
Instance profile	Creating the instance profile
Unpacking the Oracle software*	Storing the software in the appropriate directories
runInstaller	Installation of the Oracle software
Generating the SAP R/3 database*	Checking the size of the expected data files for the database Creating an empty Oracle database Creating database users Importing data Generating statistical information
Generating a temporary SAP R/3 license*	
Starting the SAP R/3 systems*	
Manual postprocessing	

Table 4.4 Installation Phases for a Central Instance with a Database (cont.)

The installation of additional SAP R/3 instances follows the same procedure. However, because the scope of additional instances is smaller, such
installations are simpler and can be performed faster.

4.4 Changes with the SAP Web Application Server

4.4.1 SAPinst

When the SAP Web Application Server was introduced as the basis for all
mySAP solutions, such as SAP R/3 Enterprise as the successor to SAP R/3
4.6C, the installation procedure for mySAP components was transferred
to the *System Landscape Implementation Manager* (**SAPinst**) instead of
R3setup. This technology enables a simplified installation of the entire
system landscape because a configuration tool predefines the required
parameters that can be used for automatic installation.

Much like **R3setup, SAPinst** can be started locally on the server that will
perform the installation. A remote installation is also an option: the **SAP-
inst** GUI monitors a remote installation. The **SAPinst** GUI is based on Java
technology; its use requires a Java development environment (JDK) or a
Java runtime environment (JRE).

An installation of components with **SAPinst** runs just like an installation
with **R3setup**: a sequence of predefined, reusable steps (see Figure 4.6).

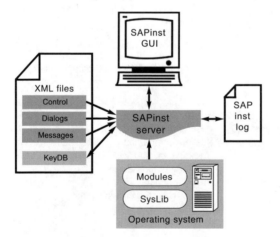

Figure 4.6 Installation with SAPinst

XML files control the flow of installation (see Table 4.5). Log data is stored
centrally in file *sapinst.log*.

File	Content
CONTROL.XML	Instructions on the installation of SAP components
KEYDB.XML	Description of the flow and status of the current installation
MESSAGES.XML	Catalog of message texts and the assignment of messages to message numbers
DIALOG.XML	Description of the dialogs with the user
PACKAGES.XML	Listing of CD labels
SAPINST.LOG	Log file of the installation run
SAPINST_DEV.LOG	Detailed log file of the installation run

Table 4.5 List of the Most Important Control and Log Files for SAPinst

Installation with **SAPinst** consists of the following phases:

1. **Input phase**
   Required entries for the type of installation, SID, instance number, host name, and so on are prompted from the user and written to the description file *KEYDB.XML* (see Figure 4.7 and Listing 4.4).

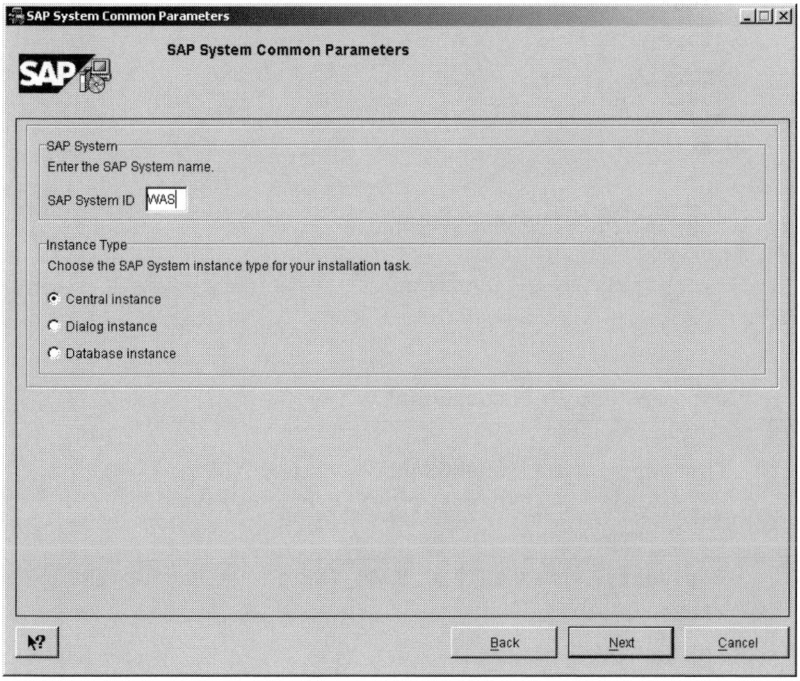

Figure 4.7 Entering Parameters

2. **Processing phase**

All the steps required for the installation are processed on the basis of the configured description files without additional user input.

The differences between **R3setup** and **SAPinst** are inherently technical and deal primarily with the way each program works in the installation procedure:

► Unlike **R3setup**, **SAPinst** does not terminate when an error occurs. Instead, it creates a pop-up that prompts you to solve the problem and try again.

► **SAPinst** allows users to scroll back during the input phase.

Listing 4.3 Excerpt from KEYDB.XML

```
   - <strval>
       <![CDATA[ WAS  ]]>
       </strval>
     </fld>
 - <fld name="WapsInstanceNumber">
     - <properties>
         <property name="GUIENG_USER_INPUT" value="GUIENG_
         TRUE" />
       <properties>
     - <strval>
         <![CDATA[ 00  ]]>
       </strval>
     </fld>
 - <fld name="WapsInstanceName">
     - <strval>
         <![CDATA[ DVEBMGS00  ]]>
       </strval>
     </fld>
 - <fld name="WapsInstanceHost">
     - <properties>
         <property name="CHANGEABLE" value="YES" />
         <property name="CONTEXT_PARAM_CHANGEABLE"
         value="YES" />
         <property name="GUIENG_USER_INPUT" value="GUIENG_
         TRUE" />
       </properties>
     - <strval>
```

```
    <![CDATA[ P6020792 ]]>
   </strval>
 </fld>
```

The *sapinst.log* contains an entry for every step executed.

Listing 4.4 Error Notation in the sapinst.log Log File (see Listing 4.2)

```
TRACE
showing dialog with index 33
TRACE
The controller is about to execute the dialog step
WebAs|ind|ind|ora|WebAs|620|0|SAPCompo-
nent|ind|ind|ind|ind|ind|0|DatabaseSys-
tem|ind|ind|ora|ind|ind|0|DatabaseCommonParameters|ind|in
d|ora|ind|ind|0|dialogGetCommonParamsPostprocess
TRACE
CALLING
COraCommonParameters::computeDependantParametersAfterDia-
log
***** Transaction begin ******************************
TRACE
CDomainObjectCache::readFromKeyDb: Reading from tGlobalDb-
Parameters WHERE dbSid = 'WAS'
ERROR 2002-11-05 12:49:22
MDB-06169  The Oracle Home name '' is not the name of
an Oracle Home directory registered on this host.
***** Transaction end ******************************
TRACE
JS Callback has thrown exception
ERROR 2002-11-05 12:49:23
FJS-00012  Error when executing script.
```

4.4.2 MCOD: Multiple Components on One Database

SAP Web Application Server 6.20 offers complete support for installing several mySAP systems on one shared database. This procedure allows for simpler administration of the database; however, it doesn't save many system resources—the sum of the requirements of individual components determines the requirements for sizing the server.

Installation of a mySAP system within a MCOD configuration runs much like the installation of a system with a dedicated database. The only dif-

SIDs

ferences are the naming conventions for the SAP system and the shared database. The name of the database is the same for all the SAP systems used within the MCOD installation, but the SIDs of the SAP components differ. The MCOD installation is an integral part of **SAPinst**. Since the SAP R/3 4.6C SR2 release, you can install the MCOD installation with **R3setup**, and you can do so manually.

SAP plans to make this configuration option available for all mySAP Business Suite components and all major databases.

4.5 Postprocessing

After the actual installation of SAP R/3 software with **R3setup** or **SAPinst**, you must make several settings on the SAP R/3 system and the RDBMS in order to make SAP R/3 operative. This phase is known as *postprocessing*.

SAP license key A request of an SAP *license key* for the new system is particularly important. The license key is a 24-character ID stored in the database of the SAP R/3 system. The value is generated from various system- and server-specific data, so that it is valid only for the current installation. If you use a hardware cluster or a standby system that is kept current with log shipping, and activated with the identity of the source system in the event of a disaster, it is mandatory that you install several licenses in parallel. To generate the license key, SAP requires the system's hardware key, which you can find at the operating-system level on the computer running the message server with the following command:

```
saplicense -get
```

You must send the key and additional data to SAP, which generates the license key and transmits it to you. SAP Service Marketplace is the easiest place in which to request a license key.

You activate the SAP license with `saplicense -install`; the program prompts you for the required parameters. Since SAP R/3 4.6C, you can execute the following actions from SAP R/3 with ▶ **License administration** (see Figure 4.8):

▶ Display downloaded licenses
▶ Download an additional (or temporary) license
▶ Delete a license
▶ Determine the hardware key

The license is active upon implementation; you don't need to restart SAP R/3.

Installation of the front-end software can occur at any time, it doesn't depend on the installation of the SAP R/3 system. Each of the following options uses a different procedure:

Front-end installation

▶ SAP GUI for Windows

▶ SAP GUI for Java

▶ SAP GUI for HTML

For a typical, common installation of the frontend on Windows PCs, you can use a local or server-based installation, or work with software distribution.

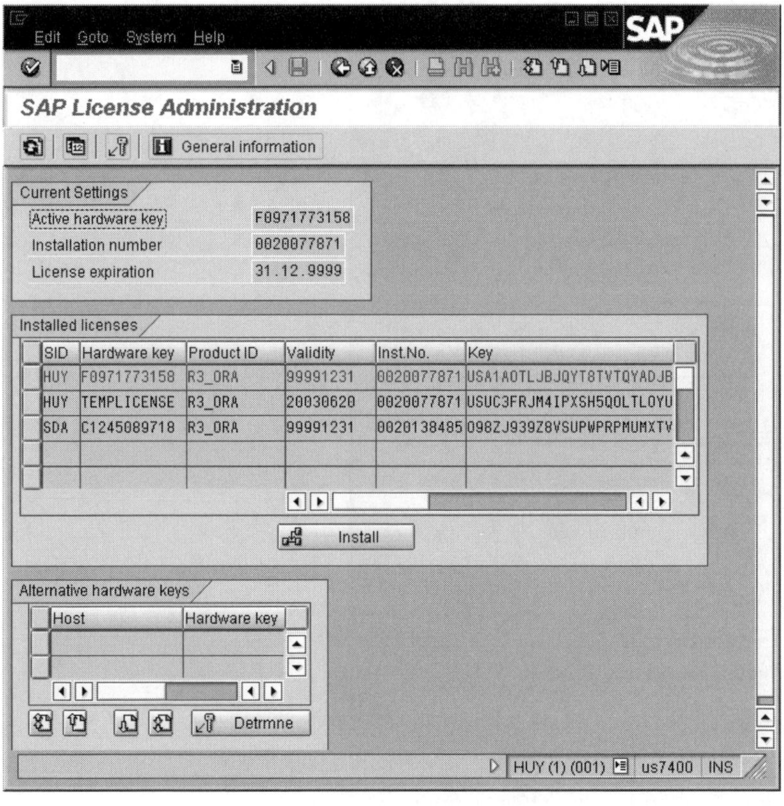

Figure 4.8 License Administration from the SAP R/3 System

The configuration of **SAPLOGON** (see Chapter 1) as part of postprocessing for a system installation first requires that you add the following properties of the new systems:

Front-end configuration SAPLOGON

▶ A description you can choose at will

▶ Application server as host name or IP address

- ▶ SAP router string

- ▶ System number

- ▶ Under **Additional command line arguments**, you can specify a code page or the front-end language. You can also define settings for Secure Network Communications (SNC) and the connection speed. Settings for a low speed connection affect the amount of data transmitted to the frontend. This setting improves response time in WAN installations, albeit at the cost of user-friendliness.

- ▶ **SAPLOGON** provides an option to select the **SAPLOGON** display language. You can also branch directly to the *sap*.ini* configuration file and, if necessary, activate front-end tracing (see Figure 4.9).

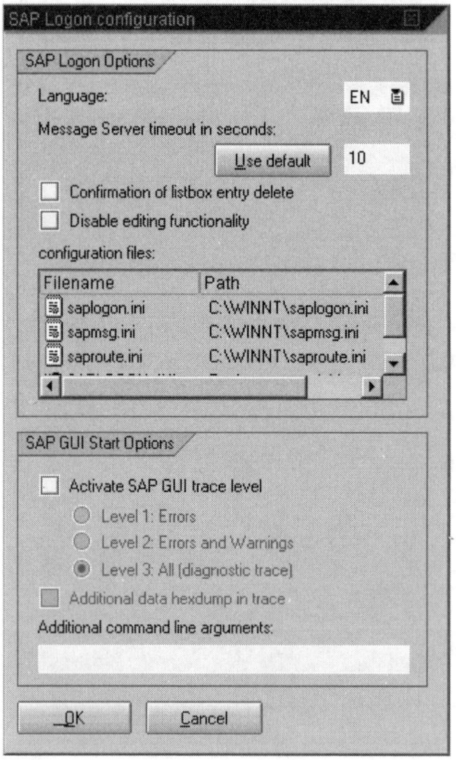

Figure 4.9 Configuration Options for SAPLOGON

Installation check

After the system has been installed successfully, you should start and stop the entire SAP R/3 system (including the database) to check its basic functions. Select ▶**Installation check** to check the installed software for the completeness and compatibility of the versions (releases of SAP R/3 and the operating system, for example). The installation check also tests if the message server can be reached. This test verifies that all types of work processes (dialog, batch, update, spool, and enqueue) are available in the installed system. It also examines the generated entries for the enqueue server and update service to determine if they agree with the actual conditions, and if the critical structure definitions are consistent.

An additional, important point involves changing the passwords of the default users (see Chapter 8) to protect the new SAP R/3 system from unauthorized access. You can do so immediately when logging on as one of these users. One of the first tasks of system administrators after the installation of the system is to create their own SAP R/3 user. With this ID, they can then perform all other administrative tasks.

The standard installation of SAP R/3 completely integrates all language-dependent elements in English and German. When they log on, users can select either English or German. If an SAP R/3 system requires additional languages, you must perform a *language import*. This task imports the required and available language elements of the preferred language into the tables of the SAP R/3 database, so you must have enough disk space available for the new data. Of the 28 languages available in SAP R/3 4.6C, only English and German are complete. Not all the screens, menu entries, or F1 Help are completely translated in the other supported languages. Rather, only portions of the text in the remaining 26 languages are translated. Given this situation, you must specify a default language (that appears whenever a text is unavailable in the local language) along with the import of the available language modules to supplement the portions of the target language that are not translated.

Language import

Beginning with SAP R/3 4.6C, the technical procedure for importing additional languages was changed to the Correction and Transport System (CTS) (see Chapter 6), so that supplemental imports occur with transport requests. Select ▶ **Language management** (see Figure 4.10) to start the import and supplementation of languages. If you plan to use languages displayed with different code pages (English, Russian, and Chinese, for example) within the SAP R/3 system, you must make special settings and deal with some limitations. SAP R/3 Enterprise features a complete Unicode implementation that supports all combinations of languages.

Because language elements are imported only into client 000, you must first process all the required languages (after the installation) and only then create the required additional clients as copies of client 000.

Client copy   Postprocessing for an installation includes copying the clients (see Chapter 7) needed for continuing operations from either of the default clients: 000 or 001.

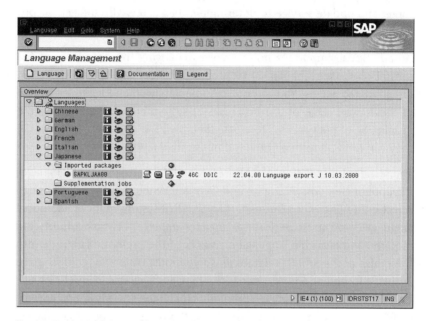

Figure 4.10 Initial Screen of Language Maintenance

Backup   Once the installation and postprocessing are completed, you must perform a complete offline backup of the newly installed system. In Windows NT systems, you should also back up registry entries; you can use the `rdisk` command to do so. To guarantee high availability of a Windows NT system, it is advisable to install a second Windows NT operating system on a separate hard drive. Should the disk with the operating system fail, you can then use the second installation to start the computer. Depending on the backup software that you decide to use, you can also back up the operating system with the SAP and database entries. At the very least, you should create an *emergency repair disk* with which to start the computer without the operating system in the event of an emergency. Here too, you can use the `rdisk` command.

For performance and security reasons, neither the SAP R/3 database server or the application server in Windows NT environments should function as the primary domain controller or the backup domain controller. However, giving limited rights to the user and group definitions required to operate SAP R/3 mitigates the importance of this point.

Online documentation is available in HTML format and can be displayed with a Web browser. To access online documentation directly from the SAP R/3 system, you must store it in the format that you want (standard HTML or compiled HTML) and make some settings in the SAP R/3 system. Since SAP R/3 4.6C, you no longer need to define system parameters. You simply make the settings with ▶ **Setting options for help (SAP Library)**. Entries in the *sapdoccd.ini* configuration file can override system settings to access online documentation.

Installation of online documentation

The postprocessing phase, which is briefly discussed here, includes several more steps. The installation guidelines describe the most important steps. Although the SAP R/3 system can function once this work has been performed, you must now define its role in the system landscape, initialize CTS, set up users, and so on. The following chapters describe these tasks.

4.6 Tips

▶ **License key**
Creation of the license key also involves a hardware key. Copying the SAP R/3 system to other hardware means that you must request and download a new license key. Until the key is implemented, only limited use of the system is possible (only user SAP* can log on).

▶ **Changes in the R3setup control files**
You can use any text editor to change entries in the **R3setup** control files. Windows systems also provide R3Sedit for this task.

▶ **Changes in SAPinst control files**
You can use any text editor to change entries in the **SAPinst** control files, but XML editors simplify the task. You can find helpful links to download test versions under Quicklink */sapinstfeedback* in SAP Service Marketplace.

▶ **R3setup templates for other purposes**
Besides standard installation activities (see Table 4.3), **R3setup** can also perform several other related tasks. For example, it includes templates for system copies, configuration of NT clusters, database exports, or integration of SAP system in the Active Directory.

▶ **Length of the host name**
Up to SAP R/3 4.5B, the host name could be 8 characters long; as of SAP R/3 4.6C, the host name can be 13 characters long.

▶ **Installation of multiple instances on one server**
Both Windows and UNIX platforms support the installation of multiple instances of an SAP system, several components of SAP systems, or sev-

eral SAP systems on one server. However, you must note the limitations regarding the compatibility of database releases. You cannot operate 32-bit and 64-bit kernels together.

▶ **Enhanced functions for language management**
After the fundamental changes to language management in SAP R/3 4.6C, these functions have been enhanced even further:

▷ As of Basis 4.6D, language installation and supplementation can run in parallel.

▷ As of SAP Web Application Server 6.10, you can process language-relevant changes within the support package with ▶ **Language management**.

▷ SAP Web Application Server 6.20 integrates the transfer of language-relevant data to clients other than 000 (report **RSREFILL**) in ▶ **Language management**.

4.7 Transactions and Menu Paths

Installation check: SAP Menu Tools • Administration • Administration • Installation check (SM28)

Language management: SAP Menu Tools • Administration • Administration • Language administration (SMLT)

License administration: Not available over the standard SAP menu (SLIC)

Setting options for help (SAP Library): SAP Menu Tools • Accelerated SAP • Customizing SAP Reference IMG • General settings • Setting options for help (SR13)

User maintenance: SAP Menu Tools • Administration • User maintenance Users (SU01)

4.8 Additional Documentation

Quicklinks

▶ SAP Service Marketplace: alias *installation*

▶ SAP Service Marketplace: alias *platforms*

▶ SAP Service Marketplace: alias *instguides*

▶ SAP Service Marketplace: alias *sizing*

▶ SAP Service Marketplace: alias *quicksizing*

▶ SAP Service Marketplace: alias *network*

- ▶ SAP Service Marketplace: alias *sapinstfeedback*
- ▶ SAP Service Marketplace: alias *ti*
- ▶ SAP Service Marketplace: alias *licensekey*
- ▶ SAP Service Marketplace: alias *mcod*
- ▶ SAP Service Marketplace: alias *language*

SAP Service Marketplace Notes

The following table (Table 4.6) provides an overview of important SAP Service Marketplace notes related to the installation of an SAP R/3 landscape:

Content	Note
Helpful log files for installation problems	331082
Configuration of the LDAP Connectors	188371
Directory integrations	448360
Windows language versions and SAP server products	427452
How many work processes should be configured?	39412
Improving the performance of **SAPLOGON**	559711
Installation of multiple components in one database	388866
Several instances or systems on one UNIX computer	21960
Two SAP R/3 systems on one Windows NT computer	28392
SAP GUI 6.10/6.20	402189
Requesting additional resources	89305, 113795, 323263, and 517085
Requesting a license key	94998

Table 4.6 SAP Notes on Installation

4.9 Questions

1. Which statement is true?

For a minimal installation of SAP R/3:

   a. Installation of the RDBMS is sufficient.

b. Installation of a database instance and a central instance is required.

c. The database instance and the central instance can reside on one system.

d. A database instance, a central instance, and at least one application server must be installed.

2. Which statement is true?

a. SAP R/3 naming conventions can be changed at any time with tools available at the operating-system level.

b. SAP R/3 naming conventions are a fixed component of various SAP R/3 tools and cannot be changed at will.

c. SAP R/3 naming conventions help users to find logs and messages quickly.

3. Which statement is correct?

a. Use of RAID systems increases the reliability of SAP R/3 systems.

b. Running the SAP R/3 database on a RAID system is not recommended, because it results in poor performance.

c. RAID systems are only recommended for the data area of the SAP R/3 database. For performance reasons, they are not recommended for log areas.

5   Setting Up the System Landscape

Operating the production system reliably and with optimal performance is one of the system administrator's most important tasks. Other vital tasks include avoiding problems that arise due to insufficient testing and ensuring the optimal distribution of the available resources. Both a well-planned setup of the system landscape and regulated processes for new developments and modifications of system settings can help the system administrator expedite these tasks.

The installation of the SAP R/3 license and the following installation checks complete the actual installation procedure for an SAP R/3 system. All the required data and programs are now available. The next step involves the maintenance of all customer-specific, technical settings. Until this step is completed, no one should work with the system. In particular, no *Customizing* (business settings) should be performed. An important part of postprocessing for a newly installed SAP R/3 system is the initialization of the *Change and Transport System* (CTS). This step lays the foundation for collaboration with other systems.

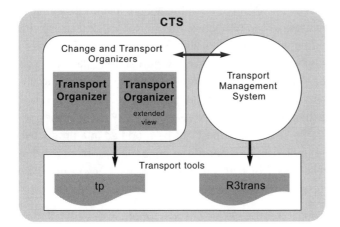

Figure 5.1 Components of the Change and Transport System

The CTS consists of the following three blocks (see Figure 5.1):

▶ Transport Organizer (and Transport Organizer—extended view)
▶ Transport Management System
▶ Transport tools

The *Transport Organizer* is one of the most important tools for project staff who deal with Customizing and development, and for system administrators who are responsible for transports. Chapter 6 addresses the characteristics and options of the Transport Organizer.

The *Transport Management System* (TMS) lays the foundation for regulated distribution throughout the system landscape of new system settings, developments, and modifications bundled in *transports*. The system administrator is responsible for creating a transport landscape that can optimally map the requirements of an application. After its initial configuration, you can use the TMS to schedule, execute, and monitor all import activities.

The **tp** and **R3trans** programs work at the operating-system level to export transport requests into files and import them into the target system. During the system installation, a transport directory is created under a fixed path; this directory contains all the CTS files.

5.1 Initializing the Change and Transport System

During the last step of an installation, the global and object-class-specific *system change option* of each SAP R/3 system in the landscape must be defined. The objects in SAP R/3 that are integral here include cross-client data, such as programs, screen templates, menus, tables, and structures, along with client-independent Customizing (see Chapter 7). The system change option is defined manually in each SAP R/3 system. Basically, you must first consider if the objects in an SAP R/3 system should be modifiable at all. The term *modifiability* means the possibility to create and adapt new objects or further develop objects delivered by SAP to meet the specific needs of customers. This data must not be modified in a productive environment. The modifications permitted in a development system depend on the type and scope of the developments. For example, are modifications of objects delivered by SAP permitted?

You have two options to set the system change option: with ▶ **Installation postprocessing** (up to SAP R/3 4.6C) or ▶ **Transport Organizer Tools · Administration · Set system change option**. First, you make a global setting to define whether modifications are permissible. Repository objects are grouped in software components and assigned to a namespace. The system in which an object was created is called the *original system* (see Chapter 6) of the object. You can use these settings to give the modifiability settings greater granularity. An object is modifiable only when:

1. The global system change option is set to "modifiable."
2. The software components to which the object belongs have the value of "modifiable."
3. The namespace in which the object lies has the value of "modifiable."

Table 5.1 describes this context.

		Software Components		
		Modifiable	Restricted modifiability	Not modifiable
Name-space	Modifiable	Existing objects can be repaired New objects receive the system ID for the original system	Existing objects can be repaired New objects receive "SAP" for the original system	–
	Not modifiable	–	–	–

Table 5.1 System Change Option at the Level of Namespace and Software Components

A software component describes a set of logically connected objects that are delivered and processed together. Objects are assigned to a namespace by appending the prefix of the namespace to the beginning of the name of the object. Name ranges are subsets of a namespace.

An SAP R/3 system distinguishes the following software components:

▶ **Customer developments (HOME)**
Includes all customer-specific developments made with all the tools available in the SAP R/3 system that can be transported.

▶ **Local developments (no automatic transport: LOCAL)**
Includes all customer-specific objects that are not transportable (local).

▶ **Cross-application components (SAP_ABA)**
This option allows you to make modifications with the tools of the ABAP Workbench (Development Workbench) to all the application components delivered by SAP.

▶ **Logistics and accounting (SAP_APPL)**

▶ **SAP Basis components (SAP_BASIS)**
Enables modifications of all Basis components with all the tools available. All components of the Development Workbench, ABAP Query, and use of the Function Builder are permitted.

▶ **Human Resources (SAP_HR)**

The most important namespaces and ranges include:

► **Customer namespace**
All objects without a prefix whose names begin with Y or Z.

► **General SAP namespace**
All objects without a prefix and whose names do not begin with Y or Z.

► **ABAP and GUI tools: prefix /1BCABA/**
Permits only the processing of SAP objects with the ABAP Editor, Screen Painter, and Menu Painter. Modifications of functions are not permitted.

► **Development Workbench: prefix /1BCDWB/**
Includes processing SAP objects with all the tools in the Development Workbench (ABAP Editor, Screen Painter, and Menu Painter) and modifications of Repository objects. Modifications of functions are not permitted.

► **Enqueue functions groups: prefix /1BCDBWEN/**
Includes SAP functions that serve enqueue management by SAP R/3.

If you want to set the change option of your system so that only customer objects can be modified, set the software components HOME and LOCAL and the customer name range to "modifiable."

Initialization   If you installed your SAP R/3 system from a CD with **R3setup** or **SAPinst**, initialization of the CTS is not required. If the system was created as a copy of an existing system, you must use ►**Installation Postprocessing** to regenerate the basic settings of the CTS and to close any foreign requests and tasks in the system.

To do so, select **Database copy or migration** in ►**Installation Postprocessing** and execute it. You can display and analyze a log of the actions performed with **Extras · Display logs**.

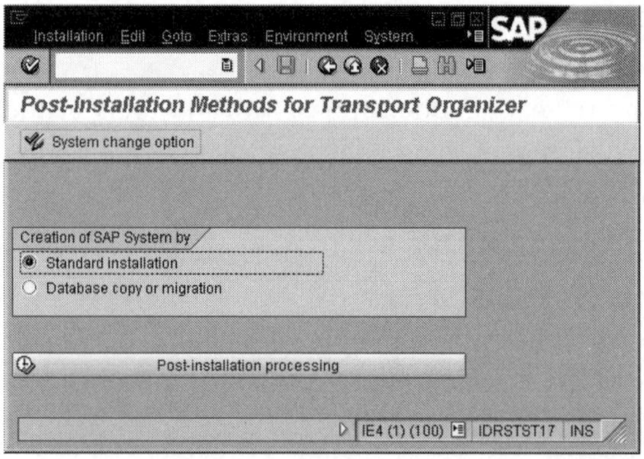

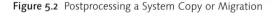

Figure 5.2 Postprocessing a System Copy or Migration

5.2 Tasks of a System Landscape

Every installed SAP R/3 system contains all the resources it needs to be able to handle all SAP R/3 functions. In addition to business applications, software development and management, quality assurance for self-developed SAP R/3 components, and special system settings are supported. To meet these different requirements and stay productive without risk to the operation, we recommend that you create separate SAP R/3 systems for each of these particular environments. A single system is justified only for training or demonstration purposes.

The reasons for the recommendation result from the different requirements of different systems. Consider what would ensue if production and testing occurred on one system:

1. All modifications of the Repository affect the entire runtime environment of the SAP R/3 system and therefore production.
2. Developers can use reports to access all production data.
3. Development work has a negative effect on the performance of a system. For example, if programs are being processed in debugging mode for a test, a dialog work process can be assigned to a user for the entire time. The dialog work process would then work only for this user. Simultaneous training sessions on a single SAP R/3 system also have a negative effect on performance.

Accordingly, you would have to stop development work in a one-system configuration.

It is therefore advisable to distribute different tasks across different systems and to transfer modifications made in the test system to the production system-only after the modifications have been tested. In this case, one speaks of *transporting* the modifications. The CTS supports both the administration of all modifications and developments in the systems and their transport between systems (see Figure 5.1).

The basic recommendation of SAP is to install a system landscape with at least two systems. Development and testing occurs on one system; productive operations occur on the other system.

Two-system landscape

In a two-system landscape, the CTS considers the development and test system as an integration system, and the production system as a consolidation system.

If developments have reached an acceptable level, the changes are transported to the subsequent system—the consolidation system. In a two-system landscape, the production system already realizes the consolidation system (see Figure 5.2), so that this scenario does not support testing transports as such. In the event of complex developments, which include dependencies, complete testing in a two-system landscape cannot occur.

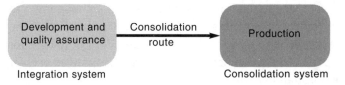

Figure 5.3 Two-System Landscape

In the same way, the intermediate states of an ABAP program cannot be tested while development of the same object is ongoing.

Three-system landscape

Only the recommended three-system landscape covers these requirements sufficiently. In this case, a distinction is made at the technical level:

▶ **Integration system**
For development and customer-specific settings (Customizing)

▶ **Consolidation system**
To test and verify developments and customer-specific settings in an environment similar to that of production

▶ **Delivery system**
As an independent production system

The roles of the systems (development, quality assurance, and production) are strictly separated here. Developments can first be tested in a separate system before they are used in the production system. To benefit from these advantages, the technical system settings and the organizational approach must adhere to this model of roles.

Figure 5.4 Three-System Landscape

Adherence means following these basic rules:

▶ All development and customizing work occurs in the integration system. The correctness of functions and properties is verified with the help of a test data pool.

▶ The developments and system settings that have undergone basic testing are transported to the dedicated consolidation system for quality assurance, where they are tested in an environment that resembles production. If an error is discovered, it is corrected in the integration system, and the modified version of the development or system setting is once again transported to the consolidation system.

▶ Only verified modifications are transported from the consolidation system into the production system. No modifications are made on the production system itself.

You can support adherence to these basic rules technically with the settings for system change option (see Section 5.1), settings for client modifiability (see Chapter 7), and the definition of transport routes between the systems of your landscape (see Section 5.3).

When making a decision for a particular system landscape, you must consider the costs and benefits in light of the requirements. Although a three-system landscape offers advantages, the hardware costs and administrative effort increase with the complexity of the system landscape. Therefore, you must balance the requirements and the effort involved.

Of course, some configurations should consist of more than three systems. For example, it might be advisable to run several production systems separated by location to handle the various sites of a company. In such cases, the distinction between integration, consolidation, and delivery systems remains because the technical functions are identical. In these types of landscapes, several systems of one class exist in parallel. The roles of each system might not be easily defined because they often play a double role.

Multisystem landscapes

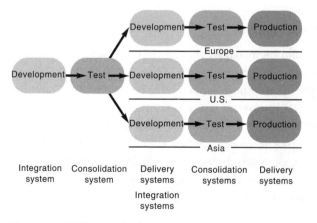

Figure 5.5 Multisystem landscape

Figure 5.5 shows an example of a multisystem landscape. A central integration system functions as the entry point; it might be used for international development work. A subordinate consolidation system handles quality assurance for the developments. Independent system landscapes are connected for country-specific developments.

5.3 Configuration of the Transport Management System

The *Transport Management System* (TMS) realizes a central administrative view of the settings and transports in an SAP system landscape. You can combine SAP systems whose transport properties should be administered centrally into *transport domains*. Typically, several systems are grouped into a transport domain, and such transport domains are linked via transport routes. From an administrative viewpoint, however, you can manage several of these groups of systems in one transport domain.

To map the preferred system environment in transport management, you must perform the following basic steps:

1. Decide which systems should be combined into a transport domain so that you can administer their transport properties centrally. If the systems are not physically present when you model the transport landscape and map them in the TMS, you can configure virtual dummy systems.
2. Determine which system you will use for central administration.
3. Define which systems or clients will be linked by transports, and which role (integration, consolidation, or delivery) they will play in the transport group.

5.3.1 Transport Domains

Transport Domain Controller (TDC)

All systems that should be managed via a central TMS are configured in one transport domain. For technical reasons, the system IDs of the systems participating in the transport domain must be unique. The *Transport Domain Controller* (TDC) is the special system of a transport domain that manages all its TMS settings. To maintain a consistent view of all systems in the domain, the TMS reference configuration resides on the TDC; a copy of the configuration is distributed to all members of the domain. All the required settings, such as the definition of the transport routes (see Section 5.3.2), are therefore made on the TDC.

Communication between the TDC and the other SAP systems in the domain occurs over RFC connections (see Chapter 13). TMS configuration automatically creates the required RFC connections.

As the TDC, you should select a highly available SAP system with good security features from the system landscape. This system should also be the most current release possible. Accordingly, production and quality assurance systems are usually more appropriate for this role than are development systems. The load created in an SAP R/3 system by the TMS is limited and does not have a negative effect on performance.

If necessary, another system in the domain can take over the tasks of the TDC. This option is often used in the rebuilding of a system landscape where the development system is installed first. This development system then assumes the role of the TDC until the configuration of the production system.

To create the transport domain and its domain controller, proceed as follows:

Creating the Transport Domain

1. Configuration of the domain occurs with the ▶ **Transport Management System** in client 000 of the SAP R/3 system that is initially viewed as the TDC.

2. The system notifies you if the TMS is not yet defined and proposes a domain name as the next step. The default name is "DOMAIN_<SID>," where "<SID>" is the system ID of the system that is used to perform the configuration.

3. Select **New Domain** and enter the name and description of the domain. The name cannot contain any spaces. Once you select a domain name, you can only modify it when the TMS is completely reconfigured.

4. Save your entries.

The system from which the transport domain is created is defined as the Domain Controller. All further configuration work must be performed from this system in client 000.

You have now defined the domain and its controller. You can check the definition with ▶ **Transport Management System · Overview · Systems**. During the definition of the TDC, and later, during the integration of additional systems into the domain, the system automatically performs some tasks in the background to prepare for the functions of the TMS:

▶ The configuration data is saved in the database; some of the data is also saved in the *DOMAIN.CFG* file in subdirectory *bin* of the transport directory at the operating-system level.

▶ Special user TMSADM is created in the SAP R/3 system with type *communication* (see Chapter 8). This user has authorizations only for TMS tasks (see Figure 5.6).

▶ All the required RFC connections to other systems are created.

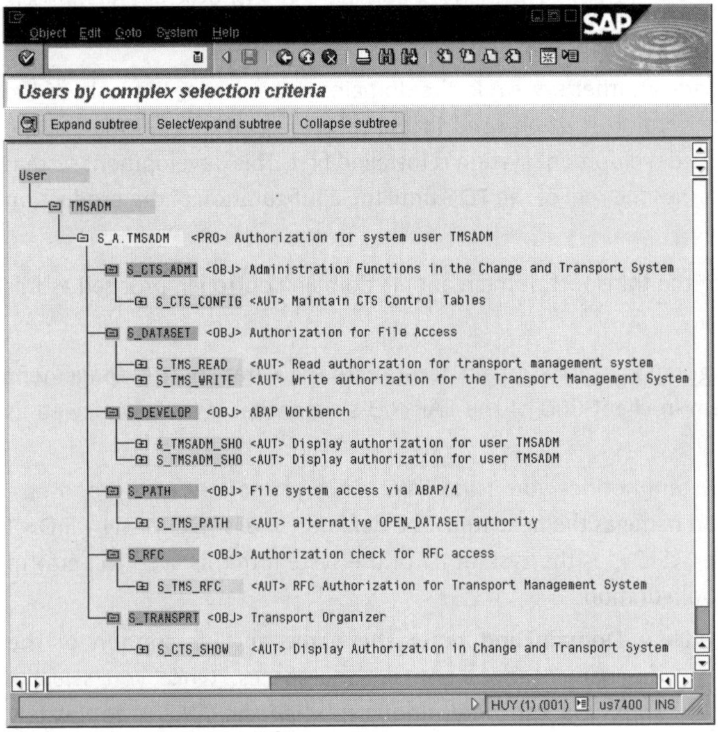

Figure 5.6 Authorizations of User TMSADM

Integrating additional systems

To integrate additional SAP R/3 systems into the domain, complete the following two steps:

1. Log on to client 000 of the system to be added and call ▶ **Transport Management System**. The system to be added automatically recognizes that the current system does not yet belong to a domain. If you use the same transport directory (see Section 5.4), the system analyzes the configuration file (*DOMAIN.CFG*) and proposes the domain provided. You can overwrite the proposal if you select another domain or create a new one. Accept the proposal, or enter the name of the domain that you want. After you're saved your entries, the new system is ready to be integrated in the domain.

2. In the second step, the TDC must confirm the integration of the new system so that it is completely integrated into the domain. To do so, restart the ▶Transport Management System on the TDC in client 000 and select Overview · Systems. The new system appears in the list with the status: *System waiting for inclusion in the transport domain.* Select the system and then SAP System · Approve to record it in the domain.

The configuration modification is now complete on the TDC. To ensure a consistent view of TMS configuration, the modification must be passed on to all the systems in the domain. Distribution of modifications is always possible directly after the action or as part of a group. You can initiate a distribution on the TDC in client 000 with ▶Transport Management System · Overview · Systems · Extras · Distribute and activate configuration.

Detailed information on any errors that might have occurred during configuration will be displayed. In addition, the TMS alert monitor contains a history of all errors, including a note about possible causes and corrections. You can access the alert monitor from the ▶Transport Management System via Monitor · TMS Alerts · TMS Alert Viewer. The functions of the Transport Management Systems area are also linked to Computing Center Management System (CCMS) alert monitoring (see Chapter 16); you can reach that monitor directly or from the ▶Transport Management System via Monitor · TMS Alerts · CCMS Alert Monitor.

The Transport Domain Controller must always be available for configuration modifications, such as the integration of an additional system. To enable continued operations should the TDC fail, you can use a *Backup Domain Controller* (BDC). The use of a BDC enables you to transfer TDC functions to another system in the same domain. To do so, define the system as the BDC as follows: ▶Transport Management System · Overview · Systems; select a system, SAP system · Change; enter the system ID in the backup field on the Communication tab. If the BDC is to adopt the tasks of the TDC, you must activate the TDC from the system list on the BDC with Extras · Activate Backup Controller. For obvious reasons, this is the only configuration activity that is not performed on the TDC.

Backup Domain Controller

You can delete the entire TMS configuration from the system overview with Extras · Delete TMS configuration; you can delete a single system from the system overview on the TDC with SAP System · Delete. After deletion, some settings are still present in inactive form and must be overwritten with new settings if necessary.

SAP R/3 3.1H is the minimum release required to integrate an SAP system in a transport domain.

Virtual systems
To model a transport landscape in which not every system is physically present or accessible, we can define *virtual systems* as dummies. The transports intended for these systems are collected, and the transports can be imported immediately when the virtual systems are replaced with real systems. You can create virtual systems with ▶Transport Management System · Overview · Systems · SAP systems · Create · Virtual system and additionally entering a *communication system*. The communication system is necessary to make the required RFC connection available. Once a real system is ready, you must delete the virtual placeholder from the configuration and integrate the new system in the domain. Note that the SID of the new system must agree with the SID of the virtual system in order to be able to use the defined settings.

External systems
In addition to definitions of virtual systems, you can also make entries for *external systems*. An external system is a kind of virtual system: like the latter, external systems do not physically exist in the transport domain. Entries for external systems are required when:

▶ Data is to be transported between different transport domains, that is, to a system in a different transport domain.

▶ Transport data is to be exported to, or imported from, removable storage media.

The essential difference between a virtual system and an external system is the transport directory that is used. Virtual systems use the standard transport directory of their communications system; you can specify any directory for external systems. Similar to setting up a virtual system, you create an external system with ▶Transport Management System · Overview · Systems · SAP System · Create · External system. The SAP system from which you manage the external SAP system is set as the *communication system*; when you create an external system, the TDC is proposed as the communication system. You must also specify the transport directory that you want to use. This directory will store all the data and logs required for transports to or from external systems.

Figure 5.7 shows external system "QAS" in DOMAIN_A being used as a dummy for real system "QAS" in DOMAIN_B and external system "DEV" in DOMAIN_B being used as a dummy for real system "DEV" in DOMAIN_A. Data is exchanged over the directory *trans_ext*, which must be accessible from the communication system assigned to both systems.

The *domain link* provides another method for joining transport domains. **Domain Link** Two domains, each with a TDC running Basis Release 4.6C (at a minimum) can be joined with a direct link. To do so, use ▶Transport Management System · Overview · Systems · SAP System · Create · Domain Link to connect to a TDC in a remote domain that can be reached over a network connection. The TDC of the remote domain must confirm the connection: all the required RFC connections will be defined and you can address the systems of the remote domain.

The central transport directory created during installation is used as the default for storage of all the required transport data and logs. Figure 5.8 illustrates the structure of the directory tree.

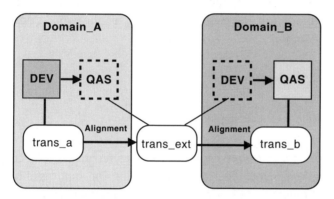

Figure 5.7 External Systems as Dummies in Other Domains

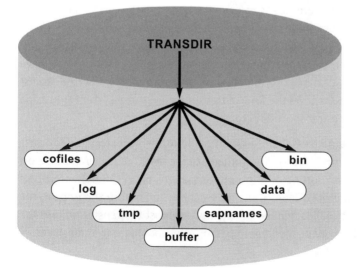

Figure 5.8 Transport Directory Tree

The following list describes the contents of the subdirectories:

▶ **bin**
Configuration file *TP_<domain>.PFL* of transport program **tp** (see Section 5.4) and configuration file *DOMAIN.CFG* of the domain.

▶ **data**
Data files of transport requests (see Chapter 6).

▶ **sapnames**
A log file for each user of the CTS. It contains the transport activities for the user's transport requests.

▶ **buffer**
One import buffer for each system. The buffers list the requests planned for import into this system, including all the work steps required for the import.

▶ **tmp**
Temporary log files and semaphores.

▶ **log**
General and request-specific log files.

▶ **cofiles**
Control files for the transport requests. The files record the object classes, the required import steps, and return values. The import status of the transport requests in the various systems of the transport group is of particular interest.

Not every SAP system needs to have its own local directory tree. In fact, it's far more appropriate to use tools at the operating-system level (*share*, *mount*, and *NFS link*) to make the transport directory tree available globally. However, systems subject to special security limitations can have their own local transport directory with appropriately limited access rights. Figure 5.9 shows the flow of transports in a three-system landscape with a common transport directory.

Transport groups The SAP systems that share a common transport directory tree form a *transport group*. A transport domain can consist of several transport groups. If the exporting and importing systems lie in different transport groups, the import queues must be synchronized before the import; the data and control files needed for the import must be transferred into the transport directory of the target system. You can initiate the transfer from the TMS.

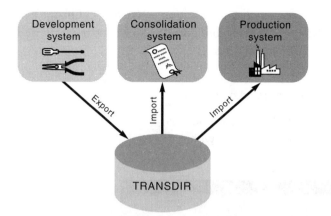

Figure 5.9 Three-System Landscape with a Common Transport Directory

5.3.2 Transport Routes

Now that we've made the SAP systems available in the landscape known, our last step is to define the transport routes between the systems. We'll assume that the configuration target is known and will show how to make the required settings for a three-system landscape.

Entries in system tables organize the control of transport routes and the role of each system. During configuration of the transport routes, you can use the hierarchical list editor or the graphical editor to generate the entries. The most important type of required information is a specification of the role of each system (configuration, consolidation, or delivery). The central configuration of the TMS means that you must provide the information only once: the information is then distributed to all the participating systems. The following description of the definition of transport routes assumes that you are logged on to the SAP system of the TDC in client 000 as a user with sufficient administrative authorizations.

Editors

To simplify the configuration of transport routes, select a predefined configuration (one, two, or three-system landscape) and enhance it as necessary.

You can use the hierarchical list editor to create a transport route between the systems as follows:

List editor

1. Select ▶Transport Management System · Overview · Transport routes to display a hierarchical tree of the links. Initially, all the defined systems and their configuration status are available only in display mode.

2. Branch to change mode with **Configuration · Display <-> Change** and use **Configuration · Standard configuration** to select the preferred model from the following options:

- ▶ Single system
- ▶ Development and production system
- ▶ Three systems in group

A role is assigned to each system within this configuration (see Figure 5.10).

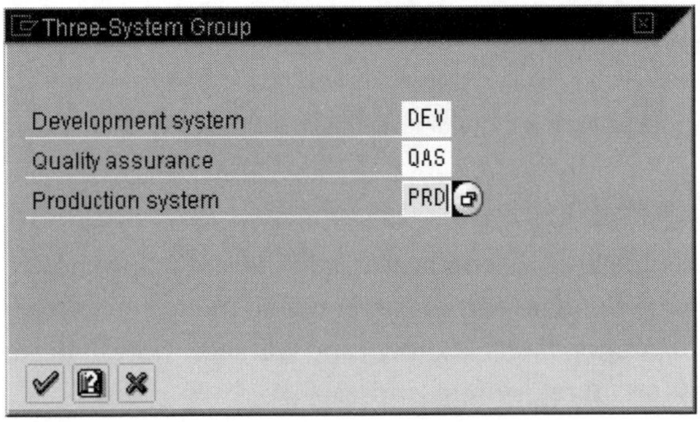

Figure 5.10 Assignment of Systems

3. Save your entries. The table entries describing the linkage between the system are generated automatically. Save the new settings with **Configuration · Check · Transport routes**.

4. Distribute the settings with **Configuration · Distribute and activate**.

Integrated version management is available to log configuration modifications and to restore an earlier version. Saved configurations are automatically numbered, as indicated in the title bar shown in Figure 5.11. When you save later modifications of the configuration of the landscape, the version number increases accordingly. A new version must also be activated—a check is performed to verify if the requested modification is consistent with system settings and partially transported requests.

Transport layer   The figure also shows that a *transport layer*, "Z<integration_system>," is generated between the integration system and the consolidation system. A transport layer always describes the transport route that the data from the development system should follow. This route is also called the *consolidation route*. The transport route from a consolidation or delivery system into another delivery system is called a *delivery route*. A delivery route can exist only in a system landscape that consists of at least three systems.

A delivery route always presumes the presence of an upstream consolidation route.

In addition to the transport layer between the integration and the consolidation system, an additional transport layer, "SAP," is also created automatically in the systems. This transport layer guarantees that modifications made to objects delivered by SAP can be imported in the systems.

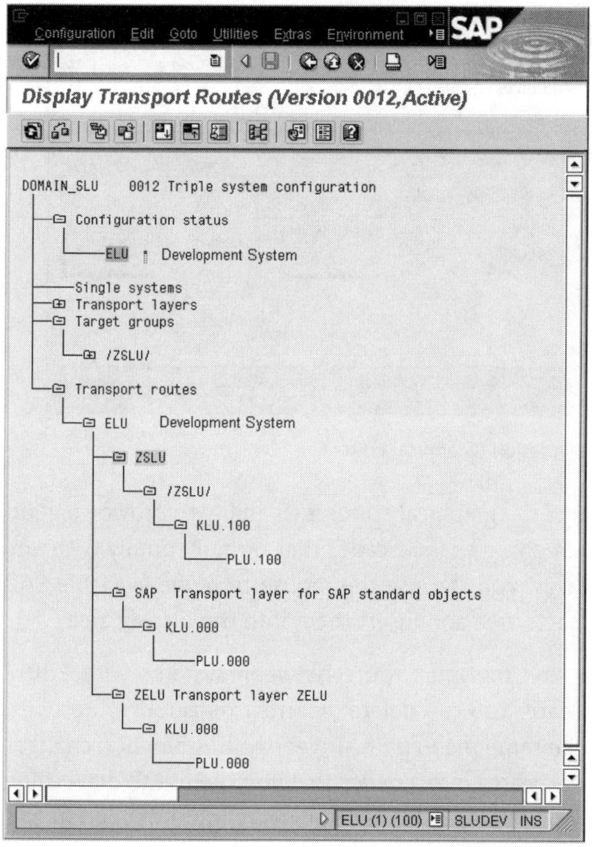

Figure 5.11 System Configuration (List Editor)

Depending on how the development project is run, it can be helpful or necessary to create several consolidation routes (see Chapter 6).

Now let's perform the same configuration using the graphical editor:

Graphical editor

1. You can reach the graphical editor from the display or maintenance of transport routes with **Goto · Graphical editor.** The upper area of the screen displays all the systems integrated into the transport domain that have not yet been used in the definition of the transport routes.

2. You can use **Configuration · Standard configuration** to select the system landscape that you want and assign roles to individual systems.

3. Save the settings with **Configuration · Save**. The required table entries are generated automatically. The configuration must now be saved and activated.

Note that Figure 5.12 displays the same configuration as Figure 5.11.

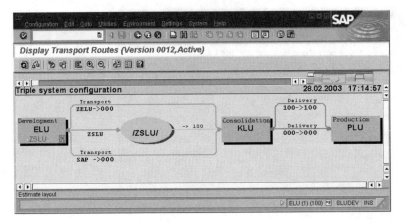

Figure 5.12 System Configuration (Graphical Editor)

The major advantage of the graphical editor is its ability to provide a good overview, especially in complex landscapes that do not comply with any standards. In such cases, you can use the mouse to move available SAP systems from the objects area and insert them into the display area.

You can now define the transport route between systems with **Edit · Transport route · Create**. You can delete incorrect transport routes with the **Delete** entry in the same menu path. Triggering this function changes the pointer in the display area into a pencil that you can use to draw a line between the preferred systems. For each transport route defined in this manner, you must determine if you're dealing with a consolidation (a transport from an integration system into a consolidation system, with the appropriate transport layer) or a delivery.

The display area depicts the flow of development data in the system landscape.

5.3.3 Extended Transport Control

In *extended transport control*, you can select a client-based procedure instead of a system-based procedure:

▶ During the definition of a consolidation or delivery route, you must specify the target client or a group of clients (*target group*) instead of the target system.

▶ You can set the standard transport layer used to define the transport target of Customizing settings to be client-dependent. In this manner, you can send Customizing requests from different clients to different transport targets.

▶ The definition of target groups under a symbolic name enables you to send requests from different transport layers in parallel to several clients of the same or different systems.

You can activate extended transport control by setting the CTC parameter to 1 in ▶**Transport Management System · Overview · Systems · SAP System · Change · Transport tool**. Mixed operations of system-based and extended transport control within one landscape is not permitted.

5.3.4 QA Approval Procedure

You can implement a QA approval procedure for technical support of the basic rules described in Section 5.3 in a transport landscape that consists of at least three systems, a consolidation system, and a delivery route.

Requests in the QA system can be released for import into the production system only after having undergone a defined number of approval steps.

Select the consolidation system that will be configured as the QA system from ▶**Transport Management System · Overview · Transport routes**. **Edit · System · Change** takes you to the system attributes of the selected system. Set a confirmation in the quality assurance field; you can then define the approval procedure (see Figure 5.13).

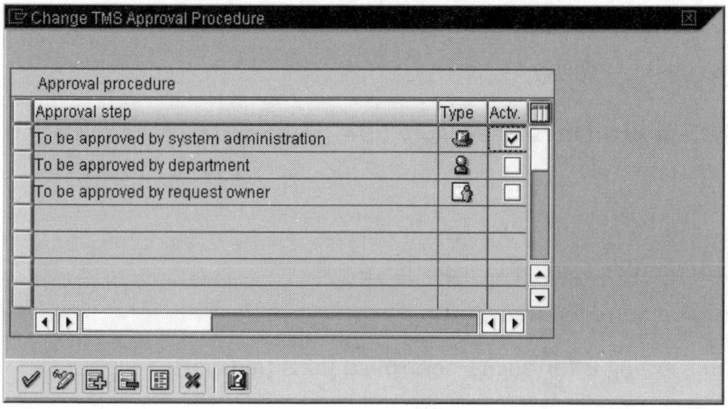

Figure 5.13 Definition of an Approval Procedure

5.3.5 Transport Strategy

Various phases of a system's life cycle, such as implementation or standard operations, reflect different volumes of transports, each with a different priority.

The implementation phase involves the transport of many time-critical new developments and modifications. The important benchmarks here include correct sequencing and quick reactions. Standard operations, however, usually involve individual transports that correct errors. Transports that involve error corrections usually do not occur frequently, and if they occur, they have to be imported quickly.

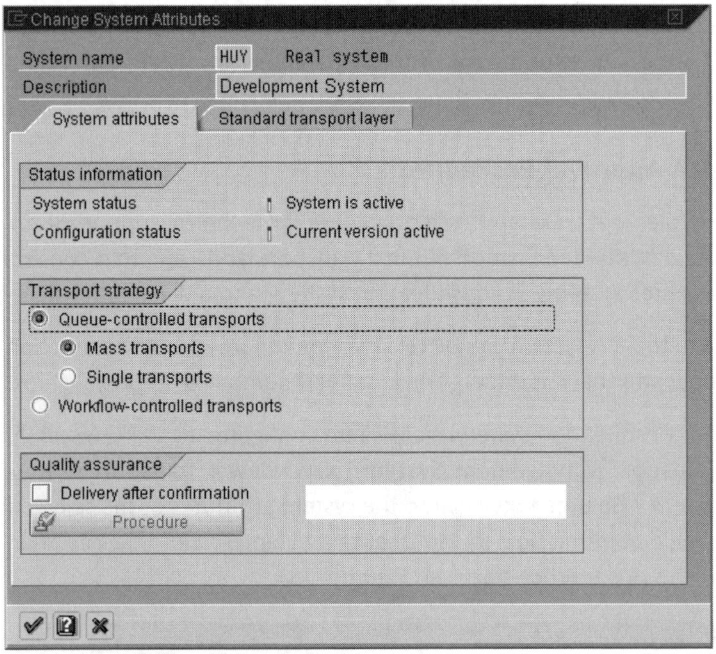

Figure 5.14 System Attributes

In the **System Attributes** (see Figure 5.14), you can select from the following variations:

▶ Queue-controlled mass transports

▶ Queue-controlled single transports

▶ Workflow-controlled transports

The default setting is for queue-controlled mass transports.

5.4 Transport Control Program tp

The tp program controls and executes transports between systems at the operating-system level. With the assistance of tools such as the **R3trans** transport program at the operating-system level and additional, integrated tools, **tp** triggers both the export of data from an SAP R/3 system and the import of data into other systems. To make available to **tp** all the required information on the system landscape, a configuration file, *TP_<domain>.PFL*, is stored in the *bin* subdirectory of the transport directory during initialization of transport management. Defaults already exist for all parameter values. You can modify and enhance parameters by making modifications in ▶Transport Management System · Overview · Systems · SAP System · Change · Transport tool.

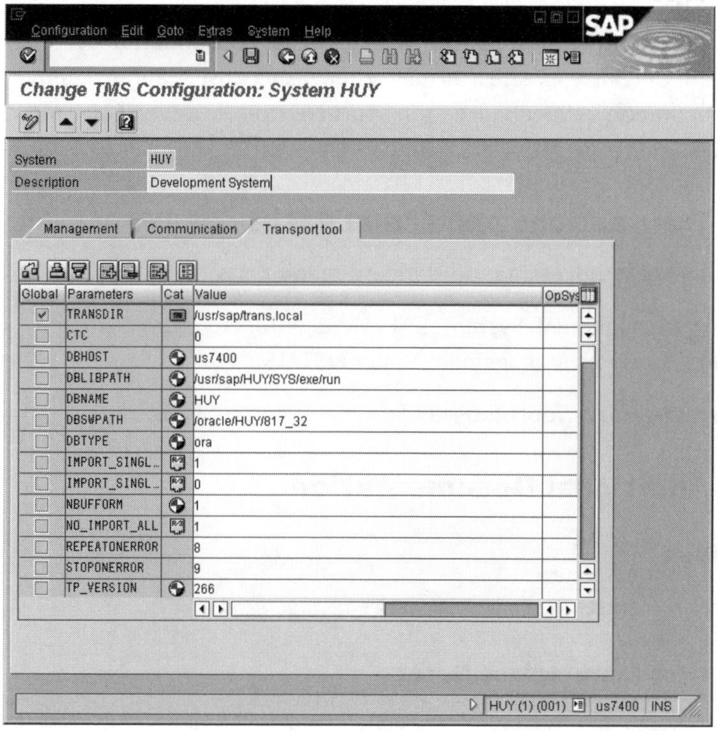

Figure 5.15 Maintaining tp Parameters

Note that prohibited or unknown parameter values do not trigger an error message—they are simply ignored. You can display the actual current values that are displayed in Figure 5.15 via **Goto · TP parameters**.

All the actions that **tp** performs are logged in the *log* subdirectory of the transport directory. By default, the *ALOG* file contains all the entries for transport requests that used **tp**. The *SLOG* file logs the starting time, work steps (and their duration), and ending time of every transport. If you want to use names other than the default file name, you can define tp parameters *alllog* und *syslog*. Consider the following example:

```
alllog = ALOG$(syear).$(yweek)
```

This definition writes a new log file as *ALOG<YY>.<WW>* for every week and year.

An additional log file, *ULOG<year>_<number>*, lists every **tp** call with its parameters and operating-system user. *<Year>* stands for the last two digits of the year; *<number>* stands for the current quarter of the year.

5.5 Tips

▶ **No enhanced transport control with a virtual consolidation system**
You can, of course, create a virtual system as a consolidation system in a configuration with enhanced transport control. However, you cannot release a transport request for this system.

5.6 Transactions and Menu Paths

Installation postprocessing: no standard menu entry (SE06)

Transport Management System: SAP Menu • Tools • Administration • Transports Transport Management System (STMS)

Transport Organizer Tools: no standard menu entry (SE03)

5.7 Additional Documentation

Quicklinks

SAP Service Marketplace: alias *swchangemanagement*

SAP Service Marketplace Notes

The following table provides an overview of important notes pertaining to the setup of transport landscapes.

Content	Note
System changeability and client control	40672
R3trans: Logging table modifications	163694

Table 5.2 SAP Notes on the Transport Management System

5.8 Questions

1. Which of the following statements about TMS configuration is accurate?

    a. Several transport groups can exist in a transport domain.

    b. All systems that access a common transport directory, /usr/sap/trans, are assigned to one transport group.

    c. At any one time, only one transport layer can be defined.

    d. The transport layer indirectly determines the route to the target system.

2. Which of the following statements is true?

In a multisystem landscape, transports:

    a. Can only be controlled by the active import or export system.

    b. Can be controlled centrally by the Domain Controller of the transport domain.

    c. Can only be controlled at the operating-system level with the **tp** program.

    d. Can be controlled by each SAP R/3 system in a transport domain.

3. Which transport routes are differentiated?

    a. Direct transport route

    b. Indirect transport route

    c. Consolidation route

    d. Delivery route

    e. Detour

4. Which program is responsible for executing transports at the operating-system level?

    a. R3load

    b. R3inst

    c. **tp**

    d. **dpmon**

    e. **sapdba**

6   Software Logistics

This chapter familiarizes the reader with software logistics: tools and methods for maintaining SAP R/3 software, the distribution of objects, and change management in the system landscape. It includes a brief overview of how a transport request is created and what this entails. It also describes how to optimize the Transport Organizer and its functions.

6.1   Implementation Guide

SAP R/3 contains standard solutions for all areas of a firm's business flows. However, "standard solution" should not be confused with "rigid" and "inflexible." In fact, several variations and versions of business flows are frequently integrated into SAP R/3. An important task during the implementation of SAP R/3 involves tailoring the system to meet a customer's needs by adjusting parameters and settings. This process is known as *Customizing*. From the available variants, Customizing is used to select the one variant that best suits the existing requirements and supplements it with customer-specific data. The *Implementation Guide* (IMG) is closely related to Customizing. The IMG serves as the foundation and precondition not only of application customizing, but also of several activities within Basis administration. Having a thorough understanding of the options available and knowing how best to use the IMG is of course advantageous to Basis administrators.

Customizing

The standard delivery of SAP R/3 includes the SAP Reference IMG, a complete guide to the implementation of all SAP R/3 application components. The structure of the IMG maps the hierarchy of the application components in your SAP R/3 system. The SAP Reference IMG also contains all the worksteps and documentation required for implementation. You can reach the IMG via ▶Implementation Guide · SAP Reference IMG.

SAP Reference IMG

One of a companie's first tasks in implementing SAP R/3 is the selection of the application areas that are relevant to its needs. To provide a structure for the overall process of Customizing, project groups within the company consider various criteria and create individual Customizing projects. The selection criteria include:

▶ Limitations to country

▶ Limitations to component

▶ Limitations to manual selection of individual activities

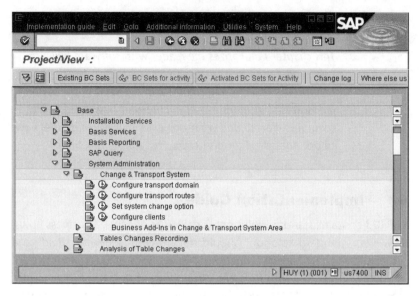

Figure 6.1 Excerpt from the SAP Reference IMG (Basis Area)

Project IMG Starting from the SAP Reference IMG, you can create *project IMGs* for these tasks. Performing all the tasks described in the project IMG is also called a "project": the system uses the terms "project" and "project IMG" synonymously. SAP R/3 provides users with a great deal of support during the execution of individual projects. For example, it offers integrated functions for scheduling, status maintenance, and documentation.

As a sample project, we'll examine setting up Basis Customizing (see Figure 6.2). You can use ▶ **Project creation** to create new project IMGs, modify existing projects, or delete projects.

1. Select ▶ **Project creation** · **Create** · **Project** to create a new project.

2. Give the project a descriptive name so that you can differentiate it from other projects later on.

3. Select the relevant countries and application components for the project, or make your selections manually in the SAP Reference IMG.

4. Save the settings and generate your project IMG.

Views You can also assign *views* of activities to each project; the views provide even more structure to the Customizing projects. The definition of a view filters the activities of a previously created project. Explicitly assigning project members to tasks enables you to enter only those tasks for which employees are directly responsible into employee work assignments. This type of assignment is particularly helpful in the following cases:

- ▶ Creation of implementation projects
- ▶ Upgrades
- ▶ Implementation of legal changes

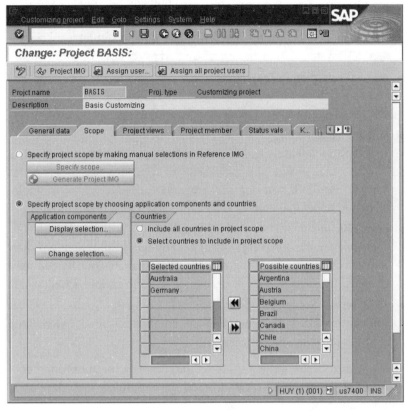

Figure 6.2 Creating a Project IMG

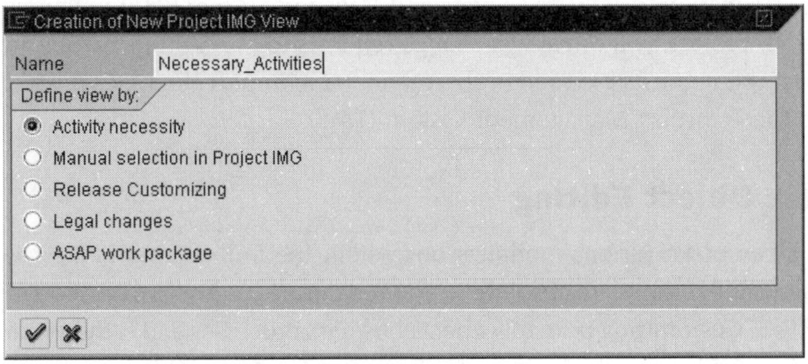

Figure 6.3 Creation of a View for a Project

The following criteria apply to the creation of views (see Figure 6.3):

▶ **Activity necessity**
Attributes are assigned to all the activities listed in the SAP Reference IMG to classify activities as: "must" (a complete SAP default setting is impossible), "can" (SAP default setting should be checked and modified if necessary), and "not required" (the SAP default setting maps a standard SAP system). Activities are also rated as "critical" or "not critical."

▶ **Manual selection in Project IMG**
You can make additional, limiting selections for the project from the subtree of all the actions available in Customizing.

▶ **Release Customizing**
You can use release-specific attributes of the IMG entries to select activities that ensure the availability of functions used in previous releases, even after an upgrade (upgrade Customizing), or to implement additional functions of the new release (delta Customizing).

▶ **Legal changes**
If you want to implement legal changes to your system, create a project view of all the Customizing activities that are affected by the legal changes. This selection also uses release-specific attributes (*law keys*).

▶ **ASAP work package**
You can use attribute values as a last criterion to group Customizing activities into the ASAP strategy.

The individual Customizing steps to set the company-specific properties of your SAP R/3 system are created based on the project IMG developed with the above steps.

Assignment of change requests | If you used the **Transport Requests** tab when you created your project via Project Creation to activate Change and Transport System (CTS) functions for your project, you can assign change requests to a CTS project. You can collect the requests grouped in this manner and import them per project with the Transport Management System (TMS).

6.2 Object Editing

Users can make various modifications within the SAP R/3 system. First, customizing settings are absolutely required during the implementation of SAP R/3. Customizing primarily affects business processes and is therefore usually client-dependent. Second, specific processes might need to be enhanced, the available functions modified, or global settings configured. These modifications affect the runtime environment and thus apply across all clients. Transports transfer these kinds of modifications or newly created objects into follow-on systems. Depending on their object type, these objects are combined into various requests.

6.2.1 Change Requests

If a client was defined with automatic recording of modifications (see Chapter 7), a task and a *Customizing request* are created as soon as a user undertakes Customizing modifications in an SAP R/3 system. The user can also control the explicit assignment of tasks to Customizing requests, when such requests have been previously created. Customizing requests therefore select client-specific settings from exactly one client (the source client of the request). The ability to transport Customizing requests into follow-on systems depends on the client-specific settings, the proposed target system, and the definition of the transport route (see Chapter 5).

Customizing requests

In addition to requiring modifications within Customizing, you might also require the development of new, company-specific objects, enhancements, or modifications of *objects in the SAP namespace (SAP objects)*. These kinds of modifications are client-independent: they affect the entire system. Much like what occurs with Customizing, the modification data here is recorded immediately; however, this time it is assigned to a *Workbench request*.

Workbench requests

Workbench requests contain Repository objects and client-independent Customizing. Workbench requests can also be mixed; client-dependent Customizing might also be present. However, this feature applies only with the limitation that all the client-specific objects must come from exactly one client-the source client of the request. The ability to transport Workbench requests into follow-on systems depends on the settings for the transport route in the TMS (see Chapter 5).

In addition to modifications that can be transported, you can also make local modifications. Tasks in *Local change requests* are available for these types of modifications. You cannot transport these modifications into other systems. Local change requests are created particularly when the configuration of the transport route has not yet been created, or has been created incorrectly. If the change requests are not released yet, you can assign them to a target system and convert them into change requests that can be transported.

Local change request

Assigning a task in a change request to a development simultaneously serves the purpose of ensuring security measures. The object is locked for users other than the owner of the task and the change request, unless the developer responsible for it explicitly grants another user rights to the task. Once a development project is closed, the task is released, followed by the change request. The object is available for additional modifications only after the change request has been released. This mechanism prevents the occurrence of simultaneous modifications of one object made by several users.

Request number All tasks and requests have a unique identifier that consists of the three-character name of the SAP R/3 system, a "K" as a key, and a sequential, six-digit number: "EA1K905975," for example. Every change request has exactly one owner, the project leader who is responsible for managing the request. The owner can be modified if necessary. A change request can combine multiple tasks, each one of which belongs to one user. Think of a change request as a project that involves various users performing separate tasks (see Figure 6.4).

If necessary, a task can be transferred to a different user.

Releasing tasks and requests Once all the tasks of a change request are completed and released, the project can be closed and the change request itself released. If the change request is not a local change request, when you release it, the preparations for a transport will take place. The version of the objects contained in the request, at the point of the release, is exported to files at the operating-system level, and the request is marked for import in the target system.

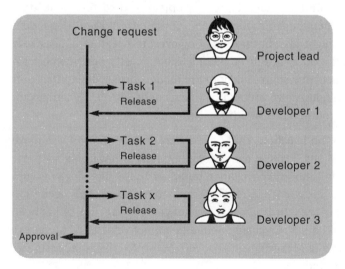

Figure 6.4 Project Management

The import must be started explicitly (see Section 6.3); the version of the objects, at the time of the export, is imported. The same applies even if the objects in the source system have been modified again—between the release and the import.

6.2.2 Editing Requests with the Transport Organizer

Up to SAP R/3 4.6B, Customizing and Workbench requests were managed by separate tools: the *Customizing Organizer* and the *Workbench Organizer*. As of SAP R/3 4.6C, you can edit all change requests and the tasks contained in them with the *Transport Organizer* (TO). A practical example is the easiest way to illustrate how to work with the TO.

Verifiable archive files are to be generated in the archiving area. To do so, we must perform a modification in cross-object Customizing of data archiving. Modifications like this are typical in Customizing.

There are two basic ways in which to generate a Customizing request: Generating a Customizing request

1. Perform the modification and let the SAP R/3 system generate the Customizing request and the task for the modification.

2. Use the Transport Organizer (TO) to create a Customizing request with a task included in it. The modification is then executed and explicitly assigned to the task generated previously.

The choice of one of these approaches depends primarily on the user concept. The assignment of authorizations can prohibit users from creating their own change requests, only a selected group of users is allowed to do so. This approach has the advantage of maintaining control of Customizing requests and their assignment. You can remove authorizations to create change requests of any type from a given developer. In such cases, the developer can make modifications only when an authorized person (typically, the project leader) generates the change requests and provides them to the developer. This feature allows for improved coordination of developments in an SAP R/3 system (see Figure 6.4).

You can also use the Transport Organizer (TO) to create *unclassified tasks*. Unclassified tasks are assigned a type only when they are assigned to a modification. For our example, you can use the second approach listed above:

1. Call the ▶ Transport Organizer.

2. Use **Request/Task · Create**, or first select **Display** and then **Request/Task · Create**.

3. Select **Customizing requests** from the list of request types.

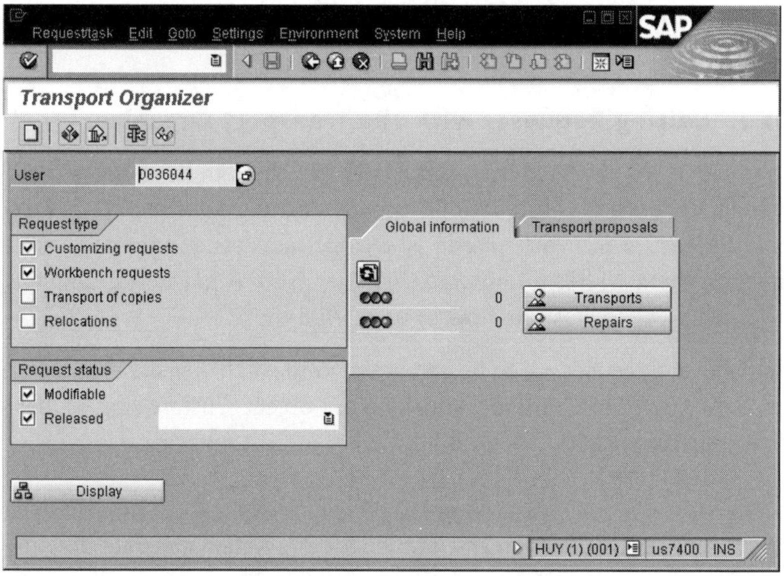

Figure 6.5 Transport Organizer (Initial Screen)

4. You will be prompted to enter a comment that describes the contents more closely and to name the persons involved in the request. A task for each person is created in the Customizing request.

5. Save your entries: the Customizing request has been generated.

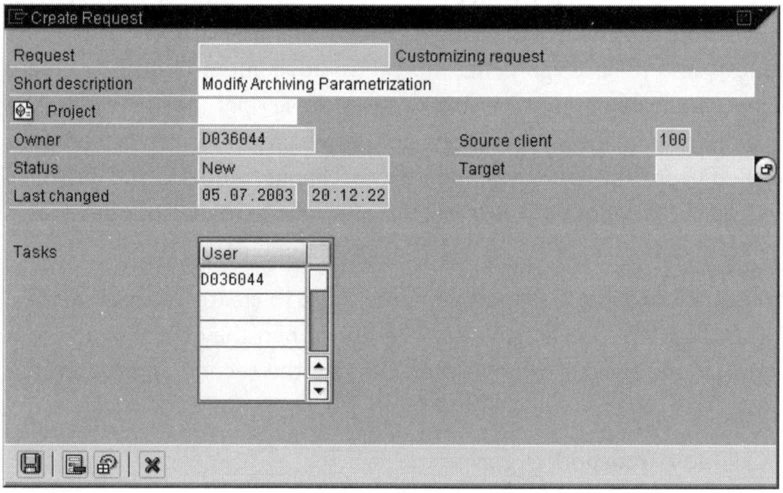

Figure 6.6 Details of the Customizing Request Being Created

Figure 6.6 shows the screen used to enter the required data for such a change request. The **Source client** field shows the client assigned to the

Customizing request. The **Target** field displays the name of the SAP system into which the Customizing request is to be transported once it has been released. The field is blank in our example; the assignment can be made later.

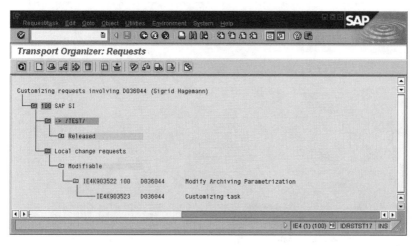

Figure 6.7 Display of all Change Requests

Figure 6.7 displays the hierarchical display mode of the TO. It shows Customizing request IE4K903522 in client 100 with owner D036044. Task IE4K903523 is assigned to that user. If necessary, you can modify the owner of a request or a task. You can also add additional tasks to a request by selecting it and then calling **Request/Task · Create**.

Now let's look at how a Customizing modification is assigned to a request.

In the example, we want to modify the archiving settings. Proceed as follows:

Assignment to a Customizing request

1. Starting at ▶**Implementation Guide · SAP Reference IMG**, we go through the IMG structure until we reach **Cross-Object Customizing Data Archiving** and activate the entry **Create verifiable files** (see Figure 6.8).

2. When you save the entries, you are prompted to assign a change request or create a new one (see Figure 6.9).

3. We select and confirm the request we have created, IE4K903522. This task completes the assignment of the modification to a Customizing request. Only now are the modifications actually saved physically, that is, modifications to objects are permanent only when they are logged in change requests.

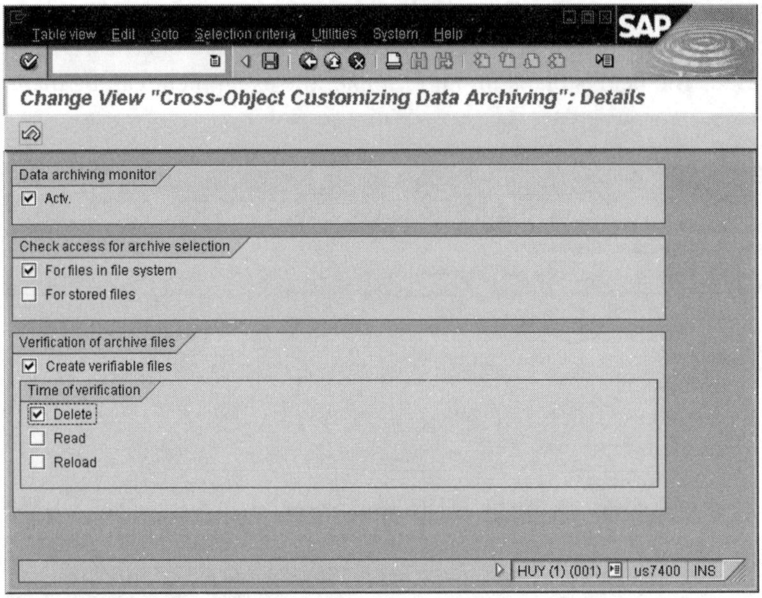

Figure 6.8 Customizing Modification

Figure 6.9 Assignment of a Change Request

Releasing the Customizing request

This step ends the Customizing procedure for our example: the Customizing request can be *closed*, which means that it can be *released*. To release a request, the person responsible for its maintenance should proceed as follows:

1. Select the preferred category of requests and their statuses in ▶Transport Organizer if you want to limit the number of requests displayed as compared with those actually required. Select **Display**.

2. All tasks of the selected Customizing requests must be closed, that is, released, by their owners. If that is not the case, as in our example, select the corresponding task, here, IE4K903523, and release it with **Request/Task · Release**.

3. You will be prompted to document the content of the modifications.

4. Activate and save the final form of the documentation and close the screen. Doing so transfers all the modifications contained in the task to the Customizing request assigned to them. You can expand the tree for more information on the relevant object (see Figure 6.10). The modifications affected object ARCH_PARAM in our example.

5. Once all the tasks have been released, the actual Customizing request can be released in the same manner. Select the Customizing request, then call **Request/Task · Release**, and document the modifications of the request.

The Customizing request is then exported along with the release. You can also release a Customizing request to a Workbench request that will be released and transported later. The advantage of this approach is that you can collect several Customizing requests and then export them as a group later.

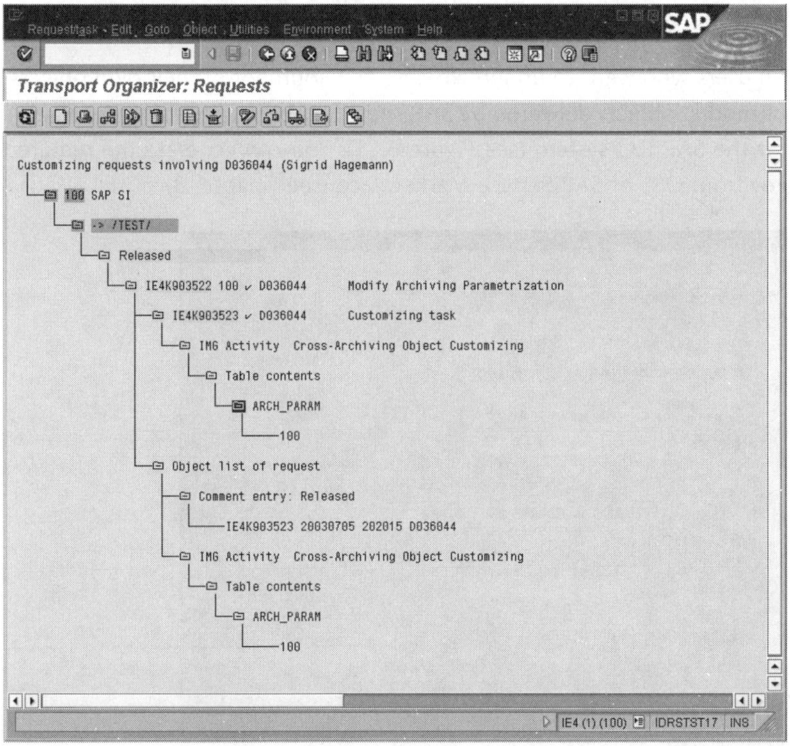

Figure 6.10 Released Request: IE4K903522

Developments and modifications

The ABAP Workbench offers developers the following tools:

- **Repository Browser and Dictionary**
  To develop tables, structures, indices, domains, matchcodes, and so on
- **ABAP Editor and Function Builder**
  To edit programs and functions
- **Screen Painter**
  To develop screens
- **Menu Painter**
  To generate menu trees
- **Testing tools**

All these tools support the development or modification of functions in the SAP R/3 system. Of course, the development of SAP R/3 functions does not generally fall under the responsibilities of the SAP R/3 system administrator. However, because administrators are responsible for *upgrades* to new releases or implementing error corrections, they will, by necessity, come into contact with the tools.

All users who want to undertake new development of their own objects, or modify objects delivered by SAP, must first be registered as developers for the SAP R/3 system (see Figure 6.11). You can generate the required key from OSS or SAP Service Marketplace (see Chapter 3).

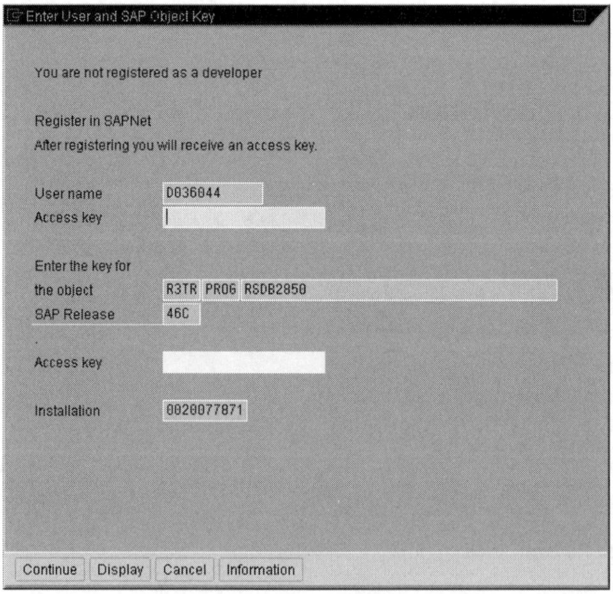

Figure 6.11 Developer and Object Registration

In this manner, both SAP R/3 administrators and SAP itself have an overview of how much development is occurring in an SAP R/3 system. The following procedures require a decision on whether an SAP object is to be modified or a new development (the creation of a new object) should occur.

Modifications of SAP objects must also be registered. You can get the access key via the OSS or SAP Service Marketplace. Enter the specifications for the object of your choice (see Figure 6.12) and transfer the access key that is generated to the screen shown in Figure 6.11.

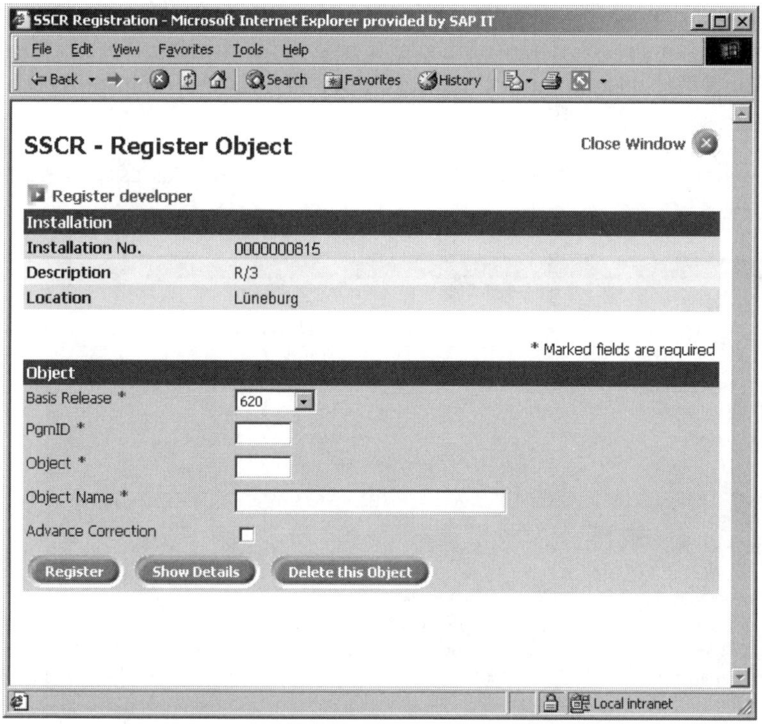

Modification of SAP objects

Figure 6.12 Requesting an Object Key in SAP Service Marketplace

An SAP object can be edited only after the access key has been generated. This security measure ensures that a log of customer-specific modifications exists so that possible problems that arise in the future can be better addressed.

New developments in a system landscape require exact planning to avoid conflicts with both SAP objects and customer-specific objects. As a basic rule, you should undertake new development only in a two-system landscape; however, a three-system landscape is preferable. You should also

New developments

always avoid mixing development and productive work in one system. Let's assume that the system landscape has already been completely configured as described in Chapter 5, and that the transport routes between the systems have already been defined.

Development class / packet A *development class* combines objects that are to be developed, maintained, and transported together. Accordingly, before a new object can be created, a development class must be created in the integration system in which the development is to occur. Development classes are also objects, and can therefore be transported.

To ensure that all the objects of a development class can be transported along the same route, a transport layer is assigned to the class (see Chapter 5). The *$TMP* development class is used for all local (non-transportable) objects.

The enhanced concept of *packets* replaced development classes with Basis Release 6.10.

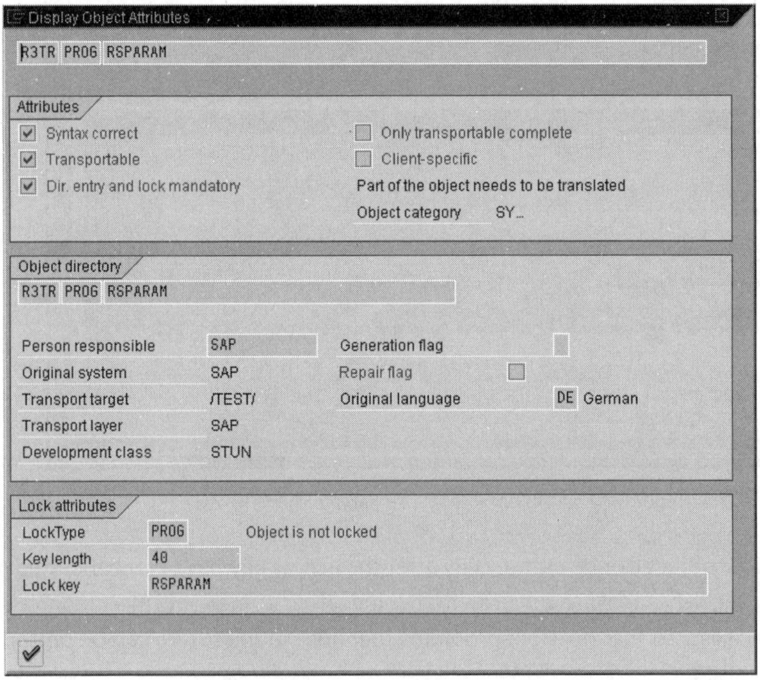

Figure 6.13 Object Catalog Entry of Program RSPARAM

Customer namespace SAP provides a separate *customer namespace* for the creation of objects, including a development class. The customer namespace guarantees that the names of SAP and customer objects do not conflict and that customer objects can be identified clearly during an upgrade. The following rules apply to the creation of names of development classes and objects from the Workbench:

▶ The namespace beginning with a Y or a Z is available to all customers.

▶ Customers can request their own namespace for particularly comprehensive developments. The namespace is a prefix (of at least five and no more than ten characters) enclosed in slashes; it is added at the beginning of the customer's name of the object. An SAP license key protects the namespace from unauthorized use. Customer-specific namespaces are reserved for complex, customer-specific development projects or developments by SAP partners.

An entry in the *object catalog* (see Figure 6.13) exists for every object in the SAP R/3 system. The entry contains all the important information about the object. In addition to the object's development class and the assigned transport layer, the object's original system is of particular importance to the systems group.

Object catalog

The *original* of an object is maintained in only one system. Various protective measures are linked to the assignment. If you consider the situation in a system landscape, the objects in an integration system are original if the development and transport strategy has been created correctly. The objects are developed in the integration system. A modification of an original object is called a *correction*. Copies of the original object are transported into follow-on systems for testing and eventual use. If the copies of the object require modifications in the target systems, they are called *repairs*. Unless the originals in the integration system have also been modified, these repairs can be overwritten by a new transport from the integration system.

Original

The release and transport of developments or modifications of cross-client objects occur in the same manner as the release and transport of Customizing requests.

Release and Export

Note that the release of a local change request does not write any data at the operating-system level.

6.2.3 Transport Logs

All transports (both exports and imports) occur in several steps, and all steps are logged. After a transport, the system produces a return (exit) code that you can use to analyze the overall status of the transport. We strongly recommend that you analyze the export log and correct any

Action log

errors that occurred. Otherwise, you might have to deal with incomplete data during later imports into the target system. To view the logs, select the respective transport request in the display of all transport requests in the ▶ **Transport Organizer.** Then, select **Goto · Action log** to display all the actions related to the transport request that have occurred so far. Figure 6.14 shows the log for our request, IE4K903522. The log files are stored in the *log* subdirectory of the transport directory (see Chapter 5).

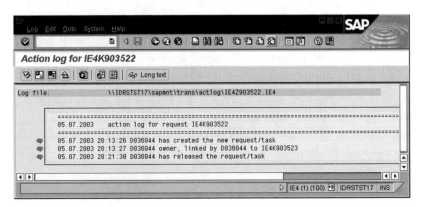

Figure 6.14 Action Log for Request IE4K903522

Transport logs In addition to the action log, another log file for each transport and the steps it consists of is stored in the same subdirectory. The name of the log file is composed of the following syntax:

`<SID of the source system><step><number of the transport request>.<SID of the source or target system>`

In the preceding lines, `<step>` stands for the step executed, according to the following naming conventions:

- ▶ A Activation of the Repository
- ▶ C Transport of C source text
- ▶ D Import of application-defined objects
- ▶ E Main export
- ▶ G Generation of programs and screens
- ▶ H Repository import
- ▶ I Main import
- ▶ L Import of the command file
- ▶ M Activation of the enqueue modules
- ▶ P Test import

- ▶ R   Version balancing during an upgrade of SAP R/3
- ▶ T   Import of table entries
- ▶ V   Setting the version ID for imported objects
- ▶ X   Export of application-defined objects

The logs are stored in a legible form at the operating-system level, so you can use the tools available to analyze the files. However, because it's more user-friendly, it's far more common to look at the files with the ▶Transport Organizer, by selecting the request that you want to analyze and then selecting **Goto · Transport logs**. The steps are first displayed in a compressed form, and can be expanded into four levels. Our example deals with only one export, therefore one log file, *IE4E903522.IE4*, was created. The content of the file corresponds to the highest level of resolution for viewing logs from the SAP R/3 system. The following listing is an excerpt of the complete export log. Information of particular importance for the analysis is highlighted in bold type.

Listing 6.1 Excerpt from an Export Log

```
Name: IE4E903522.IE4
1 ETP199X#############################################
1 ETP182 CHECK WRITEABILITY OF BUFFERS
1 ETP101 transport order    : "IE4K903522"
1 ETP102 system             : "IE4"
1 ETP108 tp path            : "tp"
1 ETP109 version and release : "305.12.57" "46D"
1 ETP198
4 ETP201 Check target systems buffer: \\psasb009\sap-
mnt\trans\buffer\DUM
3 ETP203 Buffer "\\psasb009\sapmnt\trans\buffer\DUM" is
writeable

...

1 ETP182 CHECK WRITEABILITY OF BUFFERS
1 ETP110 end date and time  : "20030223133946"
1 ETP111 exit code          : "0"
1 ETP199X#############################################
1 ETP150 MAIN EXPORT
1 ETP101 transport order    : "IE4K903522"
1 ETP102 system             : "IE4"
1 ETP108 tp path            : "tp"
1 ETP109 version and release : "305.12.57" "46D"
1 ETP198
```

```
4 ETW000 R3trans.exe version 6.05 (release 46D - 17.07.02
- 14:00:00).
4 ETW000 control file: \\psasb009\sap-
mnt\trans\tmp\IE4KK903522.IE4
4 ETW000 > #pid 811 on psasb009 (APServiceIE4)
4 ETW000 > export
4 ETW000 > file='\\psasb009\sapmnt\trans\data\R903522.IE4'
4 ETW000 > client=100
4 ETW000 > buffersync=yes
4 ETW000 >
4 ETW000 > use comm 'IE4K903522'
4 ETW000 R3trans was called as follows: R3trans.exe -w
\\psasb009\sapmnt\trans\tmp\IE4E903522.IE4
\\psasb009\sapmnt\trans\tmp\IE4KK903522.IE4
4 ETW000 date&time    : 23.02.2003 - 13:40:08
4 ETW000 Connected to DBMS = ORACLE --- dbs_ora_tnsname =
'IE4' --- SYSTEM = 'IE4'.
4 ETW000  trace at level 1 opened for a given file pointer
4 ETW000 =================== STEP 1 =====================
4 ETW000 date&time    : 23.02.2003 - 13:40:15
4 ETW000 function    : EXPORT
4 ETW000 data file    : \\psasb009\sap-
mnt\trans\data\R903522.IE4
4 ETW000 buffersync  : YES
4 ETW000 client      : 100
4 ETW000 Language    :
ABCDEFGHIJKLMNOPQRSTUVWXYZ0123456789abcdefghijklmnopqrstu
vwxyz
4 ETW000 Compression : L
4 ETW000 l.s.m.      : VECTOR
4 ETW000 commit      : 100000
4 ETW000 table cache : dynamic
4 ETW000
3 ETW673XUse Commandfile "IE4K903522"
4 ETW000     /* Conversion of archiving parameters */
4 ETW000     trfunction: 'W' (customizing transport)
4 ETW000     trstatus : 'O'
4 ETW000     tarsystem : /TEST/
4 ETW000     user     : D036044
4 ETW000     date     : 23.02.2003 - 13:39:51
4 ETW000  1 entry from E070 exported (IE4K903522).
```

```
...
4 ETW000   1 entry from E07T exported (IE4K903522).
4 ETW000  [developertrace,0] Sun Feb 23 13:40:18 2003
2201862   2.201862
4 ETW000  [developertrace,0] dbrclu3.c : info : my major
identification is 387318425, minor one 262100.
4 ETW000 DOCUTD TA T IE4K903522 exported
...
3 ETW678Xstart export of "R3TRTABUARCH_PARAM" ...
4 ETW000   1 entry from ARCH_PARAM exported (100).
4 ETW679 end export of "R3TRTABUARCH_PARAM".
4 ETW000 IE4K903522 touched.
4 ETW000 IE4K903522 released.
4 ETW000 1776 bytes written.
4 ETW000 Transport overhead 56.6 %.
4 ETW000 Data compressed to 13.1 %.
4 ETW000 Duration: 3 sec (592 bytes/sec).
4 ETW000   0 tables in P-buffer synchronized.
4 ETW000   0 tables in R-buffer synchronized.
4 ETW690 "512" "512"
4 ETW000 COMMIT (1776).
4 ETW000
4 ETW000 Summary:
4 ETW000
4 ETW000   1 COMML exported
4 ETW000   1 COMMT exported
4 ETW000   1 DOCUT exported
4 ETW000 Totally 4 Objects exported
4 ETW000 Totally 1 tabentry exported
4 ETW000
4 ETW000  [developertrace,0] Disconnecting from ALL con-
nections:
...
4 ETW000 End of Transport (0000).
4 ETW000 date&time: 23.02.2003 - 13:40:19
1 ETP150 MAIN EXPORT
1 ETP110 end date and time   : "20030223134033"
1 ETP111 exit code          : "0"
1 ETP199 ###########################################
```

The return (exit) code is of particular importance for the administrator. A return code of "0," as shown in our example, means that the transport occurred without any errors. Warnings are marked with a "W" when they cause a return code of "4." Serious errors that are likely to cause an incomplete transport are marked with an "E." In this case, the return code is equal to or greater than "8." The log files indicate the cause of errors. If errors occur, you must correct them and then repeat the export. Possible causes include problems in the database. An aborted transport request would appear in the Transport Organizer (TO) with the status *export not completed*.

Cofile and data file An export produces log files, a *data file*, and a *cofile*; the latter file contains metadata of the objects contained in the request. The data file and cofile constitute the actual data to be transported. They contain all the information that is necessary for an import. Cofiles are always stored in the *cofiles* subdirectory and data files are stored in the *data* subdirectory of the transport directory tree (see Chapter 5). The files are named according to the following convention:

```
<type of file><number of the transport request>.<SID of
the source system>
```

"K" represents cofiles; "R" and "D" represent data files. Our example created cofile *K903522.IE4* and data file *R903522.IE4*.

6.2.4 Transport Organizer (Extended View)

The extended view of the Transport Organizer (TO) offers additional transport options beyond the familiar options for administering Customizing and Workbench requests. These options share a common approach: they do not follow a predefined transport route.

The options include the following:

▶ **Transports of copies and relocation of originals**
For various reasons, you might have to transport specific objects into another system. Depending on the requirements, the objects might also retain their original system or have it assigned to the new system. The possible scenarios include the following:

 ▶ A simple copy of objects into another system; you can choose any system that you want.

 ▶ Relocating objects without changing the development class or packet—allows you to store development projects in another system temporarily. The objects' original system is changed to the new system.

▶ Relocating objects with a change of the development class or packet—allows you to store development projects in another system permanently. The objects' original system is changed to the new system; you do not have to adjust the transport properties if you select a packet with an assigned transport layer.

▶ Relocating complete development classes or packets for permanent storage of the entire packet in another system. The objects' original system is changed to the new system and the transport layer is adjusted.

Except for relocations of entire packets, the objects involved must be handled manually.

You can create requests for transports of copies and relocations of originals from the Transport Organizer.

▶ **Functions to evaluate client transports**
In addition to the options provided by client administration (see Chapter 7), you can also see an overview here of the client transports that have been performed.

▶ **Generating object lists**
Object lists are a collection of objects that can be linked to transport requests as a template. Object lists of all the objects of a development class, or according to another set of common properties of objects, can be generated automatically. You can also create lists of objects manually.

Object lists have an entry in the object catalog and are therefore assigned to a packet; they cannot be transported.

▶ **Management of deliveries from SAP or its partners to customers**
Corrections and patches delivered by SAP and its partners require special management, because they contain objects in the SAP namespace. You can recognize this type of transport request best by its name, which consists of SAPK<number>.

6.2.5 Transport Tools

You will find a complete collection of practical tools for working with the Change and Transport System (CTS) under ▶ **Transport Organizer · Goto · Transport Organizer · Tools**. Depending on the authorizations granted to users, you may have access to tools that are risky to use.

All functions are described in detail with the list entry and can be started by selecting **Tool · Execute**.

Figure 6.15 CTS Tools

For example, under **Administration · Display/change request attributes**, you can display or change the attributes of change requests, or set mandatory attributes. For example, you can define whether the assignment of a project to a transport request is a precondition to release the request.

6.3   Importing Transport Requests

With the release of a change request in a transport landscape, the data is not only exported; the new request is also recorded in the import queue of the target system(s).

You can administer and analyze the import queue of all the systems in a transport domain (see Chapter 5) and, of course, start imports from any participating system with ▶Transport Management System · Overview · Imports.

Figure 6.16 Import Overview in a Three-System Landscape

Figure 6.16 shows 11 requests for the quality assurance system and 22 requests for the production system in the queue for the next import. You can display more exact information on the type and scope of the requests by selecting the system that you want.

Figure 6.17 shows the import queue for a sample system, "ER3." Starting from the display, the administrator can coordinate all outstanding imports. The following describes the most important work steps in normal operations.

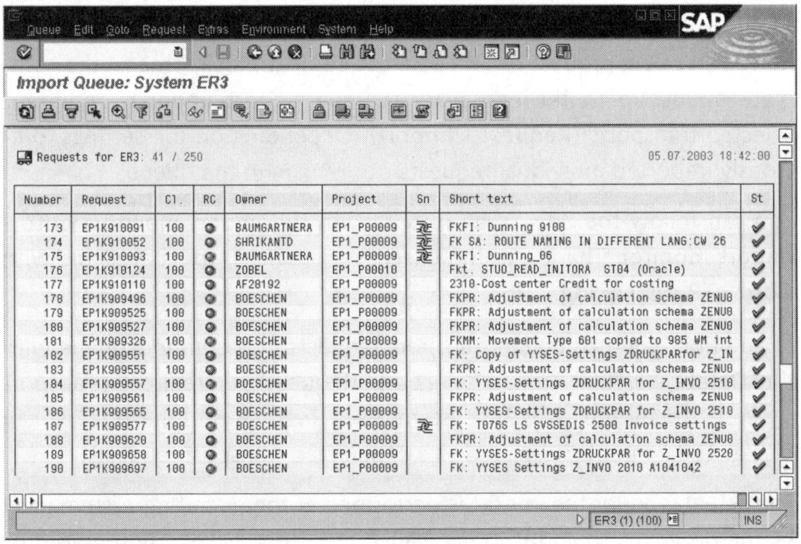

Figure 6.17 Import Queue of the "ER3" System

The sequence of the requests in the import queue depends on the time of the export of the request from the source system. The temporal sequence

Sequence in the import queue

of the export is also the sequence in which the requests will be imported. Released transport requests from the same transport group (see Chapter 5) are automatically checked into the import queue of the target system. If the target system is assigned to a different transport group, and therefore uses a different transport directory, the administrator must first use **Extras · Other requests · Find in other groups** to search for and find the outstanding requests. The same sequence of events applies when transport domains are joined by domain links. If additional requests for the system are found, they are recorded in the import queue of the selected system.

Opening and closing the import queue

The import of closed development requests should follow a fixed schedule that is coordinated by the developers. Imports are executed according to the schedule in defined periods. To avoid inconsistencies and achieve a defined, intermediate status of the SAP R/3 system, you should use the so-called *end marks* to close the import queue temporarily at these times. All requests that enter the queue after this point are scheduled for the next import. You can insert an end mark in an import queue with **Queue · Close**. With **Queue · Move end mark**, you can set the end mark before any request that you want. You can open an already-closed import queue with **Queue · Open**.

Importing

You can start an import into a system for a subset of the outstanding requests. You can also combine individual requests with **Edit · Select · Select/Deselect request** or **Edit · Select · Select block**, process the complete queue up to the end mark (**Queue · Start import**), or import selected transports (**Request · Import**). Depending on the settings, previously imported individual requests can remain in the queue.

Status and logs

You can follow the flow of an import with the import monitor: **Goto · Import monitor**. The log of the executing program, **tp**, is available with **Goto · TP system log**.

In addition, you can delete transport requests in the import queue with the **Delete** function (menu selection: **Request**), or redirect (transport requests) to another SAP R/3 system. As is the case with the TO, you can display the contents, logs, and size of selected transport requests.

RDDIMPDP

The actual work of the import is performed at the operating-system level by the programs **tp** and **R3trans** (called implicitly by **tp**). These two programs collaborate with the program **RDDIMPDP** which runs within R/3. The **RDDIMPDP** program must be scheduled in client 000 of the target system and RDDIMPDP_CLIENT_<number of the client> must be scheduled in all clients that receive transports. The **RDDIMPDP*** programs are event-driven and scheduled in the background (see Chapter 9). They wait for a notification from **tp** that a transport has arrived. Accordingly, every import requires a free batch process. If a transport hangs for no apparent reason, ensure that **RDDIMPDP** is functioning correctly.

6.4 Manual Operation of the Transport Control Program tp

As complex and user-friendly as the Transport Management System (TMS) is, situations will undoubtedly arise in which you'll have to process imports manually with **tp** at the operating-system level. What follows is a brief description of the options available with **tp**.

A parameter file, *TP_<domain>.PFL* (*TPPARAM* in older releases of SAP R/3), in the *bin* subdirectory of the transport directory controls the transport control program **tp**. Before you use **tp** for the first time, it's a good idea to test if a connection to the chosen target system is possible. To do so, you can use the following command:

```
tp connect <target system> pf=<complete path of the param-
eter file>
```

The addition of `pf=...` enables you to use any parameter file of your choosing.

To insert a request into the import queue of an SAP R/3 system, use the following command:

```
tp addtobuffer <request> <target system> pf=< complete
path of the parameter file>
```

Successful execution of this command assumes that the data file of the request is located in the *data* subdirectory and that the corresponding cofile is located in the *cofiles* subdirectory of the transport directory.

You can use the following command to import a selected request:

```
tp import <request> <target system> pf=<complete path of
the parameter file>
```

You can add `all` to import the entire import queue in the current sequence:

```
tp import all <target system> pf=< complete path of the
parameter file>
```

You can add the following to specify a special client:

```
client=<number of the client>
```

If you do not specify a client, the data is copied to the client with the same number as the client from which the data was exported. If the client into which you want to import does not exist in the target system, the import terminates with an error message.

Deleting obsolete requests
In the course of a lengthy development period, several old transport requests can accumulate in the transport directory. It would require a lot of manual work, using the Transport Organizer, to find each request and then manually delete obsolete requests. Instead, you can use `tp check-all` to find obsolete transport requests, and then delete them with `tp clearold all`. You can control the lifetime (retention period) for data, cofiles, and log files with the **tp** parameters *datalifetime*, *olddatalifetime*, *cofilelifetime*, and *logfilelifetime*. Data files older than *datalifetime* are first moved to the *olddata* directory and deleted permanently at the next call of the program, as long as the *olddatalifetime* is exceeded.

6.5 Importing Support Packages and Industry Solutions

Transports from the CTS also handle the import of support packages to correct errors in various software components (see Section 5.1), industry solutions, and plug-ins to communicate with other SAP systems, such as SAP Business Information Warehouse (SAP BW).

The import occurs in client 000; all other clients have only a display function.

Updating the installation tools
Current versions of the installation tools are required for the installation of support packages or add-ons. Accordingly, the first step in working with support packages or add-ons updates these tools; the update is integrated into the ▶Support Package Manager.

6.5.1 Importing Support Packages

SAP regularly delivers support packages with error corrections and performance improvements for all the software components available in SAP R/3. Depending on the product and the Basis release, different types of packages exist for your installation. Component packages (COP) SAP_BASIS (*Basis Support Package*), and SAP_ABA (*Application Interface SP*) exist in every system.

Essentially, the installation consists of the following steps:

- Loading the packages
- Updating the installation tools
- Defining a queue
- Installing the queue
- Confirmation

You navigate to the import procedure via the ▶ **Support Package Manager** (see Figure 6.18).

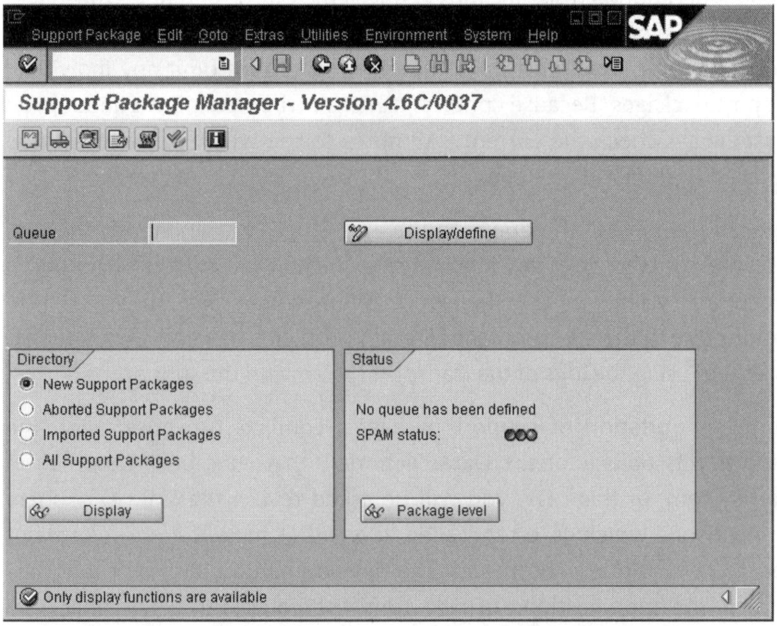

Figure 6.18 Support Package Manager

Loading support packages

First, you must load the required support packages into your system. You can use one of three options to do so:

- Copy the packages from SAP Service Marketplace or from one of the regularly delivered support CDs into the transport directory. You must also decompress the files there. You can then load the packages into your system from the application server with **Support Package · Load packages · From application server**.
- Copy the packages from SAP Service Marketplace or from the CD to the local frontend and then load them from the frontend with **Support Package · Load packages · From Frontend**.

▶ Request the support packages from SAPNet R/3 Frontend and load them from SAPNet R/3 Frontend with **Support Package · Load packages · From SAPNet R/3 Frontend**. Because of the network demands, this option is only supported for smaller support packages.

The latest version of the Support Package Manager must also be loaded in the same manner. In the first step, you can install it with **Support Package · Import SPAM/SAINT Update.**

Importing by queue

You don't have to process each support package individually. Instead, you can define a queue that the Support Package Manager will import as a group. This approach significantly reduces the effort required. Only packages of one type (Basis support packages, for example) can be imported in a queue. The queue must be complete: you cannot omit any individual support packages. Because conflicts can arise when defining a queue, you must always check the current SAP notes to see which packages can be installed together in a queue.

You can then install the queue in the next step. For the import, the tool uses the software logistics mechanisms. Technically, transport requests, which are visible in the Transport Management System (TMS), are imported with the `tp` command. Should problems develop, you can analyze them using the logs of the transport system and the support packages.

During importation of support packages, conflicts can arise when the import edits objects of the Data Dictionary that have been modified in your system. In this case, you will be asked to use the Data Dictionary Comparison, which is often called the *SPDD modification adjustment* because of the transaction used. The development department that performed the modifications usually runs the comparison. Similarly, you might have to compare imported repository objects with repository modifications (the *SPAU modification adjustment)* after an import.

After a successful installation, you must still confirm the status. You can import additional support packages only after confirmation.

6.5.2 Importing Add-Ons

You use the ▶**Add-On Installation Tool** to import add-ons. In this transaction, everything that does not belong to the SAP standard is considered an add-on. Add-ons include Industry Solutions, plug-ins, and, in systems with a Basis release earlier than 6.10, the installation of the Note Assistant (see Chapter 3). You can use the ▶**Add-On Installation Tool** to install and upgrade add-ons. From the initial screen (see Figure 6.19), you must first load the required packages with the menu entry **Installation Package** from the frontend or the application server, just as you did with support packages.

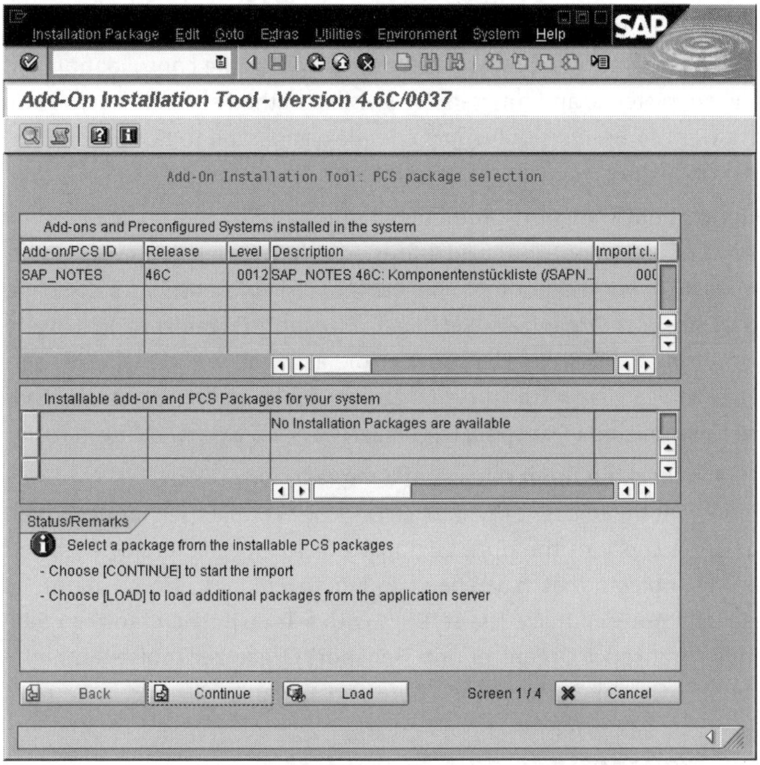

Figure 6.19 Add-On Installation Tool

After loading, the Add-On Installation Tool creates a queue that you can install with the **Continue** button.

The import occurs similarly to the way it operated with support packages. A modification adjustment might also be required here. After the installation, you must check the logs with **Goto · Import logs** and then confirm the installation in the last screen (screen 4/4) of the installation tool. You can import additional add-ons or support packages only after confirmation.

6.6 Tips

▶ **Deactivation of a mass transport**
You can set the **tp** parameter *NO_IMPORT_ALL* to the value of "1" to prohibit mass processing of all outstanding imports. This is the standard parameterization in a transport strategy with individual requests.

▶ **Versioning**

Typically, versioning is executed only on the source system of a transport request. With *versioning*, a new version of the object is created when it is stored in a transport request. All old versions are visible in the object history and can be compared or rolled back if necessary. By default, only the most recent version is stored in the consolidation and delivery systems, and this version is visible in the version history. If you also want to use versioning in a complex landscape to trace the modification history, you can set versions with **tp** parameter *VERS_AT_IMP*.

▶ **Popup about transport problems at logon**

For automatic notification of transports that terminated with errors, you can configure a popup for all users or individual users. To do so, go to ▶ **Transport Organizer · Settings · Transport Organizer** and activate the setting for **Display transport errors at logon** for user-specific settings. You can use ▶ **Transport Organizer Tools · Administration · Global Customizing (Transport Organizer)** to activate this setting globally.

▶ **Object checking upon release of a request**

To prevent the release of syntactically incorrect objects in requests, you can set a check of the objects globally or for specific users. With this setting, objects that have been found to contain errors cannot be released. You can make the settings with ▶ **Transport Organizer · Settings · Transport Organizer** or ▶ **Transport Organizer Tools · Administration · Global Customizing (Transport Organizer)**.

6.7 Transactions and Menu Paths

Add-on Installation Tool: no entry in standard menus (SAINT)

Extended Transport Organizer: SAP Menu • Tools • Administration • Transports • Transport Organizer (SE01)

Implementation Guide: SAP Menu • Tools • AcceleratedSAP • Customizing • Edit project (SPRO)

Project creation: SAP Menu • Tools • AcceleratedSAP • Customizing • Project management (SPRO_ADMIN)

SPAU modification adjustment: SAP Menu • Tools • ABAP Workbench • Utilities • Maintenance Upgrade Utilities • Program • Compare (SPAU)

SPDD modification adjustment: SAP Menu • Tools • ABAP Workbench • Utilities • Maintenance Upgrade Utilities • Dictionary • Compare (SPDD)

Support Package Manager: SAP Menu • Tools • ABAP Workbench • Utilities • Maintenance Support Packages (SPAM)

Transport Management System: SAP Menu • Tools • Administration • Transports • Transport Management System (STMS)

Transport Organizer: SAP Menu • Tools • ABAP Workbench • Overview • Transport Organizer (SE09)

Transport Organizer Tools: no entry in standard menus (SE03)

6.8 Additional Documentation

Quicklinks

▶ SAP Service Marketplace: alias *spmanager*

▶ SAP Service Marketplace: alias *patches*

▶ SAP Service Marketplace: alias *ocs*

▶ SAP Service Marketplace: alias *ocs-schedules*

SAP Service Marketplace Notes

The following table provides an overview of important notes on software logistics from SAP Service Marketplace.

Content	Note
FAQs on the Change and Transport System (CTS)	556734
Inactive import of reports	361735

Table 6.1 Important SAP Notes on Software Logistics

6.9 Questions

1. Which statement is correct?

   a. The SAP R/3 transport system is equivalent to copying clients.

   b. The SAP R/3 transport system helps exchange development and Customizing data between various SAP R/3 systems.

   c. The SAP R/3 transport system is used to exchange data between various clients of a single SAP R/3 system.

2. Which statement is correct?

A development class is:

a. A defined group of developers

b. Client-independent

c. To be assigned when modifying an original SAP object

d. Is assigned to a transport layer

3. Which statement is correct?

Modifications of SAP objects:

a. Must be registered in the OSS

b. Are not permitted

c. Are highly recommended to realize company-specific processes

4. Which statement is correct?

A Repository object of an SAP R/3 system:

a. Is automatically locked while a developer modifies it. The lock is removed automatically when the modifications are saved.

b. Can only be changed when it has been assigned to an appropriate change request. This approach ensures that other users are automatically blocked from modifying the objects until the developer releases the assigned task and the change request.

c. Can only be changed when it has been assigned to an appropriate change request; only users who are involved in the change request can modify the object.

7   Client Administration

In the previous chapters, we have frequently discussed clients. In this chapter, we take a more in-depth look at both clients and client management. One important aspect that you should note is the copying of clients within an R/3 system, or the transfer of clients to another system.

In the R/3 database, we can differentiate the data by various data classes. Some data is valid throughout the system. Most of this data belongs to the R/3 Repository. The Repository includes, among other things, ABAP programs, function modules, and the objects in the ABAP Data Dictionary. Therefore, changes to the configuration in this area influence the whole system. These changes are referred to as *client-independent* or *cross-client* changes. Other data is client-specific, which means that it can be viewed from just one client. Within *client-specific* data, we can differentiate among Customizing data, application data, and user data. There are close relationships between client-specific data groups. Application and user data are strongly influenced by client-specific Customizing settings. Application data is therefore usually only consistent in its specific Customizing environment. Figure 7.1 shows how the different data classes relate to each other.

Data classes

A *client* is a commercially self-contained unit, which may also include an annual report. Specific settings, based on a company's business requirements, added to the initially supplied standard functionality, are referred to as *Customizing*. In Customizing, you can also make system-wide settings such as selecting the factory calendar, ArchiveLink configuration, and so on. Almost all technical R/3 settings are client-independent. Therefore, in an R/3 system, the use of clients is suitable for realizing relatively independent factory sections, for example, but not for implementing the business processes of completely independent companies.

Client

Technically, each client is identified by a three-digit number. This number is used as a key in tables containing application data. This type of table is said to be *client-specific*. The first column in these tables is the MANDT (German abbreviation for client) field. This is also the first field in what is known as the *primary key* of the table. A user only has access to the data assigned to the client that he or she has selected at logon. In addition to the client-specific tables, there are also cross-client tables. The data found in cross-client tables is equally valid for all clients. Therefore, the first column, MANDT, is not included. The content of these tables affects the entire system.

Technical realization

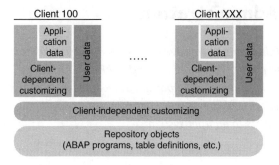

Figure 7.1 Data Classes in the R/3 Database

Standard clients SAP supplies the following prefigured clients as standard:

▶ Reference client 000 for administrative purposes and as a template for other clients

▶ Client 001 for final preparation and as a template for other clients (up to R/3 release 4.6C)

▶ Client 066 for SAP remote services

When these clients are delivered, clients 000 and 001 are identical in content. Neither client should be used for actual productive operation. Client 000 already contains default settings and sample entries and is supplied with the latest sample customizing via release upgrades, implementation of support packages, and so on. If other languages are imported, in addition to German and English, then language-related customizing, such as units of measure, is also only available in client 000. Therefore, client 000 cannot be considered for productive operation. All of these specific settings must be explicitly transferred to other clients.

Standard user Users and their configuration–such as passwords and authorizations—are client-specific, which means that users who have been created can only work in the clients in which they have been created. As standard, the users SAP* and DDIC are predefined in the clients 000 and 001 with the passwords "06071992" and "19920706", the user EARLYWATCH with the password "support" (see also Table 8.2) is available in client 066. For security reasons, we recommend that the standard user passwords be changed as soon as possible after installation.

7.1　Creating New Clients

To be able to work with an R/3 system productively, you must inevitably create your own clients in which company-specific settings can be made. To do this, you would typically copy an existing client, which at first is usually client 000, or transfer a previously configured client from another R/3 system. You can simply copy clients within a system or across system boundaries, or you can use a special transport request to transport clients to a remote system. The creation of your own clients is one of the first steps when customizing a system and is therefore one of the basic functions in the *Implementation Guide* (IMG, see Chapter 6). SAP recommends that you create a client in a development system for customizing. Once customizing has been completed in this system, you can copy all settings made to the clients in the subsequent R/3 systems assigned, in particular, to the production system. All changes have first to be tested in the consolidation system. In this way, the uniformity of the R/3 system settings in the infrastructure can also be guaranteed-something that is vital for test environments at a later stage. Copying a client should always be considered as just the first initialization of a client. If additional changes are made to the source client after the copy process, and which should also be transferred to the target client, the Change and Transport System (CTS) should be used. The creation and copying of clients are typical tasks in the R/3 implementation phase when setting up the system infrastructure. In Figure 7.2, you can see an example of these processes in chronological order for a three-system infrastructure. After copying a client, there is always a review phase during which additional maintenance work or corrections to the new client may be necessary to implement.

Creating a new client consists of two steps. In the first step, the new client is introduced in the R/3 system and important basic settings are defined. In the second step, the client is filled with data and postprocessing occurs. A client is only operable after this second step.

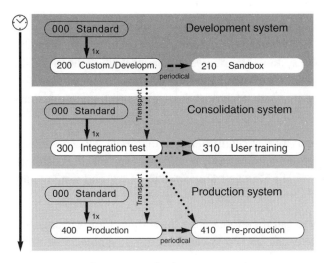

Figure 7.2 Example Structure of a Three-System Infrastructure

Role When planning an SAP R/3 system infrastructure, from the outset you should consider how the different activities should be divided up among the systems and clients. When creating a client, this is reflected in the *roles* assigned to it. These roles already reflect the purpose of the client, and therefore the attributes that describe it. The following classifications are possible:

▶ Production

▶ Test

▶ Customizing

▶ Demo

▶ Training/Education

▶ SAP reference

The classification of clients, apart from documentation, also serves to protect the production clients in a system with several additional (test) clients. For example, a client identified as a production client cannot be overwritten by a local or remote client copy. Customizing activities that are called directly from the application as current settings (for example, exchange rates, posting periods) can be implemented directly in production clients, even though customizing is not allowed due to general client settings.

In system verification, a system is categorized as productive if at least one of the clients is classified as a production client.

Client classification can be changed at any time and adjusted to reflect the way in which it would be used by the user.

Changeability One of the basic characteristics of a client is setting the *changeability* of its data and objects, which must be considered along with the changeability defined for the R/3 system. The degree of changeability defined for the R/3 system controls whether the objects in the Repository and cross-client customizing can be changed. It has no influence on client-specific customizing changes.

In the training, demo, or test clients of a system, it is certainly not always recommended that you automatically record all client-specific customizing changes—they might even be transported to a back-end system unintentionally.

In client control, you can therefore define the settings for the change and transport of client-specific and cross-client customizing objects.

For a detailed setting of clients for the maintenance and transport of client-specific objects, the following options can exist: Client-specific

▶ Changes without automatic recording

▶ Automatic recording of changes

▶ No changes allowed

▶ Changes without automatic recording, no transport allowed

In the clients in which customizing is carried out, all changes must be recorded for possible subsequent transport to other systems (Automatic recording of changes option). If changes are allowed, but aren't recorded, with a client setting, you can define whether a manual transport of changes should be allowed. For a production client, we recommend that you set a client lock, or at least that you record all changes automatically.

Controlling the maintenance of cross-client objects (Repository and cross-client customizing) is done separately: Cross-client

▶ Changes to the Repository and cross-client Customizing allowed

▶ No changes to cross-client Customizing objects

▶ No changes to Repository objects

▶ No changes to Repository and cross-client Customizing objects

As an enhancement to the possible settings in system changeability (see Section 5.1), which regulates changes to systems on the basis of objects, you can use these settings to define a client, preferably in the development system, as the only client in a system infrastructure in which cross-client Customizing and Repository changes can be carried out. In this way, you can avoid having to deal with unintentional side effects.

To prevent, for example, a production or Customizing client from being accidentally or deliberately overwritten by a copy, you can protect clients with an additional setting. The following additional settings are possible:

▶ Protection level 0: No restriction

▶ Protection level 1: No overwriting

▶ Protection level 2: No overwriting, no external availability

A client in protection levels 1 or 2 can no longer be selected as a target client for a client copy. Protection level 2 also prevents external access to this client for comparisons. R/3 offers a special comparison tool for clients. Thus, for example, you can verify if customizing is identical in two clients or, if not, what differences exist between them. This information can be important for tests in which the test environment must be identical to the production environment. Protection level 2 does not allow the use of the ▶ **Customizing Cross-System Viewer** for the clients in question. This level of data protection prevents the disclosure of client customizing and unauthorized access to the customer data contained in it. Where necessary, you should limit the use of the new client to the following areas:

▶ **Restrictions when starting CATT and eCATT**
CATT stands for *Computer Aided Test Tool*. By executing CATT operations, specified test runs can be repeated several times. In some cases, this involves a massive database change that is not permissible, at least not in production clients.

▶ **Protection against SAP upgrade**
This setting is only possible for clients that are classified as test or SAP reference clients. In the event of an upgrade of the SAP release, a flagged client is not provided with changes; after the upgrade, you can no longer work with it. This function is only intended for exceptional cases, such as to provide a basis for a comparison after the execution of an upgrade.

Note   In the R/3 Enterprise, thanks to the eCATT functionality (*Extended CATT*) since Basis release Web Application Server 6.20, the restrictions in CATT and eCATT runs can be adjusted in greater detail.

When preparing a new client, you must define the properties that were just described before you can fill the client with data. To do so, proceed as follows:

1. Select ▶ **Client maintenance**. An overview of all clients currently available in the system (see Figure 7.3) is displayed.

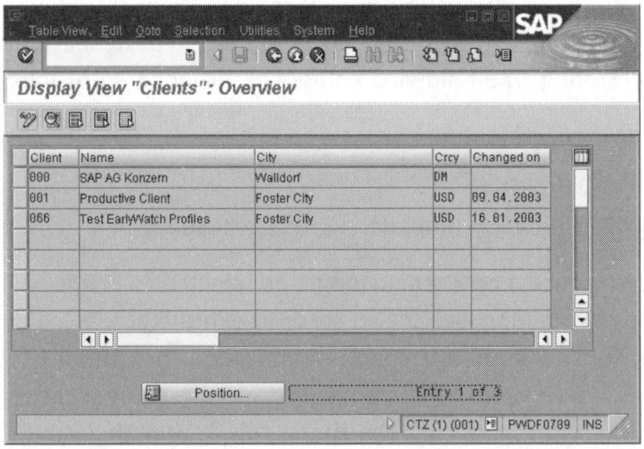

Figure 7.3 Initial Screen of Client Maintenance

2. Create a new entry here and define the attributes of the new client in the template for maintaining the technical attributes of clients (see Figure 7.4).

3. Assign a role to the client.

4. Select the level of changeability of the client.

5. Define the scope of possible changes to cross-client objects in this client.

6. If required, protect the new client from copying and being compared with other clients.

7. Save all your entries.

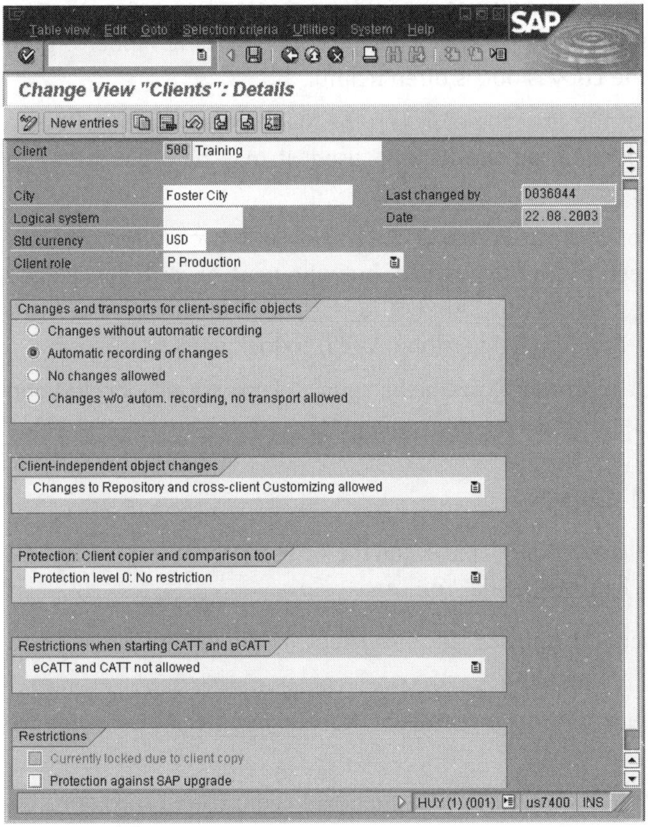

Figure 7.4 Detail Maintenance

All settings for a new client have now been made. At first, the steps described only produce an entry in table T000, which describes the properties of the new client. The new client does not contain any client-specific data, and in particular, it contains no user data. In the R/3 system, the only permanently coded user is SAP*, with the password "pass". You will need it to log on to the newly created client at the start of the copy run. In the copy process, this user is replaced by the specification of the SAP* user in the source client, if a copy profile with user master data is used.

In a second step, the necessary data must be copied to achieve client operability.

Preparation Client copies in an ongoing implementation project, or during productive system operation, do involve some hazards that can be minimized with good preparation.

▶ As system administrator, you should ensure that reconciled client copies are announced in advance by a system message, in order for users to be able to adjust their system use accordingly. A reminder on the day before the copy is due is often helpful.

▶ Ensure that at the time the copy is to be made, there is a current data backup. Depending on the RDBMS used, it may be a good idea to deactivate logging.

▶ Directly before you make the copy, you should forcibly log off users who have been previously warned, but who have nevertheless logged on to the system. Up to SAP R/3 Release 4.6C, you can also use a transaction from Euro conversion (EWZ5) to lock users.

▶ Ensure that background jobs in the source client are deallocated and that external interfaces are not running.

7.2 Local Copy

As was just explained, there are several methods that you can use to fill a newly created client with data. You can:

▶ Create a client by copying another client in the same system (local copy).

▶ Create a client by copying a client from a remote system (remote copy).

▶ Transfer a client from a system to the target client (client transport) via a transport request.

The method you choose will depend on the existing system infrastructure and the type of data to be copied. The steps in each method are quite similar. To avoid inconsistencies, no work should be done in either the target client or the source client during the copy process.

Based on the data structures in the R/3 database, certain data types can be Copy profile selected for the copying process. R/3 provides what are known as *copy profiles* for this purpose. Figure 7.5 shows the profiles that are currently available for copying clients.

It is not possible to create your own profiles, and existing profiles cannot be changed. It is possible, however, to use user master data and miscellaneous application data from different clients and store the resulting combination of sources in a usable form as a characteristic value. One element of this combination must always be the source client of the user master data. You cannot mix application data from different clients in this way. The copy profiles are described in Table 7.1.

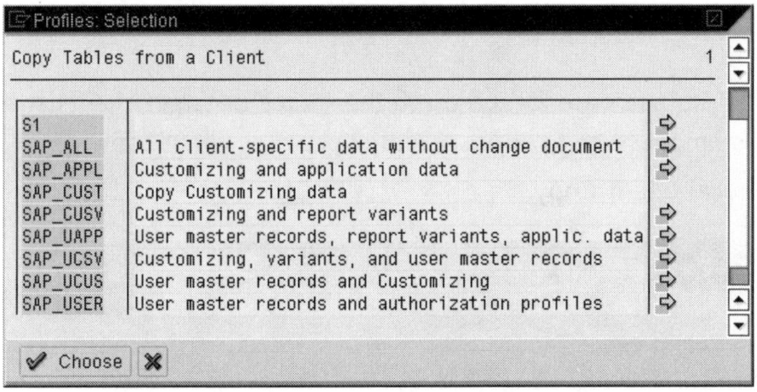

Figure 7.5 Copy Profiles Delivered by SAP

Profile name	Description
SAP_ALL	All data specific to a client is copied to the target client (except: change documents and local data).
SAP_APPL	Same as SAP_ALL, but without the user master data.
SAP_CUST	Client-specific Customizing (including the authorization profiles) is copied to the target client. The application data is deleted; the user data remains.
SAP_CUSV	Same as SAP_CUST, but the variants are also copied.
SAP_UAPP	Same as SAP_ALL (no longer used since R/3 Enterprise).
SAP_UCUS	Same as SAP_CUST, but the user master data is also copied.
SAP_UCSV	Same as SAP_UCUS, but the variants are also copied.
SAP_USER	Users, roles, and authorization profiles are copied.

Table 7.1 Copy Profiles for Local Copies

In all profiles, with the exception of SAP_USER, all Customizing and application data is deleted in the target client before the actual copy.

Change documents are not included in a client copy. If they are needed in the target client, they can be copied subsequently in a transport, provided that the source client and the target client have the same name.

The user master data in the target client is only overwritten if a copy profile with user master data is selected.

Method of procedure for local copies

First, we will look at the procedure for a local copy of a client, assuming that the target client has already been set up, as described in the previous section.

1. Log on to the newly defined client as user SAP* with the password "pass".

2. Ensure that no users are logged on to the source or target clients and send a system message to announce the upcoming client copy.

3. Select ▶ **Local Client Copy**.

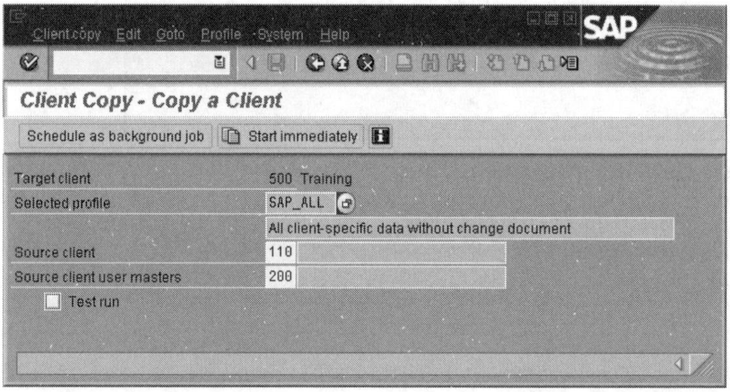

Figure 7.6 Local Client Copy

4. Use the profile to select the data to be copied from the source client (see Figure 7.6). If you are unsure about the nature of the data selection in the available profiles, you can get a more detailed description of the content by selecting **Profile · Display**.

5. Run the client copy in the background by selecting **Schedule as background job**.

6. Using ▶ **Client copy log analysis**, you can monitor the current status of the copy at any time and analyze the logs of past copy runs. Detailed logs are created for the copying process.

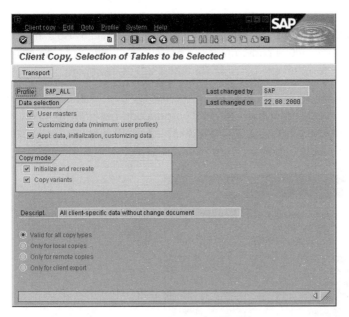

Figure 7.7 Detailed Description of the Profile SAP_ALL

In theory, you can also execute a client copy process in the foreground by selecting **Start immediately**; however, the copy process will then automatically be adopted by the current instance. In the background, any instance in the R/3 system offering the background service can be selected. Depending on the volume of data to be copied and the performance of the hardware, the process may take several hours. If the copy process were to run in the foreground, a dialog process would be blocked during this time. In addition, processing time in a dialog work process is limited by the instance parameter *rdisp/max_wp_runtime*. If a transaction exceeds this time limit, it is terminated and rolled back. If you execute it in the background, the time at which the copy process starts can be selected at will. If you select **Schedule as background job** to execute the copy in the background, the data defining the job start options can be entered.

Should the copy process be terminated because of some problem, you can execute it using the **Restart mode** option, which the system will automatically prompt you to use. In this case, the copy process would continue where it left off and would not have to start over from the beginning again.

Using the option **Test run,** you can first perform a test run of the entire process. The **Resource check** and **Simulation** options are available (see Figure 7.8).

During the copy run, you can take a look at the log from all other clients and obtain information on the progress of the action. You can also activate the monitor for an active copy run. It can present the progress of the process in graphic form on the basis of the tables still to be copied.

The following log shows excerpts from the file log of a local client copy executed in the background. It refers to a production system with its own customer data. Data from client 100 was copied to the newly created client 600. Particularly important information is depicted in bold font.

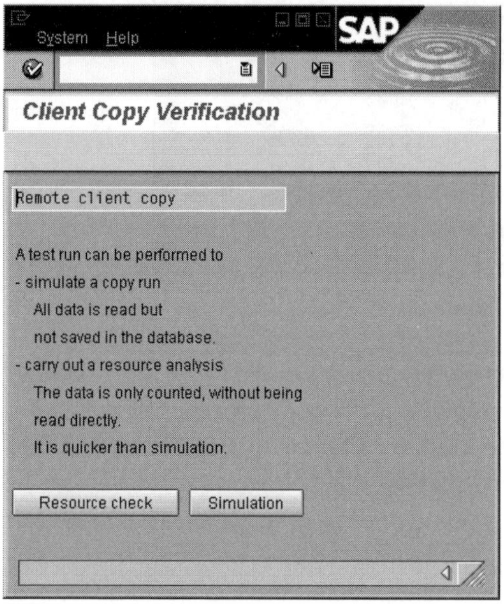

Figure 7.8 Test Run of a Remote Client Copy

Listing 7.1 Excerpt from the Log of a Local Client Copy

```
Client copy from " 15.07.2002" " 17:30:45"
SYSID.................................PLU
SAP Release..........................46C
Host.................................SLUPLU
User.................................SAP*
Parameter
Source client........................100
Source client user master data.........100
Target client........................600
Copy profile:........................SAP_ALL
Table selection
Customizing data.....................X
```

```
with application data.................X
Initialization and recreate............X
Change documents not copied
ADDR_CLIENTCOPY_SELECT_TABLES executed   25(0)
Entries transferred
Runtime            0 seconds
Exit program ADDR_CLIENTCOPY_SELECT_TABLES
successfully executed
SCCB_VARIANT_
CLIENTCOPY executed      4(   9.324) Entries transferred
Runtime           200 seconds
Exit program SCCB_VARIANT_CLIENTCOPY successfully executed
CLIENTCOPY_SELECT_TEXTTAB executed       3(0)
Entries transferred
Runtime            0 seconds
Exit program CLIENTCOPY_SELECT_
TEXTTAB successfully executed
table             Inserts Delete  Total Function   Kbyte
---------------------------------------------------------
Excluded from copy: STXB
Excluded from copy: STXH
Excluded from copy: STXL
Table BSEC not copied explicitly, copied as a cluster table
Table BSED not copied explicitly, copied as a cluster table
.........
A000    0      0      0 COPY      0        0
A002    6      0      6 COPY      0        0
A003  516      0    516 COPY     12        1
.........
WYT5    0      0      0 DEL.      0        1
WYT6    0      0      0 COPY      0        0
Z5D11  86      0     86 COPY      6        0
.........
Exit program RSSOUSCO_FOR_CC successfully executed
Selected objects      :        18.398
Edited objects        :        17.937
Tables  deleted       :           461
Storage required (KB) :     2.172.391
Program ran successfully.
Runtime (seconds)     :         4.797
End  of processing: 06:50:35
```

7.3　Remote Copy

Each R/3 system in a multi-system infrastructure has specific, clearly defined tasks. Therefore, for example, Customizing, quality assurance, and production should be executed on separate R/3 systems. To ensure that settings made in the R/3 systems are really identical, you can copy clients outside the realm of the system that you're working on. One possible way to carry out this data transfer is with a "remote copy".

Note A client can only be copied cross-system if both R/3 systems are of the same release and the repositories have not developed along different lines as a result of patches or transports.

An RFC connection is used as an interface between the R/3 systems. As a result, an RFC connection must be defined from the target system for the source client in the source system (see Chapter 13). Data transfer using the RFC interface is slower than it is with a local copy or client transport between systems. Therefore, and because a considerable amount of data has to be copied to the remote system, the runtime is proportionately long as well. In any case, a remote copy process is bound to be slower than a local copy, because of the network connection used alone. During this time, neither the source client nor the target client can be used. It is also preferable with this method to run the copy process in the background, in order to avoid blocking a dialog process. Due to the long runtime, the process would also easily exceed the allowed runtime for dialog processes defined in the R/3 system. Should the process be terminated, with this method, you can also restart the process at the termination point if the appropriate Restart option is activated in the copy run. You should also note that even with background processing, the RFC process occupies a dialog work process during the time it takes to read a table on the source system. Therefore, you should adjust the maximum dialog time in the source system depending on the size of the largest table.

Method of procedure for a remote copy The only difference between a local copy process and copying a client from a different R/3 system is that for the latter, an RFC connection is necessary. You should proceed as follows:

1. In the target system, create the new client, as described in Section 7.1.

2. In the target system, log on to the newly defined client as user SAP* with the password "pass".

3. If you have not already done so, you must define the RFC connection between the two R/3 systems to the source client for the scheduled copy run. See Chapter 13 for instructions on how to do this.

4. In this case also, you need to protect the source client from changes during the copy run. Ensure that no users are logged on to the source or target clients and send a system message to announce the forthcoming client copy.

5. You can then start the copy process in the target system. You can display the corresponding client copy program by selecting the ▶Remote client copy option (see Figure 7.9).

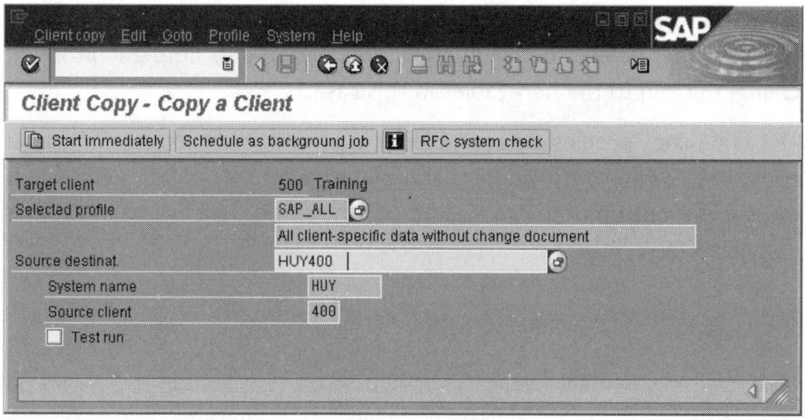

Figure 7.9 Remote Client Copy

6. Then, once again, use the profile to select the data to be transferred.

7. Select the RFC connection defining the **Source destination**. The source system name and the source client are automatically provided when you select the RFC connection.

8. Test the RFC connection before the actual copy run using the **RFC system check**. In addition to the connection test, there is also a check to verify that the R/3 systems have the same version and that the Dictionaries are compatible.

9. Start the copy run in the background.

10. Check the status of the copy process in the target system.

A remote copy run is the same as a local copy run with regard to both the execution alternatives (foreground or background) and the options available. Therefore, for the reasons outlined above, background processing is also preferable to foreground processing in this case. Here, also, you can do a test run before the actual copy run. Work must stop in both the source and target clients once the process starts, at the latest. Should the copy processes be terminated, you can also restart a remote client copy.

Note In a remote client copy, only table data is moved and not table definitions. If client-specific tables have been created in the source clients, these tables are not automatically transferred to the target client; in fact, that would cause an error. The structure of all tables to be copied is examined. If the copy would result in a loss of data, because, for example, tables are missing in the target system or the field structure of tables in the source and target systems is different, the copy process is interrupted and all differences are recorded in the log. To create Dictionary compatibility, you must transport the missing table structures from the source system to the target system before the client copy. You should also note any program changes linked to the new tables in this case.

Copy profiles The same copy profiles are available for a remote client copy as for a local copy. In R/3 Enterprise, additional profiles have been added, with which cross-client customizing can also be transferred in the context of a client copy (see Table 7.2):

Profile name	Description
SAP_RMBC	Same as SAP_UCSV with cross-client customizing.
SAP_RMPA	Same as SAP_ALL with cross-client customizing.
SAP_RMPC	Same as SAP_CUSV with cross-client customizing.

Table 7.2 Additional Copy Profiles for a Remote Client Copy (since Web AS 6.10)

7.4 Client Transport

With a client transport, the data to be copied is not transferred directly to the remote target system; rather, the transport control tool **tp** is used to first create data and control files for the client data to be exported, and these files are then stored in the global transport directory. You can import this data into the target system at a later time. Client transport can also be used to transport client-specific data to a system outside of the system infrastructure, using an external data carrier, or it can be used to create a backup copy for the client.

Note For this method, the R/3 releases of the source and target systems must also be consistent. As with the remote copy, for a client transport, the Dictionaries of both systems must also be compatible. If the target system is already known and an RFC connection is possible, this condition can be checked using the **RFC system check**—as was possible with the remote copy.

The method of procedure for transferring client data using a client export differs in some ways from the procedure in a local or remote copy.

1. Your first step should once again be to create the target client in the target system. Unlike the local and remote copies, however, this step can also be done after you have created the transport request in the source system.

2. Then, log on to the source system in the source client with a user that has transport authorization (not SAP* or DDIC).

3. Check to ensure that nobody other than you is logged on to the source client, and send a system message to other system users regarding the forthcoming client export.

4. Start the ▶ **Client export**.

5. As with local and remote copies, in this case you also select the data to be copied using the data profile (see Figure 7.10). In contrast to local and remote copies, with client export, you can create copies of cross-client data even before R/3 Enterprise. Profiles are also available for this (see Table 7.3):

Profile name	Description
SAP_EXBC	As SAP_UCSV with cross-client customizing.
SAP_EXPA	As SAP_ALL with cross-client customizing.
SAP_EXPC	As SAP_CUSV with cross-client customizing.

Table 7.3 Additional Copy Profiles for a Client Export Copy

6. The target system can be any system described in the definition of the system infrastructure, including virtual or external systems. The system only offers R/3 systems for selection if they have the same release version as the source system. With this method, both online and background execution are possible, with the same advantages and disadvantages as listed above.

7. Confirm your selection. You will then be informed which transport requests have been created for this task (see Figure 7.11).

8. Check the log that has been created for the export run.

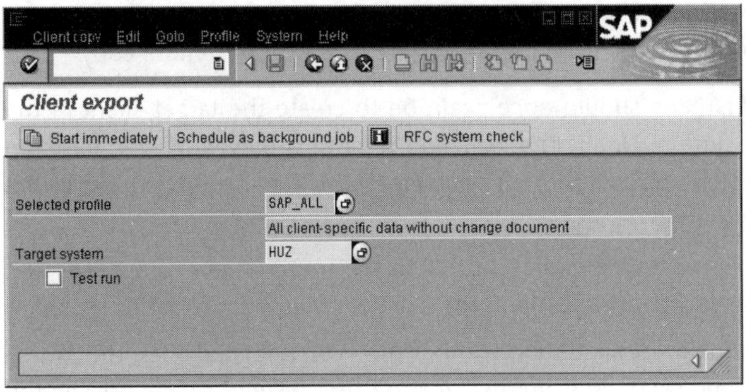

Figure 7.10 Client Export

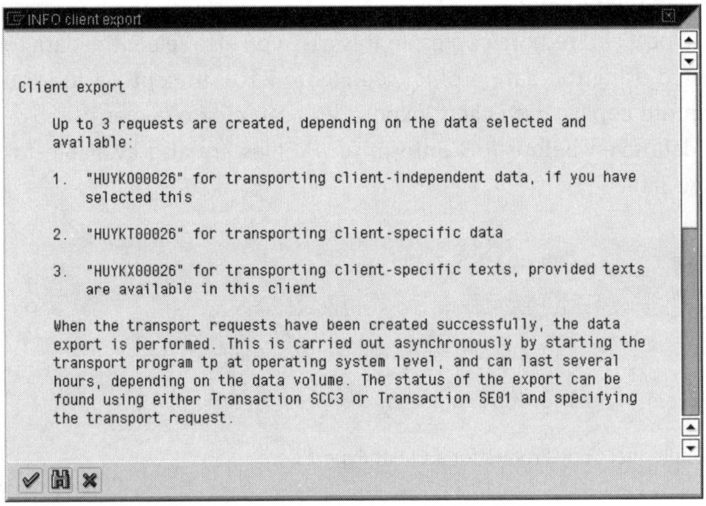

Figure 7.11 Information on the Requests Created

With this method of copying the data of a client, logs are also created. The following log shows the copy log for a client export with the profile SAP_CUST.

Listing 7.2 Copy Log for a Client Export

```
Client export from "10/03/2002" "03:56:14"
System ID............................. "KLU"
R/3 Release........................... "46C"
Host.................................. "SLUQAS"
User.................................. SHAGEM
Parameter
Source client......................... "600"
Copy profile:......................... "SAP_CUST"
```

```
Table selection
Customizing data ....................."X"
with application data............... " "
Initialize and recreate........ "X"
With cross-client tables.............." "
"ADDR_CLIENTCOPY_SELECT_
TABLES" executed "        25"("        0") entries copied
Runtime "              0" seconds
Exit program "ADDR_CLIENTCOPY_SELECT_
TABLES" successfully executed
"RKC_CC_EXCLUDE_
TABLES" executed "         0"("        0") entries copied
Runtime "             10" seconds
Exit program "RKC_CC_EXCLUDE_TABLES" successfully executed
"RKE_CC_EXCLUDE_
TABLES" executed "         4"("        0") entries copied
Runtime "             12" seconds
Exit program "RKE_CC_EXCLUDE_TABLES" successfully executed
"RV_COND_RECORDS_
TRANS" executed "         4"("    1.046") entries copied
Runtime "             11" seconds
Exit program "RV_COND_RECORDS_TRANS" successfully executed
"SCCB_VARIANT_
CLIENTCOPY" executed "    4"("    5.573") entries copied
Runtime "            121" seconds
Exit program "SCCB_VARIANT_
CLIENTCOPY" successfully executed
"CLIENTCOPY_SELECT_TEXTID_
STD" executed. "         1" entries found
Runtime "              0" seconds
Exit program "CLIENTCOPY_SELECT_TEXTID_
STD" successfully executed
"CLIENTTRA_SELECT_TEXTID_
FORM" executed. "         6" entries found
Runtime "              0" seconds
Exit program "CLIENTCOPY_SELECT_TEXTID_
STD" successfully executed
"CLIENTTRA_SELECT_TEXTID_
FORM" executed. "         0" entries found
Runtime "              0" seconds
Exit program "CLIENTTRA_SELECT_TEXTID_
STYL" successfully executed
```

```
Command file for "tp" is written under: "KLUKT00116"
For client transport, "           12.508" entries entered in
command file
Command file for "RSTXR3TR" is written under: "KLUKX00116"
For client transport, "                7" entries entered in
command file
Selected objects          : "           30.961"
Program ran successfully
Runtime (seconds)         : "              352"
```

The main content of the log, apart from any errors that occur, consists of the names of the transport requests created for the client export. In addition to the already familiar possibility of using ▶Client Copy Log Analysis for a client copy to determine the status and progress of an action, in this case, you must also use the **Client** function of the ▶Transport Organizer **(extended view)** to evaluate the results. The log of the client copy program describes only the creation of the command files for the transport program **tp**. The transport program does the actual export of the client. You can find the log for the export run itself by using the Transport Organizer. Listing 7.3 shows an example of this.

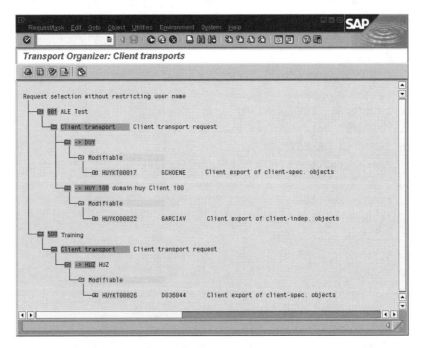

Figure 7.12 Client Export in the Transport Organizer

Listing 7.3 tp Client Export Log

```
Directory  \\SLUQAS\sapmnt\trans\log
Name: KLUEX00116.KLU1
ETP199X/#############################################
1 ETP183 EXPORT PREPARATION
1 ETP101 transport order    : "KLUKX00116"
1 ETP102 system             : "KLU"
1 ETP108 tp path            : "tp"
1 ETP109 version and release : "305.12.42" "46D"
1 ETP198
2 EPU230XExecution of the export pre-
processing methods for request "KLUKX00116"
4 EPU111   on the application server: "SLUQAS"
4 EPU138   in client          : "000"
.........
2 EPU232 End:  Adapting the object directory for the obje
cts of the request "KLUKX00116"
1 ETP183 EXPORT PREPARATION
1 ETP110 end date and time   : "20021003160206"
1 ETP111 exit code           : "0"1
ETP199X/#############################################
1 ETP150 MAIN EXPORT
1 ETP101 transport order    : "KLUKX00116"
1 ETP102 system             : "KLU"
1 ETP108 tp path            : "tp"
1 ETP109 version and release : "305.12.42" "46D"
4 ETW000 R3trans.exe version 6.05 (release 46D -
10/18/01 -
 11:30:00).   ============================================
=====
4 ETW000 control file: \\SLUQAS\sapmnt\trans\tmp\KLUKKX00
116.KLU
4 ETW000 > #pid 4380 on SLUQAS (APServiceKLU)
4 ETW000 > export
4 ETW000 > file='\\SLUQAS\sapmnt\trans\data\RX00116.KLU'
4 ETW000 > client=600
4 ETW000 > buffersync=yes
4 ETW000 >
4 ETW000 > use comm 'KLUKX00116'
4 ETW000 R3trans was called as follows: R3trans.exe -
```

```
u 1 -
w \\SLUQAS\sapmnt\trans\tmp\KLUEX00116.KLU \\SLUQAS\sapmn
t\trans\tmp\KLUKKX00116.KL
4 ETW000 date&time    : 10/03/2002 - 04:02:14
4 ETW000 active unconditional modes: 1
4 ETW000 Connected to DBMS = MSSQL     SERVER = 'SLUQAS\
KLU' DBNAME = 'KLU'    SYSTEM = 'KLU'.
4 ETW000  trace at level 1 opened for a given file pointe
r
4 ETW000 ================== STEP 1 ====================
4 ETW000 date&time    : 10/03/2002 - 04:02:14
4 ETW000 function     : EXPORT
4 ETW000 data file    : \\SLUQAS\sapmnt\trans\data\RX00116
.KLU
4 ETW000 buffersync   : YES
4 ETW000 client       : 600
4 ETW000 Language     : ABCDEFGHIJKLMNOPQRSTUVWXYZ01234567
89abcdefghijklmnopqrstuvwxyz
4 ETW000 Compression : L
4 ETW000 l.s.m.       : VECTOR
4 ETW000 commit       : 100000
4 ETW000 table cache : dynamic
4 ETW000
3WETW129 transport request "KLUKX00116" has trstatus "D".
3 ETW673XUse Commandfile "KLUKX00116"
4 ETW000       /* client export texts */
4 ETW000       trfunction: 'M' (client transport)
4 ETW000       trstatus  : 'D'
4 ETW000       tarsystem : PLU.600
4 ETW000       user      : SHAGEM
4 ETW000       date      : 10/03/2002 - 04:01:52
4 ETW000   1 entry from E070 exported (KLUKX00116).
4 ETW000   7 entries from E071 exported (KLUKX00116
*).
.........
4 ETW000 Disconnected from database.
4 ETW000 End of Transport (0004).
4 ETW000 date&time: 10/03/2002 - 04:02:16
4 ETW000 1 warning occurred.
1 ETP150 MAIN EXPORT
```

```
1 ETP110 end date and time   : "20021003160216"
1 ETP111 exit code           : "4"
1 ETP199 ###############################################
```

Note If the operating system used with the R/3 system still has limitations on file size—2 GB may be conceivable, for example—the data files created for the transport request cannot exceed this limit either. In this case, because the file size exceeded the limit, the transport request would terminate.

The data files created during the client export are necessary in order for the data to be imported into another R/3 system. Table 7.4 lists and describes the files created in the transport directory in a complete client export.

Subdirectory	File name	Description
\data	RO<Request number>.<SID>	client-independent data
\data	RT<Request number>.<SID>	client-specific data
\data	RX<request number>.<SID>	texts and forms
\cofiles	KO<Request number>.<SID>	client-independent meta information
\cofiles	KT<request number>.<SID>	client-specific meta information
\cofiles	KX<Request number>.<SID>	meta information on texts and forms

Table 7.4 Files That Are Important for an Import

Only those files for which data exists in the system, and which are to be exported in accordance with the copy profile, are created. If no client-independent data is exported in a client export, as in our example using the profile SAP_CUST, the corresponding data files are not included. Therefore, in the example, no file RO0116.PLU was created. Proceed as follows to import this data into another R/3 system:

1. If the source system and target system are in the same transport domain, then, in the ▶ **Transport Management System**, you can select any transport request that pertains to the client export. The other requests associated with it will automatically be imported in the correct order.

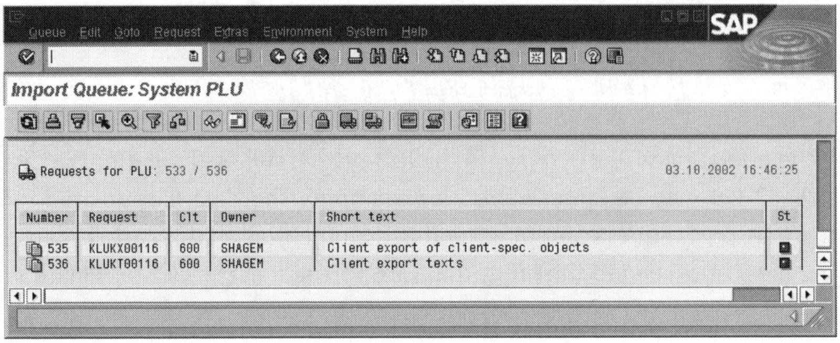

Figure 7.13 Import Using the Transport Management System

2. If the exported client is imported into a system that is not in the same transport domain, you must carry out manual actions on operating-system level. To do this, you must copy the necessary files into the appropriate subdirectory of the local transport directory in the target system.

3. On operating-system level, from the *bin* subdirectory in the local transport directory in the target system, the commands

   ```
   tp addtobuffer <request> <target system>
   ```

   and

   ```
   tp import <target system> client <target client>
   ```

   are executed for the client-independent data transport request and then for the transport request with the client-specific data. These actions usually take a fairly long time, just like the execution of the export. The transport request for texts and forms is imported and generated by the postprocessing described in the next step.

4. Subsequent to the actual import and to avoid authorization problems, using the Transport Management System or manually using **tp**, you must adapt the R/3 runtime environment to the current state of the data by calling ▶ **Import editing** as user SAP* or DDIC. Import postprocessing must always be performed. During import postprocessing, there should be no users working in the target client either.

5. You can find the import log using ▶ **Transport Management System**, even if the import is initiated directly using **tp**. The postprocessing work carried out is listed in the ▶ **Client copy log analysis**.

The client import is now finished. In practice, client import is rather risky, especially if client-independent data is included. Cross-client data influences the entire R/3 system, which means that all clients in the target system are inevitably affected by the imported data. In the worst case, other clients may not be able to operate when cross-client data is imported from another R/3 system. If you decide not to transfer cross-client data from the source system, on the other hand, the functionality of the imported client may be affected if there are significant differences between the source and target system. The conclusion that can be drawn here is that for client import and export, particular attention should be paid to the differences between the source and target system.

After successfully copying the client, you should now focus on the necessary postprocessing:

Postprocessing

▶ If the client settings for the copy were initially given a transition value to allow for the copy, the settings must now finally be adjusted.

▶ If you have deactivated database logging for the client copy, you must reactivate it for productive operation, after running a complete backup.

▶ Schedule client-specific background jobs.

▶ If logical systems are used (see Chapter 13), in non-production systems you can adjust the names of the logical systems after the client copy using ▶ **Conversion of logical system names**.

▶ If using SAP Workflow, you must maintain the default workbench.

▶ Check the connection of interfaces for client-specific settings and maintain them if necessary.

▶ If the database used works with a cost-based optimizer, after the client copy, the statistics will have to be generated again.

Copying clients is not suitable for merging data from different clients or for transferring difference quantity from one client to another. Copying clients should be regarded as a first step in the development of a system infrastructure. Once the copy process has been completed, the data in the client must be maintained using CTS and transported, as required.

Conclusion

7.5 Special Functions

Some special functions are offered as part of client administration.

▶ **Copy as of transport request**
With ▶ **Copy as of transport request**, customizing changes recorded in a transport request can be transferred between two clients in a system. Apart from the object list of the request itself, the object lists of unreleased tasks in the request can also be copied. The request itself does

not have to be released. Entries in the target client are overwritten or deleted depending on the key entries in the transport request.

▶ **Delete client**
Now and then, it may happen that a client must be completely deleted, for example, in R/3 systems that result from copying another system. Please note that this is a critical function. With this function, almost as many changes accrue in the database as with a client copy. With some relational database management systems, unnecessary disk space that resulted from deleting a client is only released for use again after a reorganization.

▶ **Client comparison**
R/3 offers various functions for comparing the Customizing settings of two clients in the same system or across different R/3 systems, all of which will require an RFC communication between the two clients. Using the ▶**Customizing Cross-System Viewer**, you can compare complex customizing environments, controlled with different criteria. The client setting "Protection level 2: No overwriting, no external avail- ability" does not allow the use of the Customizing Cross-System Viewer. Any two tables can be compared using ▶**Object comparison**.

7.6 Tips

Given the volume of data that is moved when a client is copied, the pro- cess should be considered critical. The most common error is to underes- timate the growth in data when a copy is made. The database turns out to be too small and therefore, not only is the copy process terminated, but in some cases it is not possible to do any further work with the system until more space has been added to the database. Therefore, you should conduct a test run to determine the volume of incoming data. Check to see if there is enough space on the database for it!

▶ **Client size**
The results of the test run are based on estimates, in particular, when determining the expected resource requirement. To help get a more precise idea of the size of a client, with the Enterprise release, R/3 offers the report programs **RSTABLESIZE** (see Figures 7.14 and 7.15) and **RSSPACECHECK** (see Figure 7.16), which can be used for a more exact actual evaluation at table level. In the R/3 releases 4.x, the rou- tines **YSTABSIZ** and **YKSPACEC** can be used as instructed in SAP Note 118823. They are not included in the standard release.

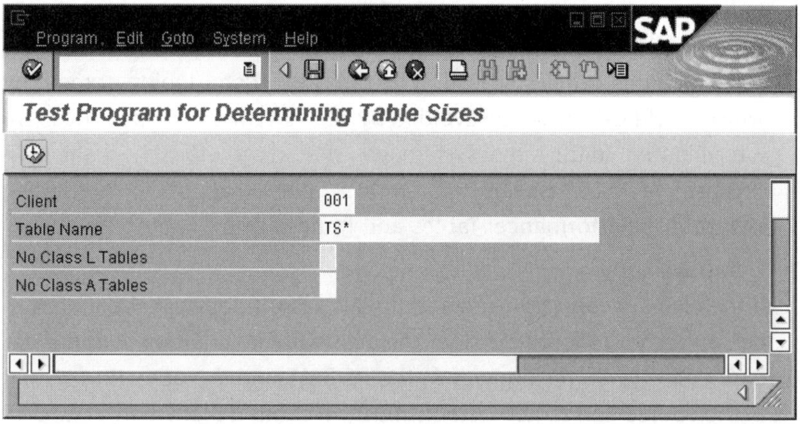

Figure 7.14 Determining Size Using RSTABLESIZE

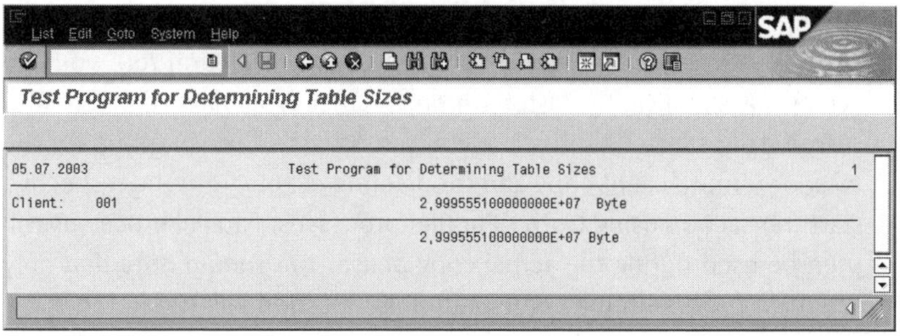

Figure 7.15 Result of Size Determination

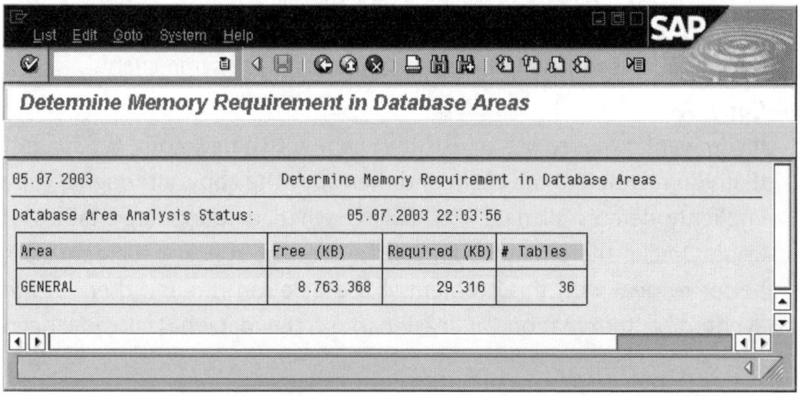

Figure 7.16 Determining Memory Requirement Using RSSPACECHECK

► Indices

Sometimes indices are missing from the database. If you restart a client copy run, this can result in double data records in tables, something which could otherwise be avoided by the system. The copy procedure is terminated. In the target system, you should therefore check the consistency of database objects and in particular of indices using ►**Database Performance: Tables and Indices** (see Chapter 15).

► Database copy

If the client is very large and additional client-independent data has to be copied, you should consider the possibility of a homogeneous database copy. To do this, however, the RDBMS and the operating system in the source and target systems must be compatible, whereas remote client copy and client transport between different system configurations is possible.

► Tuning

If you use parallel processes in a client copy or deletion run, you can achieve a significantly faster runtime. Once you have defined RFC server groups (see Chapter 13), you can activate a server group for the local or remote client copy and for deleting clients from the respective start transaction using **Goto · Parallel processes**. Parallel processes will then be used during the actual copy phase. You should note that only the main process in the configuration in question will run in the background, whereas all other parallel processes occupy dialog work processes. The serial scheduling of individual client copies with parallel processes is preferable to the parallel scheduling of several client copies (with different source clients), that do not use parallel processes. It is not possible to run simultaneous copies from the same client.

► Copy over

If you want to overwrite an existing client with a new copy, we suggest that you first delete the client and then start the copy, although a copy implicitly deletes all data. Particularly when deleting large tables, if using Oracle, there may be an overflow of the rollback segment. It is better to deal with this problem in the deletion run and then, in the event of a termination, at least part of the data has already been deleted.

► Restarting a client export

If a client export is terminated and restarted, you should ensure that all corresponding **tp** runs are completed before restarting the export. Otherwise, you run a risk of having generated inconsistent transport files that cannot be imported.

▶ Copy large tables

For extremely large tables, you can improve performance by deleting the secondary indices before the client copy and then creating them again, to avoid having to change the index for every data record copied. From Web AS 6.20, tuning parameters for a client copy can be implemented using the report program RSCCEXPT. If you do use these options, however, you must proceed with caution. In particular, you should remember to undo settings after the end of the client copy.

7.7 Transactions and Menu Paths

Client copy log analysis: SAP Menu • Tools • Administration • Administration • Client Administration • Copy Logs (SCC3)

Client export: SAP Menu • Tools • Administration • Administration • Client Administration • Client Transport • Client Export (SCC8)

Client maintenance: SAP Menu • Tools Administration • Administration • Client Administration • Client Maintenance (SCC4)

Conversion of logical system names: not accessible via the SAP standard menu (BDLS)

Copy as per transport request: SAP Menu • Tools • Administration • Administration • Client administration • Special functions • Copy transport request (SCC1)

Customizing Cross-System Viewer: SAP Menu • Tools • Customizing • Customizing Cross-System Viewer (SCU0)

Database performance: Tables and indices: SAP Menu • Tools • Administration • Monitor • Performance • Database • Tables/Indexes (DB02)

Import editing: SAP Menu • Tools • Administration • Administration • Client Administration • Client Transport • Import Editing (SCC7)

Local client copy: SAP Menu • Tools • Administration • Administration • Client Administration • Client Copy • Local Copy (SCCL)

Object comparison: SAP Menu • Tools • Administration • Administration • Client Administration • Customizing Objects • Object Comparison (SCMP)

Remote client copy: SAP Menu • Tools • Administration • Administration • Client administration • Client Copy • Remote Copy (SCC9)

Transport Management System: SAP Menu • Tools • Administration • Transport • Transport Management System (STMS)

Transport Organizer (extended view): SAP Menu • Tools • Administration • Transports • Transport Organizer (SE01)

7.8 Additional Documentation

SAP Service Marketplace Notes

Table 7.5 provides an overview of important SAP Service Marketplace Notes related to R/3 client maintenance.

Content	Note
R/3 multi-client capability	31557
Copying large and productive clients (from Web AS 6.10)	489690
Copying large and productive clients (up to R/3 4.6D)	67205
Size of a client	118823
Parallel processes (up to R/3 4.6D)	212727
Parallel processes (from Web AS 6.10)	541311

Table 7.5 SAP Notes on Client Maintenance

7.9 Questions

1. Which of the following statements referring to the R/3 client concept are true?

   a. Customizing settings are basically client-independent.

   b. A client is a commercially self-contained unit in an R/3 system.

   c. Each client has its own application data.

   d. Each client has its own technical data, independent of other clients.

   e. Each client has its own application tables.

2. What methods does R/3 offer for copying clients?

   a. Local copy

   b. Remote copy

   c. Data exchange procedure

   d. Client export

   e. Data backup

3. What data can be transferred in a remote client copy?

    a. Client-specific application data

    b. Client-specific table definitions

    c. Client-independent data

    d. All data in the R/3 system

8   R/3 Users and Authorizations

*Different types of users exist in the R/3 system environment:
users at operating-system level, database users, and R/3 users.
Here, as is the case throughout this book, "user" does not refer
to an actual person. Like "client," it is a technical term. This
chapter describes R/3 users exclusively.*

The *user concept* is one of the fundamental components within the R/3
security concept. To achieve a high level of security, R/3 system administrators must be familiar with the features of the user concept and therefore, be better prepared to implement this concept conscientiously. This
chapter teaches you what you need to know to carry out these tasks.

8.1   Basics

From the perspective of the SAP system, a *user* is a technical identifier   User
under which an action is executed. The *user ID* is assigned properties,
which are saved in the *user master record*. The user can be an actual physical user, or a technical user who is only used for background processing.

The user is identified uniquely via the *user name*, which is both the string   User name
that an actual user uses to log on to the system and the identifier used
internally by the system.

The most important properties of a user include that user's authorizations,
which are assigned as *profiles*. The administration and assignment of these
profiles is another topic that will be explored in this chapter.

R/3 has its own user concept. When you first install the R/3 system, only
superusers SAP* and DDIC are initially available (see Chapter 7). You can
use one of these two superusers to start creating other users. In the previous chapters, the descriptions always assumed that the utilized R/3 user
had blanket privileges in R/3, in particular all the privileges required to
perform the described activities. While this approach is acceptable for the
initial phase, it poses a major security gap in live operations—a gap that
you will now close.

8.2   User Maintenance

Directly after installation, several standard clients and standard users are available in the R/3 system (see Chapter 7). Users are always client-specific—that is, they are only valid in the client(s) where they were defined. Another important user property is the password, which is queried during logon and can be changed at any time—including during logon. Users can also select an available language in the given R/3 installation during logon. The user name and the properties it is assigned form the *user master record*. A user master record contains all the data and default settings that are necessary to log on a user in a client. This master record is formed from the following element groups, which also appear in the tabs for address maintenance (see Table 8.1).

Tab page	Data elements
Address	Address data
SNC	Settings for Secure Network Communications (SNC), which are only visible when SNC is active
Logon data	Password and validity period of the user
Defaults	Default settings for a default printer, logon language, and so on
Parameters	User-specific values for standard fields
Roles	Roles assigned to the user (until Basis Release 4.6B: **Activity groups**)
Profiles	Profiles assigned to the user
Groups	Assignment of user to groups for mass maintenance
Personalization	Individual settings for personalization objects
License data	Classification (until Basis Release 4.6C: only possible in change mode with Measurement Data button)

Table 8.1 Tab Pages of Address Maintenance

User maintenance, which is described in the next section, involves creating, changing, and deleting users, in addition to maintaining their properties in the user master record. You don't have to select values for all of these properties; however, entering an expiration date, for example, in order to restrict the temporal validity of a user, is optional. The complex variations of the possible settings for a user enables you to adapt the R/3 system to the individual users' needs and, simultaneously, restrict their authorizations to their assigned application areas.

8.2.1 Creating Users

You start user administration with ▶ User Maintenance (see Figure 8.1). This menu contains all the functions for creating, changing, and deleting users, as well as maintaining their properties.

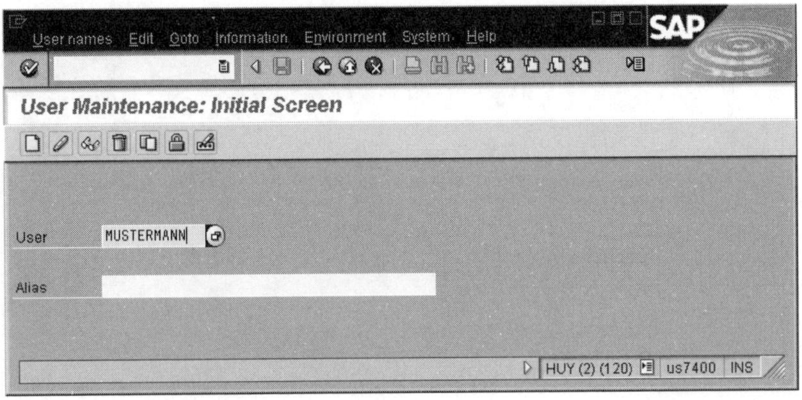

Figure 8.1 User Maintenance: Initial Screen

You specify the user by entering the unique user name in the **User** field. You can use the **Alias** field (in Basis Release 4.6C and later) to select users with an alternate identifier, such as those users created from Internet transactions in the self-service area. You cannot create an alias at this point. The following example assumes that user MUSTERMANN is created with **User names · Create** or with the corresponding icon.

The various properties of the user are displayed on tab pages, grouped by subject area. To change the subject areas, select the appropriate tab page.

When you create user MUSTERMANN, a screen similar to Figure 8.2 is displayed in which you can enter the user's address data. Technically, you must maintain at least the user's last name and password in the **Logon data** tab page. You should enter all known address data, in case it becomes necessary to contact the user.

User address

You do not have to enter the same address for each user. Instead, you can now define ▶ **Company Addresses** and assign them to users.

In the **Logon data** tab page, you must specify a password and user type for each user. In Basis Release 4.6C and later, you must also maintain a user group for new users. Figure 8.3 shows the settings for creating user MUSTERMANN.

Logon data

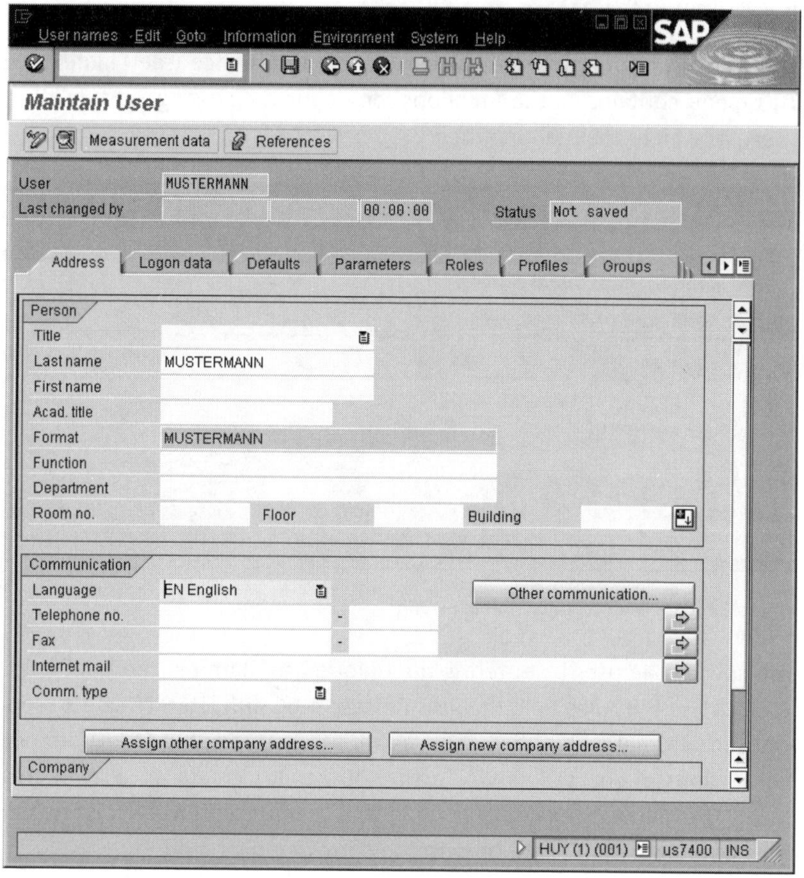

Figure 8.2 Address Maintenance for a User

When the user enters his or her password, it is masked by asterisks. The user type determines the permitted method of using the R/3 system. Possible types are:

▶ **Dialog**

A user with type *Dialog* can use the R/3 system in any manner. This includes background processing, batch input processing, CPI-C services, and working in dialog, as long as it is not explicitly restricted again via the assignment of specific authorizations. SAP licensing conditions prohibit multiple concurrent use of the same user ID in live systems.

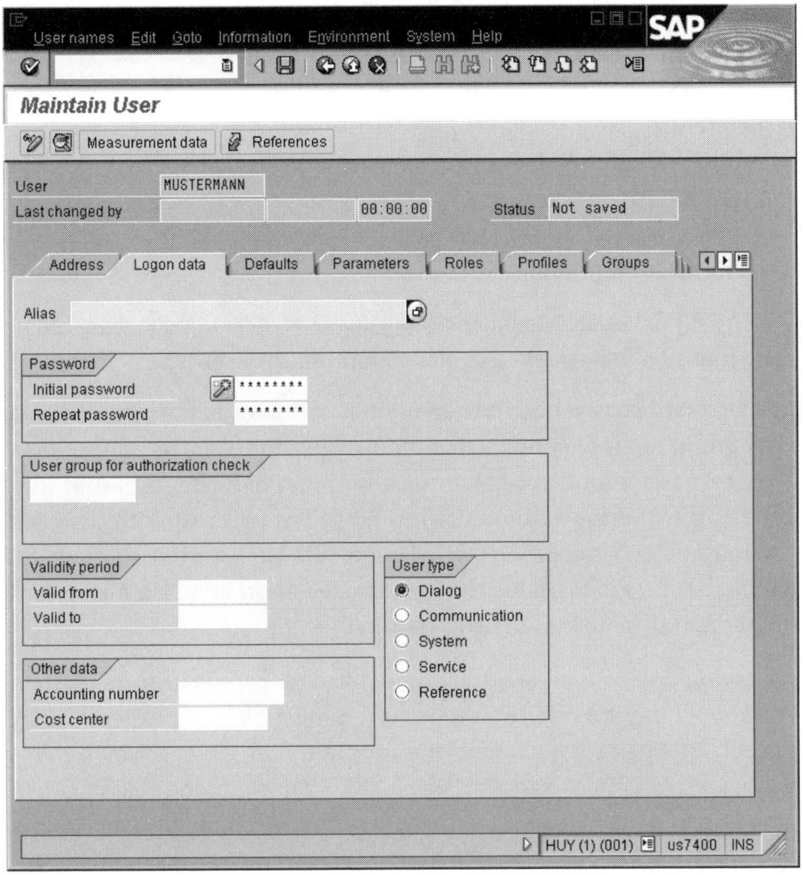

Figure 8.3 Logon Data for a User

▶ **Communication**

A user with type *Communication* can be used for dialog-free communication between systems, such as via Remote Function Call (RFC, see Chapter 13). This user is not allowed to log on to the R/3 system or start dialog processing.

▶ **System**

A user with type *System* can employ dialog-free communication within a system and for background processing. The general settings for the validity period of a password don't apply for this user type. Logon in dialog is not possible.

▶ **Service**

A user with type *Service* is a dialog user who is available to a large, anonymous group of users, for example, for access via Internet Transaction Server (ITS). For this user type, no check of expired or initial passwords is performed, and multiple logons are explicitly permitted. For security reasons, however, you should only assign such users with great caution and with limited authorizations.

▶ **Reference**

A user with type *Reference* is a general, non-person-specific user. This user type cannot be used for logon. It serves only as a reference for granting authorizations, for example, to equip Internet users with identical authorizations.

User MUSTERMANN is defined as a dialog user. Accordingly, there are no restrictions on R/3 system use that stem from the user type.

User group   In addition to serving both documentation and information purposes, the **User group** helps to coordinate authorizations for maintaining user data. A user from one user group can only maintain the data for a user from another group if the authorization to do so has been explicitly assigned. You must enter a user group in the **Logon data** tab page; the user can add additional user groups in the **Groups** tab page. In addition, arranging users in user groups simplifies the ▶**Mass Change** of users.

User group SUPER is initially the only defined user group in an R/3 system. You should use it for all users who have similar blanket privileges in the system. The logical assignment of a user to a user group enables you to deduce activity areas and privileges later. You enter and maintain user groups in user maintenance (with menu path **Environment · User Groups**) or using ▶**User Group**. Create a user group called *MM*, for example. You will use this user group later for new users who are responsible for activities in materials management. This enables you to define a user administrator who can only maintain the users from this user group.

The other data (accounting number, cost center) can be analyzed by reports for statistical purposes. The data has no effect on the functionality of the user.

Defaults   You can use the **Defaults** tab to define default settings for output devices, time zones, and date format and decimal notation. You can also set a default value for the user's logon language. In this case, the user no longer has to enter a logon language during logon. Users can adjust the user defaults to meet their specific needs by using the ▶**Own Data** menu (see Section 8.4).

Parameters   The **Parameters** tab page can be used to define user-specific default values for frequently used input fields. Users can adjust this data themselves with menu item ▶**Own Data** (see Section 8.4).

If Secure Network Communications (SNC) is used (if not, the tab is not displayed), you can use the **SNC** tab to define the name used to authenticate the user with the external security product.

SNC

Users can enter individual settings for personalization objects in the **Personalization** tab page. The personalization objects must be predefined and implemented in the application component in order to be selected here. The tab page and all interfaces are already available in Basis Release 4.6C, whereas standard personalization objects that can be adjusted in this manner are included in Release 6.10 and later.

Personalization

You use tab pages **Roles** (until Basis Release 4.6B: **Activity groups**) and **Profiles** to assign the required authorizations to the user. This process is described in more detail in the following sections.

8.2.2 License Data

The SAP software contains a measurement program, which is used to generate information that is critical for the billing of each installation. The measurement program analyzes the number and types of users and the utilized components. Therefore, all users must be classified for measurement. You do so using the **Measurement data** button in user maintenance. To avoid additional work during measurement, you should always classify users as soon as you create them.

The actual measurement is performed using ▶**System Measurement**, or the ▶**License Administration Workbench** for more complex system landscapes (i.e., Service Data Control Center (SDCC) in SAP Web AS and later).

The rules for classification and measurement depend on the specific release and contract, and are described in detail in the "Introduction to System Measurement."

8.2.3 Changes to Users/Mass Changes

All the data described in the previous sections can be changed again later in the same transactions. Changing many users simultaneously can be extremely time-consuming. Fortunately, a specific ▶**Mass Change** function is available to meet this need. It enables you to create and perform most changes within user administration for a selected set of users.

You can select the users by address data or authorization data. Selection is particularly simple when the users have been divided into suitable user groups (see Section 8.2.1).

You can use the mass change function to create, delete, lock, and unlock users, as well as change logon data, parameters, roles, profiles, and groups.

Changes to a user master record don't take effect until the next logon. In particular, changes to roles and authorizations of active users don't take effect immediately. The users must log off the system and then log on again.

8.2.4 Logon and Password Protection

When creating a new user, the administrator assigns an initial password, which the user must change during the first logon. This password, along with the user name, is required to log on to the SAP system. Several rules apply to the password. Some of these rules are predefined and not changeable, while others can be adjusted via the use of profile parameters. The predefined rules include:

▶ The first three characters of the user name cannot appear in the same sequence in any position of the user ID.

▶ The password cannot be PASS or SAP*.

▶ Users can only change their passwords once a day.

For an overview of possible profile parameters and recommended settings, refer to the "Data Protection Guidelines for SAP R/3" and the "SAP Security Guide." Several of the most important profile parameters for password protection are described below:

▶ *login/min_password_lng*
Defines the minimum length of the password
(minimum: 3; maximum: 8 characters)

▶ *login/password_expiration_time*
Defines the validity period of passwords in days

▶ *login/disable_multi_gui_login*
Controls whether multiple logons of the same user are allowed

As an alternative to logging on with a password, you can also implement logon using Single Sign-On (SSO). With this method, the user only logs on with a user name and password once to the security system. From here, the logon data is routed as a logon ticket or certificate to the subsequent systems where the user logs on; additional authentication is no longer required. Secure Network Communications (SNC) is required when using SSO.

8.2.5 Standard Users

Standard users

Among the user IDs, the standard users SAP* and DDIC (also called *super-users*) play a special role. SAP* and DDIC are created automatically in every client of the R/3 system (see Table 8.2). SAP* possesses all authorizations in the R/3 system. The DDIC user is equipped with full privileges for managing the R/3 Repository (see Chapter 7). For the superusers, some components of the Change and Transport System (CTS) are only to be called in display mode, in order to avoid customer developments under this ID.

Client	User	Standard password
000	SAP*	06071992
000	DDIC	19920706
001	SAP*	06071992
001	DDIC	19920706
066	EARLYWATCH	support

Table 8.2 Standard Users and Their Predefined Passwords

One of the first activities after installation is to secure these users, and prevent unauthorized access to the system, by changing the default passwords. We also recommend changing the standard password "SUPPORT" of user EARLYWATCH in client 066. The EARLYWATCH user has display authorizations for performance-monitoring functions only, however, so it does pose a slight security risk. Contrary to the EARLYWATCH password, the passwords of users SAP* and DDIC should be stored with great caution; however, you should ensure that they're available immediately in case of an emergency.

8.3 Authorizations

Division of responsibility

Creating users is the R/3 system administrator's or user administrator's responsibility. By granting authorizations, the administrator determines which activities a user can perform within a user type and user group. The authorization administrator, a person who should be separate from the system administrator, should grant the authorizations. We recommend that you divide these tasks between at least two people in order to reduce the security risk. If a user were authorized to create new users and grant them authorizations, that user could assign herself/himself all authorizations for the R/3 system, thereby giving her/him unlimited access to the data. Splitting these responsibilities among several people avoids this potential hazard. Authorizations can only be maintained in close cooperation with or entirely by the user department. As far as the user departments are concerned, authorizations involve business activities that a user is either allowed or prohibited to perform. From an R/3 administrator's point of view, however, assigning and administering authorizations is more important. Administrators do not decide which business authorizations a user does or does not need. Rather, the user departments must decide which authorizations to grant for which functions. Therefore, the following sections concentrate on the technical aspects of the authorization concept and its handling.

Authorizations are among the most important properties that have to be maintained for a defined user. As in any software product, there are two ways to look at assigning authorizations in SAP R/3, namely: The tasks that a user is authorized to perform should be tailored to reflect the tasks that a user actually performs; however, a lack of authorizations must not prevent the user from doing his or her job. The authorization administrator is responsible for coordinating these two views as effectively and as seamlessly as possible. The authorization concept in the R/3 system is a highly complex system that consists of many single authorizations, which you can then combine to form more complex units, thereby allowing for a highly detailed level of control.

8.3.1 Overview of the Authorization Check

An authorization check occurs each time a transaction is called in the SAP system. The check is a two-step process: first, the authorization for a transaction is checked (when the transaction is called); second, when an action is triggered, the authorization for an activity in the authorization object is checked.

Role concept   Authorizations are assigned to users as roles (called *activity groups* up to Basis Release 4.6B). Authorizations are grouped together as roles and entered in the user master records. In this context, a *role* is a job description that can be assigned to different users. In addition to authorizations, the roles also contain the definition of the user menu (which are described in more detail in the context of role maintenance) and workflows.

For historical reasons and to improve technical handling, the authorizations of a role are grouped together in profiles, which are generated automatically during role maintenance. In earlier releases, these profiles had to be maintained manually. While manual maintenance is still possible, it is now only rarely necessary.

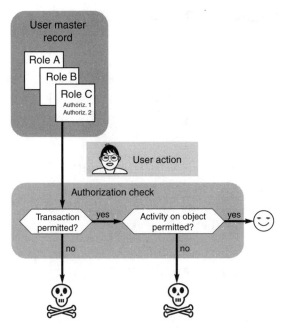

Figure 8.4 Two-Step Authorization Check

Ideally, the administrator should only have to select one of the predefined roles and assign it to a user for administration. Then, during the user comparison (see Section 8.3.8), the authorizations would be recorded in the respective user contexts as profiles.

To explain the technical connections, the following sections initially deal with the underlying technical layers of the authorization check—namely the authorization objects and profiles—before you learn about the important administrative task of assigning roles to users.

8.3.2 Authorizations and Authorization Objects

Each authorization in the R/3 system is based on an authorization object. An *authorization object* is a module that consists of a name, authorization fields, and possible values, which represent actions. The assignment of an authorization object to an activity (report, transaction, update, and so on) is predefined. Technically, an *authorization* is a set of values for a specific authorization object, which grant a user permission to perform an action in the SAP system. The SAP authorization system works exclusively with authorizations; there are no defined prohibitions of activities. Of course, this also means that all activities that are not explicitly allowed through authorizations are prohibited.

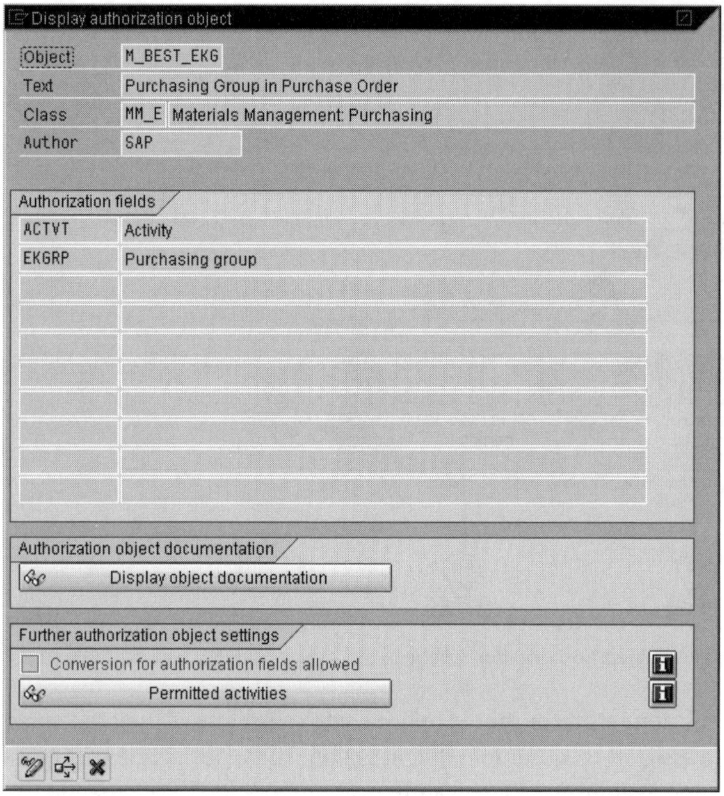

Figure 8.5 Authorization Object M_BEST_EKG

The number of authorization objects in an R/3 system is very large, due to the range of functions of the R/3 system. To better differentiate among the object classes, they are divided into subject areas, or *object classes*. For an overview of all the authorization objects that are available in the SAP system, see ▶ **Object Classes**. Choose MM_E, for example, for the Materials Management-Purchasing area. When you select this area, all the available authorization objects are displayed. Short texts indicate the descriptions of the authorization objects. Authorization object M_BEST_EKG for purchase order handling consists of authorization field ACTVT, which is present in every authorization object, and the specific field EKGRP (see Figure 8.5). For information on the field descriptions and the values they can assume, refer to the documentation for the respective object.

In our example, field EKGRP can contain the name or name range of defined purchasing groups. Click the **Permitted activities** button to determine all the possible values for the activity. The values in field **ACTVT** have the descriptions listed in Table 8.3 below.

Value	Description
1	Create or generate
2	Change
3	Display
...	Other values for other specific activities may be defined here, depending on the specific authorization object involved
*	All possible activities

Table 8.3 Possible Values in the ACTVT Field and Their Descriptions

Most of the authorizations are predefined with value "*". You only have to add company-specific values as necessary. You can use ▶ **Role Maintenance · Environment · Auth. Objects** to display all existing authorizations for an authorization object, change existing authorizations, or add new ones.

When you consider the complexity of the R/3 system, it is apparent that although you can define and assign all necessary authorizations to each individual user, the tremendous effort required does not warrant this approach. This is the reason why authorizations can be grouped together. You can use role maintenance to maintain entire sets of authorizations simultaneously. Earlier Basis releases used authorization profiles for this purpose; the R/3 system continues to use these authorization profiles as a technical tool.

8.3.3 Authorization Profiles

Authorizations can be grouped together to form *authorization profiles*. In turn, several authorization profiles can be grouped together to form a *composite profile*. SAP systems feature a comprehensive set of predefined authorization profiles, which meet most standard requirements.

These profiles are generated automatically later. during role maintenance, which is described below. This is both the simplest and the most recommended procedure. In exceptional cases, however, such as for customer developments, it may be necessary to change existing profiles manually or create new ones. Manual profile maintenance is possible within ▶ **User Maintenance**, using **Environment · Profiles · Maintain profiles** (in Basis Release 6.10 and later, a warning message is displayed, indicating that you should use roles to maintain authorizations).

Profiles can exist in different states in the R/3 system:

▶ Active or inactive
▶ Maintained (in the sense of adjusted to actual conditions) or left as the standard version

In a standard (unmodified) system, none of the profiles have been maintained yet. If you create new profiles, you must activate them (that is, have them declared in the system) before they are available system-wide.

While you can technically change existing profiles, you should not do so under any circumstances, as your changes can then be overwritten in role maintenance and during upgrades. If you must maintain profiles directly, use copies of existing profiles in the customer namespace.

Composite profiles

You can also create new profiles as a grouping of customer-defined or predefined authorizations and authorization profiles. This type of profile is called a *composite profile*. You assign the defined profiles to users manually in the **Profiles** tab when you create a user. Figure 8.6 shows the profiles assigned to user SAP*. This user has been assigned profile SAP_ALL, which includes all possible activities in an R/3 system.

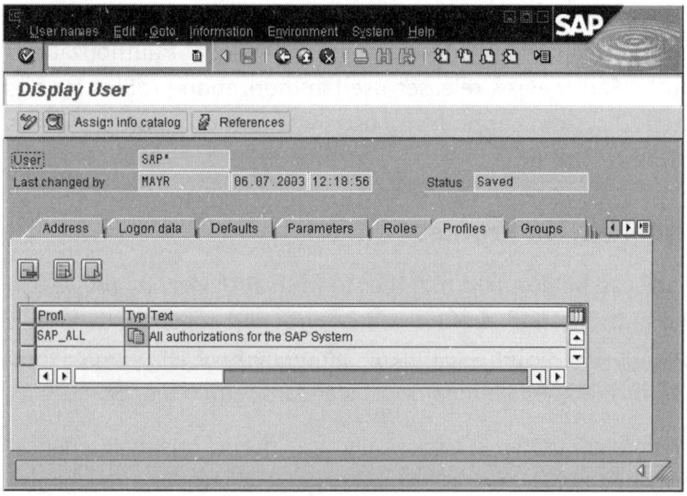

Figure 8.6 Authorization Profile of User SAP*

Accordingly, Figure 8.7 illustrates the hierarchical arrangement of authorizations.

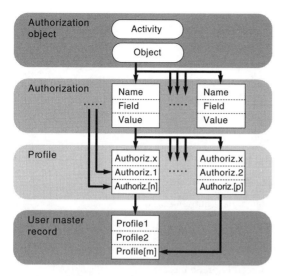

Figure 8.7 Hierarchical Arrangement of Authorizations and Profiles

The authorization objects (which are logically divided into object classes) consist of a standard field *Activity* and additional authorization fields. An authorization is defined based on values for the fields of an authorization object, which represent permission for an action. By defining different values, you can create different authorizations for an authorization object.

Authorization fields

To simplify administration, authorizations are grouped together as profiles or generated automatically during role maintenance. These profiles are recorded in the user's master record—either automatically, if roles are used, or manually.

8.3.4　Important Profiles for System Administration

The authorizations for system administration should also be divided to reflect areas of responsibility, and distributed using roles (see Section 8.3.8). The SAP system has several profiles that are especially important for administration, however, and which occasionally have to be assigned explicitly. These profiles are listed and described in Table 8.4.

Profile name	Description
SAP_ALL	All authorizations in the SAP system
SAP_NEW	Authorization profile for all new authorization objects for existing functions added in the course of an R/3 Release upgrade

Table 8.4 Important Authorization Profiles from the Administration Area

Profile name	Description
S_A.ADMIN	Operator without configuration authorizations in the R/3 system
S_A.CUSTOMIZ	Customizing (for all system configuration activities)
S_A.DEVELOP	Developer with all authorizations for working with the ABAP Workbench
S_A.DOKU	Documentation developer
S_A.SHOW	Basis: Display authorizations only
S_A.SYSTEM	System administrator (superuser)
S_A.USER	Person in charge (Basis authorization)
S_ABAP_ALL	All authorizations in the ABAP area
S_ADDR_ALL	All authorizations for central address management
S_ADMI_SAP	Administration authorization (except spool configuration)
S_ADMI_SPO_A	Spool: All administration authorizations
S_ADMI_SPO_D	Spool: Device administration
S_ADMI_SPO_E	Spool: Extended administration
S_ADMI_SPO_J	Spool: Cross-client job administration
S_ADMI_SPO_T	Spool: Device type administration
S_LANG_ALL	All authorizations for language administration
S_SPOOL_ALL	Spool: All authorizations for administering spool requests, including reading the received output requests
S_SPOOL_LOC	Spool: All authorizations except general read authorization
S_SPO_ATTR_A	Spool: Change all attributes
S_SPO_AUTH_A	Spool: Change authorization of all spool requests
S_SPO_BASE_A	Spool: Visibility and one-time printing
S_SPO_DELE_A	Spool: Authorization to delete spool requests
S_SPO_DEV_A	Spool: Management of all output devices
S_SPO_DISP_A	Spool: Display content of all spool requests
S_SPO_FEP	Spool: Front-end printing
S_SPO_PAG_AL	Spool: Unlimited number of pages on all devices
S_SPO_PRNT_A	Spool: One-time printing
S_SPO_REDI_A	Spool: Redirect all requests
S_SPO_REPR_A	Spool: Print all requests multiple times

Table 8.4 Important Authorization Profiles from the Administration Area (cont.)

8.3.5 Role Maintenance

A *role* (up to Basis Release 4.6B: *activity group*) is the description of a work environment, which can be assigned to a user. The definition of roles makes user administration much easier. If you must change authorizations, you only need to modify the roles. After the modified roles are generated, you can run the user comparison to make the changes effective automatically for all assigned users. A role contains the following information:

Role

▶ Name of the role

▶ Descriptive text for the role

▶ Role-specific menu

▶ Workflow activities of the role

▶ Authorization profiles

▶ Users to which the role is assigned

▶ Personalization data

▶ MiniApps (in Basis Release 6.10 and later)

When a user logs on to the system, he or she is assigned all menu items and the total set of authorizations resulting from the assigned profiles.

To activate role maintenance with the Profile Generator, you must first enable the deactivation of authorization checks. To do so, set the following parameter in the instance profile:

Preparation for role maintenance

```
auth/no_check_in_some_cases = Y
```

This is the default setting in newer Basis releases, which means that the authorization profile generator is active. This parameter enables you to suppress the authorization check for individual transactions (this function is required for role maintenance).

The next step in preparing to use the Profile Generator is to copy the check indicators for the authorization objects of a transaction and the authorization field values for the Profile Generator provided by SAP (SAP values) to the customer tables. To copy the check indicators, use the utilities from the ▶ **SAP values** (see Figure 8.8).

SAP values

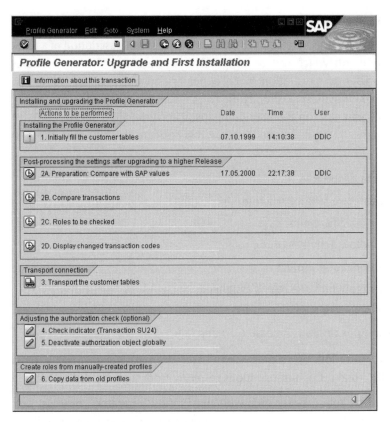

Figure 8.8 Integrating the SAP Values

After an initial installation, all the authorizations defined by SAP—including all the proposed values—are copied to customer tables, where they can be changed using the Profile Generator.

You merely have to synchronize these values after an upgrade. Objects in the customer namespace are not changed.

You can then manually change authorization objects or composite profiles for individual transactions. To do this, you maintain the ▶Check Indicators in Customizing (see Figure 8.9).

This function enables you to manually change the assignment of a transaction authorization. For example, you could change the full authorization for maintaining all purchasing groups into an authorization for maintaining specific purchasing groups that start with "A."

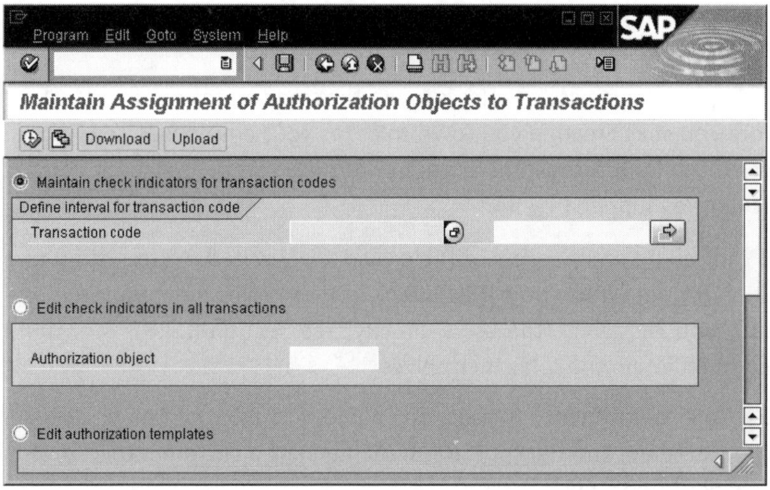

Figure 8.9 Maintaining the Assignment of Authorization Objects to Transactions

To make these changes transportable, you must assign them to a customer development class (in Basis Release 6.10 and later: *package*). Therefore, you must first define at least one customer development class.

Figure 8.10, for example, shows the check indicators for all the authorization objects used by Transaction AL09 (**Download Monitoring Data**). The check indicator can have one of the following status values:

▶ U — Check indicator unspecified, similar to check for N

▶ N — Authorization object is not checked under transaction

▶ C — Authorization object is checked under transaction

▶ CM — Authorization object is checked under transaction and specified field values are proposed in the Profile Generator

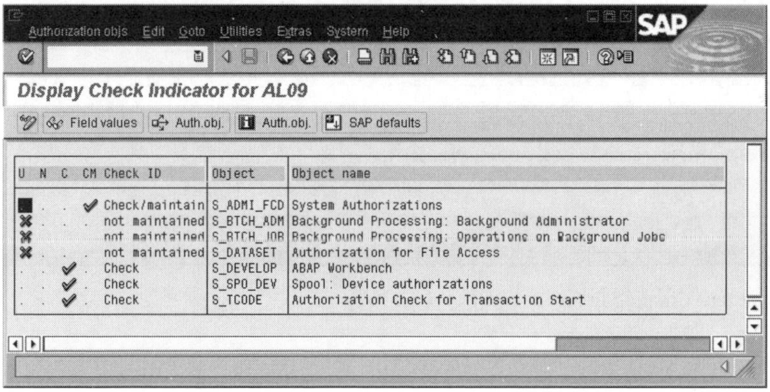

Figure 8.10 Authorization Objects and Check Indicators for Transaction AL09

In most cases, however, the proposals provided by SAP will meet your requirements, and no changes will be necessary.

Standard roles The simplest way to assign roles is to use the *standard roles* defined by SAP. Before you start creating your own roles for your employees, you should check if the job descriptions at your enterprise can be matched with the default roles supplied by SAP.

You can call up an overview of the provided roles in the info system (see Section 8.6) or with report **RSUSR070**. If these roles meet your requirements, you can assign the users directly (see Section 8.3.8); they don't need to maintain the roles themselves.

Role maintenance The ▶**Role Maintenance** transaction enables you to copy, create, change, assign, compare, and transport roles. Maintaining a customer role consists primarily of two steps:

1. Assigning the user menu

2. Adjusting the authorizations and authorization fields created by role maintenance, based on the user menu created in the first step

A relatively simple example is used to illustrate this procedure: You want to create and edit a role for the R/3 system administrators.

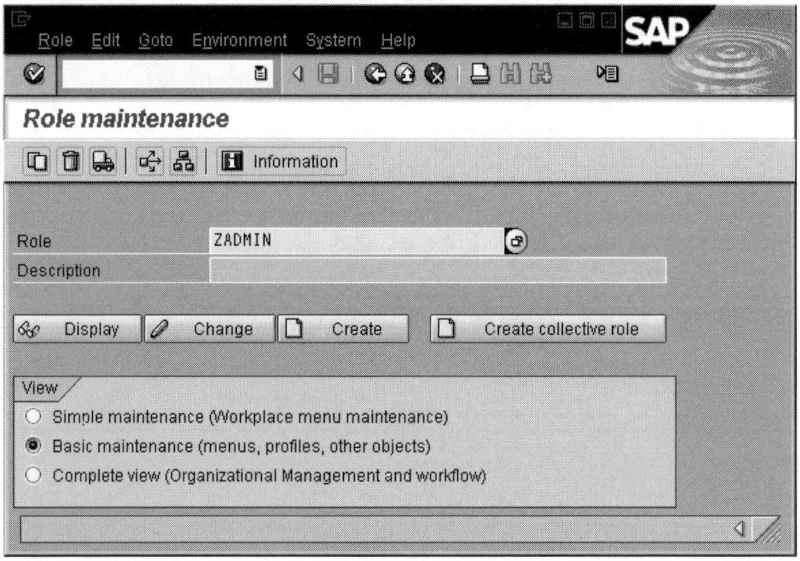

Figure 8.11 Creating Roles

In the first step, you have to create the role, or copy it from an existing role.

1. Select ▶**Role maintenance** to create roles and maintain existing ones. Figure 8.11 shows the initial screen. In this example, you will create a role called *zadmin*.

2. Enter the requested name of the role, such as *zadmin*. Role names that begin with "SAP_*" are reserved for standard roles.

3. Select the **Basic maintenance** view.

Basic mainte-nance and complete view

   Three modes are available for role processing. In *simple maintenance*, only the user menu is maintained (for the workplace, for example). *Basic maintenance* involves menus, profiles, and personalization objects. The defined role is assigned actual R/3 users later. The *complete view*, however, is much more complex and is directly linked to HR Organizational Management. Instead of assigning existing R/3 users by name, you can assign positions, jobs, or organizational units, which allow for far greater flexibility. This approach only makes sense if you use HR Organizational Management within R/3. Accordingly, the following example is limited to basic maintenance.

4. Select **Create**.

5. Each tab in role maintenance (see Figure 8.12) has a color that indicates the status of the respective part of role maintenance:

   ▶ Not maintained yet (red)

   ▶ Obsolete (yellow)

   ▶ Maintained and current (green)

   In the **Description** field, make a brief note of the purpose of the role, indicate the components it was copied from (if any), and document the change history during changes.

6. You can now create the user menu in the **Menu** tab. Use menus from the SAP menu, from other roles, from area menus, or as an import from a file. You can also add individual transactions, queries, and other objects, such as Web addresses. Select the relevant activities for the role from these options.

7. For this fictitious example, select the **Tools CCMS** section from the SAP menu and add transaction SM21 (online analysis of the system log) and the Web address of the SAP Service Marketplace (see Figure 8.13).

8. Save your selection.

9. Return to basic maintenance. When you finish your maintenance activities, the status of the **Menu** item changes to green.

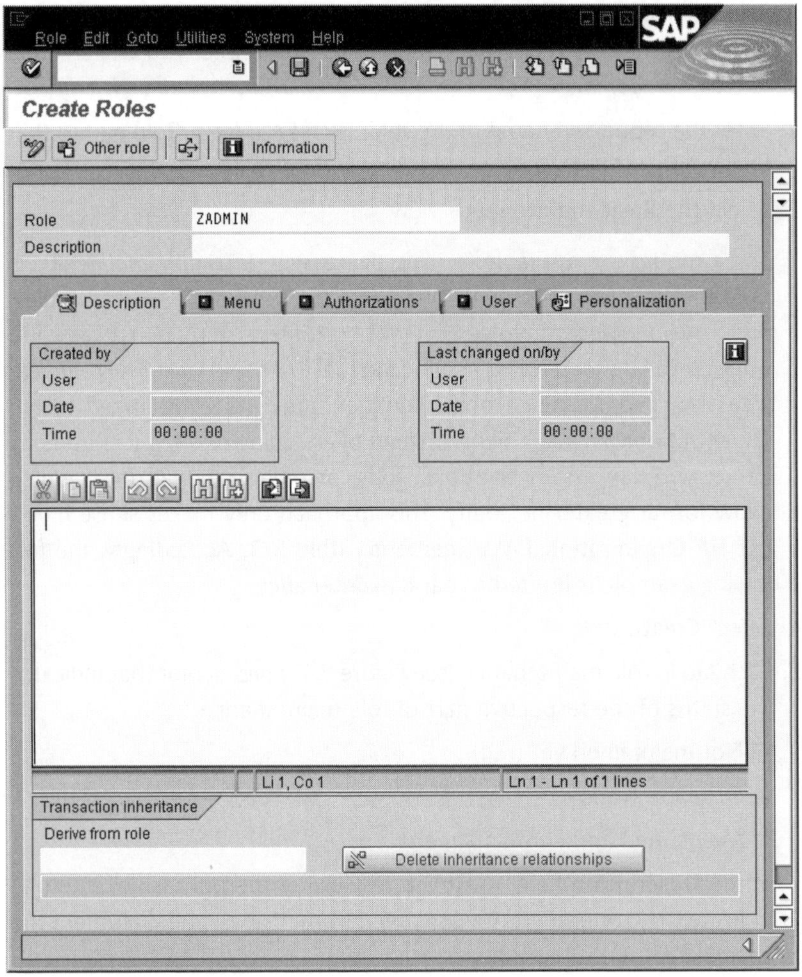

Figure 8.12 Basic Maintenance of Roles

User menu

The selection of activities that are permitted for a role is automatically saved as a menu tree that contains these exact activities. All users who are assigned to this activity group later can use this menu as a *user menu*. You can modify the user menu further in role maintenance by adding several folders for structuring. You can also move the menu nodes around by using the Drag&Drop technique, and adjusting the menu hierarchy to meet your specific needs.

10. The next steps consist of maintaining the authorizations and generating the authorization profile for the selected activities. Select the **Authorizations** tab page within role maintenance (see Figure 8.14) and enter a name for the new authorization profile. All names with "_" as

the second character are reserved for SAP standard profiles. You can have the system propose a value; however, it consists of a non-mne-monic string of digits and characters (see Figure 8.17). To simplify sub-sequent analysis, we recommend that you use your own name or a descriptive short text.

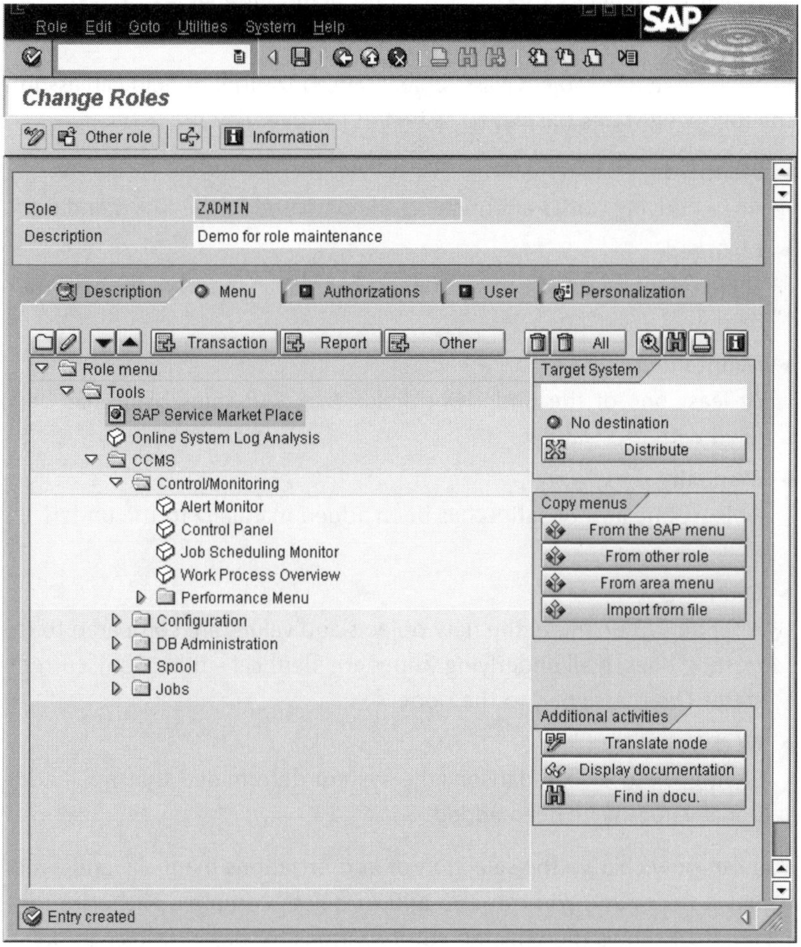

Figure 8.13 Selecting Activities

The necessary authorizations are determined automatically based on your selected activities, and displayed in hierarchical form. A traffic light indi-cates the maintenance status of the node:

▶ **Green**
The underlying authorizations have all been provided with values, but you should still check them.

▶ **Yellow**

At least one of the underlying fields could not be automatically assigned values completely (for user name or device name, for example). You have to set them manually.

▶ **Red**

At least one field exists for which no organizational levels have been maintained.

In addition, a role, object class, object, authorization, or field can assume the following states (displayed as text in the overview):

▶ **Standard**

All underlying nodes are unchanged compared to the SAP standard.

▶ **Changed**

The content of at least one node has been changed from the SAP standard.

▶ **Maintained**

At least one of the underlying fields that SAP ships blank has been filled with user values.

▶ **Manually**

At least one authorization has been added manually to the underlying nodes.

▶ **Old**

After an R/3 upgrade, the new objects and values are compared to the existing ones. If all underlying values are identical—that is, still current-status *Old* is assigned to the node.

▶ **New**

During the user comparison, the system determined that new, additional values have been added

You can now change the selection of authorizations manually and assign values if necessary. You can also add or delete complete authorizations. Figure 8.14 shows the selected authorizations for our example. To do so, proceed as follows:

1. Select the required node and open it.

2. The following activities are possible:

   ▷ Deactivate unnecessary subtrees or individual authorizations with the icon to the right of the status (the **Legend** icon displays an overview of the various symbols used in this transaction).

   ▷ Create new full authorizations or individual authorizations with **Edit · Insert · Authorizations**.

▶ Select the corresponding symbol in the line of an authorization object to add or change values for that object. In Figure 8.14, it makes sense to enter values for the device authorizations for the R/3 spool system. These values describe the device names for which the authorizations will be valid. The entry *D**, for example, would allow use of all devices whose name starts with "D."

▶ Manually remove or add individual transaction codes, which contain actions.

3. Once you have made all the necessary changes, all the traffic lights must be green. Save the settings.

4. Select the **Generate Authorizations** icon.

5. A profile with your assigned authorizations is created and saved under the name defined in the previous screen.

6. Return to basic maintenance. The status of authorization maintenance changes to green when processing is complete.

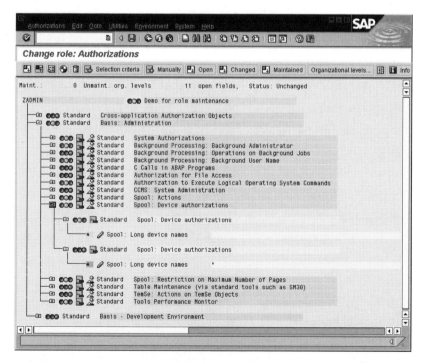

Figure 8.14 Maintaining Authorizations

To simplify administration further, you can group roles together to form composite roles. The creation and maintenance of composite roles is largely identical to the maintenance of individual roles.

Composite roles

In the initial screen for ▶Role maintenance, enter a name and click the Create collective role button to create a composite role. Use the Roles tab page to define the roles that you want to group together. You can import and process the menus of the individual roles in the Menu tab page. You cannot edit the authorizations at this point.

8.3.6 Important Roles for System Administration

In large R/3 projects, system administration responsibilities are usually separated into several areas and assigned to different individuals or groups. User SAP* has profile SAP_ALL, which includes all activities— including application-specific ones. Accordingly, this user is unsuitable for general operations and must be protected against unauthorized access. Instead, you should define the special users with roles coordinated for the specific purpose. The most important administrator roles are listed in Table 8.5 below.

Profile name	Description
SAP_BC_BASIS_ADMIN	Basis administration and system monitoring
SAP_BC_SPOOL_ADMIN	Spool administrator
SAP_BC_BATCH_ADMIN	Administrator for background processing
SAP_BC_CUS_ADMIN	Project administrator for Customizing
SAP_BC_DWB_ABAPDEVELOPER	ABAP developer
SAP_BC_SRV_GBT_ADMIN	Administrator for communication, folders, appointment planning
SAP_BC_SRV_COM_ADMIN	Administrator for external communication
SAP_BC_SRV_EDI_ADMIN	IDoc administrator
SAP_BC_MID_ALE_ADMIN	ALE administrator
SAP_BC_TRANSPORT_ADMIN	Administrator for Change and Transport System (CTS)
SAP_BC_BMT_WFM_ADMIN	System administrator for workflow
SAP_BC_BDC_ADMIN	Business Workflow administrator
SAP_BC_USER_ADMIN	User administrator
SAP_BC_AUTH_DATA_ADMIN	Authorization data administrator

Table 8.5 Important Roles from the Administration Area

8.3.7 User Assignment and User Comparison

Now that you know how to administer users and roles from the previous sessions, you will learn how to assign roles to users. There are basically two ways in which to assign roles:

1. Assign roles to users in ▶ User Maintenance
2. Assign users to roles in ▶ Role Maintenance

To assign roles in ▶ User Maintenance (see Section 8.2.1), select the Roles tab page. You can then enter the required roles for this user directly. In the process, the profiles generated for a given role are automatically added to the Profiles tab page.

Generated profiles must not be changed manually, as manual assignment or changes would invalidate the control and comparison functions in the Profile Generator. In addition, any changes to generated profiles are lost the next time the role is changed.

You can assign users to a role in the User tab in role maintenance.

1. Select the User tab page.
2. Enter the new user under User ID (see Figure 8.15 for our example user MUSTERMANN). The user must already be defined.

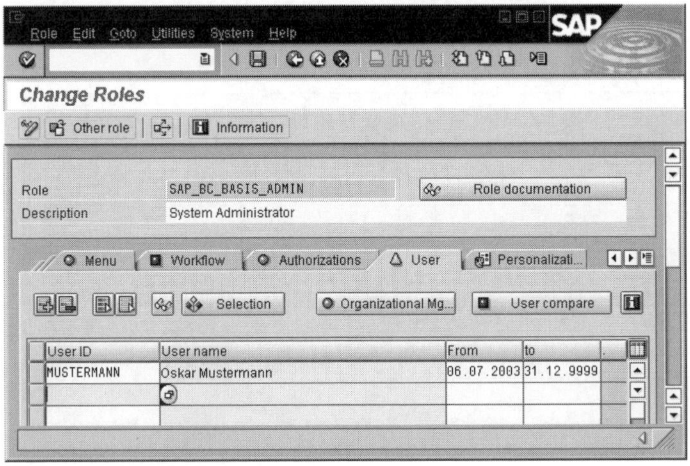

Figure 8.15 User Assignment

This view for role maintenance allows you to define time restrictions for the validity of roles and their assignments to users. This enables you, for example, to schedule authorizations that will be required in the future or should only be valid up to a certain date.

Validity periods

3. Then, click the **User compare** button to assign the generated authorization profiles for the role to the selected users (see Figure 8.16). This process is called the *comparison of the user master*.

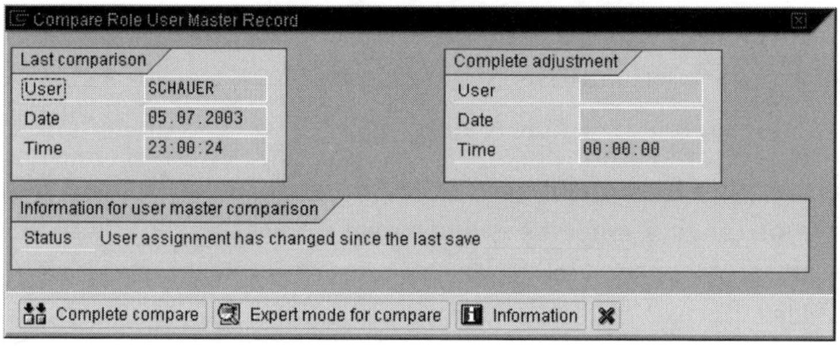

Figure 8.16 User Master Comparison

4. Exit role maintenance.

This concludes the example. You can use the user maintenance transaction to confirm that your changes have been saved. All assigned users have received the selected role and the generated profile. Figure 8.17 illustrates this for user MUSTERMANN.

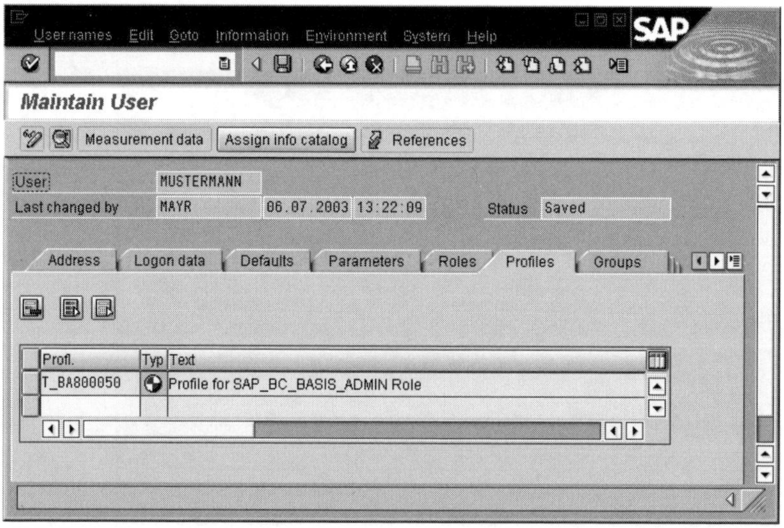

Figure 8.17 After Comparison of the User Master

In the preceding example, you started a user comparison during user assignment. The generated profile for a role is not recorded in the user master record until you run a comparison. As a result, changes in the user assignment, changes to roles, and the generation of profiles all require a user comparison. There are various ways of performing this user comparison:

- User comparison during user assignment with the **User compare** button (see example above). In this case, the status display of the button indicates whether another comparison is required. This method is well suited for role maintenance in the development system.

- Choose the **Automatic User Master Adjustment when Saving Role** option in ▶ **Role Maintenance** in the SAP menu under **Utilities · Settings**. The comparison is then performed automatically each time a role is saved.

- User comparison with report **PFCG_TIME_DEPENDENCY**. You should schedule this job periodically (daily if possible) as a background job. This is the only way to ensure that users are kept up-to-date-especially in consolidation and production systems, where profile changes are imported as transports. This report performs a full user comparison, deleting all assignments that have become invalid.

8.3.8 Transporting Roles

Roles are maintained in the development system and can be transported from there to the consolidation and production systems. All automatically generated profiles are transported in the process. Therefore, you should not enter a role in a transport request until you have maintained it completely and generated the profiles. The profiles do not have to be generated in the target system. When you create the transport request, you can decide whether you want to transport the user assignment as well. If you choose this option, any existing user assignment is overwritten in the target system.

If you use Central User Administration (CUA, see Section 8.7.4), you can only assign users in the central system.

Users do not receive the new authorizations in the target system until a user comparison has been confirmed (see Section 8.3.7) and they log on again.

8.3.9 Upgrade Procedures

Authorization management has undergone several changes over the past few releases. Therefore, after an upgrade, you must perform some post-processing for authorization management and transfer the existing profiles or roles to the new authorization management environment. This activity differs depending on whether the Profile Generator was already used in the start release.

Conversion to the Profile Generator Upgrading from an R/3 system release that does not use the Profile Generator to a release that does is extremely difficult. In this case, SAP recommends that you completely reimplement your authorization management.

Alternatively, you can use the ▶ **SAP values** (see Figure 8.8) under step 6 to convert the existing profiles to roles. The advantage of this approach is that you can continue using the existing, proven profiles. Please note, however, that you cannot use the SAP default values here; also note that menus can only be created when the profile contains the corresponding authorizations for the transaction code.

If your start release uses the Profile Generator, you can use the ▶ **SAP values** (with steps 2A through 2C) to compare the existing authorization data with the new data.

The postprocessing, that is, synchronizing the existing and supplementary data and assigning new roles and profiles, can be very time-consuming. Accordingly, every upgrade is shipped with profile SAP_NEW, which contains all the authorizations for the new authorization checks in existing transactions. You can assign this profile to all users temporarily, until the synchronization of authorization data is complete.

8.3.10 Troubleshooting and Traces

You will frequently encounter situations whereby users don't have all the authorizations they need, especially during the initial phases of an R/3 implementation. In this case, after a transaction is canceled due to a lack of authorization, the affected user or the system administrator can select ▶ **Authorization Data** to display a list of the missing authorizations. The transaction shows which authorization is required to perform the selected action.

You can use the ▶ **SAP System Trace** (see Chapter 15), among other things, to record all authorization checks. In this case, all checked authorization projects are recorded, including the checked values. You can use the Edit filters menu to restrict the trace to individual users, processes, or transactions. Administrators can then further restrict the selection, for instance, by user, during the trace analysis. The SAP System Trace is handy for determining all the necessary authorizations for an action, based on an executed authorization check.

8.4 Personal Settings

The data in the user master record described so far is largely maintained by a user administrator. Users from the application department are usually not authorized to maintain this data themselves, aside from the company address. In addition to this user master data, each user can define his or her own personal settings to simplify working with the R/3 system. Such settings include the selection of a custom start menu, a logon language, a standard printer, and the date format or default settings for certain input fields. Each user can enter his or her own requested data with ▶**Own Data**. This displays the **Maintenance** screen, where you can define values for the areas *Address*, *Defaults,* and *Parameters*. These tab pages correspond to the respective tab pages from user maintenance (see Section 8.2.1).

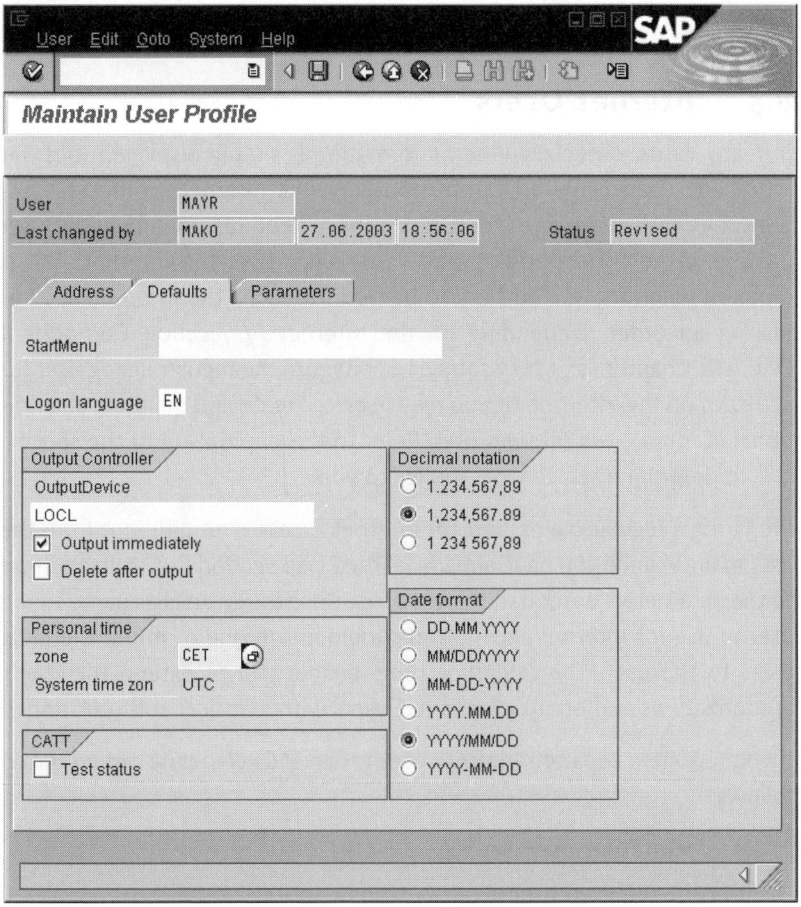

Figure 8.18 Maintaining User Defaults

Figure 8.18 shows the maintenance screen for the user defaults. This screen is opened in a separate session, so you do not have to interrupt a workstep-in-progress in order to maintain the user defaults. The original session remains unchanged.

By maintaining parameters in the user defaults, each user can define his or her own custom default settings for the input fields. Accordingly, users don't have to enter the corresponding field value explicitly when working with the application; instead, the field is filled automatically with the defined value. You can define user defaults for the company code, cost center, and other values. To display the necessary technical information for an input field in a screen, select the field in the screen and activate the technical information button within the F1 context-sensitive help. The **Parameter ID** field contains the parameter name, as required to specify it. "BUK", for example, stands for the company code. You can then use this ID to specify a default setting in the user defaults.

8.5 Internet Users

In many cases, especially when information is simply displayed (but not modified), users can work anonymously on the Internet. In the SAP system environment, however, access usually requires an individual user name and the corresponding password—even over the Internet. This is required when transactions are to be performed via the Internet, such as placing an order. Depending on the Internet Application Component (IAC, see Chapter 1), it may suffice to configure the regular dialog user for activities on the Internet, or you may need to create and maintain an additional account—the *Internet user*. Refer to the description of the specific IAC to determine which case applies to you.

Preparing a regular dialog user for Internet access is no different from the user maintenance you have already learned (see Section 8.2.1). In addition to the parameters described there, you can also assign an alias name to the user to use for Internet access. You should assign one or more reference users to the user. The reference users enable you to extend the user's authorizations and equip all Internet users with identical authorizations.

If you require a separate Internet user for an IAC, you can configure it as follows:

1. Select ▶Internet user (see Figure 8.19).
2. Enter the required user ID.

3. Select the user type. The type often corresponds to a work area and limits the user's authorizations. Specifying "KNA1", for example, signifies that the user can only use this Internet transaction. The user type depends on the IACs that the user wants to perform.

4. Select **Initialize** to initialize the user.

5. The user account becomes active. The system generates a password automatically. You can use **Change password** to change this default password at any time.

You can lock and unlock an Internet user. No other data has to be maintained for Internet users at this time.

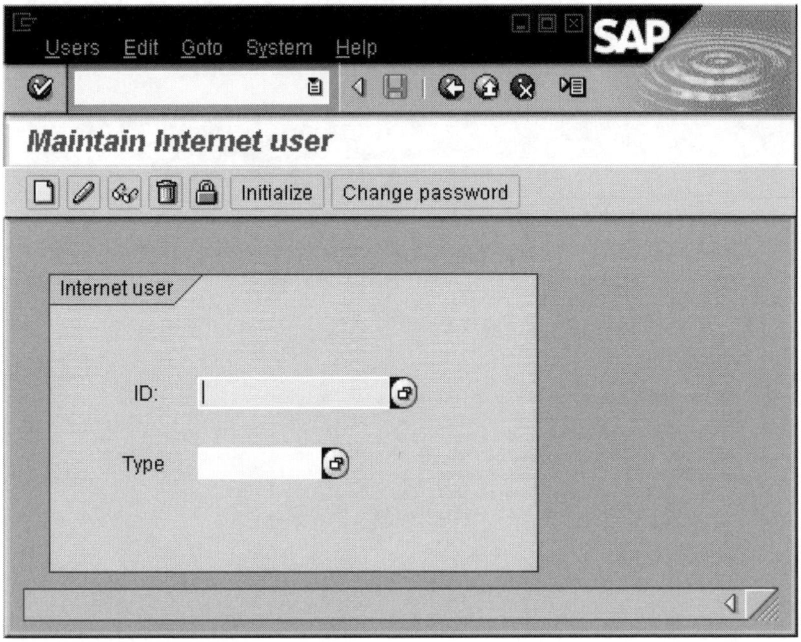

Figure 8.19 Maintaining Internet Users

8.6   Information About Users and Authorizations

The more users work in an R/3 system, the more difficult and complex it becomes to manage users and monitor security-critical users. The SAP system features additional tools to meet these needs.

8.6.1   Information System

To provide system administrators with an overview of all users and authorizations, the R/3 system offers a specific ▶ **Information system**. You can analyze and compare the users and authorizations granted in the system for a wide variety of criteria. Figure 8.20 shows the initial screen for this tool.

The *user information system* makes it possible, for example, to select all the users who have been assigned a specific role, or determine all the roles that contain a specific authorization.

Another important function in the information system is the analysis of change documents. Every time a user master record is changed, a change document is created with a time stamp and the user name of the person who made the changes. The information system allows you to analyze this information at any time to find out who created, changed, or deleted a user. Change documents cannot be deleted (they can be archived, however), which means that they are available in perpetuity.

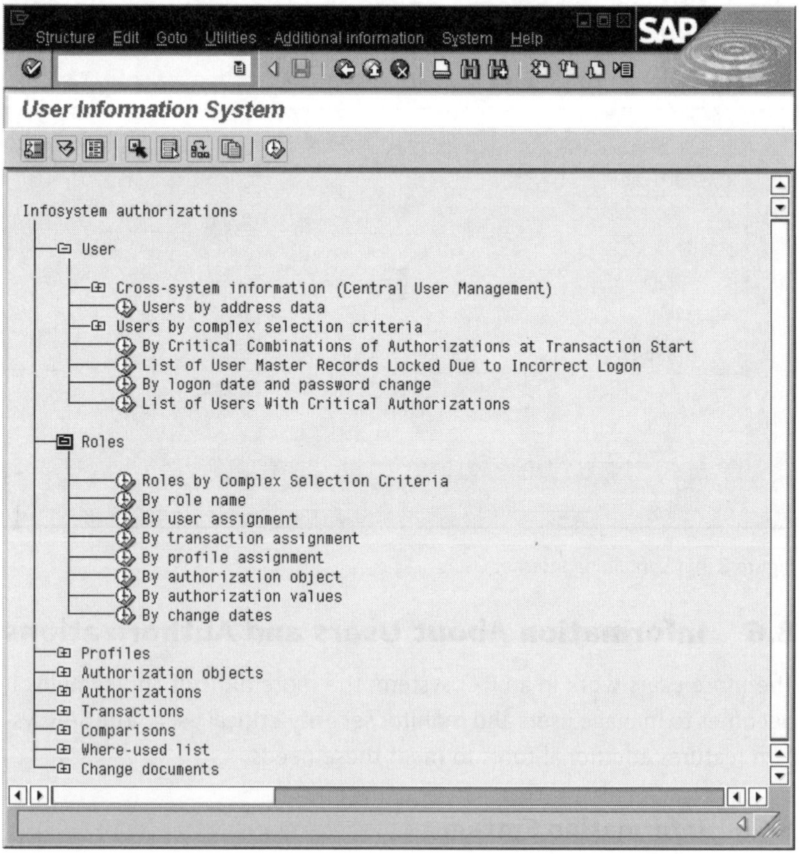

Figure 8.20 User Information System

8.6.2 Security Audit Log

The *Security Audit Log* enables you to log all user activities that are relevant to security in the system. Auditors often demand such logging, especially for users with critical authorizations, to ensure the auditability of the system. It is neither sensible nor technically possible to log all user actions using the Security Audit Log. Instead, the audit log is used more frequently to monitor critical users who have many authorizations, especially the emergency users and support users, as well as create transparency for specific security-critical events, such as failed logon attempts.

To do so, you can use the ▶ **Security Audit Configuration** to define which types of activities will be recorded for which users in the Security Audit Log. These users and activities are then monitored constantly. You can use the ▶ **Security Audit Analysis** to analyze the audit logs according to various criteria.

You must create a profile first in the ▶ **Security Audit Configuration** (see Figure 8.21). You then use this profile name to save the settings below.

You can use filters to define which events in which audit classes (dialog logons, transaction starts, RFCs, and so forth) will be logged for which users in which clients. You can use placeholders (*) for user and client, but you cannot use wildcard entries like "MILLER*". As a result, the number of users who can be logged with a profile is restricted by the number of filters. You must select each filter via **Filter active** explicitly. **Filters**

After you have configured the filter criteria, save the profile. The additional icons for administering the profile reappear in the application toolbar. To start logging in accordance with the configured filters, you now have to activate the selected profile via menu or icon. The activated profile is then used after the next system startup. **Profile**

As an alternative to static configuration, you can also change these settings dynamically at runtime with the **Dyn. Configuration** tab. The parameterization using filters for dynamic configuration is identical to that of the static configuration. **Dynamic configuration**

The logged data is saved in files at operating-system level. The ▶ **Security Audit Analysis** lets you select via the known filter parameters, as well as by date/time and the user terminal. The selected data is formatted in accordance with the system log settings (see Chapter 15).

Profile parameters To use the Security Audit Log, you must activate it via the profile parameters and specify how many filters can be used. The most important profile parameters are:

▶ *rsau/enable*
Activate Security Audit Log

▶ *rsau/max_diskspace/local*
Maximum amount of space that can be assigned to audit files

▶ *rsau/selection_slots*
Number of filters allowed for the Security Audit Log (maximum: 5)

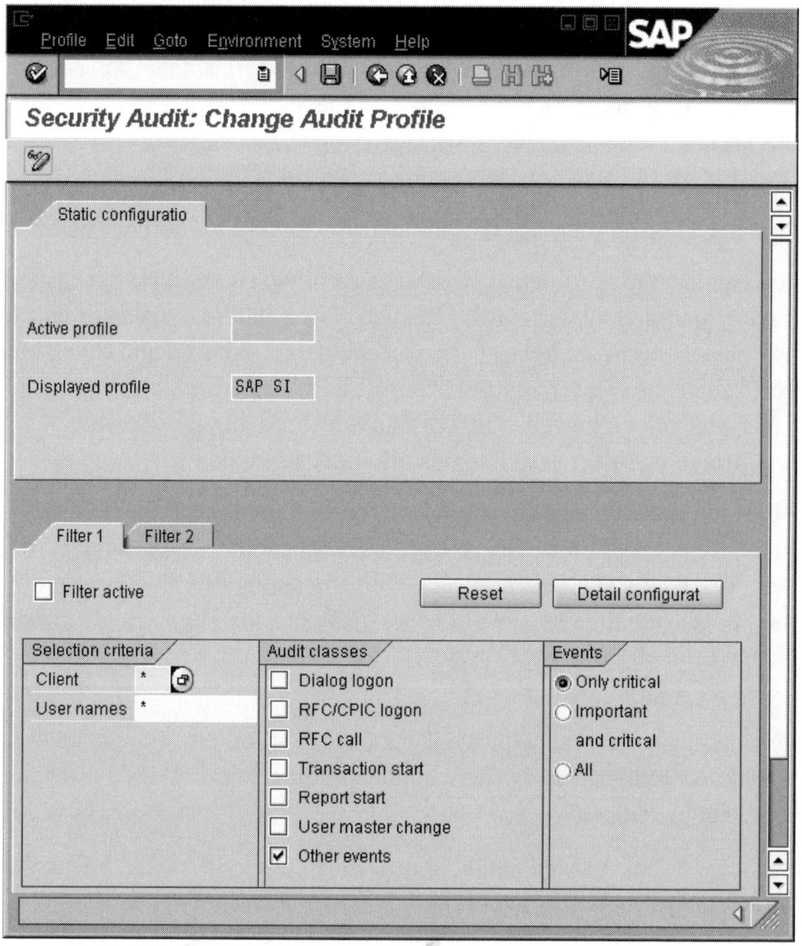

Figure 8.21 Configuration of the Security Audit Log

Before you activate the Security Audit Log, ensure that you adhere to your local laws governing data protection and employee co-determination as an organizational prerequisite.

The analysis files can grow rapidly, depending on the configured filter criteria. Therefore, you should back up these files regularly in order to delete them at operating-system level.

8.7 Central User Administration

In large system landscapes with many users, the local user administration described above can be very time-intensive. Maintaining identical users in different systems and synchronizing changes between the systems—which means administrators have to log on to each local system—can make user maintenance both tedious and error-prone. Fortunately, *Central User Administration* (CUA) provides relief. In Basis Release 4.6 and later, you can perform all user maintenance activities in one defined client of one system, and then distribute the data to the other clients of the same or other systems. This specific client is the sender (the central system), while all other clients (the child systems) are recipients of the data. *Application Link Enabling* (ALE, see Chapter 13) is the technology used to exchange data. The clients that exchange the data are configured and managed as logical systems.

Once you configure CUA, users can only be created or deleted in the central system. You can define for each user attribute (in CUA administration) whether this attribute is maintained only centrally, only locally, or both centrally and locally. Therefore, the required roles and authorizations must exist in active form in all child systems. As a result, each user only has to be administered once, centrally, which gives administrators a much clearer overview of all users and authorizations.

Benefits

These benefits of CUA are offset somewhat by the increased effort required to configure the ALE scenario and synchronize existing users, as well as the additional skills required for administration. The following criteria can help you to determine whether it makes sense to configure CUA in your enterprise landscape:

▶ Number of users per system
▶ Number of logical systems
▶ Frequency of changes to users and authorizations
▶ Duration of a development (and thus the time in which developers are required as users in the systems)

Configuring CUA   Configuring CUA involves the following steps:

▶ Configuring an administrative user in the central system

▶ Configuring the ALE scenario:

  ▶ Naming the logical systems

  ▶ Assigning the logical systems to clients

  ▶ Creating the communication users (which are used in the RFC interfaces) in all involved clients

  ▶ Creating the RFC interfaces

  ▶ Creating the new model views of the ALE distribution model

  ▶ Maintaining and generating the Partner profiles between all clients participating in CUA

  ▶ Distributing the model views

▶ Activating CUA

▶ Configuring the distribution parameters for fields

▶ Distributing the company address

▶ Synchronizing users

These steps are described in more detail in the following sections.

8.7.1   Configuring the ALE Scenario

The features and handling of an ALE integrated system are described in Chapter 13. Therefore, only the settings specific to Central User Administration (CUA) are described here.

You first have to configure *logical systems* (see Chapter 13) for all the clients involved with CUA. You then use ▶ **Client Administration** to assign the logical systems to the clients. One RFC connection has to be set up to forward the data from the central system to each child system and in the opposite direction—you have to have separate RFC connections for each direction. No RFC connections are required between the child systems. Note that the client where CUA is located also has to be integrated as a child system in the central administration. You define a new model view for the ALE distribution model to define which data will be exchanged between the logical systems. For CUA, these are the predefined business objects *USER* and *UserCompany* with distribution method *Clone*.

You then generate the partner agreement and distribute to all logical systems, which concludes the configuration of the ALE for Central User Administration.

8.7.2 Activating and Configuring Central User Administration

To activate CUA, you merely have to assign an ALE model view to the CUA. To do this, enter the name of your model view in ▶Central Role Administration and press **Create**. In the next screen, enter all the child systems for your central administration and save them. You can now distribute the model with menu path **Distribution Model · Distribute Distribution Model** to distribute the model to the child systems. Central User Administration is now active.

The primary aspect in configuring CUA involves defining which user attributes are maintained in which system, that is, in the central system or the child system. You can use the ▶Distribution Parameters in Customizing to maintain how each user attribute will be maintained (see Figure 8.22).

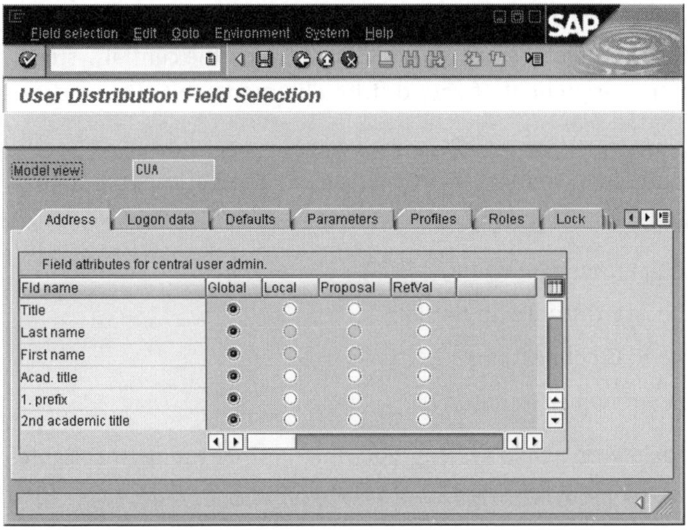

Figure 8.22 Defining Distribution Parameters

Administrators can use the following options:

Option	Maintenance and synchronization
global	The field can only be maintained in the central system. The changes are then distributed automatically.
local	Data is only maintained in the child systems and is not distributed to any other systems.

Table 8.6 Options for Field Selection

Option	Maintenance and synchronization
proposal	A field with this option is maintained and distributed with a default value when a user is created. Further maintenance takes place in the child systems. Subsequent changes are not distributed.
retval	The value can be maintained both centrally and locally. When data is changed locally, it can be sent back to the central system and then distributed to all the child systems.
everywhere	The value can be maintained both centrally and locally. Central changes are distributed to the child systems, but changes in the child systems are not returned. This option is only available for a small number of fields.

Table 8.6 Options for Field Selection (cont.)

8.7.3 Deleting Central User Administration

To delete individual child systems from Central User Administration (CUA), run report RSDELCUA on the relevant child systems. To dissolve the entire CUA completely, run report RSDELCUA on the central systems. This cancels the assignment of your distribution model to CUA and deactivates CUA.

When you completely remove CUA, you should also perform the following cleanup tasks:

▶ Delete the partner agreement.

▶ Delete the ALE distribution model.

▶ Delete the RFC connections.

▶ Lock the communication user.

If you only delete one child system, you must restrict the partner agreement, ALE model, and RFC interfaces accordingly.

8.7.4 Administering Users in Central User Administration

When you initially set up CUA and when you add a new child system, you first have to integrate all the existing users in the child system to the central system. To do so, use the **Edit Transfer Users** functionality of the CUA structure display in the central system. After you select the child systems, all the users in each child system are displayed, divided by:

▶ **New users**
These users only exist in the child system, but not in CUA yet. During the transfer, all parameters are integrated into CUA.

- **Identical users**

  A user with the same user name and real name exists in both CUA and the child system. The user can either be copied from the child system to CUA and be redistributed from there, or it can be deleted in the child system and the definition redistributed from CUA.

- **Different users**

  The same user name is contained in both CUA and the child system, but with different real names (the *real name* is the combination of first name and last name). You have to decide which user will be maintained further. You may have to create a new user in CUA.

- **Central users**

  These users are *already* registered identically in CUA and are managed centrally.

You can then integrate the users into CUA individually or all at once. In the process, the data for all users except *New users* is always taken and distributed from the central system. If two different users are actually used for the *Different users*, you have to define them again in the central system and delete the identically named users in the child system.

You continue to use ▶ **User maintenance** (see Section 8.2.1) to maintain users, even when CUA is active. Users can no longer be created in the child systems, however, and only those fields that can be maintained locally according to the definition of the distribution parameters (see Section 8.7.2) are ready for input. A new tab page, **Systems**, appears in the ▶ **User maintenance** transaction in the central system. Use this tab page to enter the systems to which you want to distribute the users. The user data can only be defined once, and is then identical in all child systems. You can assign different roles and profiles in each child system.

8.8 Outlook: Directory Services

As more and more SAP systems are integrated in heterogeneous system landscapes, the demands on user administration increase. Much of the user data is required in both SAP and non-SAP systems, and is therefore stored redundantly. This redundant data maintenance is time-intensive and not always synchronous.

Directory services make it possible for different applications within an IT landscape to access shared data, which is managed centrally. Think of the directory service as an "IT address book." If a directory service supports the *Standard Lightweight Directory Access Protocol* (LDAP), you can use the LDAP Connector to exchange data with the directory service in Basis

LDAP

Release 6.10 and later. Consequently, central user data only has to be stored once, in the central directory service, and can be synchronized directly with an SAP system or a Central User Administration with the LDAP synchronization functions. From here, the data can then be distributed to the child systems in CUA (including those with an earlier Basis release).

8.9 Tips

▶ Maintaining communication data
When you maintain communication data in ▶ **User maintenance**— especially the fax number—you must ensure that this data corresponds to the SAP conventions. You have to enter the values without any leading spaces or special characters, with a separator between company number and extension and without a country code (this can be selected in **Other Communication**), otherwise SAPconnect cannot evaluate the data (see Chapter 13).

▶ **High memory requirements due to large user menus**
User menus are saved in buffered tables. If many users have large user menus, this can result in extremely high memory requirements. In such cases, you will either have to compress the user menus, or some users will have to forgo using the user menus completely.

▶ Client for Central User Administration
The authorization concept for CUA is simplified when the CUA is set up in a separate client or even a separate system (such as a separate monitoring system).

8.10 Transactions and Menu Paths

ALE Customizing: SAP Implementation Guide (SPRO) • R/3 Basis Customizing • Application Link Enabling (SALE)

Authorization data: SAP Menu • System • Utilities • Disp. Authorization Check (SU53)

Central Role Administration: ALE Customizing (SALE) • Configure Predefined ALE Business Processes • Configure Central User Administration • Select Model Views for Central Administration (SCUA)

Check indicators: SAP Implementation Guide (SPRO) • Basis • System Administration • Users and Authorizations • Maintain Authorizations and Profiles with the Profile Generator • Edit SAP Check Indicators and Field Values • Change Check Indicators (SU24)

Client administration: SAP Menu • Tools • Administration • System Administration • Administration • Client Administration • Client Maintenance (SCC4)

Company address: SAP Menu • Tools • Administration • User Maintenance • Users • Environment • Maintain Company Address (SUCOMP)

Distribution Model: ALE Customizing (SALE) • Model Business Processes • Maintain Distribution Model and Distribute Views (BD64)

Distribution Parameters: ALE Customizing (SALE) • Configure Predefined ALE Business Processes • Configure Central User Administration • Configure Distribution Parameters for Fields (SCUM)

Information system: SAP Menu • Tools • Administration • User Maintenance • Information System (SU01 • Info • Info System)

Internet users: SAP Menu • Tools • Administration • User Maintenance • Internet Users (SU05)

License Administration Workbench (LAW): Not available in the SAP standard Menu (LICENSE_ADMIN)

Mass changes: SAP Menu • Tools • Administration • User Maintenance • Users • Environment • Mass Change (SU10)

Object classes: SAP Menu • Tools • ABAP/4 Workbench • Development • Other Tools • Authorization Objects • Objects (SU21)

Own data: SAP Menu • System • User Profile • Own Data (SU3)

Partner agreements: ALE Customizing (SALE) • Model Business Processes • Maintain Distribution Model and Distribute Views (BD64) • Generate Partner Agreement (BD82)

Role maintenance: SAP Menu • Tools • Administration • User Maintenance • Roles (PFCG)

SAP Implementation Guide: SAP Menu • Tools • AcceleratedSAP • Customizing • Edit Project (SPRO)

SAP Proposals: SAP Implementation Guide (SPRO) • System Administration • Users and Authorizations • Maintain Authorizations and Profiles with the Profile Generator • Copy SAP Check Indicators and Field Values (SU25)

SAP System Trace: SAP Menu • Tools • Administration • Monitor • Traces • SAP System Trace (ST01)

Security Audit Analysis: SAP Menu • Tools • Administration • Monitor • Security Audit Log • Analysis (SM20)

Security Audit Configuration: SAP Menu • Tools • Administration • Monitor • Security Audit Log • Configuration (SM19)

System Measurement: SAP Menu • Tools • Administration • Administration • System Measurement (USMM)

User group: SAP Menu • Tools • Administration • User Maintenance • Maintain User Groups (SUGR)

User maintenance: SAP Menu • Tools • Administration • User Maintenance • Users (SU01)

User transfer: ALE Customizing (SALE) • Configure Predefined ALE Business Processes • Configure Central User Administration • Transfer Users from New Systems (SCUG)

8.11 Additional Documentation

Quicklinks

▶ SAP Service Marketplace, alias *licenseauditing*
White Paper: "Introduction to System Measurement"

▶ SAP Service Marketplace, alias *security*

▶ SAP Service Marketplace, alias *securityguide*
White Paper: "SAP Security Guidelines"

▶ SAP Service Marketplace, alias *sso*

SAP Service Marketplace Notes

The following table provides an overview of important SAP Notes related to user administration:

Contents	Note
Additional documentation regarding the authorization concept	093769
Responsibilities replaced as of Release 4.5A	156250
High memory consumption with Easy Access menu	203617

Table 8.7 SAP Notes for User Administration

Contents	Note
CUA: Tips for problem analysis	333441
CUA: Minimum authorizations for communication users	492589

Table 8.7 SAP Notes for User Administration (cont.)

8.12 Questions

1. Which statement is correct?

   A user with type "System":

   a. Can log on without a password via RFC interface

   b. Has a password, but the settings for the validity period do not apply

   c. Cannot log on in dialog

2. Which statement is correct?

   a. A user can only be assigned one role.

   b. A user can be assigned several roles.

3. Which information is transported when roles are transported?

   a. The authorization profiles for the role

   b. The definition of the users

   c. The assignment of roles to users

4. The authorizations of a role are extended. From which point can a user who has been assigned this role, and who is already logged on to the system, start using the changed authorizations?

   a. The user can start using the changed authorizations instantly.

   b. The user can use the changed authorizations after a user comparison.

   c. The user has to log on again and can then start using the changed authorizations.

   d. A user comparison has to be performed first. The user then has to log on again. The user can then start using the changed authorizations.

9 Background Processing

In addition to dialog mode processing, the R/3 system can also process jobs in the background. This is particularly relevant for long-running programs that do not require any interactive input. This chapter focuses on the management of background jobs. You will learn how to schedule background jobs by time and by event, and how to analyze the flow traces.

9.1 Concepts

Generally, all programs that don't require explicit user dialog processing can also run in the background. Background processing is most useful when the program you're running is long and resource-intensive, and should therefore run at a time when the system load is low. Online execution would tie up a dialog process for the entire run, thereby indirectly hindering other dialog users. **Background processing**

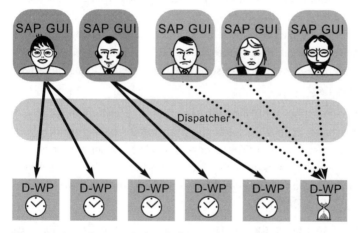

Figure 9.1 Long-Running Task in Dialog Mode

To prevent users from executing long-running reports interactively (see Figure 9.1), the dialog steps have a runtime limit. This limit is set to 600 seconds by default. Processing is terminated after this period. You can set this limit in the system profile (parameter *rdisp/max_wprun_time*). Background processing has no limits of this type.

Automating periodically required routine tasks is another obvious use for background processing. The R/3 system provides the background service with its background work processes (or simply *background processes*) for background processing. In contrast to dialog processing, in which the dispatcher assigns each logical unit of work (LUW, see Chapter 1) to the next available dialog process, background processing consists of a fixed connection with one background process during the entire execution. The system administrator or user schedules the start time for the background job. You can choose between time control and event control.

Time-controlled job scheduler In the time-controlled approach, you define a start time when you schedule a job. Each instance of the R/3 system that is configured for background work processes has an active *time-controlled job scheduler*, which checks in defined intervals whether any background jobs are waiting for processing. The descriptions of pending jobs are stored in central tables in the database. This scheduler is an ABAP program that is interpreted and processed within a selected dialog process, which is selected automatically during R/3 system startup. The interval after which the time-controlled job scheduler becomes active is set to 60 seconds by default. The administrator can change this interval to any value in the instance profile by using the parameter *rdisp/btctime*. The time interval between two job scheduler runs can result in delays when starting jobs. Therefore, if these delays are too long for your needs, you can reduce the duration of the interval. Accordingly, if a possible delay is immaterial for starting a job, you can increase the interval. Please note, however, that reducing the run frequency of the time-controlled job schedule has a nearly negligible effect on the system load.

Event-controlled job scheduler In contrast to the time-controlled job scheduler, the *event-controlled job scheduler* reacts to events. It starts the appropriate background job in response to a specific event. The event-controlled job scheduler is also processed by a dialog work process. You define the instance to use with parameter *rdisp/btcname = <server_name>* in the standard profile of the R/3 system (*DEFAULT.PFL*).

System events You first have to define the *events* that you want the R/3 system to respond to. Many kinds of events are already defined in the standard R/3 system. You can display an overview in ▶ **Event Maintenance**. The events that are included in the standard system are also called *system events*. System events are frequently used for internal R/3 control; however, they are also available for use by R/3 users.

User events In addition, users can use the same menu path to define their own new events—the *user events*. Initially, the event definition is nothing more than an entry in a table.

There are several different ways in which you can trigger an event:

▶ Manually for test purposes, with ▶**Trigger Event**

▶ Using function module BP_EVENT_RAISE from an ABAP program within the R/3 system

▶ With the external program sapevt

The **sapevt** program allows you to trigger an event in the R/3 system from within an external program. The **sapevt** program is available in the standard SAP directory for executable programs (see Chapter 1). You can use it as follows:

```
sapevt <EventID> [-p <parameter>] [-t]
pf=<profile>|name=<R/3_System_name> nr=<R/3_System_num-
ber>
```

The -t option causes the system to write a log file, *dev_evt*, in the **sapevt call directory**. You can use the -p option to pass on a parameter that specifies an R/3 module (such as FI). This makes it easier to assign the events to the work areas. This assignment is merely of a descriptive nature and has no other function

Example: The following call:

```
sapevt SAP_TRIGGER_RDDIMPDP name=Q01 nr=00
```

triggers event SAP_TRIGGER_RDDIMPDP in R/3 system Q01.

Event control is used within the R/3 system to transport objects between R/3 systems, for example. Transports performed with **tp**, the transport control program, are executed in several phases. In addition to the actual data import, the individual objects often have to be generated or activated. Accordingly, the **tp** program triggers event SAP_TRIGGER_RDDIMPDP once the data import is complete. In an R/3 system, the scheduling of job RDDIMPDP is always dependent on this event. When event SAP_TRIGGER_RDDIMPDP occurs, job RDDIMPDP is executed automatically in the background.

This technique affords you a lot of flexibility. You can't always predict when actions will be completed, and this makes it almost impossible to create dependencies between background jobs. Event control gives you entirely new perspectives to consider.

9.2 Definition of Background Jobs

To configure background jobs, use ▶Job Definition (see Figure 9.2).

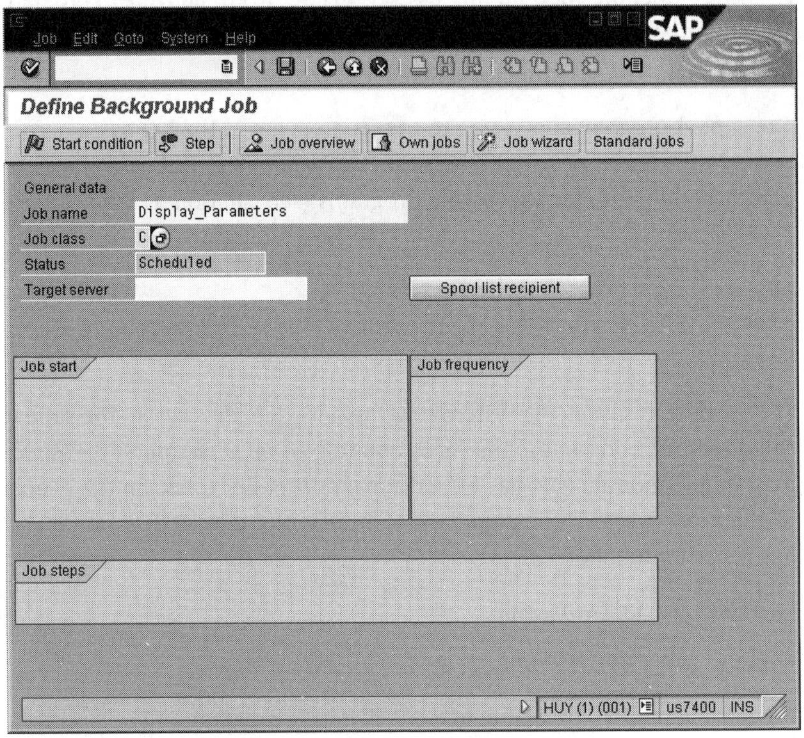

Figure 9.2 Initial Screen: Job Definition

Frequently, the scheduling of background jobs is integrated directly into the applications—to copy clients, for example, or in the user master comparison. The appearance of the screens can differ, and certain job attributes may be preassigned, depending on the application in use. The basic features and background processing options described in this chapter remain applicable, however, and can also be applied to these special cases.

The definition of background jobs consists of the following three primary attributes:

▶ General information, such as the job name, job class, and target server

▶ Information about the start time or assignment of a triggering event

▶ List of the processing steps

9.2.1 General Information

The general information is the first step in defining any background job (see Figure 9.2). You should choose as descriptive a job name as possible, as this name will be used in all logs and overviews that you will have to analyze later. From a technical standpoint, the job name is negligible; it does not have to be unique.

The priority for executing a job is initially determined from the assignment of that job to a *job class*. The following job classes are defined:

Job class

▶ **A — Highest priority**
Time-critical jobs that ensure the functionality of R/3

▶ **B — Medium priority**
Periodic jobs that ensure the functionality of R/3

▶ **C — Normal priority**
Job class C is the usual job class for R/3 users

System resources are assigned based on the job class. If many class C jobs are often being processed, which means jobs with classes A and B have to wait for background processes to become available, the system administrator can specify *n* number of background processes to reserve for class A jobs in ▶ **Operation Mode Maintenance**. This configuration ensures that *n* background processes are always available for executing class A jobs. Jobs with class B and C have to wait until at least *n+1* processes are available. This configuration is described in Section 14.2 on operation mode maintenance.

In a distributed R/3 system, you can assign the execution of a job to any R/3 instance with the background service. This R/3 instance is called the *target server* in the background processing context. If you do not explicitly specify a target server, the next available background process at execution time is selected.

Target server

The following priorities are defined for processing a request on a defined background server:

1. Job class A, target server is specified
2. Job class A, no target server is specified
3. Job class B, target server is specified
4. Job class B, no target server is specified
5. Job class C, target server is specified
6. Job class C, no target server is specified

If the pending jobs have equal priority according to the above criteria, the waiting time is used.

If a target server is specified, this value is binding. If a target server is not available when the job is started, no background process of another instance will take over the processing. The job remains in the queue until the defined target server starts working again, or processing is explicitly moved to another server.

The output generated by an ABAP program is saved as a spool request in the SAP spool system. You can use **Spool list recipient** to send the output to a user. This technique makes it possible for several people to administer a background job and analyze its results, for example. Because the output can be quite large, we recommend that you use this option with caution. For performance reasons, the length of an output list sent in SAPoffice is restricted to 1,000 lines. You specify the information for the print parameters themselves in the step definition (see Section 9.2.3).

9.2.2 Start Time

In the next step, you have to select the parameters to determine the start time. To do so, choose a **Start** condition from the initial screen for the job definition. You can specify the start date as being time- or event-controlled (see Figure 9.3). The time information and time zone used are based on the system time. In addition to specifying the start time directly, time-controlled job scheduling also enables you to schedule jobs periodically—for example, for regular analyses or the maintenance jobs described in Section 9.6. You can choose any repeat interval: a number of minutes, hourly, daily, weekly, and so on. You can use the **Restrictions** button to define exceptions from the usual period, for example, to consider legal holidays in the valid factory calendar. When time-sensitive jobs are involved, you can define the latest possible time for starting the job (**No start after**).

Instead of defining a time control, you can also specify a defined event as a trigger. In particular, operation mode changes (see Chapter 14) and the end of a job are defined as events, which means a background job can also be started as a follow-on job. You can use the **Start status-dependent** option to make the job start, given the successful completion of the previous job. If the previous job terminates, the dependent follow-on job is also set to status *cancelled* and is not executed.

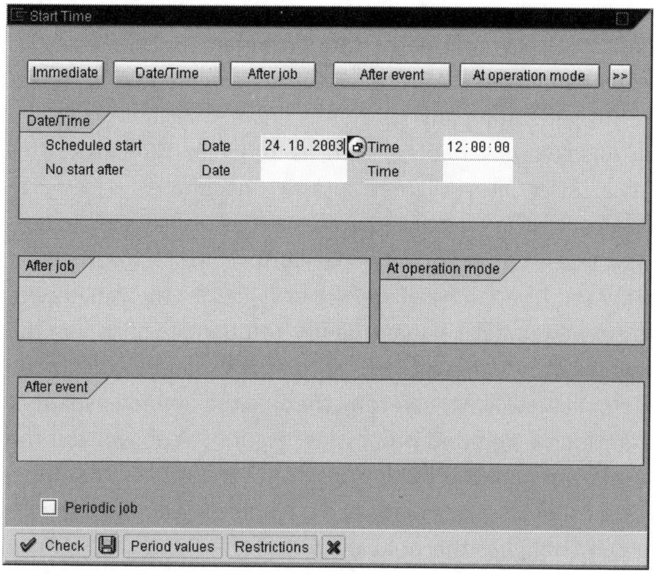

Figure 9.3 Start Dates for Scheduling Background Jobs

If jobs with start date *After job*, *After event,* or *At operation mode* cannot be started, because no background processes are available when the expected event occurs, they are noted to start immediately, and are then also started by the time-controlled job scheduler as soon as possible.

9.2.3 Processing Steps

To complete the definition of a background job, describe the processing steps that comprise the job. A *processing step* is defined as the execution of an independent program, such as an ABAP program or an external program. A background job consists of one or more such processing steps. To define the steps, choose the **Step** function in the job definition transaction (see Figure 9.2). Each processing step can be executed by a user different than the scheduler. The authorization checks are always performed based on the assigned users. This enables you to implement scenarios in which one group of users is responsible (and authorized) for job scheduling, while another group of users is responsible for job analysis. Using explicitly assigned users can also simplify the subsequent analysis of background job results, because the generated lists can be clearly assigned to those users. You can define the background users, which were described in Chapter 8, for this specific purpose.

Steps can be formed from ABAP programs, external commands, or external programs (see Figure 9.4).

ABAP program   As mentioned above, all dialog-free ABAP programs can also be executed in the background. To do so, choose the **ABAP program** function (see Figure 9.4). Enter the name of the ABAP program to execute and, if necessary, a language for generating any log that is created. Many ABAP programs are controlled with variables, such as program **RSPFPAR**. This program creates a list of all configured instance parameters. Users can restrict the namespace of the instance parameters to display before execution. To run this type of program in the background, you have to define *variants* for a program. A variant is a fixed set of values for the variables of a program that is saved under a variant name. You define variants in the ▶**ABAP Editor** with **Goto · Variants**. Then, enter the variant name and the required parameter values. Next, you can schedule the defined variant of an ABAP program for background processing. Figure 9.4 shows you the scheduling of ABAP program **RSPFPAR**, for which variant "ALL" has been defined to create a list of all current instance parameters. Generate the list in English. You can configure the print output of the list with the **Print specifications** button.

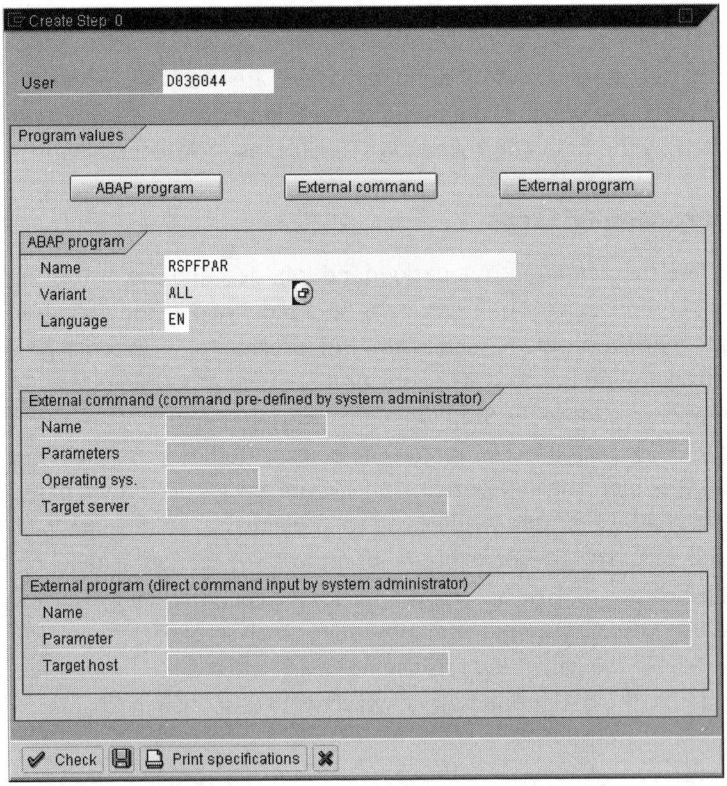

Figure 9.4 Step Definition

R/3 users with administrator authorization can select **External Program** to run any programs at operating-system level from within the R/3 system. The name of the target server is required; parameters are optional. Routine **SAPXPG** is started on the target server to execute the program, and communicates via RFC with the calling R/3 system, using the ID of special R/3 user **SAPCPIC** (see Chapter 8).

External programs

To use the internal R/3 authorization mechanism, but still enable external programs to run in a limited manner, *external commands* are preconfigured to be extendable. An external command consists of a name and an assigned external program, along with possible parameter values that can vary depending on the operating system. Before external commands can be used in background processing, you have to define them first with ▶ **Create External Operating System Commands** (see Figure 9.5).

External commands

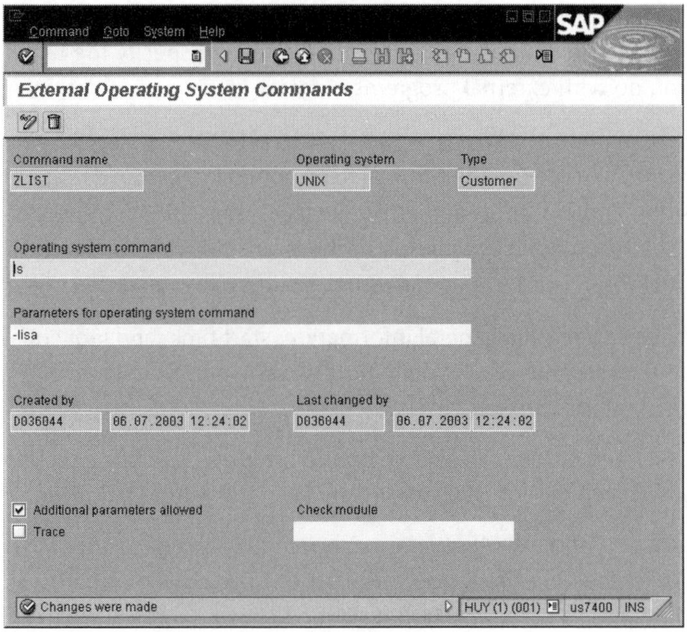

Figure 9.5 Creating an External Command

The standard R/3 system already contains many external commands. System administrators can define any other command in the customer namespace. Figure 9.5 illustrates this for a ZLIST command, which is defined for UNIX systems as the ls command with parameter -lisa, to display the contents of the current directory.

You could also create an external command with the same name for the Windows NT system, which would call the corresponding program *dir*.

Commands defined in this manner are not only used for specifying background jobs, but can also be executed from within the Computing Center Management System (CCMS). To do so, start ▶ **External Operating System Commands**, select the required command, and then choose **Edit Execute**.

You can define a check module to further restrict the use of an external command for security reasons. The check module runs before the command is started. Depending on the result of the check routine, the command is either executed or not. Routine SPXG_DUMMY_COMMAND_CHECK is a model example in the system, which you can use as a template for your own checks.

When you define a step within a background job, the external command to execute is determined from the name, such as ZLIST, and the relevant operating system, such as UNIX. You can allow users to add additional parameters to the predefined ones. You always have to specify the target server, as you do with external programs.

If external commands or external programs are used in the step list of a background job, you can use the **Control flags** option in the step definition to define whether the outputs and error messages from the operating system should be recorded in the job log of the step, and whether synchronous or asynchronous processing is needed, to improve integration.

Once you have entered the general information, start time, and individual steps of the background job, its definition is complete. Save your information when you are through.

Job Wizard

All of the described entries can also be queried step-by-step using the *Job Wizard*. You can call the Job Wizard directly from the ▶ **Job Definition**.

API

R/3 provides an interface (*Application Programming Interface*, API) that allows users to schedule background jobs from customer programs, in addition to the menu-based method described above.

9.3 Analysis

You analyze and monitor the background jobs with ▶ **Simple Job Selection** or ▶ **Extended job selection**. You can filter jobs by various criteria, including scheduling user, period, job period, event, and status (see Figure 9.6). The selection criteria are restricted by the authorization concept. If you have administrator authorization for background processing, you can display the jobs in all clients in the extended job selection. If not, you can only display the jobs in the logon client.

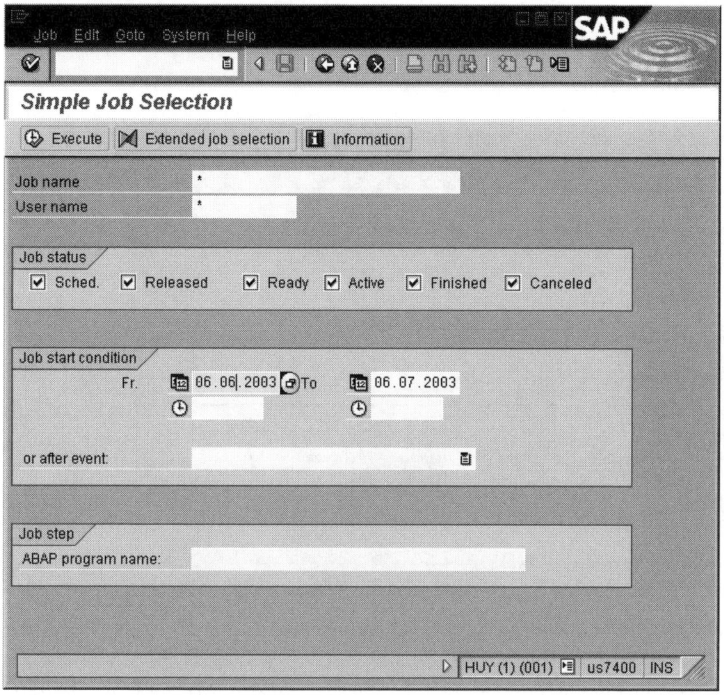

Figure 9.6 Simple Job Selection

A list of all background jobs that meet the selection criteria is generated (see Figure 9.7).

The status of a job has the following meanings:

▶ *Sched.*
The step definitions of the job have been saved; a start time has not been defined yet.

▶ *Released*
The job has been scheduled and a start time has been set explicitly, or the job is waiting for an event.

▶ *Ready*
The start time has been reached, or the awaited event has occurred; the job is waiting for system resources to start execution.

▶ *Active*
The job is currently being processed.

▶ *Finished*
The job has been completed successfully.

▶ *Canceled*

Processing was terminated due to a problem. The job was not completed successfully.

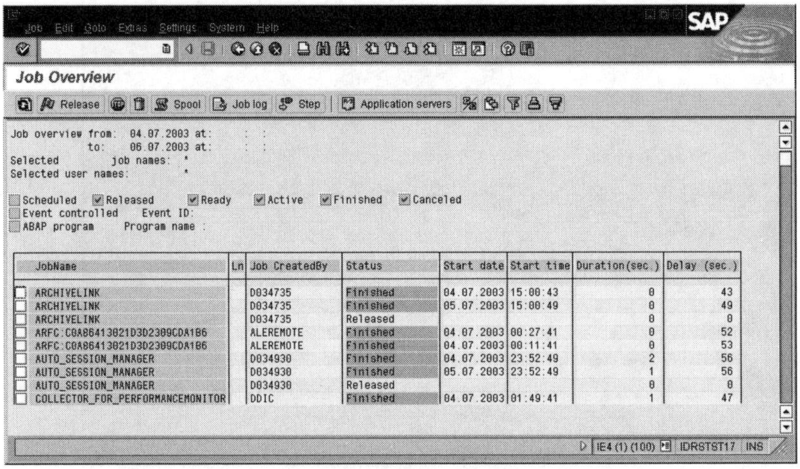

Figure 9.7 List of Background Jobs

You can double-click on a selected job to display the job log from its execution. In addition to the start and end times, terminated jobs contain valuable information about the termination cause. The job log in Figure 9.8 was created during an attempted data extraction. According to the log, duplicate records in the database caused the termination.

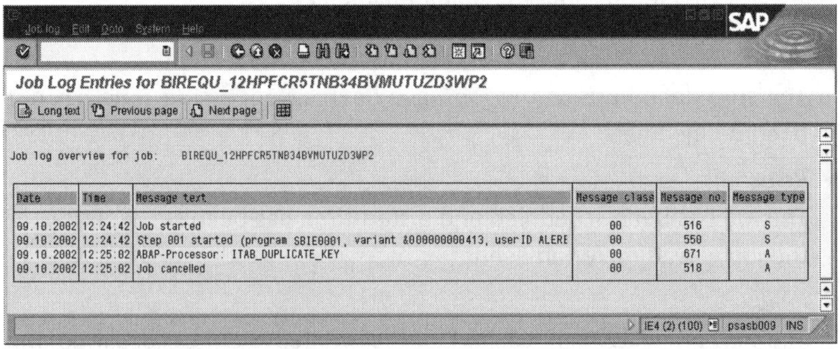

Figure 9.8 Log of a Termination

The job overview integrates all the major operations used for background jobs. This includes:

▶ Displaying the scheduling data
▶ Canceling jobs with *Active* status

- Deleting jobs with status *Sched.*, *Released*, *Finished*, or *Canceled*
- Canceling the release for one or more jobs; the job status changes to *planned*
- Comparing several jobs: you specify the general job information, the step definition, and the start requirements
- Moving to another server
- Interrupting an active job when problems are suspected (long-running tasks): A job that is currently running an ABAP program can be stopped and analyzed with the ABAP debugger. The program continues to run normally when you exit the debugger.
- Checking the status of active jobs (see Section 9.4)
- Copying planned, released, or finished jobs; the new job is set to status *Sched.*

In addition to this list overview, a graphical display is available, which enables you to change and release jobs as well as check active jobs. The graphical monitor is available in the ▶**Job Monitor** (see Figure 9.9). The job status values are displayed in color for faster comprehension.

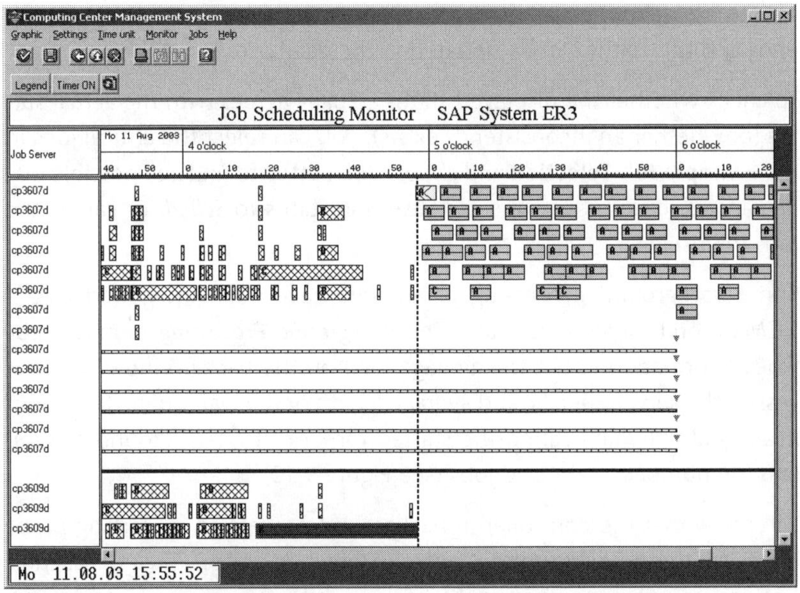

Figure 9.9 Job Scheduling Monitor

You can also select ▶**Own Jobs** or ▶**Job Definition** · **Own jobs** to display an overview of your own background jobs.

9.4 Analysis Functions

Because a user's problems in background processing—in contrast to dialog processing—are often not even apparent to the users themselves, additional analysis functions are available within the CCMS.

Runtime analysis Up to R/3 Release 4.6B, the ▶**Performance Analysis** function displays a list of all selected background jobs, along with the planned and actual start times and runtimes. Starting in R/3 Release 4.6C, this information is integrated in the ▶**Simple Job Selection.** Large variances between the planned and actual start times indicate a bottleneck in the available background processes, as they indicate that it took a while for a released job to be sent to a background process for processing. If a user can rule out performance bottlenecks during the execution of scheduled background jobs, the administrator should check the resources and increase the number of background processes if necessary (parameter *rdisp/wp_no_btc* in the instance profiles or in profile maintenance; see Chapter 14).

Zombies When you start up an R/3 system, it checks whether jobs with status *ready* or *active* are found, although they are not possible in this situation. Any such jobs that are found are set to status *Sched.* or *canceled.* Such *zombies* can be created when an application server is shut down before the job ends and the status can be updated in the database.

Status check To check whether the displayed status actually agrees with the actual status (or whether an inconsistency exists), you can select the critical jobs in the ▶**Simple Job Selection** and choose **Job status** to find any possible discrepancies. If necessary, you can reset job status to *Sched.* or cancel the jobs themselves.

Alerts from background processing Some background processing parameters have been integrated in the CCMS monitoring architecture. The *Background Processing* monitor provides information about the average load on the background work processes, the server-specific and average length of the wait queue for jobs in *Ready* status (which cannot be started for lack of a background server), and the number of aborted jobs (see Figure 9.10).

Control object list To ensure that the controller in background processing is working properly, use the ▶**Background Control Object Monitor.** This transaction enables you to check important background processing components— such as time-controlled and event-controlled job schedulers, zombie cleanup, start of external programs, and switching operating modes—and analyze them with additional trace outputs.

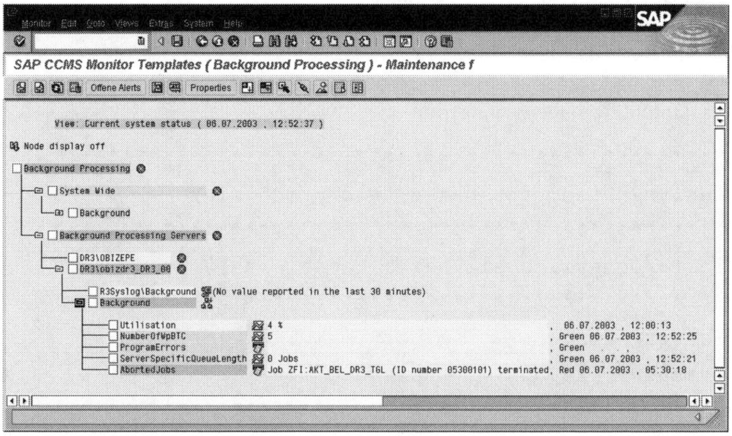

Figure 9.10 Integration of Background Processing in Alert Monitoring

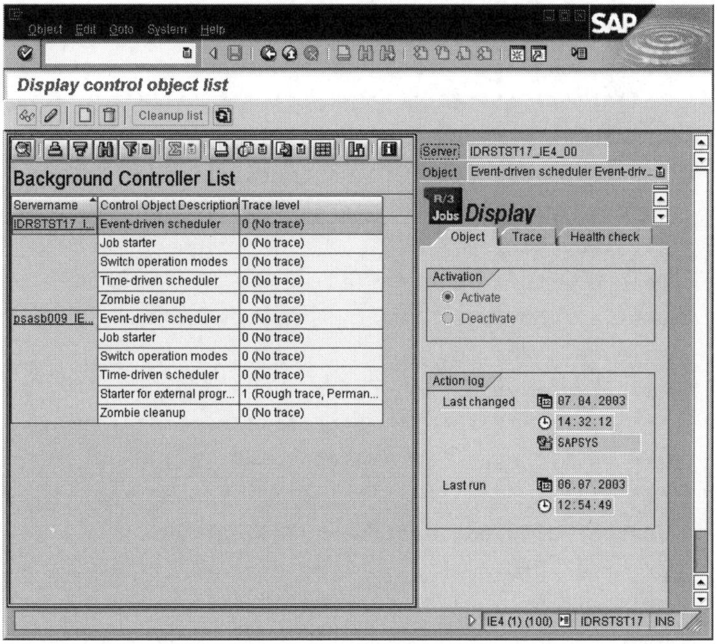

Figure 9.11 Monitor for Background Control

You can run a comprehensive analysis of all aspects of background processing with ▶**Analysis of Background Processing**. In particular, this analysis tool enables you to locate and correct inconsistencies in the database

Analysis tool for background processing

tables for job control. The following listing contains an example of the output from this tool:

Listing 9.1 Output from the Analysis Tool

```
**********************************************************
*     Analysis tool for background processing
**********************************************************
**    Test: Determine all batch-capable servers
**********************************************************
*     Server name              Host Name
*     psasb009_IE4_00          psasb009
**********************************************************
* Test: Test TemSe functionality
**********************************************************
*     ==> TemSe check ran without errors
**********************************************************
* Test: Check a user's batch authorizations
**********************************************************
*     User to check           = D036044
*     ==> Possesses the following authorizations:
*         Batch administrator    : Yes
*         EarlyWatch: Yes
*         Delete external jobs: Yes
*         Display job logs: Yes
*         Release jobs: Yes
*         Display external jobs: Yes
**********************************************************
* Test: Test environment for starting external programs
**********************************************************
*     ==> User SAPCPIC not defined in client 002
*         External programs cannot be started in
*         this client!
*     ==> User SAPCPIC not defined in client 066
*         External programs cannot be started in
*         this client!
**********************************************************
* Test: Consistency check of database tables
**********************************************************
*     ==> No inconsistencies found!
*     ==> All job contexts are consistent
```

```
**********************************************************
* Test: Check profile parameters
**********************************************************
* Server = psasb009_IE4_00 , Date = 10/13/2002 ,
* Time = 2:35:46 p.m.
**********************************************************
*     rdisp/btctime   = 60
*     rdisp/wp no btc = 6
*     ==> Server is configured correctly for
*         background processing
**********************************************************
* Test: Check local host name against message server
**********************************************************
* Server = psasb009_IE4_00 , Date = 10/13/2002 ,
* Time = 2:35:46 p.m.
**********************************************************
*     Local host name = psasb009
*     ==> Local host name agrees with name on
*         message server
**********************************************************
* Test: Determine status of batch work processes
* on a server
**********************************************************
* Server = psasb009_IE4_00 , Date = 10/13/2002 ,
* Time = 2:35:46 p.m.
**********************************************************
*     ==> Status of batch work processes:
*     WP 1 : waiting
*     WP 2 : waiting
*     WP 3 : waiting
*     WP 4 : waiting
*     WP 5 : waiting
*     WP 6 : waiting
*     Number of reserved class A work processes: 0
**********************************************************
* Test: Determine number of requests in batch queue
**********************************************************
* Server = psasb009_IE4_00 , Date = 10/13/2002 ,
* Tie = 14:35:46
```

```
* * * * * * * * * * * * * * * * * * * * * * * * * * * * * * * * * * * * * * * * * * * * * * * * * * *
*    ==> Number of requests in batch queue = 0
* * * * * * * * * * * * * * * * * * * * * * * * * * * * * * * * * * * * * * * * * * * * * * * * * * *
```

9.5   Authorizations

Authorizations also control which actions a user is allowed to perform in background processing. Table 9.1 lists and describes the most important authorizations in this area. Even without any special authorization, all users are authorized to schedule, cancel, delete, and check the status of their own jobs. Special authorization is required for the following actions:

▶ Manipulating a job scheduled by a different user

▶ Displaying the job log

▶ Displaying a spool request generated by a background job

▶ Releasing a job for execution

▶ Using an external command

Authorization	Description
S_BTCH_ADM	Batch administration
S_BTCH_JOB	Operations with background jobs, client-dependent Possible values: DELE — Delete other users' jobs LIST — Display other users' spool lists PROT — Display other users' logs RELE — Schedule own jobs and release for execution SHOW — Display other users' job details You can use the "Job Group" field to restrict the authorization to selected job names.
S_BTCH_NAM	Use of an explicit background user
S_DEVELOP	Interrupt jobs
S_LOG_COM	Execute external commands Required parameters: COMMAND — Name of the logical command OPSYSTEM — Operating system HOST — Name of target system
S_RZL_ADM	CCMS system administration
S_ADMI_FCD	System authorization for special functions

Table 9.1 Authorizations for Background Processing

In contrast to dialog mode, no passwords are checked during background processing. The relevant R/3 users merely have to be defined and not locked in the current client.

9.6 Maintenance Jobs

The system administrator is responsible for running certain jobs for maintaining the performance and functionality of the R/3 system. These jobs delete unnecessary tables, for example, or collect statistical data for the performance analysis. Table 9.2 lists and describes the most important maintenance jobs. Additional jobs may also be necessary, depending on which applications and proprietary developments you use.

Recommended Job Name/Description	ABAP	Variant	Interval
SAP_COLLECTOR_FOR_PERFMONITOR Collects general statistical data for performance analysis in the R/3 system. Cross-client Schedule in client 000 as DDIC.	RSCOLL00	No	Hourly
SAP_COLLECTOR_FOR_JOBSTATISTIC Collects statistical data to analyze the average runtime of periodically scheduled jobs. Cross-client	RSBPCOLL	No	Daily
SAP_REORG_JOBS Deletes all logs of successfully executed jobs. System administrators can use variants to define the number of days to elapse before deleting a log. Cross-client	RSBTCDEL	Yes	Daily
SAP_REORG_JOBSTATISTIC Reorganizes the runtime statistics of the background jobs. All objects that are older than the specified date are deleted. Cross-client	RSBPSTDE	Yes	Monthly

Table 9.2 Important Maintenance Jobs

SAP_REORG_BATCHINPUT Deletes processed batch input sessions and their logs, as well as all logs for which sessions no longer exist. Client-specific	RSBDCREO	Yes	Daily, but only during times where there is no batch input activity
SAP_REORG_SPOOL Deletes outdated spool objects. Client-specific	RSPO0041 / RSPO1041	Yes	Daily
No standard name. Deletes spool lists that are relics of terminated background programs. Consistency check of spooler tables Cross-client	RSPO0043 / RSPO1043	Yes	Daily
SAP_REORG_ABAPDUMPS Deletes entries (short dumps) from runtime errors. Cross-client	RSSNAPDL	Yes	Daily
SAP_REORG_PRIPARAMS Reorganizes the print parameters. Cross-client	RSBTCPRIDEL	No	Monthly
SAP_CCMS_MONI_BATCH_DP System monitoring Client-specific	RSAL_BATCH TOOL_DIS-PATCHING	No	Hourly
No standard name. Implements transport requests.	RDDIMPDP		Event controlled
EU_PUT Administration job for updating object lists and navigation indexes. Cross-client	SAPRSLOG		Daily
EU_REORG Administration job for updating object lists after a transport. Cross-client	SAPRSEUT		Daily

Table 9.2 Important Maintenance Jobs (cont.)

For more information on the properties and parameters of these jobs, refer to the documentation of the individual program. You can do so in the ▶ABAP Editor. Enter the program name and choose **Documentation · Display**.

In R/3 Release 4.6C and later, you can schedule all of the above jobs individually, or automatically with standard parameters, with ▶Job Definition · Standard jobs.

In addition to the Basis-related maintenance jobs, application-specific reorganizations can also improve system performance. One important example is report **SBAL_DELETE**, which deletes the application log.

9.7 External Interface

The SAP BC-XBP interface enables you to integrate R/3 background jobs with external job management systems. The following functions are supported:

▶ Defining jobs

▶ Changing, editing, and deleting jobs

▶ Starting jobs

▶ Terminating active jobs

▶ Accessing job information (status, log files, and so on)

To display a list of the products certified for this interface, visit the SAP Service Marketplace under alias *background*.

9.8 Tips

▶ **Defining jobs with a target server**
If you often specify a target server in your job definitions, you must modify the job definitions when your system configuration changes. This is the case, for example, when:

   ▶ You move an application server to other hardware (change of server name)

   ▶ You change the distribution of work processes in the definition of the operation modes

▶ **Deleting jobs that are no longer current and have status** *Sched.*
When you display the current job queue in the ▶Simple Job Selection, the **Job Status: Planned** checkbox is usually not checked, which means the administrator may not notice unnecessary jobs with this status. Another common mistake is to forget the checkbox **Or after event**, which means event-triggered jobs are not displayed.

▶ **Scheduling jobs under a non-generic user**
When you schedule periodic jobs that will run over a long period, it makes sense to assign the individual steps to generic background users. This will help you to avoid problems later on if the users who schedule the jobs are deleted.

▶ **Minimum number of processes**
You have to configure at least two background work processes for the transport system, even if you do not plan to use background processing actively.

▶ **Deallocation and rescheduling of all released jobs**
Report **BTCTRNS1** is used during upgrades in R/3 Release 4.5B and later. It changes the status of all jobs to a status that the job scheduler does not recognize, in order to prevent unwanted starts. After the upgrade, report **BTCTRNS2** is used to change the jobs back to their original status. Of course, you can also use these functions for other purposes.

▶ **Moving the start times of individual, time-controlled job schedulers**
If several instances with background processes are used, it may make sense to set parameter *rdisp/btctime* to different values in the instance profiles, in order to achieve better load distribution.

▶ **Problems with self-planning periodic jobs with a limited start time**
If you use periodic jobs that schedule themselves again automatically at the end of each run, and you define a time after which such jobs can no longer be started, these jobs may stop running altogether after a long system shutdown. You must monitor these jobs manually.

9.9 Transactions and Menu Paths

ABAP Editor: SAP Menu • Tools • ABAP Workbench • Development ABAP Editor (SE38)

Analysis of background processing: SAP Menu • Tools • CCMS • Jobs • Check Environment (SM65)

Background control object monitor: SAP Menu • Tools • CCMS • Jobs • Background Objects (SM61)

Create external operating system commands: SAP Menu • Tools • CCMS • Configuration • External Commands (SM69)

Event maintenance: SAP Menu • Tools • CCMS • Jobs • Maintain Event (SM62)

Extended job selection: SAP Menu • Tools • CCMS • Jobs • Maintenance • Extended job selection (SM37C)

External operating system commands: SAP Menu • Tools • CCMS • Jobs • External Commands (SM49)

Job definition: SAP Menu • Tools • CCMS • Jobs • Definition (SM36)

Job monitor: SAP Menu • Tools • CCMS • Control/Monitoring • Job Scheduling Monitor (RZ01)

Operation mode maintenance: SAP Menu • Tools • CCMS • Configuration • Operation Modes/Instances (RZ04)

Own jobs: System • Own Jobs (SMX)

Performance analysis: SAP Menu • Tools • CCMS • Jobs • Performance Analysis (SM39)

Simple job selection: SAP Menu • Tools • CCMS • Jobs • Maintenance (SM37)

Trigger event: SAP Menu • Tools • CCMS • Jobs • Trigger Event (SM64)

9.10 Other Documentation

Quicklinks

▶ SAP Service Marketplace, alias *background*

SAP Service Marketplace Notes

Table 9.3 lists important SAP Service Marketplace Notes for R/3 background processing:

Contents	Note
Standard jobs, reorganization jobs	16083
Distribution of background jobs on application servers	24092
Error analysis: Background processing system	37104
Behavior of transactions SM37 and SM37C	422000

Table 9.3 SAP Notes for User Background Processing

9.11 Questions

1. Which transaction can you use to analyze the job logs?

    a. SE38

    b. SM37

    c S000

2. Which external program can you use to trigger events in the R/3 system?

    a. sapevt

    b. sapxpg

    c. sapstart

    d. spmon

3. What does status *Ready* mean for a background job?

    a. Job scheduling was completed and saved.

    b. The job was executed and is ready to print the log.

    c The job is waiting for system resources to become available to start execution.

10   Update

Every change performed by an SAP transaction ultimately results in a write modification in the database. The SAP update system ensures the consistency of changes within an SAP logical unit of work (LUW). This chapter describes the particularities that are associated with monitoring and troubleshooting the update task.

The SAP update module is a central component of the R/3 system; however, it is not an independent component. Instead, it is always considered with other services collectively in the R/3 system, such as dialog, background, and especially enqueue. The update task works closely with all of these services.

A business process in the SAP system is mapped to an SAP logical unit of work (LUW, see Chapter 1), which can consist of several screen changes. This dialog or background processing results in a data change that can only be written to the database completely—that is, with all changes from the LUW—or not at all. The SAP update system ensures that the changes are not written to the database until the SAP LUW is complete, and that no data is changed if the SAP transaction is terminated. In most cases, the update is performed asynchronously at the end of an LUW (see Section 1.4). This results in significantly improved performance for dialog users, who can continue their work in the next LUW while the update system is still writing the change in the database.

SAP LUW

Until the update is performed, the objects to be changed remain locked; other users cannot access the objects, or at least, they cannot change them, depending on the type of lock involved. Because update problems can disrupt the entire system, their resolution always has the highest priority. This chapter introduces the basic concepts of the update and teaches you how to use the necessary tools for monitoring the update task that are integrated in the R/3 system.

10.1   Update Concepts

In the R/3 environment, the term *update* describes the execution of changes in the R/3 database, which the SAP system usually carries out asynchronously after data is entered or changed. A special update system is required in order to map the R/3 LUW to the database transactions.

Definition

Logical R/3 work units are mapped to independent R/3 LUWs, which themselves can consist of multiple database transactions. This is only possible with a separate update system; otherwise, every R/3 LUW would have to be mapped to exactly one database transaction. The update system makes it possible to manage data entry separately from the update itself and consolidate update processes.

When a user enters data, for example, the data is initially received by a dialog process. However, the dialog process does not execute the necessary changes to the database. Instead, special update work processes perform this task, which means the changes are executed asynchronously (see Figure 10.1).

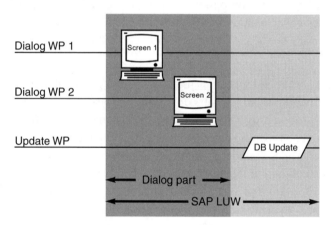

Figure 10.1 Asynchronous Update

When the SAP LUW is processed in dialog, the changes to be implemented are saved as modules—defined as function modules and the corresponding data—in the update request. At the conclusion of the dialog part of an SAP transaction, the update request is closed, the update header (see Figure 10.2) is written, and the update task itself is called, which executes the changes in the database as specified in the update request. Lock entries from dialog or background processing are inherited by the update task, which unlocks the objects again once the update is complete.

The asynchronous method of implementing changes results in a far better performance for users when compared with synchronous data modification, that is, immediate change by the dialog process itself. As users enter, change, or delete data in rapid sequence, they don't have to wait for their changes to be updated in the database. The update work process takes care of updating changes in the database asynchronously. This asynchronous update method has an especially positive effect on performance when large amounts of data are changed in dialog, such as during order entry. In addition, the asynchronous update improves the scalability of the R/3 system. Typically, however, users have no influence over whether their database changes are executed synchronously or asynchronously—this depends on the implementation of the relevant ABAP program.

The data to be changed by an SAP LUW is saved in an *update request* (also **Update request** called an *update record*). The update requests consist of the update header and one or more V1, V2, and collective run modules (see Figure 10.2).

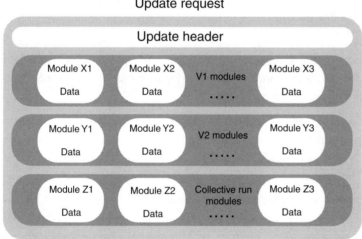

Figure 10.2 Update Request

The information regarding the update requests is saved in the *update* **Update tables** *tables*:

▶ VBHDR
Update headers

▶ VBMOD
Update modules

▶ VBDATA
Data transferred to the modules

▶ VBERROR
Error information that is generated if an update is canceled

Because these tables change constantly, you must not generate any database statistics for them (see Chapter 15). The processing programs are designed to deal with relatively small update tables. This is another reason why it is important to monitor the update task and clean up canceled updates.

10.1.1 Update Mode and Update Modules

Update mode

ABAP programs support three types of updates:

- ▶ Local update
- ▶ Asynchronous update
- ▶ Synchronous update

The ABAP program determines which mode is used, and cannot be changed by the administrator or user.

Local update

During *local update*, changes to the database are triggered directly from the respective work process, circumventing the mechanisms described above. These updates are not visible in update monitoring (see Section 10.3) and cannot be administered.

Asynchronous update

Asynchronous update is the most frequently used update mode and offers the best performance for dialog applications. You must monitor the update system and its update requests in order to maintain the functionality of the system.

Synchronous update

Synchronous update uses the same mechanisms as does asynchronous update. In this case, however, after the update request is sent to the update task, the calling program waits until the update work process returns the update status. Synchronous updates are flagged accordingly in the information column in update management.

V1 and V2 Updates

The system differentiates between the V1 and V2 update modules. There are also collective runs for frequently used function modules, sometimes called *V3 updates*. The *V1 updates* contain the critical changes with control functions. They involve business transactions such as changes to material stocks. Changes to such objects have to be implemented as quickly as possible. In contrast, *V2 updates* are usually of a statistical nature and therefore have a lower priority. Accordingly, V1 updates are to be handled with a higher priority than V2 updates.

Each update module corresponds to an update function module. Whether a V1, V2, or V3 update is involved is a property of the function module, and cannot be influenced by the administrator.

At the system level, processing of V1 and V2 modules can be distributed to separate update work processes in classes UPD and UPD2 (see Chapter 15). You use profile parameters to define the number of UPD and UPD2 update processes (see Section 10.3). You can check the work process distribution with ▶Process Overview (see Chapter 15). If no UPD2 work processes are configured in a system, the V2 update is performed in a UPD work process.

V2 updates are not performed until after the V1 updates. When the V1 component is processed, the system automatically attempts to process the V2 components from this update request.

In the *collective run modules* (V3), the update is not performed in an update process; instead, it is performed asynchronously in a batch job (report **RSM13005**). In this approach, the collected calls of the function module are consolidated first. If the same entry is changed several times, the resulting value is calculated first and only this one is written to the database once. Otherwise, the administration and handling of the function modules is identical to the V2 update modules. In particular, this means that the update requests remain in the update tables until they have been processed in the collective run.

Collective run modules

Whether V3 modules are used for a collective run is defined in either the ABAP program or in Customizing for the application (one example is the delta extraction in Logistics using Transaction LBWE). If use of the V3 modules is specified, the SAP administrator is responsible for scheduling and monitoring the regular collective runs.

From the system administrator's perspective, it is immaterial which user transactions generate the update records. Similarly, how the update process is executed within the R/3 system is irrelevant to the users. What users do care about are throughput and results, both of which the system administrator is responsible for ensuring. The following sections explain the tools and methods that are available.

10.2 Configuring the Update System

Under the default configuration, the SAP system distributes the update requests equally among all update work processes. This is called *update dispatching* and it utilizes load balancing.

You define the number of UPD and UPD2 update processes with parameters *rdisp/wp_no_vb* and *rdisp/wp_no_vb2* (respectively) in the instance profile. The number of update records to process is the critical factor in determining the number and distribution of update processes (see Section 10.3.1). The upper limit is set by the hardware performance—that is, the resources available to the R/3 system. Accordingly, you must monitor the update processes. As a point of reference for the initial settings, we recommend that you configure around one update work process for every four dialog processes. Because the V2 update is not time-critical, one UPD2 work process per system will usually suffice.

Multiplexing   In rare cases, it can make sense to deactivate automatic dispatching and instead conduct *multiplexing* using manually configured server groups (for installations with several database instances, for example). This is an exceptional case, however, that is not covered in detail here.

A good overview of the profile parameters for controlling the update task and a short description of each parameter are available in ▶Update Program Administration. Several of the most important configuration parameters are described below:

Configuration   ▶ rdisp/vbmail
parameters
You can configure the R/3 system to automatically send a message to a user when that user's update request causes an error. To do this, set rdisp/vbmail = 1. The value 0, however, deactivates the sending of messages to the user in case of an error. The default setting for this parameter is 1.

▶ rdisp/vbdelete
This parameter specifies an interval in days, after which incompletely execute update requests are deleted when the R/3 system or one of its instances is restarted. The default value for this parameter is 50 days. Whether automatic deletion of update requests is allowed depends on your business environment, and may also have to be discussed with your auditors. If you never want incomplete update records to be deleted, set the parameter to 0.

▶ rdisp/vbreorg
This parameter controls whether incompletely created update requests will be deleted when the R/3 system or one of its instances is restarted. 0 = do not delete requests; 1 = delete requests. You can also delete incomplete update requests with the ▶Update Program Administration, administration of the ▶Update Records, or report RSM13002. Incomplete update requests are caused by user-triggered terminations (*rollbacks*), in which part of the update request has already been written to the database.

► rdisp/vb_stop_active

This parameter defines whether the update task can be deactivated. When you set the value to 1, the update task can be deactivated automatically, in case of serious database problems, or manually. Unlike earlier releases, this deactivation of the update task prevents database problems from resulting in many canceled updates. If you set the value to 0, the update task cannot be deactivated.

10.3 Monitoring and Troubleshooting for the Update

Failure of the update task will quickly result in a system hangup, because the objects to be changed remain locked and the update tables continue to grow in size. Usually, the update task in an R/3 system does not require any regular maintenance. However, if database problems do occur, they must be corrected as quickly as possible.

Possible causes of failed updates—or even the failure of the entire update system—include database problems and lock conflicts in the application.

Causes of errors

We differentiate between two main problem areas:

► System-wide problems, such as those caused by database problems, often deactivate the update task. A good example of this is reaching the maximum size of a table in an Oracle database. Therefore, if the update task stops, you should first check the R/3 system log (see Chapter 15) and the database log files and look for general system problems. Once the problem is corrected, you have to restart the update service manually.

► The other type of update problem is of a more isolated, local nature—one that is frequently caused by programming errors in customer objects—which requires developer and user intervention to jointly decide what to do with the update records. You can use the overview of ►Update Records to delete, update, post, or reset individual or all records. *Updating* means continuing the update; *posting* means the update record is still in its initial stage (status *init*). If the update or posting attempt also fails, you must delete the relevant records, or reset and process them again.

10.3.1 Monitoring the Update

You can access both general monitoring of the update process and detailed troubleshooting via either administration for ►Update Records (see Figure 10.3) or from ▶ **Update Program Administration** (see Figure 10.4).

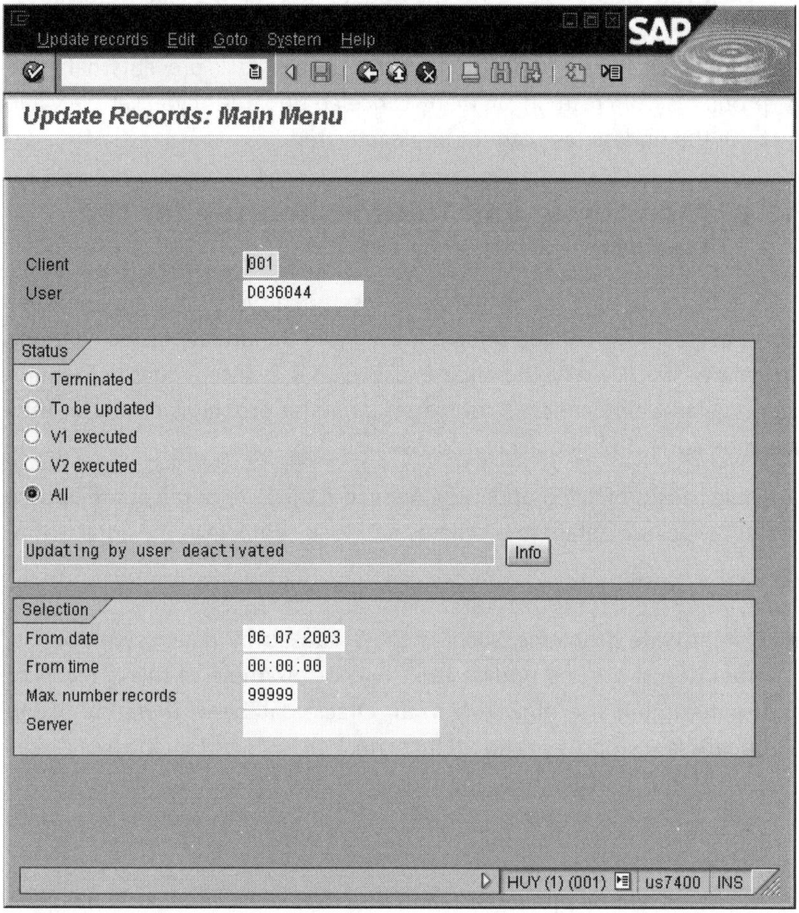

Figure 10.3 Administration of Update Records

The most important piece of information is the current status of the update service. In extreme errors, the update service is deactivated automatically. In this case, any user who tries to update data sees an information message in the status bar indicating that the update service has been stopped, and is asked to wait. The session remains blocked until the update resumes.

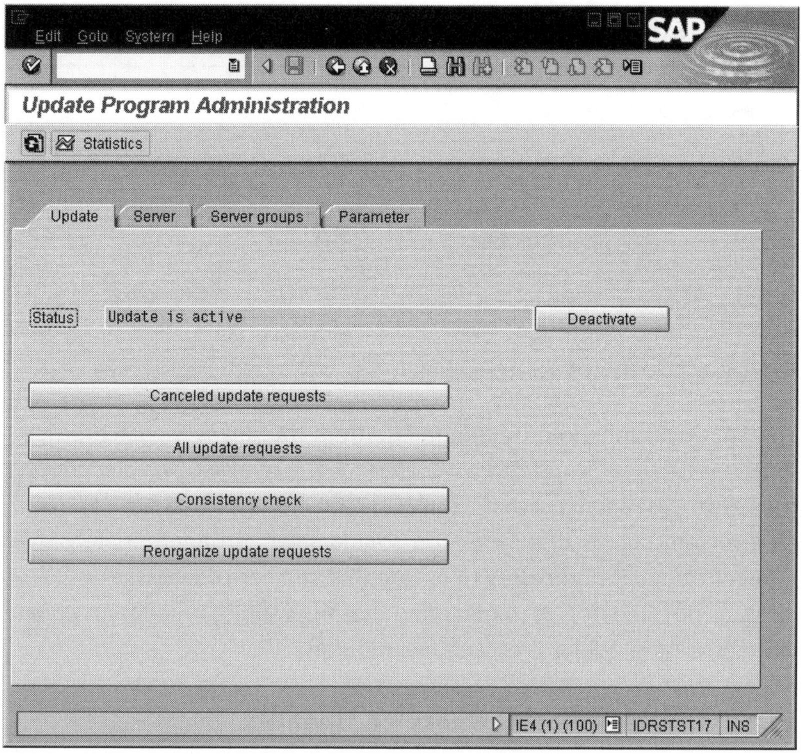

Figure 10.4 Initial Menu for Update Program Administration

If system-wide errors occur, you can also deactivate the update manually in the management of ▶Update Records, with **Update Records · Update · Deactivate**, and then reactivate it after the problems are corrected with **Update Records · Activate** (see Figure 10.3). Update terminations and problems with the update are recorded in the R/3 system log (see Chapter 15).

To get an overview of the current situation, you should display all the update requests first. When you start administration of the ▶Update Records, ensure that you select all previous update records for all users and in all clients. For you, however, only your own update records from the current date and the current client are displayed under the default settings. The amount of data that is waiting to be updated at any given time is a good indication of whether the number of update processes satisfies your requirements (see Figure 10.5).

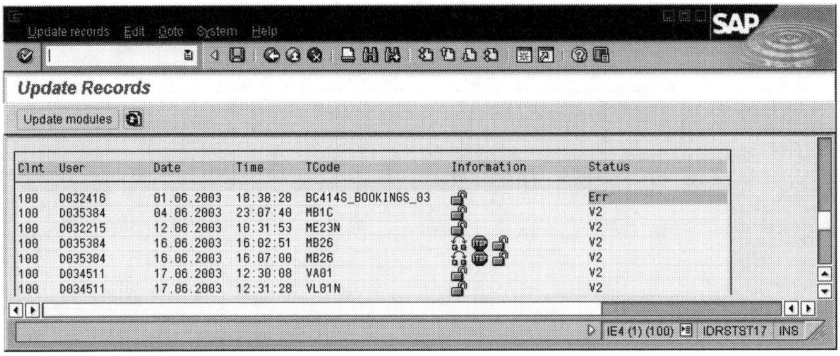

Figure 10.5 Overview of Update Records

The SAP locks inherited by the update from the dialog or batch process remain until the V1 update is executed for the relevant objects. If a user tries to process an object that is locked because it is waiting to be updated, an error message is displayed. You should select an appropriately large number of update processes to ensure that such error messages occur as rarely as possible. It is recommended that the waiting time for an update work process should not exceed five minutes.

10.3.2 Troubleshooting Canceled Updates

Canceled updates are particularly critical. When updates are canceled, the necessary processes for updating the data record could not be executed, which means that the changes were not implemented in the R/3 database (see Figure 10.6).

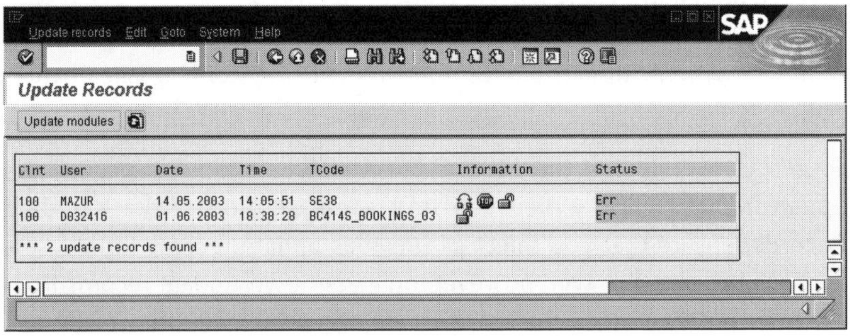

Figure 10.6 Canceled Updates

To analyze canceled updates, you can select the respective update operations by using various criteria in the initial screen for ▶ **Update Program Administration**. The following information is displayed for each data record to be updated (update record): client, executing user, time received, transaction code that resulted in the update record, any additional information for the update request, and its current status. The following status values are possible:

▶ *init*

The record is waiting to be updated.

Status of update records

▶ *auto*

When the update task is activated again after the update server is shut down, the record will be updated automatically.

▶ *run*

The record is being processed.

▶ *err*

An error occurred that caused the request to be canceled.

▶ *V1*

The V1 modules of the order were executed free of errors; the request is waiting for the V2 update.

▶ *V2*

The request is waiting for a collective run (V3 update).

The information column contains additional information on the type of update created and its current status. Table 10.1 shows the possible icons and their descriptions:

Icon	Short text from ▶ Update Records	Description
	Synchronous update	Update request with synchronous update.
	No restart possible	Update request was canceled in V1 module and cannot be updated.
	Update request with enqueues	SAP locks exist for this request.
	Enqueues released	The SAP locks for this request have been released.
	External commit	The update request was created by an external system.
	Generated by batch input	The update request was generated by a batch input session; the request cannot be updated.

Table 10.1 Descriptions of the Information Icons

Troubleshooting   You must always investigate the cause of terminations. After you correct the cause, you must decide what to do with the canceled update records. The business aspects are critical, therefore, the corresponding user department must also be involved in the analysis. Proceed as follows:

1. In ▶ **Update Records** management, select status *Terminated*, the appropriate client, the user, and the relevant period.

2. Choose **Execute**.

3. A list of all canceled updates appears (see Figure 10.6). The following information is displayed for each record: the client, the user, a time stamp, the transaction that created the update, and the status.

4. Analyze the termination of the update together with the responsible user department.

5. Select individual update records and test them with **Update Records · Test**. You can also run an update in debugging mode with **Update Records · Debugging**. Use this function with caution, however, as it places a heavy load on system resources.

6. If you still haven't resolved the cause of the problem, check the data record's update header. The update header contains all the administrative data of the update record. To display it, choose **Goto · Update Header** (see Figure 10.7).

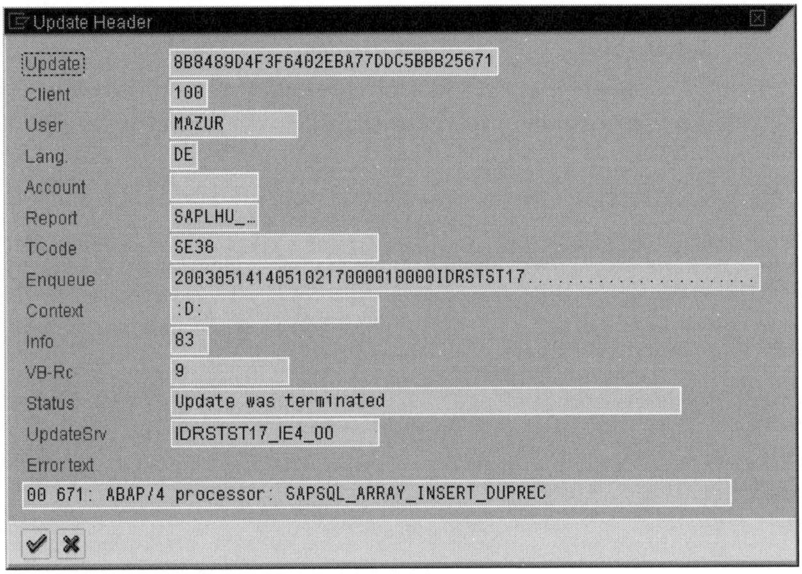

Update	8B8489D4F3F6402EBA77DDC5BBB25671
Client	100
User	MAZUR
Lang.	DE
Account	
Report	SAPLHU_…
TCode	SE38
Enqueue	20030514140510217000010000IDRSTST17........................
Context	:D:
Info	83
VB-Rc	9
Status	Update was terminated
UpdateSrv	IDRSTST17_IE4_00
Error text	
	00 671: ABAP/4 processor: SAPSQL_ARRAY_INSERT_DUPREC

Figure 10.7 Update Header

7. To see which function modules (update modules) should have been used to update a record, check the **Update Modules** from the overview of terminated ▶**Update Records**. Figure 10.8 shows this for a record from Figure 10.6. The overview reflects the structure of an update request from Figure 10.2. In this case, the record that was not updated consists of two V1 components and one V2 component.

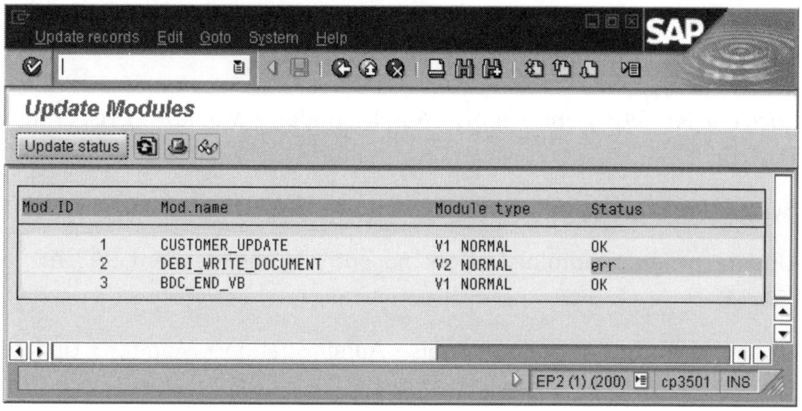

Figure 10.8 Update Modules

8. Choose **Goto · Display Data** to check the actual data of the update record.

9. Check the ▶**System Log** of the R/3 system for error messages that occurred around the time of the update termination.

In typical R/3 system operations, you have to monitor three major items for the update service:

Note

1. Is the update service active?

2. Have update terminations occurred?

3. How large is the queue of requests waiting for processing?

Monitoring the update activities is one of a system administrator's daily activities.

10.4 Tips

▶ **Overview of all open updates**

To get an initial overview when you start SM13, you should enter "*" for user and client and select a date prior to the system installation. Otherwise, under the default settings, you will only see a list of your own update records in the current client from today's date.

▶ Deleting lock entries

During the update, SAP locks are inherited by the update request. If lock entries are simply deleted, the corresponding objects can be edited by other users, and the system can no longer determine how an update request should be processed. Therefore, lock entries and update records must always be processed together—in case of manual intervention.

10.5 Transactions and Menu Paths

Lock entries: SAP Menu • Tools • Administration • Monitor • Lock Entries (SM12)

System log: SAP Menu • Info • System Log (SM21)

Update program administration: no entry in the standard SAP menu (SM14)

Update records: SAP Menu • Tools • Administration • Monitor • Update (SM13)

10.6 Additional Documentation

Quicklinks

▶ SAP Service Marketplace, alias *installation*
▶ SAP Service Marketplace, alias *technology*

SAP Service Marketplace Notes

Table 10.2 provides an overview of important SAP Service Marketplace Notes related to the update system:

Contents	Note
V3 update, questions, and answers	396647
Update groups for asynchronous updates	109515

Table 10.2 SAP Notes for the Update System

10.7 Questions

1. Update was deactivated due to a tablespace overflow. Which actions are required after you extend the tablespace?

   a. No actions are required; the update service is reactivated automatically.

   b. You must activate the update service.

   c You must repost all the update records manually.

2. Which status does an update record have when it is waiting to be updated?

   a. Active

   b. Released

   c. init

   d. start

3. Which R/3 profile parameters can you use to control whether an R/3 user receives a notification when his or her update task is terminated?

   a. rdisp/vbmail

   b. A message is always sent to the user.

   c. rdisp/rbdelete

11 Output Configuration and Management

When they work with an SAP R/3 system, users create many output requests of varying degrees of importance. Examples include invoices, documents, master data reports, and logs. The integrated spool system, therefore, handles an essential, basic function of the SAP R/3 system. The system administrator and the operating-system administrator must configure and administer the spool landscape jointly, and then monitor it and ensure that it operates correctly.

Print requests created within an SAP R/3 system are converted into a device-specific data stream and output via the host spool system. To enable this functionality, the SAP R/3 system must be cognizant of the properties of the various devices. In addition to a definition of the output devices at the operating-system level, a specification of these devices is always required within the SAP R/3 system.

11.1 Basics

Numerous output requirements arise in dialog and background processing: a list must be printed, the results of a settlement run must be output, or a fax must be sent. From within the dialog application, users print the data they want with or without their specifying an output device in the SAP R/3 system (see Figure 11.1). Users can also specify a printer when they define a background request.

The dialog or background process then executes the output request. The active work process first creates a *spool request* from the user's entries. It then stores the raw data intended for output in the *TemSe* (short for *temporary sequential object*) in the database or at the file-system level (see Section 11.4). It stores the description of the request in the SAP R/3 database. If the spool request is then to be printed, the spool work process assigned to the selected output device takes over the formatting of the data into a printable form and directs it to the operating-system spooler that is responsible for the output device. In this manner, the spool work process creates an *output request*.

Spool and output request

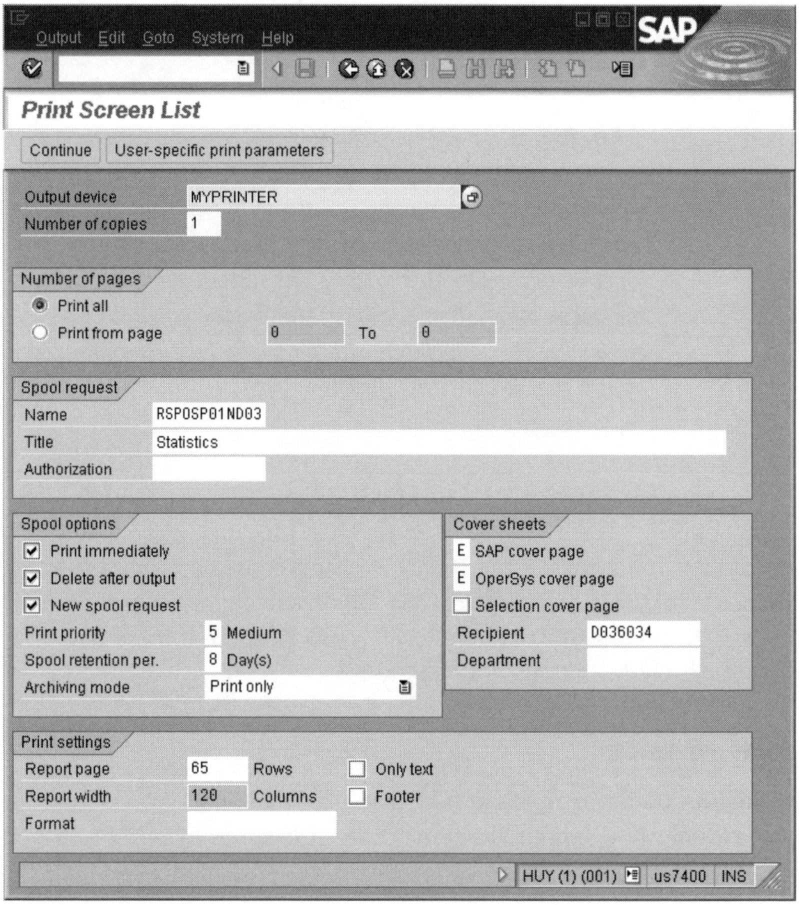

Figure 11.1 Output Request in Dialog (SAP R/3 Release 4.6D)

Every output occurs in two steps (see Figure 11.2):

1. Generation of a spool request—the request information (author, number of copies, and date of the request) is stored in the database; the device-dependent printing data is stored in the TemSe.

2. Generation and processing of an output request from a spool request— if the output device has been defined and is ready to receive the data.

This separation into spool and output requests enables you to see the output before it is actually printed. If necessary, you can also create several output requests with different parameters from one spool request, without having to recreate the spool request itself.

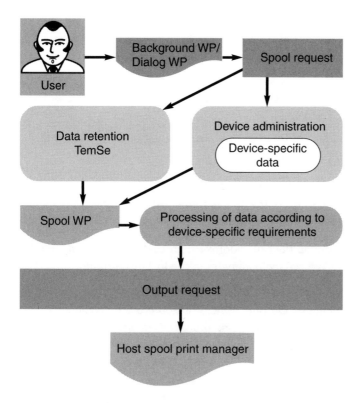

Figure 11.2 Dataflow During Printing

If the host spool's print manager cannot address an output device at the operating-system level, printing from the SAP R/3 system cannot succeed.

11.2 Configuring Spool Work Processes

Output management handles the formatting, coordination, execution, and monitoring of output requests. It uses spool work processes to do so.

In theory, you can use as many spool work processes as you want for each instance of an SAP R/3 system. Depending on the particular requirements of your spool environment, you must consider the following criteria for an optimal configuration:

► A sufficiently high number of spool work processes must be configured to process incoming requests in an acceptable time, even during periods of peak load.

- Because not all servers that run an instance of SAP R/3 are able to reach all the printers being used in the operating system, a failure of an instance can mean the inability to reach an output device.

- Spool work processes are responsible for formatting print requests, forwarding requests to the host spool system, and for additional administrative tasks:

  - Reorganization of the spool system (deleting obsolete requests)

  - Redirecting requests if a server fails

  - Searching for unprocessed requests

  In addition, the status of the queue of the host spool system is checked following the default setting at regular intervals.

You can define the number of spool work processes to be configured by setting the *rdisp/wp_no_spo* parameter in the instance profile.

Request management

The spool work processes of an instance form a unit; they cannot be addressed separately. Output devices are therefore assigned to an instance, not to a dedicated work process (see Section 11.4). Every instance with spool services manages its incoming output requests in its own queue of spool requests, as objects in main memory. If an overload develops and the spool request queue overflows, a dispatcher queue is used as a collector for incoming requests so that no spool requests are lost. Once the spool request queue can accommodate all the output requests, the spool work processes can once more transfer requests from the dispatcher queue into the spool request queue. The processing of spool requests continues only when the dispatcher queue is empty, or the spool request queue is full.

Sequential processing

The configured spool work processes can process requests within an instance sequentially, and sometimes in parallel. Therefore, there is no guarantee that output requests will be processed in the same order in which they were entered, when you have several spool work processes that are run within an instance. Some requests can be processed out of order. If required, you can activate an option when creating a device to force a sequential processing of requests in the order in which they have been created. In this case, a spool work process always processes all the requests for this device in the spool queue before it accepts other requests. Doing so, however, limits the parallelism between several spool work processes, therefore, you should use this option only when it is truly necessary (see Section 11.4).

11.3　Configuring the Spool Server

A *real spool server* is an SAP application server with at last one spool work process. Every output request on a spool server is processed using one of the spool work processes configured on the instance. Every output device is assigned a spool server that processes the requests for that device.

You can define a logical spool architecture for the following purposes:

▶ Load balancing between spool servers

▶ Availability of an alternative should a spool server fail

▶ Option of simply transporting a defined printer landscape

A *logical server* is a hierarchy of one or more logical servers and exactly one real spool server, which eventually processes the output requests. When you set up a logical spool architecture, you can use logical servers to represent a real spool server. When you define a logical server, you can assign an alternate spool server in addition to the spool server that the logical server is supposed to represent. If necessary, the alternative server can take over the tasks of an actual spool server that fails, or you can configure appropriate settings to use this alternative server for load distribution.

Logical server

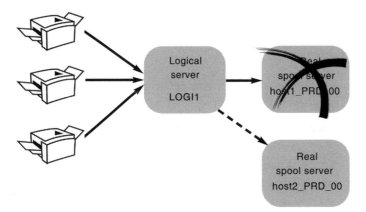

Figure 11.3　Failure Scenario with a Logical Spool Server

Figure 11.3 illustrates the realization of a failure scenario with the definition of a logical server and its alternative server. Logical server "LOGI1" is assigned to the printers; "LOGI1" represents "host1_PRD_00," the real spool server. Real spool server "host2_PRD_00" is the alternative server. If spool server "host1_PRD_00" fails, all print requests intended for the devices assigned to logical server "LOGI1" are processed by the alternative server, "host2_PRD_00."

If the definition of "LOGI1" also permits load distribution, the system will always determine the more appropriate spool server and divide the requests accordingly between "host1_PRD_00" and "host2_PRD_00" (see Figure 11.4).

If the printers were assigned directly to the spool server "host1_PRD_00," the outstanding output requests would not be processed if the spool server fails.

The load of a spool server is determined by the number of spool work processes of the instance, the number of requests to be processed, and the number of pages to be output.

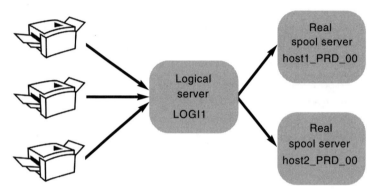

Figure 11.4 Load Balancing

The use of logical servers enables you to define the landscape of output devices more flexibly.

Classification   To simplify the organization of the output infrastructure, spool servers should be classified according to their intended use. *Classification* mirrors the definition of devices and supports you in optimal planning of the landscape. If you assign an output device to a classified spool server, the conformity of the classification will be checked. A warning is issued should discrepancies appear (see Figure 11.5).

The following variants are available for classifying real and logical spool servers:

- ▶ Production printing: documents and cover letters, for example
- ▶ Mass printing: lists of cost centers, for example
- ▶ Desktop printing: SAPoffice documents, for example
- ▶ Test server for test print
- ▶ Production printing and mass printing

- ▶ Production printing and desktop printing
- ▶ Mass printing and desktop printing
- ▶ Production printing, mass printing, and desktop printing
- ▶ Production printing and test printing
- ▶ Unclassified

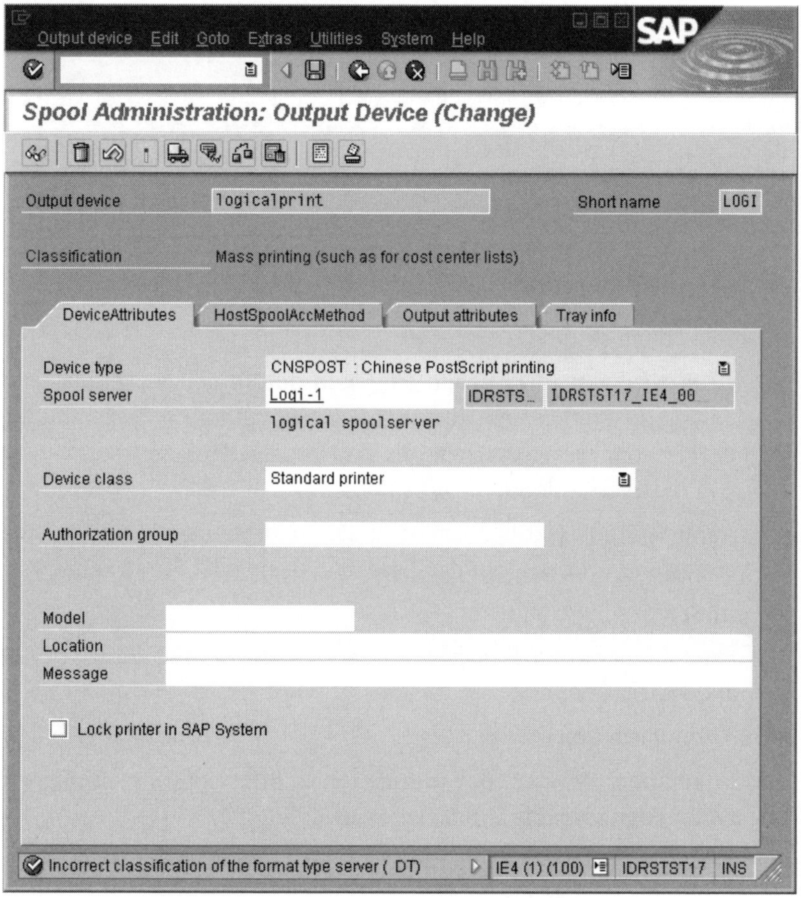

Figure 11.5 Warning About Dissonant Classifications

You can administer the SAP spool system with ▶**Spool administration.** You have three different layers for simple, extended, and full administration (see Figure 11.6).

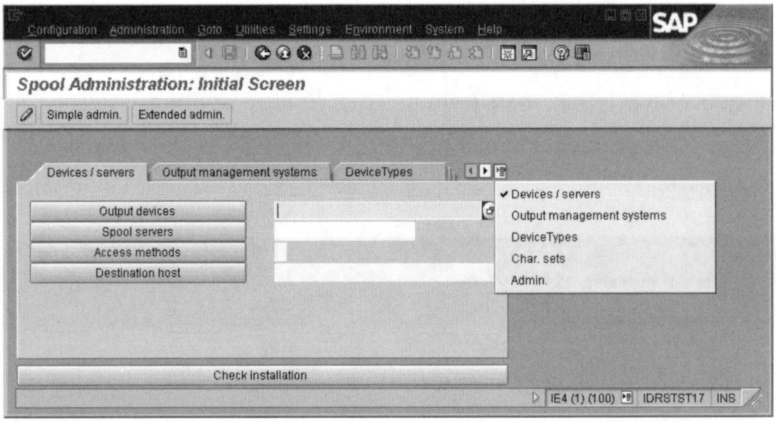

Figure 11.6 Spool Administration (Full Administration)

The following summarizes the differences between the layers:

▶ Simple administration

  ▶ Devices/servers (display and editing of output devices, display and editing of spool servers, display of access methods and distributing devices to these access methods, and display of the destination host and the distribution of devices to it).

  ▶ Administration (settings, deleting old spool requests, checking the consistency of the spool database, and overview of print requests).

▶ Extended Administration

  ▶ In addition: output management systems (display and editing of real and logical OMS).

▶ Full Administration

  ▶ In addition: device types (device types, print controls, formatting types, page formats, and texts for cover letters).

  ▶ In addition: character sets (character sets, SAP characters, and manufacturers of character sets).

Definition of spool servers

After the configuration of the spool work processes at the profile level, you define the logical and real spool servers.

1. From simple, extended, or full administration, within **Spool Administration**, select **Configuration · Spool servers** or the **Spool Servers** button. From the list of already-known spool servers, switch to change mode with **Spool Server · Create** to the screen for **Spool Administration · Server (Change) · Full Administration: Create Server** (see Figure 11.7).

2. Maintain the properties of the server. If you activate the option for **Logical Server**, the screen displays an additional entry field, **Mapping**, for this information after you press the **Enter** key.

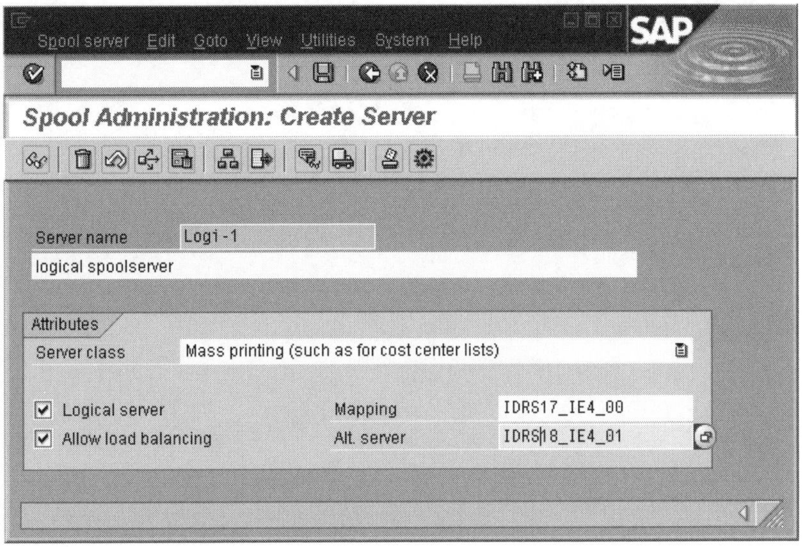

Figure 11.7 Spool Administration: Create Server

3. In the **Mapping** field, enter the real spool server that the logical spool server is to be mapped to.

4. In the **Alt. server** field, you can specify an alternative server as a replacement, should the actual or real spool server fail.

5. Activation of the load balancing option enables load-controlled selection of the spool server or the alternate server.

Due to the possibility of using both real and logical spool servers, as an alternative or a mapping of logical spool servers, a rather complex spool landscape can result in some situations. You can display various graphical illustrations of the landscape to avoid losing an overview of the situation. You can use ▶ **Spool Administration · Spool servers · View · Mapping relationship** to display the overview. The mapping relationships between logical or real spool servers are illustrated horizontally; relationships to alternatives are illustrated vertically (see Figure 11.8).

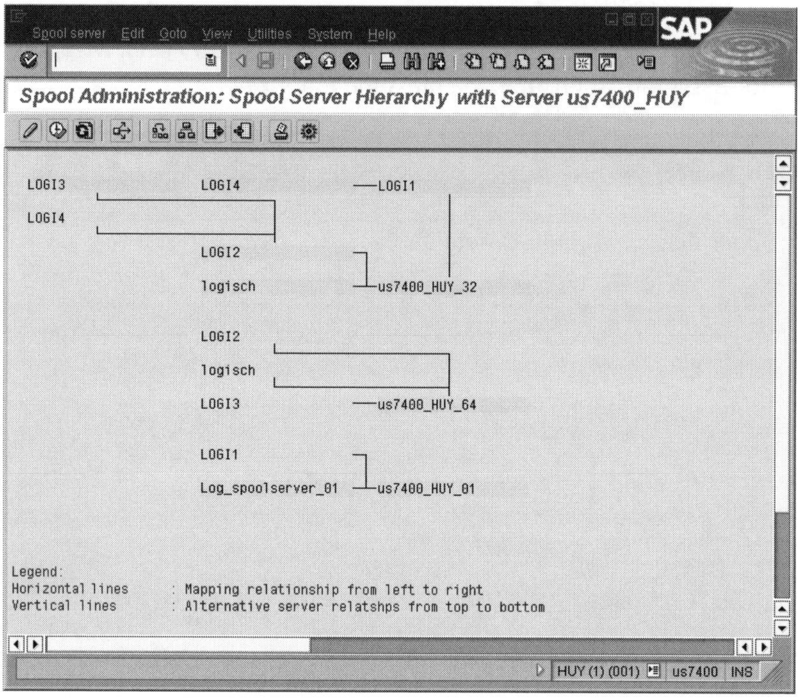

Figure 11.8 Structure of Logical Spool Servers

Use of logical spool architecture offers the following options:

▶ The assignment of printers to logical spool servers enables you to group output devices, such as local and network printers. Although the structure assigns the groups to different logical servers, they all reference the same real spool server. You can then adjust the mapping, if necessary, to assign the groups to different spool servers.

▶ If a real spool server cannot be addressed because it's down for maintenance, you can change the mapping definition to redirect all the devices assigned to it by a logical server to another spool server. You can withdraw the redirection in the same manner.

▶ Because the name of the logical servers does not depend on the instance name of the SAP R/3 system (unlike the case for real spool servers) and the name can be identical across all systems, you can define a standardized and transportable printer architecture with logical servers. You would simply have to adjust the mapping definitions to the physical properties of the transport targets.

However, if you plan a simple and manageable spool landscape with a configuration of only a limited number of possible spool servers, it is hardly possible to take full advantage of the properties of logical spool architecture.

It is not required to map a logical structure.

11.4 Configuring the Output Devices Landscape

Because the SAP spool system manages output devices itself, you have to also define printers, faxes, and archiving devices not only on the operating system level, but within the SAP R/3 spool as well. Configuration of a device within the SAP R/3 spool system means that the device is assigned an SAP device type and that a connection is defined. Doing so indirectly determines how the data of the spool request in the TemSe is to be formatted for a specific device so that the respective output request for the device can be generated.

To ensure optimal printer throughput, you should plan the printer landscape carefully, especially when you coordinate the various types of print assignments that occur, such as time-critical printing, mass printing, or quick printing from a frontend. Classification of the output devices according to the following technical criteria is the starting point for the configuration of the landscape:

Classification

▶ **Production printing**
Use a local access method (see below) to operate printers that handle time-critical output (such as shipping documents) in order to improve performance.

▶ **Mass printing**
Classify printers that are to print large documents as *mass printers*. To avoid creating a bottleneck when processing long lists, we recommend that you use a dedicated spool server for mass printing. You can choose any access method.

▶ **Desktop printing**
Desktop printers are found locally at the user's workplace. They handle relatively small print jobs and those that don't take a great deal of time.

▶ **Test printing**
You can create a separate class of printers for new printers, or when you modify the output configuration.

In the broadest terms, the *access method* that is assigned to an output device describes the method or the protocol used to transfer the data for the output request from the spool server to the host printer. The spool work process of the assigned spool server can transfer the data directly to

Access methods

a host spool system, an output management system, a network printer, or to the transfer program **SAPLPD**. **SAPLPD** operates between a spool work process and the Windows print manager. **SAPLPD** is started on the Windows computer.

Local access methods

If the spool server transfers the data directly to the host's spooler or print manager, we refer to this process as a *local access method*. Whether the data is output to a local or a remote printer is immaterial. Typically, the local method is the fastest and the most reliable method.

▶ **Access method L: Local printing using commands**
The spool service stores the data to be printed in a file on the host. It is printed from there with the appropriate host spool command, by default `lp` or `lpr` on UNIX systems, or `print` in a Windows NT environment. An operating-system command also determines the status of the output. If the device needs commands for printing and a query that deviate from the default, you can define *command sets*. To do so, select ▶ **Spool Administration · Output devices** to select your preferred printer and use **Edit · Command Set** to assign an existing command set to the printer. Alternatively, you can enter a letter in the command set ID field and then double-click to define a new command set; enter the print command that you want to use and the command to query the status. All devices created with access method L can then use the new command. The default settings for print commands and status query commands are stored in instance parameters *rspo/host_spool/print* and *rspo/host_spool/query*. For example, the print command for Windows NT systems is:

```
rspo/host_spool/print = print /d:&P &F
```

Where `/d` represents the printer connection option, `&P` serves as a macro for the port being used (LPT1, COM1, and so on), and `&F` defines the file to be printed.

▶ **Access method C: Direct operating system call**
Access method C differs from access method L: the data is transferred directly to the print manager of the system via the print API, without any intermediate storage in the file system of the host. This access method is only available for Windows NT systems.

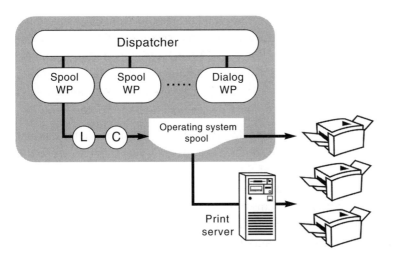

Figure 11.9 Local Access Method: Spool Server and Host Spool Running on the Same Computer

▶ **Access method E: External output management system**
If a device served by an output management system (OMS) is to be made available for printing from an SAP R/3 system, you can assign the local access method E to the device after installing the OMS and defining its properties in the SAP R/3 system. Much like the process with access method L, here the spool server stores the data in the file system: a local installation of the OMS fetches it from there.

▶ **Access method P: Device pool**
Access method P handles a logical grouping of printing devices (of the same type, if possible) into a device pool. Output requests can be specified as follows:

  ▶ In parallel, to all the output devices in the pool

  ▶ Switching between various devices in the pool

All the devices in a pool are created in the SAP R/3 system with their own access method; they can be addressed separately by their printer names.

▶ **Access method F: Frontend printing**
You can use access method F to direct output to printers that can be reached from your frontend PCs, but aren't necessarily defined in your SAP R/3 system. This access method is therefore not permitted for immediate printing from within background jobs. Processing of frontend printing is also handled by a spool work process. You can use instance parameter *rdisp/wp_no_spo_Fro_max* to limit the number of

available work processes for frontend printing to avoid blocking regular print requests. Immediate output with access method F (and on Windows frontends) is transferred to **SAPLPD**, which is started automatically if required. It sends the request to the default printer, __DEFAULT. If no default printer is defined, as is the case in UNIX systems, a host printer must be specified in the device definition for frontend printing.

Remote access methods Unlike the process described for local access methods, *remote access methods* transfer data from spool work processes over the network to the spooler or print manager of the printer host (see Figure 11.10). Consequently, these access methods can be quite sensitive to network problems. If connection problems arise, the active spool work process must wait—until a timeout notification in the worst case. Accordingly, you should use local access methods for production printing or large print jobs. If the receiving print server does not have sufficient memory for the incoming request, the spool service can transmit the data only as quickly as the printer can output it.

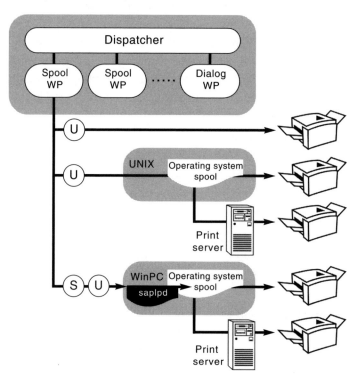

Figure 11.10 Remote Access Method: Spool Server and Host Spool Running on Different Computers

▶ **Access method S: Printing with the SAP protocol**
This access method is used for printers that function as workplace printers on a Windows system. The data is sent over the network in compressed form to the delivery program **SAPLPD**, which is started automatically if needed.

▶ **Access method U: Printing with the Berkeley protocol**
Access method U serves as the protocol for spool systems on UNIX systems. Unlike access method S, the data is not compressed here. You can use this access method together with the delivery program **SAPLPD** on Windows systems; however, in this case, access method S is more appropriate. Network printers with their own operating system spooler are also linked with access method U.

In addition to the local and remote access methods described above, you can use additional variations that do not apply to printers as output devices:

Exotic access methods

▶ **Access method X: Fax connection with SAPcomm**
Access method X connects fax devices over the SAPcomm interface. This interface is no longer supported as of Basis Release 6.10; you can use SAPconnect (see Chapter 13) instead.

▶ **Access method I: Connection with ArchiveLink**
This access method is used with SAP ArchiveLink (see Chapter 12). The spool system is used as an intermediate storage location for the documents to be archived. SAP ArchiveLink handles further processing.

Proceed as follows to define the output devices and assign them to selected spool servers:

Definition of the output device

1. From simple, extended, or full administration, within ▶ **Spool administration**, select menu entries **Configuration · Output devices** or the **Output devices** button. Switch to change mode. In the list of already-defined printers, choose **Output device · Create** to arrive at the screen for **Spool Administration: Create Output device** (see Figure 11.11).

2. First, give the new output device a name. The system will determine the short name if you leave the field blank.

3. Select the appropriate SAP device type for the printer and assign it to a logical or real spool server. In typical cases, an appropriate device type is already defined in the SAP R/3 system because device types represent a family of models rather than a specific model. If required, you can also download additional device types from the SAP service computers, *sapserv[x]* (see Chapter 3), use the compatibility mode of many

models, or enter device type *SWIN* (in Windows environments) to establish formatting by the print manager and the Windows driver instead of the SAP R/3 spool work process. You can also define your own device types, although doing so is no trivial task.

4. Device classes distinguish between the following:

   ▶ Standard printer

   ▶ Archiving program

   ▶ Fax

   ▶ Telex

   ▶ Device pool (as an individual device class as of Basis Release 6.10)

   ▶ Logical output device (as an individual device class as of Basis Release 6.10)

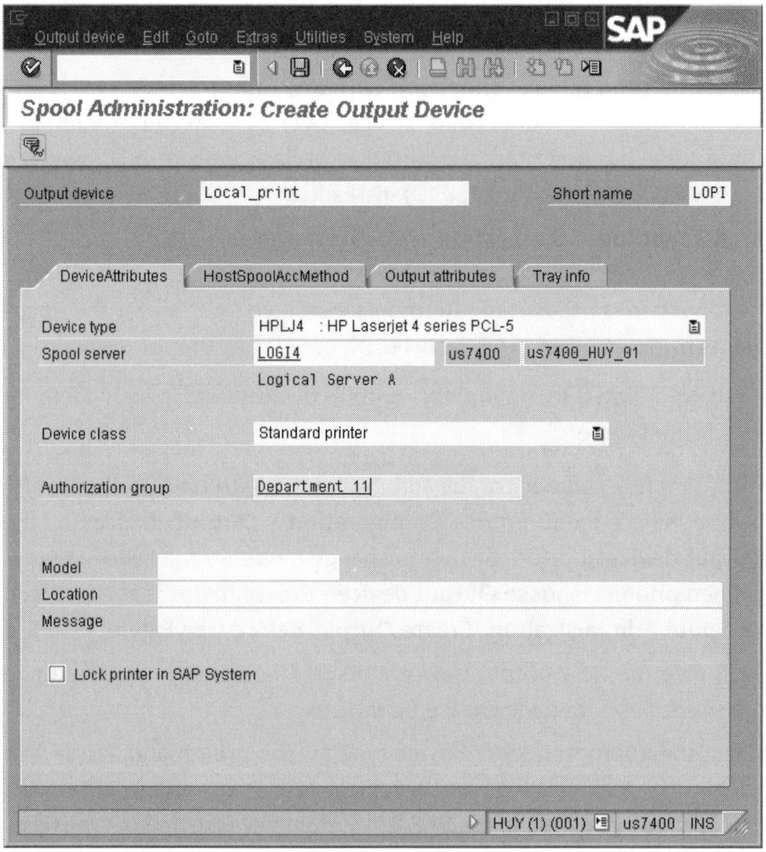

Figure 11.11 Creating a Local Printer — Device Attributes

5. Use the **Authorization group** field to summarize a group of output devices that can be entered in an authorization definition instead of entering an individual device.

6. Use the **Model**, **Location**, and **Message** fields for explanatory texts. The overview list of all defined output devices will display the content of the message field; it will display the location if the message field is empty. The printer can be blocked for maintenance work from the SAP R/3 side.

7. The **Host spool access method** field defines communications between the spool server and the host spool (see Figure 11.12).

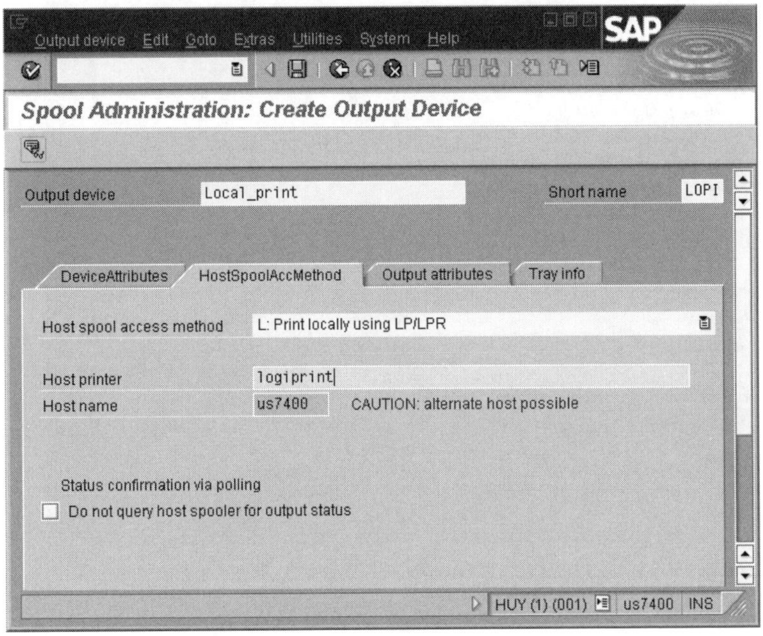

Figure 11.12 Creating a Local Printer — Host Spool Access

8. Use the **Host printer** field to enter the name of the device as it is known at the operating-system level, *host**printername* or _*DEFAULT*, for example. For local access, the computer on which the spool server and the host spool are running is displayed here. For remote access, you must explicitly specify the destination host that receives the data.

9. From within the SAP R/3 system, you can trace the status of a print request after it has been transferred to the host spool system. You do this via an explicit query of the active spool work process. To avoid doing so and thereby not affect performance, you can activate the flag

Do not query host spooler for output status. An explicit query cannot occur with front-end printing. Here, and with deactivation of the query on the host spool, a request in the spool system is considered to be completed when it is transferred to the host spool process.

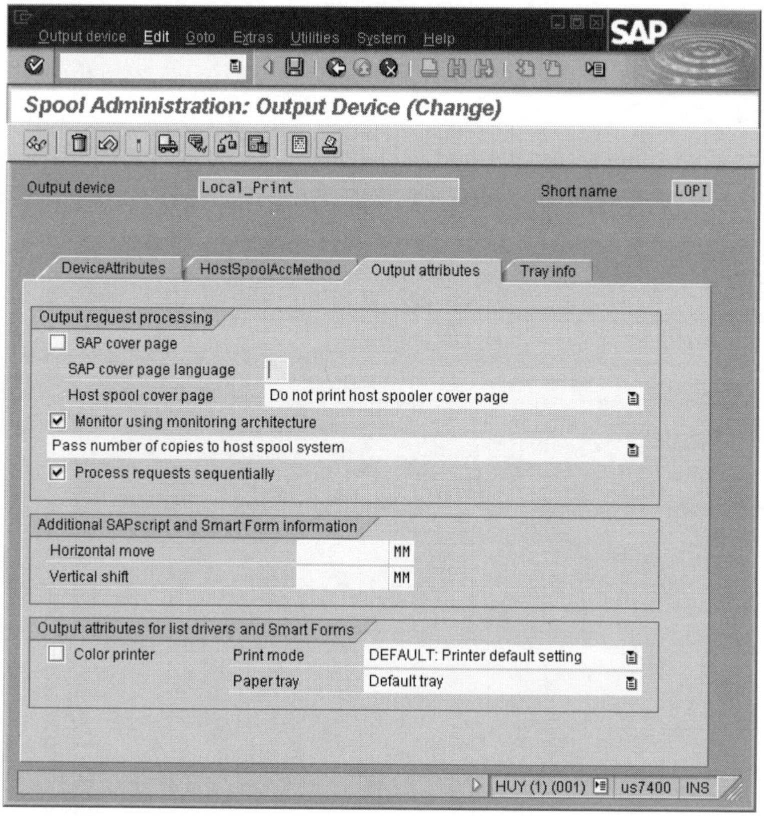

Figure 11.13 Creating a Local Printer — Output Attributes

10. You can select **Monitor using monitoring architecture** for important output devices (see Figure 11.13).

11. The **Process requests sequentially** option ensures that requests for this device are executed in the order in which they were requested. Here, the device setting has precedence over the load-balancing definition of the spool server.

12. You can use the **Tray info** tab to address the output device's paper trays directly.

13. You classify a device with **Edit · Classification**.

14. For each device, you can explicitly define where the data to be printed is placed into intermediate storage: according to system settings (see Section 11.5), in the database, or in the file system. Select **Edit · Data storage**.

If necessary, you can assign individual or all device definitions to a transport request and transport them to other SAP R/3 systems.

If you want to add greater flexibility to the spool architecture, you can define logical output devices with an assignment to physical output devices as of Basis Release 6.10. In Basis releases prior to Release 6.10, conversion of a physical device into a logical device and vice versa is possible.

The XOM-API interface enables you to connect external output management systems (OMS) to the spool system in SAP R/3. OMS are used primarily in complex IT landscapes. Connecting SAP systems to an OMS provides access to the advantages of an OMS from the SAP R/3 system, particularly the more exact and more direct information that an OMS provides for print requests.

Output management systems

To use an OMS with SAP R/3 and ensure that they work together correctly, SAP must certify the interface. The SAP R/3 system must know the properties of the OMS. Note the following distinction. The actual interface between the spool work process and the external output management system (real OMS, or ROMS) as a set of all the communication commands and property definitions differs from the special characteristics of the ROMS related to individual output devices (logical OMS, or LOMS). Depending on the device scenario, several LOMS can exist for one ROMS, but each LOMS is a subset of the ROMS.

ROMS and LOMS

If you want to use an external OMS, you must also define the ROMS (and the LOMS, if required) in the SAP R/3 system. This is part of extended or full spooler administration. The definition of an external OMS requires exact knowledge of the spool system on each server. You should always consult the documentation of the OMS to ensure that you comprehend the properties of the ROMS correctly. Figure 11.14 shows how to get started with ROMS administration: you can begin with ▶ **Spool Administration Configuration · Output Management Systems** or use the **Output Management System** tag.

Defining an external OMS

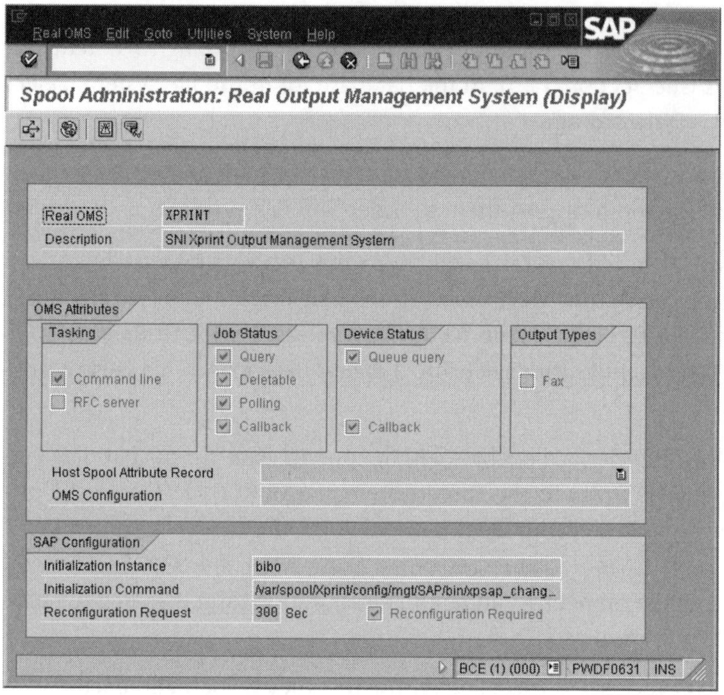

Figure 11.14 Defining an ROMS

11.5 Analysis and Error Correction

11.5.1 Usage Statistics

You have two ways of tracing the operations of the SAP R/3 spool:

1. ▶ Output control

2. ▶ Spool administration · Administration · Request overview for statistical purposes

▶ Output control can display all spool and output requests or selected requests according to various criteria, such as user, date, output device, or request number (see Figure 11.15). Authorizations determine if one user may view another user's requests and regulate the actions permitted for outstanding spool requests. Such actions might include outputting a spool request again, redirecting it to another printer, and viewing its contents.

Users can also navigate with **System · Own Spool Requests** to an overview of their own spool requests.

Table 11.1 lists the statuses of a spool or output request.

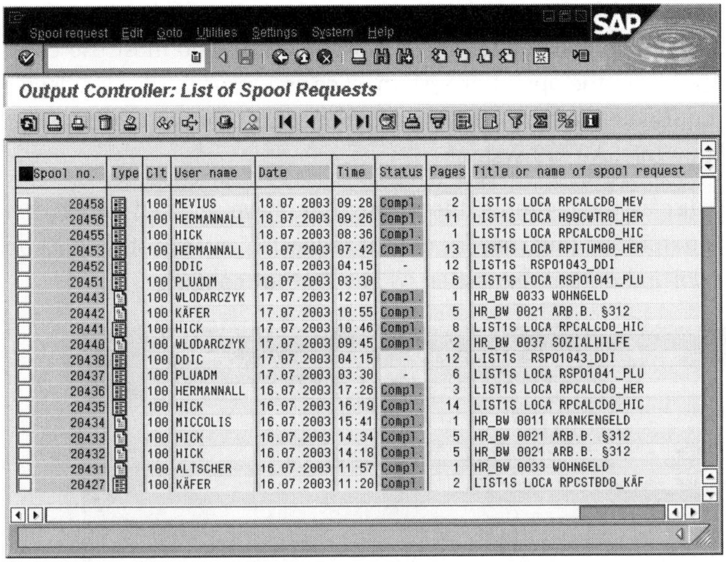

Figure 11.15 Overview of Spool Requests

ID	Status
–	No output request exists.
+	Spool request being generated.
waiting	Output request is not yet processed.
in proc	Request being formatted.
printing	Request being printed by host spooler.
compl.	Request was printed successfully, or transferred to the host spooler.
<F5>	The spool request generated several output requests, each with a different status.
Problem	The request was printed despite a minor problem, but the output probably contains errors.
Error	The spool request could not be printed.
Archive	The request was processed and is waiting for archiving.
Time	A specific time was scheduled to output the request.

Table 11.1 Status of Spool and Output Requests

Missing or corrupt output indicates errors with output control. In these cases, the administrator with the proper authorizations can examine the output log to view the indications it gives about the causes of errors.

For printing problems, you should always check the operability of the device at the operating-system level first. To do so, you must use commands specific to the operating system, such as `lpr` or `print`. If a device cannot be reached at the operating-system level, it cannot be addressed from within the SAP R/3 system.

You can display the contents, the settings you have selected for generation, the output log (but only for output requests), and statistical data on every spool and output request listed in ▶ **Output control.**

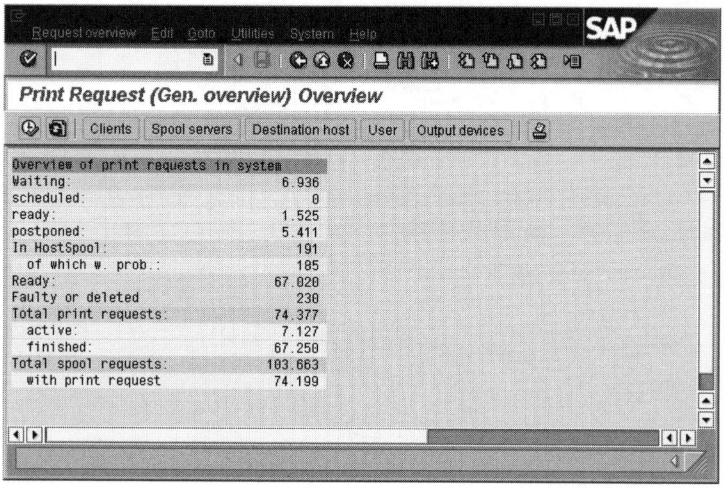

Figure 11.16 Overview of Print Requests

The overview of output requests in ▶ **Spool administration** includes configuration functions of the spool system and statistical information, such as the number of print requests per device, per destination host, or per user (see Figure 11.16).

This information is of interest when evaluating the overall landscape of output devices. The load should be divided as evenly as possible across SAP R/3 instances.

11.5.2 Administrative Tasks

Installation check

Immediately after first setting up a system, or after major changes in the spool landscape, we recommend that you examine the configuration with ▶ **Installation check.** This check does not include spool data (spool and output requests or TemSe).

TemSe

The data of a spool request is stored (unformatted) in temporary sequential objects (*TemSe*). These objects contain spool data and similar data, such as logs of background jobs, and temporary FI and HR data. Physically, the TemSe is either a table in the database or a file (outside the database) in the file system of the application server or in the global directory of the SAP R/3 system. The exact location depends on instance parameter *rspo/store_location*. The default value is "db," which means storage in the database. Setting the parameter to "G" stores the data in the *global* subdirectory of the SAP directory tree (see Chapter 1). If the data is stored in the database, it is subject to the administrative techniques and security measures of the RDBMS: transaction management, log management, and regular backups. However, it also means that the RDBMS must perform some work, so access to the TemSe in the file system is faster. If the TemSe is stored in the file system, there's less work for the RDBMS, but none of the advantages that the RDBMS offers are available. For example, the data must be backed up separately and it is not included automatically in a system copy.

You can find statistical information on the fill level and content of the TemSe with ▶ **TemSe Management** or ▶ **Spool administration · Environment · TemSe administration**. Select **TemSe database · Memory allocation** (or **TemSe data storage · Memory Occupation** as of Basis Release 6.10) to view a list of all the data stored in the TemSe by user and client, including the space for data storage that user and client each require. When the TemSe is stored in the SAP R/3 database, the size of the database segments limits the size of TemSe data storage. If the data is stored in files at the operating-system level, the maximum size of the file system is the maximum size of the TemSe. However, performance concerns suggest keeping the TemSe database as small as possible.

As an administrator, you must ensure that spool requests are removed from the TemSe once they are no longer required. First, you should schedule report **RSPO1041** regularly (see Chapter 9 and Figure 11.17). The essential selection criteria include the age of the spool request (depending upon its status) and whether it has become obsolete. A spool request is obsolete when its expiration date has been exceeded. The default setting for the expiration of a spool request is eight days (see Figure 11.1). You can also automate the deletion of obsolete spool requests with ▶ **Spool Administration · Settings · Spool system · Admin**.

Reorganization of the spool system

Report **RSPO1041** only deletes spool data from the TemSe. To delete other types of data, use the report for background processing logs, **RSBTCDEL** (see Chapter 9).

Follow the menu path ►**TemSe management · TemSe database · Reorganization** to use **RSTS0022**. This menu path does not start **RSPO1041** or its predecessor **RSPO0041**. Note that you must handle report **RSTS0022** with more caution than is necessary with the other two reports, because it deletes *all* obsolete entries from the TemSe, without considering dependencies to other tables.

Consistency check To respond to potential problems in optimal time, you should schedule consistency checks of the spool system and TemSe data storage on a regular basis.

► **Consistency check of the spool system**
Schedule report **RSPO1043** daily (see Chapter 9).

► **Consistency check of TemSe data storage**
You can schedule this report regularly via ►**TemSe management · TemSe database · Consistency check** or by specifying report RSTS0020.

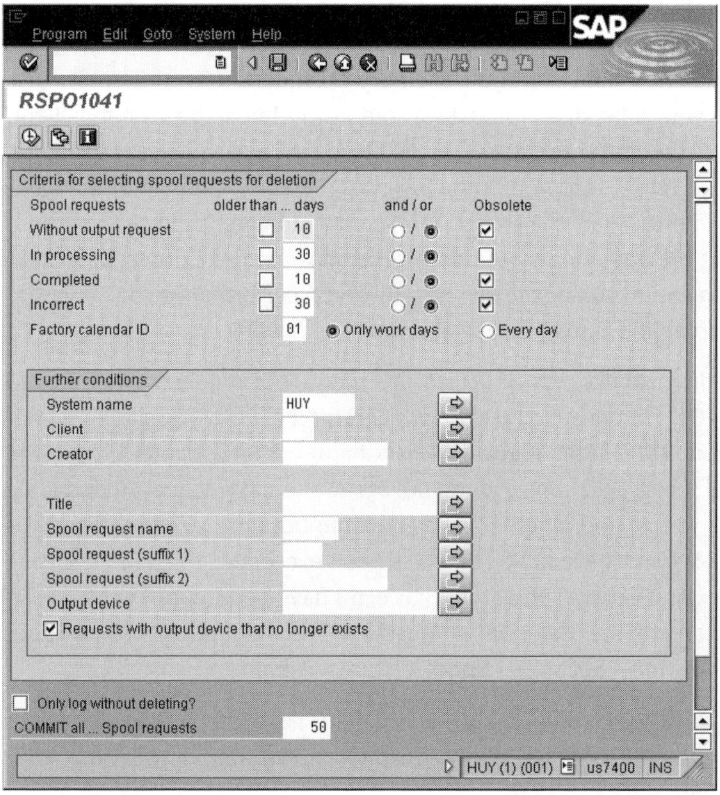

Figure 11.17 Selection Criteria for Deleting Spool Requests

11.6 Authorizations

As is true of all activities in SAP R/3, specific authorizations are used to control activity in this area. Note the distinctions between the following authorization areas:

- ▶ Device authorizations: S_SPO_DEV
- ▶ Selection authorizations: S_ADMI_FCD
- ▶ Authorizations for operations on spool requests: S_SPO_ACT
- ▶ Authorizations to manage the TemSe: T_TMS_ACT
- ▶ Authorizations to limit the maximum number of pages to be printed: S_SPO_PAGE

Device authorizations define the devices for which a user can generate requests. To do so, the real or generic name of one or several output devices, or of an authorization group, is assigned to the authorization object (see Figure 11.11). It's advantageous to use a naming convention when you define output devices. If the first character of a printer name reflects a group assignment, such as "D" for all desktop printers, it's easier to define authorizations for specific groups of output devices.

Device authorizations

Authorization object S_ADMI_FCD controls the output devices that a user can display. Basically, all users may call information about their own spool requests via **System · Own spool request**. The display of spool requests in general is handled with ▶**Output control**. Authorization values SP0R and SP01 permit cross-user selection in one's own client or cross-client and cross-user selection.

Selection authorizations

Authorization object S_SPO_ACT regulates the actions that users can execute for the spool requests visible to them. Table 11.2 lists and describes the available authorization values.

Action authorizations

Authorization value	Description
BASE	Authorization to display all spool requests
ATTR	Modification of request attributes
AUTH	Change authorization value
DISP	Display of the content of a spool request
DELE	Deletion of spool requests
PRNT	First-time output

Table 11.2 Authorization Values and Their Descriptions for Object S_SPO_ACT

Authorization value	Description
REDI	Redirection of a spool request to another device
REPR	Authorization to repeat the output of a request

Table 11.2 Authorization Values and Their Descriptions for Object S_SPO_ACT (cont.)

11.7 Tips

▶ **Maximum number of spool requests**

The maximum number of spool requests that you can manage in the system is 32,000. With some additional effort, you can increase the number to 99,000.

▶ **Priorities**

You can assign each spool request a priority between 0 and 9: 0 is the highest priority. The default setting is 5. The value is forwarded to the host spool; the SAP spool system itself does not evaluate it.

▶ **Limit the visibility of printers in clients**

If you want to make printers that are set up over the entire system accessible only from specific clients, use the menu path ▶ **Output control · Configuration · Output devices**. Select the device and then the **Extras · Display client field**.

▶ **Network load**

To minimize network load, you should use access method S (rather than U) whenever possible, because access method U transmits uncompressed data. Because a great deal of administrative overhead develops with a large number of small print requests, you should rather transmit a few large print requests instead.

▶ **Outputting non-Latin 1 codepages to standard printers**

If an output device is connected with access method S, the data is formatted in the server. The device itself receives a graphic that it can print—even if it doesn't support the selected character set.

11.8 Transactions and Menu Paths

Installation check: no entry in the standard SAP menu (SPIC)

Output control: SAP Menu • Tools • CCMS • Output controller (SP01)

Spool administration: SAP Menu • Tools • CCMS • Spool • Spool Administration (SPAD)

TemSe management: SAP Menu • Tools • CCMS • Spool • TemSe administration (SP12)

11.9   Additional Documentation

Quicklinks

▶ SAP Service Marketplace: alias *output*

SAP Service Marketplace Notes

The following table provides an overview of important SAP Notes on the spool system:

Content	Note
Collective note on spool and printing	504952
Flexible design of the spool service in SAP R/3	118057
R/3 does not print	26009
How many spool work processes per instance?	108799
Front-end printing: collective note	114426
Front-end printing with HTML GUI	351230
Setting up front-end printing as of SAP R/3 4.6B	351492
Printing under Windows Terminal Server	150533
Printing over e-mail	311037; 513352 only to SAP R/3 4.5B
LPD for remote printing	2863
Printing to a file	161516
Cannot reach SAPLPD	10758
Device type SAPWIN	21738
List of supported printers	8928
Printing Asian languages	423003, 83502
Printing to a file on tape	6753
Authorizations of spool requests	29666
Reorganization of TemSe and spool	48400

Table 11.3 SAP Notes on the Spool System

11.10 Questions

1. Which access methods are differentiated?

   a. Local access methods

   b. Remote access methods

   c. Special access methods

   d. Access methods with formatting

   e. Access methods without formatting

   f. Internal access methods

   g. External access methods

2. For which authorizations does SAP R/3 provide authorization objects?

   a. Device authorizations

   b. Display authorizations for spool requests

   c. TemSe management authorization

   d. Authorizations for operations with spool requests

3. Which of the following statements is correct?

   An output request:

   a. Is generated by a spool work process from a spool request

   b. Can be printed multiple times

   c. Can be output to any printer

4. Which access methods are recommended for mass printing?

   a. Local access method L for transfer to the host spool, using the appropriate command interface

   b. Local access method C for direct transfer to the print manager of the host spool, using the appropriate command interface

   c. Local access method F for front-end printing

   d. Remote access method S for desktop printing with SAPLPD

   e. Remote access method U, based on the Berkeley protocol

5. What is a dedicated spool server?

   A dedicated spool server is:

   a. A selected application server of the SAP R/3 system that is used for central spool administration

b. An application server assigned to an output device defined in the SAP R/3 system. The spool service of a dedicated spool server formats and manages the spool requests sent to this device.

c. The front-end computer (desktop) that currently processes front-end printing

d. An application server of the SAP R/3 system that is explicitly assigned to the user as a spool server

12   Data Archiving

This chapter focuses on archiving—the storage and warehousing of database data—and the tool used for archiving—the Archive Development Kit (ADK). Both the main features and the background of data maintenance are described.

Depending on the user's point of view, archiving in the R/3 environment can refer to the following three areas:

▶ In Oracle database administration, *archiving* often refers to saving offline redo logs.

▶ The storage of incoming and outgoing documents, such as scanned-in invoices and order confirmations, or list outputs created in the R/3 system on external storage systems (previously in paper form or on microfiche; now usually on optical media), is also a form of archiving.
Using SAP's *ArchiveLink* interface, in accordance with situation-specific Customizing, you can create a link between archived documents and application documents entered in the SAP system. Original documents stored externally are linked in this way with R/3 business objects and can be accessed from the business transaction or the application document. From R/3 Release 4.6C, the ArchiveLink interface is based on HTTP Content Server technology. Storage of archive files on external systems is carried out by the Content Management Service (CMS).

▶ The system administrator's most important task is the storing and warehousing of data from business processes that were completed in the R/3 system. Because this data will not be changed again, it is no longer needed in the database. Therefore, it can be compressed and stored in archive files on the operating-system level and, as required, transferred to external storage systems.

Usually, the R/3 database grows continuously over the years. After a certain duration, determined by legal regulations and company-specific requirements, a lot of data can become irrelevant and even obsolete, and therefore unnecessary for the daily work. The larger a table is, the more time, and therefore the more money, is spent navigating through it. Large volumes of data also occupy more resources, such as main memory, and hard drive or backup media. Administrative work also increases as the size of the database expands. For these reasons, it is necessary to clear the database of data that is no longer needed in the system—but which must

Reasons for archiving

nevertheless be maintained in a format that is easy to read and evaluate—and to store the data in archive files that can later be accessed.

Requirements For legal reasons, it is often necessary to keep data and have it available for reading if required. Frequently, it is also necessary to ensure that this data cannot be changed. In these cases, using archives on the basis of WORM (*Write Once, Read Multiple*), DVD, or CD-ROM is an option.

In data archiving, data held in the R/3 system database, which is no longer needed for immediate access, is identified, extracted, and initially stored in compressed form in files on the operating-system level. From there, it can, for example, be transferred to one of the external memory systems mentioned above. Once it has been successfully extracted and archived, the data is deleted from the database itself. Depending on the RDBMS used, the newly freed space on the database is available for use again after reorganization.

12.1 Archive Development Kit

Archiving objects *Archiving objects* are the basic component of data archiving in the R/3 solution. An *archiving object* is a logical unit of related physical data—such as financial accounting documents, bank master data, purchase requisitions, trip data, or payroll results—and all programs needed for archiving this data, such as formatting, read, write, and delete programs (see Figure 12.1). The data in archiving objects can only be archived all together, therefore, the logical consistency of the database is maintained. An example of an archiving object from the area of mySAP Financials is the object FI_DOCUMNT (financial accounting documents). It is made up of data from tables BKPF, BSEG, and BSET, among others, in addition to SAPscript texts and change documents and programs to:

▶ Archive (select data from the tables and subsequently write them to archive files)

▶ Delete (compare the data written in archive files with the data still in the database, and delete the latter if data is consistent)

▶ Reload (in cases of emergency)

▶ Take apart and rebuild the index (for direct access after archiving)

In addition, more than ten analysis programs are supplied. You can also use Transaction FB03 to read archived documents directly.

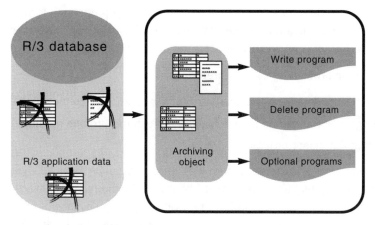

Figure 12.1 Structure of an Archiving Object

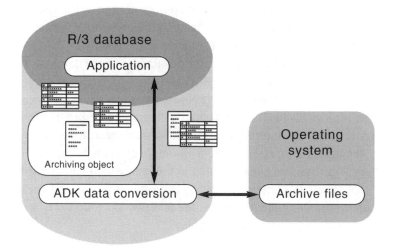

Figure 12.2 Archive Development Kit

If data archiving is to be carried out for data belonging to a business object that is not predefined in the SAP standard, you must first specify which physical data belongs to the object, in what form it should be archived, and what processing functions are needed. Archiving objects are already predefined for the SAP standard business processes. Additional archiving objects for added customer-specific processes can be created as required using ▶ Definition of archiving objects.

The *Archive Development Kit* (ADK) forms the interface between the SAP application, the database, and the archive files in which extracted application data is to be stored. The ADK provides the function modules used by the programs in the archiving objects, which enable you to write the

Archive Development Kit (ADK)

archive data to directories outside of the database in a predefined format (see Figure 12.2). In addition, the ADK manages the archiving files on the operating-system level and administers the archiving sessions.

The archiving procedure follows three steps:

1. Extraction of data from the database and the creation of archive file(s).
2. The optional transfer of archive file(s) to an external storage medium.
3. Starting the delete program.

Phase 1 The relevant user department determines what data can be archived. Typically, the R/3 system administrator is responsible for the technical execution of the archiving process and not for evaluating the relevance of business data. The volume of data to be archived is determined by the relevant archiving objects and the definition of an archiving period. All data created during this period is archived. A background process started by the system administrator copies the data defined in this way in a predefined format to a specified directory on the hard drive, outside of the database. The predefined data corresponds to the data being extracted from the database in a meta format, independent of the RDBMS and the hardware. Apart from the actual data, details of the code pages used, record structure, or number formats are also saved. These details are necessary to ensure that the archived data is correctly interpreted in any subsequent read access. Concurrently, the data is compressed up to a maximum of factor 5, except for cluster tables—as they are already stored in the database in compressed format. Since release R/3 Enterprise, data in Unicode can also be archived. You can access archiving files with Unicode and non-Unicode data. You don't have to convert existing archiving files.

Phase 2 Once the archive files have been created, you can transfer the data to an external archiving system (this is optional). There are different variants that can be automated to differing degrees, controlled by the corresponding Customizing.

If an external storage system is linked to the SAP system, after a successful write process, the files created can be transferred there using the ArchiveLink/CMS. Storage can occur automatically or manually, depending on the settings.

To ensure regulated communication between the SAP system and the archiving system, SAP AG offers a certification process for archive providers. You can find more information on certified providers on the Internet at *http://www.sap.com*, under the path *partners/software/directory*.

If a Hierarchical Storage Management System (HSM System) is used, you can simply store the archive files to a directory in the HSM system. ArchiveLink is not used. The migration of archive files to back-end levels (hard disk, jukebox, tapes) is controlled by access strategies and realized by the HSM. To the R/3 system, the HSM appears as an infinitely large file system in which archive files, independent of their actual location, are always addressed under the same file name.

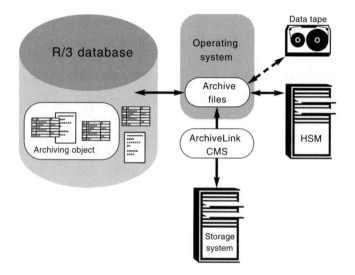

Figure 12.3 Transfer of Archive Files

Apart from connecting an archiving system, the manual storage of the archive files created in phase 1 to another medium, such as data tapes, is also conceivable.

Once the data has been successfully extracted and stored in files, it can be deleted from the database. In general archiving Customizing you can set whether the delete process is started automatically after archiving, after transfer to an external storage system, or manually at a later point in time. There are different methods of procedure for the delete process, in which security or performance aspects are the main focus, as appropriate. **Phase 3**

▶ Delete the data from the database once the archiving file has been completed.

As a security measure, the archived data is read from the archive file and compared with the original data in the database. Therefore, only data that has been stored correctly in the archiving file is deleted from the database.

► Delete the data from the database after transferring an archive file to the external storage system.

As a security measure, the archived data is read from the archive file in the storage system and compared with the original data in the database. Therefore, only data that has correctly been stored in the archiving file and transferred to the storage system is deleted from the database.

Since R/3 Enterprise, the delete program can be scheduled as a periodic background job, independently of the actual archiving.

12.2 Customizing

Data selection   The need for data archiving in an R/3 system results from the increased workload of managing the growing database, combined with the knowledge that some of the data is no longer actually needed. What application-specific data can be archived, however, cannot be determined by the R/3 system administrator, or by the database administrator. This task is the responsibility of the relevant department, which works in collaboration with the R/3 system administrator especially during archiving.

First, there is a changeover from a somewhat application-oriented point of view to an R/3 database approach. It has to be decided which archiving objects will best meet the current requirements. It is important to remember that there must be coherence in logical and temporal terms between archiving objects. Let us take the archiving object MM_MATNR (material master record from the mySAP Logistics component) as an example. An object of this type cannot be archived so long as objects referring to the material master record exist that have not yet been archived. Therefore, if there is still a purchasing document (object MM_EKKO) that refers to the material master record set for archiving and that has not yet been archived itself, the archiving session for MM_MATNR would be terminated with an error.

The interrelations between archiving objects can be illustrated with a network graphic (see Figure 12.4), which can be accessed via ►**Archive Administration Initial screen · Goto · Network graphic.** In a hierarchical display of archiving objects and how they interconnect, you can see in what order they should be archived to achieve optimal data storage. Each archiving object is symbolized by a node inside the network graphic. The colored rectangle in each node shows the archiving status of the object.

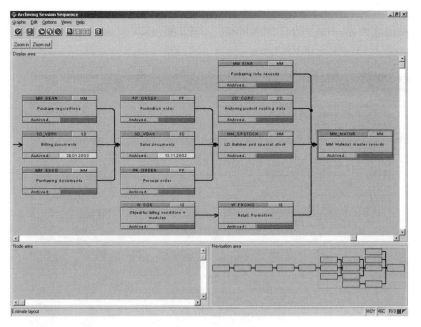

Figure 12.4 Network Graphic for Object MM_MATNR

The relationship between the archiving object and the relevant tables can be analyzed using the ADK subcomponent ▶**Tables and archiving objects.** All tables from which data is included in a selected archiving object are listed here; all archiving objects containing data from a selected table are also displayed. In principle, only consistent objects can be archived.

Figure 12.5 shows the existing archiving object for table RFBLG, which is FI_DOCUMNT—a financial accounting document. It also shows all the tables in object FI_DOCUMNT.

Once you have decided to archive an object, you must estimate the volume of data that you think will or should be archived. In order to assess whether you should archive, you will need information about the current physical and logical size of the archiving object's tables in the database. The *physical size* refers to the actual memory space occupied in the database. The *logical size* refers to the number of data records in the table. There are two methods for determining the size; the availability and development of each method will depend on the database used.

Data volume

Use **Online space** in ▶**Tables and Archiving Objects** (see Figure 12.5) to determine the current size of the selected table, if the database enables you to analyze its size. Depending on which RDBMS is used, either the actual physical table size or a database-specific statistical value will be displayed. It may take several minutes for the display, depending on the process and the size of the table.

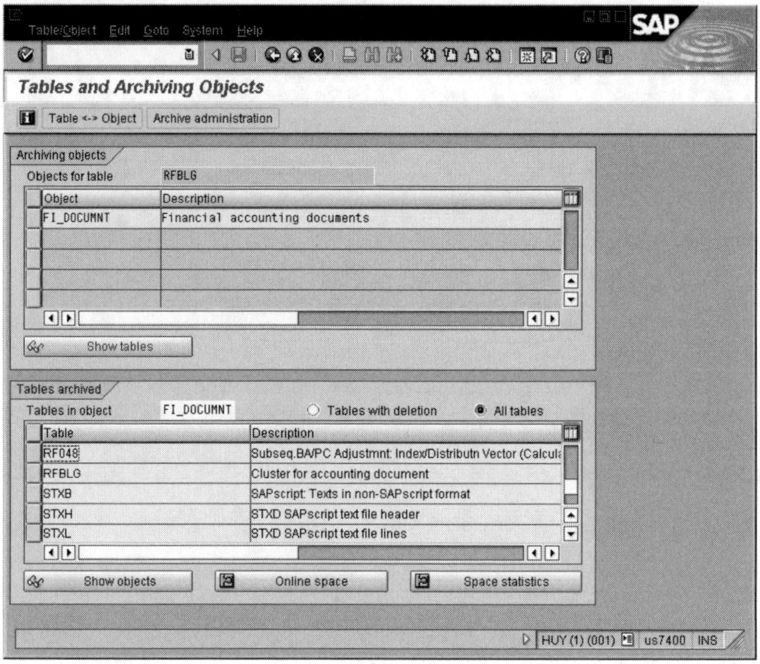

Figure 12.5 Tables and Archiving Objects

Use **Space statistics** if the statistical information used by the SQL optimizer will suffice to meet your needs. The data regarding size is based on statistical information; however, often, only the status or an estimate is provided, based on a random sample taken when the optimizer was last updated. If that was a long time ago, the size of the table may have changed greatly since then. Therefore, you must consider this possibility when estimating the size of the tables. All Relational Database Management Systems used with R/3 systems work with cost-based optimizers; access to table contents is achieved via statistical data, which describes how tables have grown and how data is distributed within a table. Depending on the database system used, the database administrator must ensure that this statistical data is updated at regular intervals.

Archive configuration

Once you have collected the necessary information regarding the archiving object and the associated tables, you need to determine the archive configuration. Figure 12.6 shows the initial screen of archive administration, in which no specific archiving object has been selected. By entering the name of an archiving object, the possible actions are automatically extended accordingly.

The **Database tables** option once again shows all the tables contained in the archiving object. By selecting **Information system**, you can go directly to the archiving information system. To start an archiving run for the selected objects, you must establish some settings. In particular, you must decide where the data to be archived will be written to. This is done in Customizing, which is divided into four areas:

▶ Cross-archiving object Customizing

▶ Archiving object-specific Customizing

▶ Basis Customizing

▶ Application-specific Customizing

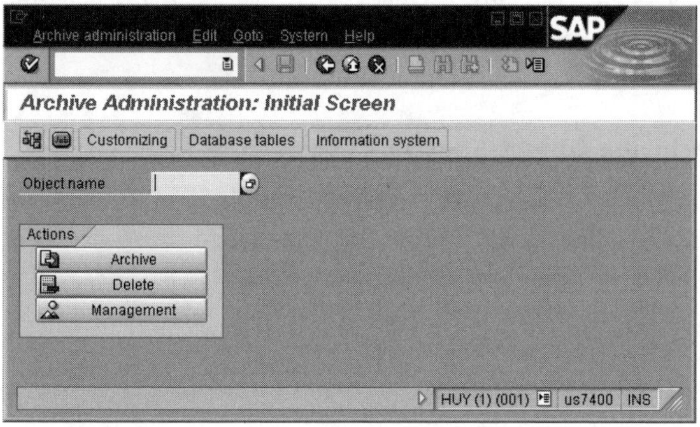

Figure 12.6 Archive Administration-Initial Screen

12.2.1 Cross-Archiving Object Customizing

The parameters set here are valid across all applications and for all archiving objects. They pertain to the following areas:

▶ CCMS data archiving monitor

▶ Access check when archive is selected

▶ Verification of archive files

The Computing Center Management System (CCMS) monitoring of data archiving (see Chapter 16) offers information on the archiving sessions, an alert mechanism in the event of an error, and monitoring of write and delete jobs. In cross-archiving object Customizing, you can activate or deactivate this monitoring.

If you need to access an archive file to read, delete, reload, or analyze it, here you can define whether you should do a search for the required archive file in the storage system or on an operating-system level. The access check on stored files when the archive is selected indicates that accessing the storage system may be time-consuming.

If the archive file is also given verification information when it is written, this information can be analyzed when the file is deleted, read, or reloaded. In this way, you can avoid deleting data from the database that is found to be erroneous in the storage system. If you are using an external storage system, note that using the setting **Verify when reading** can admittedly lead to high response time.

For R/3 Enterprise, you can specify a maximum duration, in hours, or you can specify the maximum size of the archive file for the archiving session (write phase). Once the first of these limits has been reached, the archiving run is stopped and at a set time, it can be restarted at the same point.

12.2.2 Archiving Object-Specific Customizing

Under this heading, you can make technical settings, such as the size of the archive file to be created, and set the sequence for the subsequent delete program.

In Figure 12.7 you can see the possible technical settings for the archiving object FI_DOCUMNT. To store archive files, it is necessary to define a path name for the storage directory and file names within this storage directory for the actual archive data. The logical file name ARCHIVE_DATA_FILE is the default setting for the operating system-independent name for the archive file to be created. The path is assigned the logical name ARCHIVE_ GLOBAL_PATH. A platform-specific name is generated at runtime. The size of an archive file is limited by hardware factors, like the maximum file system size and the capacity of back-end media (CD, DVD, WORM). If no size is specified, the size of the archive file is limited to 2 GB. If the archiving program observes that with the next object to be written the maximum size set for the archive file or the maximum number of data objects defined here will be exceeded, a new archive file is started. For both parameters—**Maximum size in MB** and **Maximum number of data objects**—object-specific default settings are suggested.

With **Server selection**, you can define the background server to be used for all archiving sessions, or for the current archiving object. If background work processes are configured on the database server, the archiving program is started on the database server, and the delete sessions are distributed over the other servers in the server group.

In the first phase of archiving, a copy of the data to be archived is merely created in files outside the database. The last phase of archiving, the deletion of the successfully copied data, can be configured to run automatically after phase 1. If the archive files are transferred to an external storage system, you can elect to delete the data in the database—either before or after storage. The archive files at the operating-system level or in the storage system are used for the data comparison before deleting.

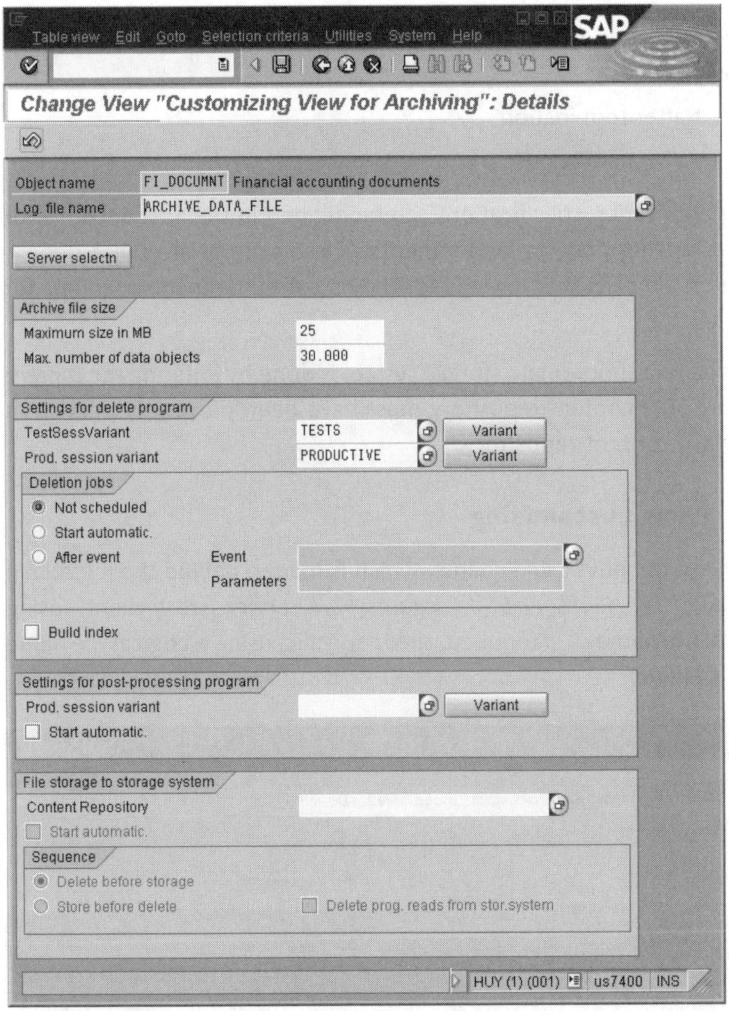

Figure 12.7 Archiving Object-Specific Customizing

Index   With the delete process, you can start building an index with a selection of archiving objects, using the option **Build index**. An index allows you to select individual data objects in the archive file, using the ADK. From the vantage point of the database, deleting, unlike copying data, is a change transaction and is recorded in the RDBMS log. Consequently, the database administrator must ensure that the areas that are necessary to sustain the before image in the event of a database transaction rollback—for example, the rollback segment in Oracle—are configured to an ample size. You can use the variants to make the following settings for test and productive sessions:

► Test session

► Detail log

► Restart after termination

► Delete own matchcodes

Further application specifications can be defined in the area **Settings for post-processing program** and **Variants**. These settings are client-dependent, which means that if required, they must be defined separately for each client.

Content repository   Allocation to a subordinate storage system is done by entering the *content repository*. The content repository must have been previously defined in ►**Maintain content repository**.

12.2.3 Basis Customizing

You can set the physical file name, which is hidden behind the logical file name *ARCHIVE_DATA_FILE* in Figure 12.7, either cross-client, using ►**Logical file name** or, if required, client-specific, using ►**Logical file name (client-specific)**.

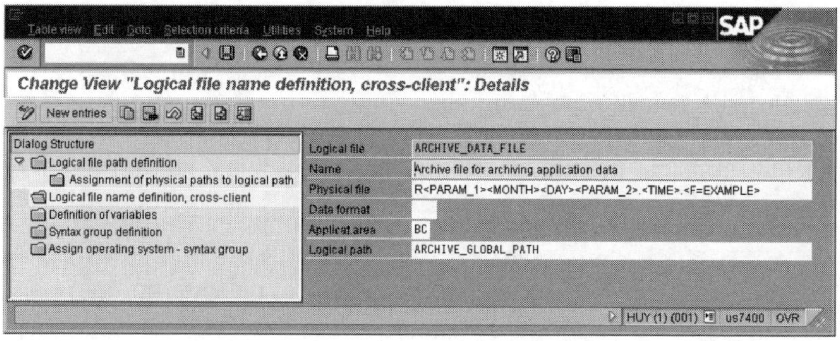

Figure 12.8 Assigning Logical File Names

Figure 12.8 shows the cross-client definition of file names and paths. A physical, cross-client file name can be assigned to each logical file name.

12.2.4 Application-Specific Customizing

Depending on the archiving object selected, client-specific application settings must also be made. The application manager is responsible for these settings. Only the technical settings are important to the system administrator.

When customizing an archiving session, you must therefore meet the following requirements:

Summary

▶ Prepare sufficient disk space, on locally accessible disks if possible, to optimize performance.

▶ Set the database parameters, especially for the delete sessions.

▶ Customize the archiving parameters for the application.

12.3 Control and Analysis

The *control and analysis* of an archiving session is carried out from ▶**Archive administration**. The specific flow and content of the actions depend on the archiving object selected, therefore, the scenarios presented here should only serve as examples. You can learn about object-specific procedures using ▶**Definition of archiving objects** (see Figure 12.9).

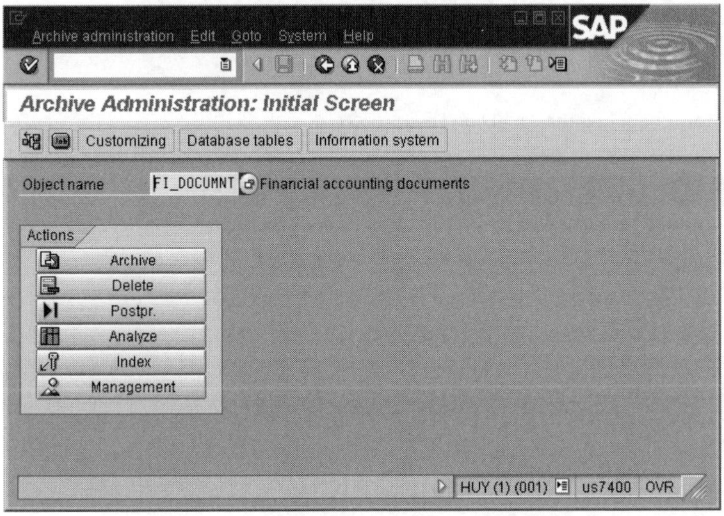

Figure 12.9 Object-Specific Initial Screen of Archive Administration

The following list is an overview of the programs available for the control and analysis of archiving sessions:

▶ **Pre-processing (optional)**

With a *pre-processing* program, you can prepare the data objects to be archived for the archiving session, for example, by setting a delete indicator. You must define the start date and the output parameter. Whether the pre-processing function is offered depends on the archiving object selected.

▶ **Archive**

Define the start date for the archiving session and possible spool parameters (see Figure 12.10).

In variant maintenance, you define the application-specific selection of data. Figure 12.11 shows the background job automatically scheduled from this data (▶**Job overview**).

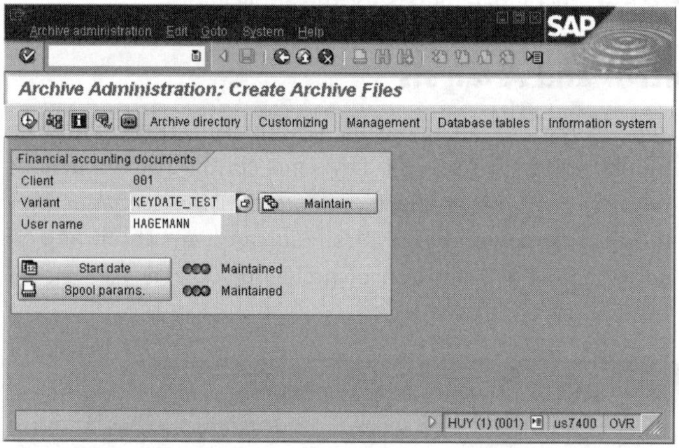

Figure 12.10 Scheduling the Archiving Session

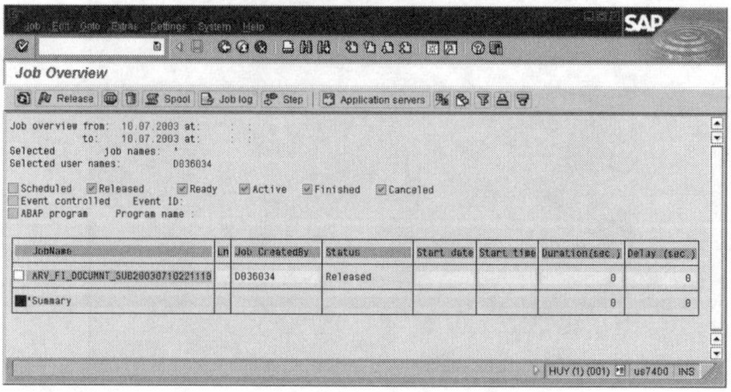

Figure 12.11 Job Overview for the Scheduled Archiving Session

▶ **Delete**

If data should not be automatically deleted immediately after archiving, here you can set the start date and spool parameters for deleting the archive marked in **Archive selection**.

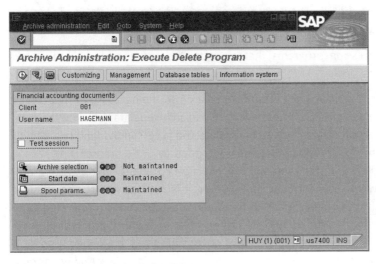

Figure 12.12 Scheduling the Delete Session

▶ **Post-processing (optional)**

Post-processing includes application-specific operations that may be required after an archiving session. This includes, for example, updating statistics. Whether the post-processing function is offered depends on the archiving object selected.

▶ **Analyze**

Depending on the archiving object selected, different application-specific analysis programs are available. For the archiving object FI_DOC-UMNT, for example, these programs are the compact document journal or a line item journal.

▶ **Index (optional)**

An index can be built subsequently for existing archive files. You can also remove an existing index. Depending on the application, the archive index is stored in application tables (for example, FI documents), or in the cross-application archive index table.

▶ **Storage system**

If the transfer of the archive files to an external storage system is not scheduled in archiving-object-specific Customizing, the files can be transferred here, provided that the content repository to be used has already been maintained in archiving-object-Customizing.

▶ **Management**
Archive administration offers an overview of all archiving sessions (see Figure 12.13). They are ordered according to their status. To display details of the sessions, double-click on the session in question.

All processing programs that are activated are executed in the background.

Reload When you *reload*, data is imported back into the database from archives. In general, you should not have to reload archived data back into the database, as you can analyze archived data and access individual data directly with the ADK. Reloading is only intended to undo an archiving session immediately, if, for example, the selection criteria for the archiving program were set incorrectly. If, however, it is necessary to reload archived data after a longer period of time, you must first ensure that all data to which the data to be reloaded refers, is available in the database. A re-import after a change of release is never supported. If a reload is possible for an archiving object, you can activate the action via ▶**Archive administration Initial screen · Goto · Reload**.

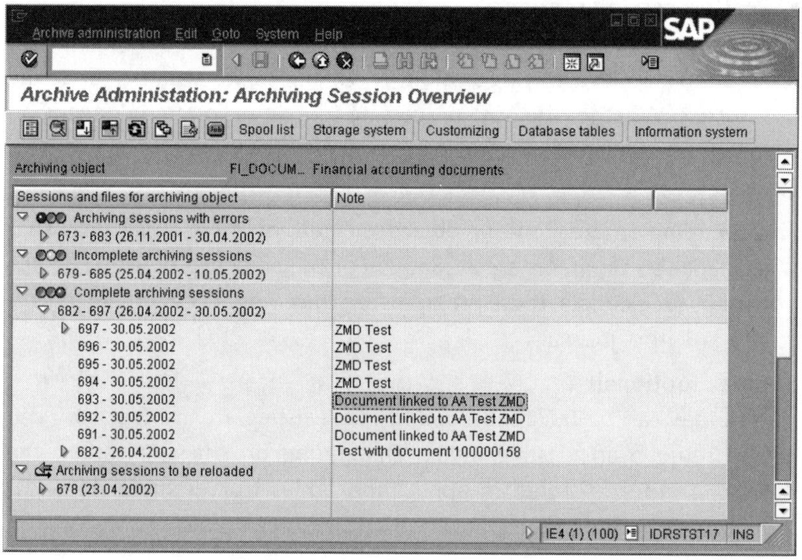

Figure 12.13 Managing Archiving Sessions

12.4 Tips

Statistics

From R/3 Enterprise, by selecting **Statistics** from ▶**Archive administration**, you can view extensive information on the completed archive sessions. In particular, you can see how much data has actually been removed from the database as a result of the archiving session (see Figure 12.14).

Restart after termination

If a termination of the archiving or the delete programs occurs, you can differentiate between the following scenarios:

▶ **Termination during the write process**
The archive files are created sequentially; only the file in process has the status *created*. Only when the write process has been successfully completed is the status set to *active* and the file written can be processed or analyzed using the ADK. If the write program terminates, only the file currently being recorded is affected. The sequence of the process is:

  ▶ Start the delete session for all correctly closed archive files.

  ▶ Mark the file from the interrupted job as invalid in Archive administration.

  ▶ Delete the erroneous archive file on the operating-system level.

  ▶ On completion of all delete sessions, restart the archiving session with the same selection criteria as used in the first session.

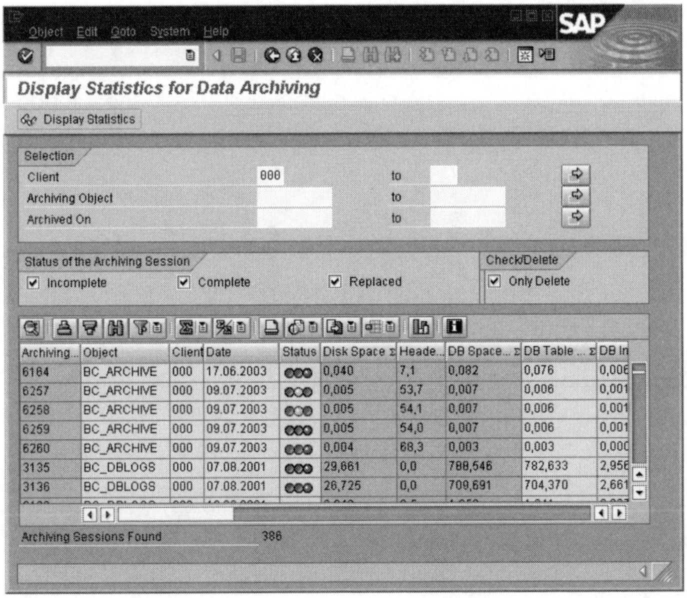

Figure 12.14 Archive Statistics

▶ **Termination during the delete session**

If a termination occurs during the delete session, you must analyze and correct the problem with the help of object-specific SAP notes. If the archive files can be accessed, once you have resolved the problem, you can restart the delete session at any time. If you cannot access the actual archive files, you can mitigate the problem via copying the readable part of the data to a new archive file. Until the termination, only the database data that was readable in the archive file has been deleted. Then, start the delete session again with the help of this file. Additional reports will be needed to repair the archive files. You can get them from SAP support.

Archive Information System

The *SAP Archive Information System* (SAP AS) is a tool for searching R/3 data archives, integrated in the archiving environment. The search and display of data is conducted on the basis of *archive information structures*, which the user can define and fill with data from the archive.

Document Relationship Browser

You can use the *Document Relationship Browser* to display linked objects and documents, grouped (cross-application) according to process or business transaction. Objects that are already archived are incorporated in the display.

For additional information on data archiving in SAP systems, see the book *Archiving Your SAP Data* by Helmut Stefani, which was also published by SAP PRESS.

12.5   Transactions and Menu Paths

Administration of stored documents: SAP Menu • Tools • Business Documents • Miscellaneous • Stored documents (OAAD)

Archive administration Initial screen: SAP Menu • Tools • Administration • Administration • Archiving • (SARA)

Archive Information System: SAP Menu • Logistics • Agency business • Environment • Archive • Display (SARI), or you can go there via the ▶ Archive administration Initial screen

ArchiveLink Monitor: SAP Menu • Tools • Business Documents • Environment • ArchiveLink Monitor (OAM1)

Definition of archiving objects: not accessible via the SAP standard menu (AOBJ)

Document Relationship Browser: not accessible via the SAP standard menu (ALO1)

Job overview: SAP Menu • Tools • CCMS • Jobs • Maintenance (SM37)

Logical file names: SAP Menu • Accounting • Enterprise Controlling • Executive InfoSystem • Environment • Configuration Menu • Basic Settings • File Names • File Names—Client-independent (FILE)

Logical file names (client-specific): SAP Menu • Accounting • Enterprise Controlling • Business Planning • Environment • Configuration Menu • Basic Settings • File names • Logical file names (SF01)

Maintain content repository: SAP Menu • Tools • Business Documents • Environment • KnowledgeProvider • KPro • Content Repositories (OACO)

Tables and archiving objects: SAP Menu • Tools • CCMS • DB Administration • Data archiving (DB15)

12.6 Additional Documentation

Quicklinks

▶ SAP Service Marketplace, alias *adk*

▶ SAP Service Marketplace, alias *archivelink*

▶ SAP Service Marketplace, alias *data-archiving*

▶ SAP Service Marketplace, alias *dma*

SAP Service Marketplace Notes

Table 12.1 provides an overview of some of the most important SAP Service Marketplace Notes related to archiving.

Content	Note
Archive file cannot be read	79186
Maintaining logical path and file names	35992
Compiling information sources for archiving R/3 data	71930
Archiving outside of SARA	133707

Table 12.1 SAP Notes on Archiving

12.7 Questions

1. What is an archiving object?

    a. CD-ROM or WORM

    b. The archive files created by the archiving session

    c. A logical unit of related data and the programs needed to archive it

2. What is meant by "data archiving"?

    a. Saving archive logs

    b. Archiving any documents such as incoming and outgoing print lists, invoices, or documents from application components

    c. Removing data from the database and storing it in an archive system or on other data media

3. Which R/3 tool is used for transferring data to an archive during data archiving?

    a. SAP ArchiveLink

    b. HSM (Hierarchical Storage Management)

    c. ADK (Archive Development Kit)

    d. RFC

4. Which of the following statements is true?

    a. The entire archiving process can be performed while the SAP R/3 system is running.

    b. The R/3 system must be stopped during the entire archiving process.

    c. The R/3 system cannot be used while the archive files are being generated.

13   Data Distribution and Transfer

Data distribution and transfer are important components of the Business Framework in SAP R/3. Given their strong dependence on business background, these areas of work are not the sole responsibility of the system administrator. Rather, the scenarios must be developed as a result of close collaboration between user departments, developers, and technicians. The primary tasks of the SAP R/3 system administrator are the technical realization, the monitoring of configured processes, and the coordinating of problem resolution.

Different ways to find a solution or resolve a problem can be used to establish cross-system business processes and thereby promote the open exchange of data. Depending on the requirements, you can choose between loose or tight interconnections and synchronous or asynchronous distributed processing of process steps.

The standard scenario for a distributed application is *Application Link Enabling* (ALE). For technical realization, data structures and communication methods must be defined. As an enhancement to traditional procedures, new interfaces are also implemented using BAPI technology.

A *Business Application Programming Interface* (BAPI) allows internal and, in   **BAPI**
particular, external access to data and business processes defined in the SAP R/3 system. The underlying basic components of this object-oriented approach are the *business object types*, which represent objects from the real world in the software. Predefined examples include a chart of accounts, a sales order, or a purchasing organization. These object types can be accessed only using standardized, platform-independent methods that are also release-independent and open—BAPIs.

All business object types and the corresponding BAPIs are stored in the *Business Object Repository* (BOR) of an SAP R/3 system. Using the ▶ **BAPI Explorer**, you can get an overview of the defined object types, their methods, and their characteristics and make changes. Objects are specific instances of an object type.

In addition to object-specific methods, some BAPIs are available for all object types, such as the following:

`<Object>.Display`	For displaying an object
`<Object>.Delete`	For deleting an object
`<Object>.GetDetail`	For displaying details of an object

Technically, methods are realized as function modules. For instance, you can use BAPIs to link external programs, and ALE distribution to link business processes beyond system boundaries.

13.1 RFC Destinations

Many connections/links between two SAP R/3 systems or an SAP R/3 system and an external system are based on an SAP interface protocol: the *Remote Function Call* (RFC). Using this protocol, applications can call ABAP functions within the SAP R/3 system, and SAP R/3 systems can call external applications (see Chapter 1). The RFC functions are made available to the external programs via dynamic libraries.

An RFC calls a predefined function module in a partner system; the calling program is the RFC client; and the "answering" system called is the RFC server (see Figure 13.1).

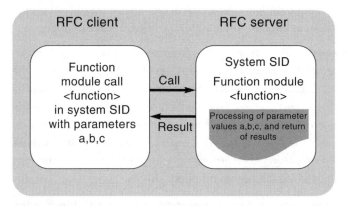

Figure 13.1 Distribution of Tasks Over Different Systems

In the SAP environment, RFC offers a CPI-C interface implemented by SAP.

RFC destinations To integrate an SAP R/3 system into an existing system landscape completely, the RFC connections provided must be identified as *RFC destinations*. Part of this definition is automatically done when the SAP R/3 system is being configured in the landscape. For example, this includes the

RFC links required for the Transport Management System (TMS, see Chapter 5), which are created when an SAP R/3 system is integrated into the transport domain. During the installation of an SAP R/3 system, RFC destinations are also generated for all pertinent application servers; however, it is often necessary to create additional destinations. Everyday examples from the system administration area are RFC links for the following:

▶ Remote client copies (see Chapter 7)

▶ Setting up Central User Administration (CUA, see Chapter 8)

▶ Monitoring remote SAP R/3 systems via the Alert Monitor
  (see Chapter 16)

To define an RFC destination, all the data necessary for communication with the partner system is compiled under a logical name. The type of the communication is established. A defined RFC link can be used by every program; it is assigned neither to unique functions nor to a specific client.

RFC connections are always unidirectional.

Each of the communication pairs mentioned above is realized with a specific connection type. The parameters needed to create a new RFC destination depend on the connection type.

Type	Description	Data required
I	Connection to application server with the same database	none
3	Connection to an SAP R/3 system	Target machine and system number
2	Connection to an SAP R/2 system	none
T	Start an external program via TCP/IP	Depends on activation type Start: Host name and program path Registration: program ID
L	Reference entry (refers to another destination)	RFC destination for which an alias is created
S:	Start an external program using SNA or APPC	none
X	RFC via special ABAP/4 driver subroutines	ABAP/4 driver
M	CMC connection	none

Table 13.1 Connection Types for RFC Destinations

You can create a new RFC destination using ▶RFC Administration.

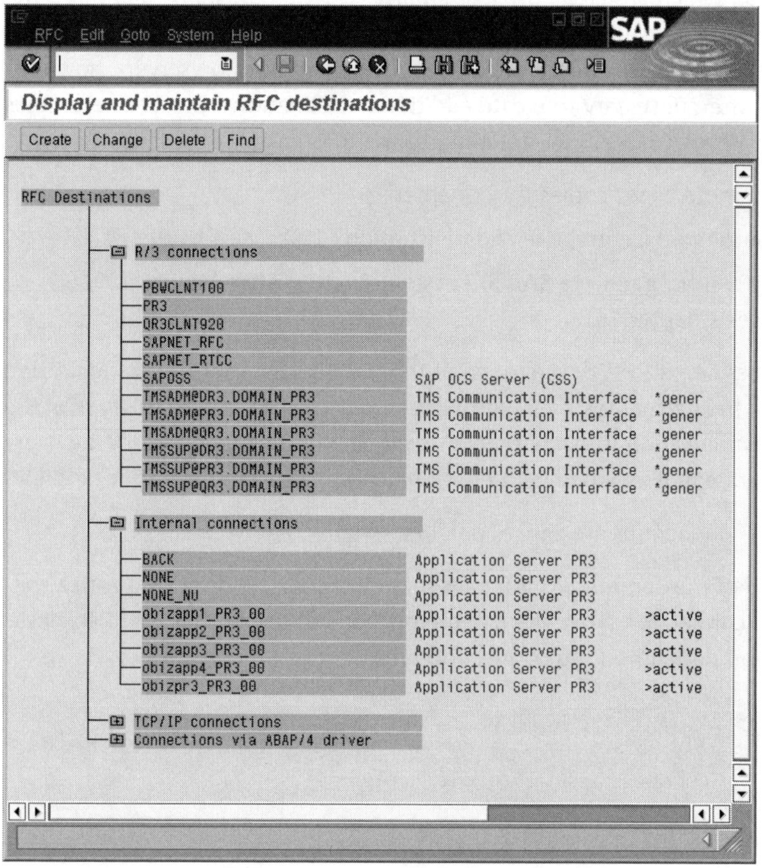

Figure 13.2 Initial Screen of RFC Destination Maintenance

As an example, let's look at the definition of a new connection between two SAP R/3 systems, "KLU" and "ELU."

1. First, using ▶RFC Administration, a list of all known RFC destinations is displayed and sorted according to connection type (see Figure 13.2).

2. Click on **Create** to open the entry field for a new RFC connection.

3. Enter the logical name of the connection in the **RFC destination** field. You should note that once it has been created, this name cannot be modified.

4. Depending on the connection type selected, the screen will automatically be extended to include the necessary input fields. Figure 13.3 shows the template for recording the data for an RFC connection to another SAP R/3 system (connection type 3).

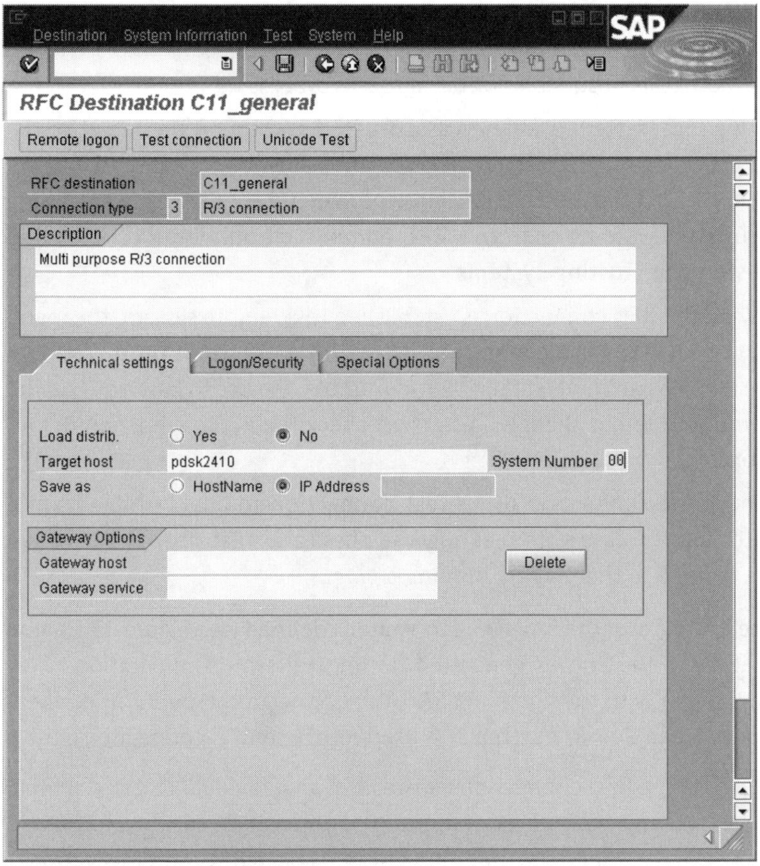

Figure 13.3 Creating a New RFC Destination

5. The effect of activating the trace option is that all program flows using this RFC connection are logged in detail in files at the operating-system level (see Section 15.5). The logs can be analyzed from both the sending and receiving system using report program **RSRFCTRC** or using ▶**RFC Administration · RFC · Display trace**.

6. Enter the **Target host** as host name or IP address and the **System Number** of the instance on this machine.

7. Typically, for an RFC connection, you must enter a logon language, target client, a user on the target system, and the user's password. Different variants are possible here:

  ▶ Enter all data in the **Logon** section explicitly. To avoid abuse, a user of type *communication* should be used here.

  ▶ Use the current user. For this approach, the current user must have the same user data in the target client.

▶ If you enter no data in the Logon section, the logon data is requested in a pop-up when the RFC connection is used. This method is unsuitable for background processing.

If the local system is defined as a **Trusted system** on the target of the RFC destination, you don't need to enter any identification data. You can maintain trust relationships between SAP R/3 systems using ▶**Trusted systems** or from ▶**RFC administration** with **RFC · Trusted systems** or **Trusting systems**.

When the RFC connection is established to a remote system, the logon data provided for a connection is used to authorize it on the remote system. Assignment is static. If, for example, the user's password on the remote system is changed, you must check the RFC connection definitions.

8. Check the connection using **Test connection** to avoid problems at a later stage. Please note that only the physical availability of a server can be verified in this way by running a *ping*.

In the overview of the SAP R/3 connections defined (see Figure 13.2), you can also see the entries generated during the TMS configuration. They always begin with the code "TMSADM." Connection type 3, for connections between SAP R/3 systems, is used for these RFC connections.

Server groups When defining RFC connections, instead of an individual target machine, you can also use the names of a group of application servers. You must, however, have generated this previously using ▶**RFC administration · RFC · RFC groups** or ▶**Maintenance of Server Groups**. The advantage of this method is that when a connection is built from the group of application servers, the machine with the lowest load is selected, so there is an automatic distribution of load. This mechanism is used, for example, when parallelizing a copy of a large client (see Chapter 7). You can control the load distribution in server groups by adjusting the predefined resource parameters. One important parameter is the number of work processes that must be kept free.

TCP/IP connections Defining other specifications for RFC connections is done in the same way. The data to be entered differs depending on the type. For an RFC destination to execute external programs (connection type T), it is first necessary to differentiate between the target servers. You can choose among the application server, front-end work station, and an explicit host that isn't used by the current SAP R/3 system. If the external program should run on an explicit host, you must enter the name or the IP address of the server when defining the RFC destination. For front-end work stations and application servers of the actual SAP R/3 system, the computer names are already known during system logon. All servers must be able to be reached over the network without a new request for user name and password. The external program to be started is assigned to the RFC connection to be defined.

Instead of explicitly starting the external RFC server program, you can also register with an SAP gateway. The registered program then waits for queries from different SAP R/3 systems targeted at this gateway by entering the registration.

It is also advisable to use entries of connection type L. These are called *logical entries* and refer to another RFC destination. To use this mechanism, an RFC destination is first defined in a way that ultimately determines only the physical target-the selected server. Then, connections of type L are created that reference this entry. The RFC connections of type L take on the target server and connection type of the RFC destination to which they refer. If necessary, a logical RFC connection can be extended to include the logon data. Therefore, you can define RFC destinations independently of one another. If, for example, an SAP R/3 system is relocated from one server to another, you only need to adjust the RFC destinations that are used as a point of reference for defining type L connections.

Logical connections

We can differentiate between several types of RFC communication, for which you can set specific, additional configuration parameters:

Types of RFC communication

▶ **Synchronous RFC**
With the synchronous RFC, the calling program waits until the requested processing step on the remote system has ended, and then continues to work locally.

▶ **Asynchronous RFC**
With the asynchronous RFC, the calling program gives the request to the remote system and immediately continues to work locally. The requested processing step is executed on the remote system in isolation. If the remote system cannot be reached at the time of the call, the asynchronous calls of the RFC client are lost.

▶ **Transactional RFC**
The transactional RFC also works asynchronously, and by allocating a *transaction ID*, it guarantees that if a request is sent several times because of network problems, it is processed only once. In contrast to asynchronous RFC, with transactional RFC, the remote system does not have to be available at the moment the RFC client program starts the call. The data is held in the source system until the target system is

available. The report program **RSARFCSE** is called in the background at regular intervals and tries to place the unsuccessful requests, identified by their transaction ID, again.

▶ **queued RFC**
The queued RFC is an extension of the transactional RFC. With this variant, requests are assembled in a queue and processed in a transactional RFC only if it is certain that all the preceding calls have been dealt with appropriately. This procedure guarantees that requests are processed in the sequence in which they are received.

You can adapt the characteristics of the defined RFC destinations from the details displayed in the connection definition using **Destination · TRFC options** or **ARFC options**.

A communications partner cannot always reach all application servers or the message server of the RFC client system. For linked external programs, it is often necessary to specify one particular application server when describing the connection. If more than just this one application server should communicate with the external program, you can define the application server known by the external program as a gateway for this RFC connection so that all communication between the RFC client and the external system takes place via this application server.

Monitoring the RFC calls
Transactional RFC is monitored using the ▶**tRFC Monitor**, the queued RFCs using ▶**qRFC Monitor Inbound**, ▶**qRFC Monitor Outbound** and the ▶**qRFC Monitor**.

13.2   Application Link Enabling

Frequently, the business processes in an enterprise cannot be represented by a single central system. Very often, the reason is the divided flow of information between relatively independent branches of a company. Another reason may be technical bottlenecks that result from the size of a single, central system. Security aspects can also play a role. In addition, it might also be necessary to communicate with external program systems (a warehouse management system, for example). If, for one or more reasons, you cannot set a central system configuration, but a constant data reconciliation or message flow is required, you might try linking the system using Application Link Enabling (ALE). Given the complexity of ALE, from both a technical and business viewpoint, the following sections only address the basics of this technology. The most important points of ALE processing are described for the future system administrator.

13.2.1 Technical basics

Application Link Enabling (ALE) is a method and technology in SAP R/3 to support the business-controlled exchange of messages between loosely coupled systems. ALE contains the business scenarios and function modules that allow for data to be transferred and reconciled from or to an SAP R/3 system, without customer-specific developments.

The starting point for designing an ALE scenario is to analyze the business requirements from an application point of view and to transfer the scenario into a suitable technical procedure. Typical questions include:

Questions on design

- ▶ What processes must be represented across systems?
- ▶ What objects are involved in these processes?
- ▶ What data must be considered in different systems?
- ▶ In what format must the data be available, and what information must be transferred for formatting?
- ▶ What transfer technique is suitable to meet the requirements? The criteria here are frequency, need for return information, promptness, and so on.
- ▶ What form will data flow take between the systems involved?

ALE technology is integrated into both the applications and in Customizing. It provides a range of distribution services and information can be sent to the sender over the course of processing. Often, not only is data transferred, but follow-up actions can also be triggered in the target system.

From the viewpoint of SAP R/3, the data to be exchanged can include:

Exchanged data

- ▶ **Transaction data**
  Data from applications and transaction data
- ▶ **Master data**
  Customer or material master data, for example
- ▶ **Customizing data**
  Data that ensures a uniform, global ALE view

Data can be exchanged between SAP R/3 systems, between SAP R/3 and SAP R/2 systems, and between SAP R/3 and external systems. The main focus of the scenarios realized is the distribution between SAP R/3 systems. The distribution of data between SAP R/3 systems is independent of the system release to the greatest possible extent, which means that it is unnecessary to upgrade all SAP R/3 systems in the system infrastructure at the same time. Systems are linked via a loose synchronous (reading) or asynchronous (changing) communication. The technical characteristics of the coupling are set in the *port definition*. The port types correspond to the communication methods selected. Currently, file interfaces, RFC, CPI-C, and Internet interfaces are used.

Message type The semantics of a message to be transferred to a remote system are described by the *message type*. Material master data stored in a central master system and which, for example, should be automatically distributed to downstream systems if changed, is one example of a message type.

IDoc types The actual information can be sent via an *Intermediate Document* (IDoc). An *IDoc type*, containing a description of the structure of the data, is assigned to a message type as a container for data to be exchanged. A specific IDoc type is available for all application areas that must prepare data for exchange. The data to be sent—including tables and fields—must be defined on the basis of IDoc types. When an IDoc type has been filled with concrete data in accordance with the rules of structure, we call it an IDoc.

Generation of IDocs Depending on the application, one of three methods can be used to generate an IDoc (see Figure 13.4).

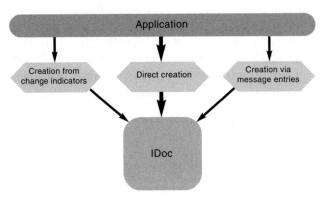

Figure 13.4 Methods for Generating IDocs

Frequently, IDocs are created directly from the application. The application program either fills an internal table in the IDoc format and transfers it to the ALE service, or it uses a BAPI with ALE interface.

The second method is the generation of IDocs from *change indicators*. The business background is the automatic synchronization of systems in terms of defined master data. For each change to the object being observed—for example, a material master record—a change indicator is logged for this record in a database table. With the help of scheduled ALE reports or manually, IDocs are generated from these change logs and replicated in one or more target systems.

With the third method, SAP R/3 *message control* is used to generate the relevant IDocs. Sending a message forms part of the standard scenarios in many applications, such as the creation of a purchase order. A message can be printed or sent in electronic form using the generic service of message control. For this method, the application in question makes *message entries* of type ALE in table NAST. Depending on the configuration, the entries can either be analyzed immediately by SAP R/3 message control, or at periodic intervals with the help of report program **RSNAST00**; IDocs are generated from the entries.

Which of the three methods is optimal will depend on the application; you cannot arbitrarily choose a method at will.

An IDoc is made up of several different segments. Each segment has its own structure definition and documentation. Several tables are used at the database level to store the data. An IDoc is organized hierarchically (see Figure 13.5).   **IDoc structure**

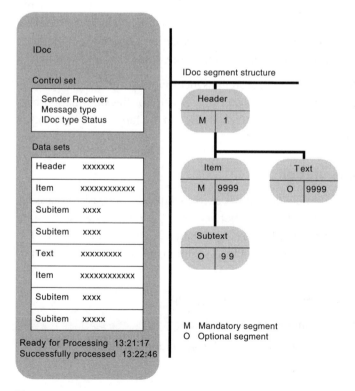

Figure 13.5 IDoc Structure

Each IDoc contains exactly one control record that consists of the technical information necessary for the transfer, such as sender, recipient, and message type. The control record establishes which processing operations are necessary for the transferred data. The actual ALE message data comes after the control record. The data is stored in different segments according to hierarchy. A cluster table defines the structure of the segment and contains the data to be distributed in one field. The name and structure of this table depends on the SAP R/3 release. The third component of the IDoc structure is the status information.

Defining the data exchange is the responsibility of Customizing. The technical definition of the ALE connections, however, is usually the SAP R/3 system administrator's responsibility, working in close collaboration with the application manager or consultant responsible for the application side.

13.2.2 Narrow and Loose Coupling Using BAPIs

If a distributed business process should be realized with a remote BAPI call, the ALE mechanism can also be used.

Narrow coupling   Instead of a message created by the application in IDoc format, the name of a business object type and a method is sent. This method is processed synchronously on the target system. Synchronously started methods should execute only reading or analyzing functions.

Loose coupling   To start a BAPI on the target system asynchronously, the necessary interface parameters can be sent as an IDoc. Receipt of this information triggers the processing of the preferred method in the target system, with the parameters transferred.

13.2.3 Configuration

In this section, a simple example is used to illustrate the basic process for configuring an ALE distribution between two SAP R/3 systems. The task will be to set up Central User Administration (CUA, see Chapter 8). The main focus here will not be on the application, but on the system administrator and his or her tasks.

The procedure consists of the following steps:

1. Defining the partner in an ALE landscape
2. Creating a model view for the ALE distribution model
3. Generating the partner profile

The entry point for ►ALE Customizing is a subnode of the Implementation Guide (see Chapter 6).

The order of the tasks more or less corresponds to the sequence of their processing. The following settings described are always based on the ALE Customizing screen.

The communication partners in an ALE scenario are referred to as *logical systems* and must first be defined. In an SAP landscape, logical systems are realized by clients. When setting up an ALE communication, it is immaterial whether the partners are physically on the same SAP R/3 system or on separate SAP R/3 systems. When assigning names for the logical system, you should, wherever possible, adhere to the naming convention <SID>CLNT<Client>. This convention makes the partner apparent just from the name used. Figure 13.7 shows the logical system's entries, which can be reached directly from the Customizing tree using the execute symbol.

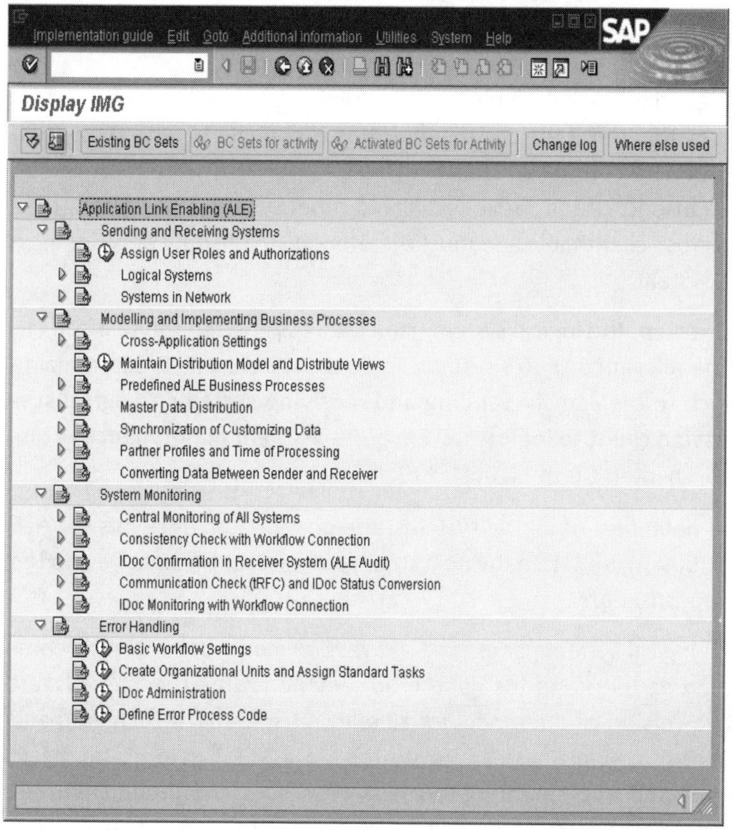

Arranging logical systems

Figure 13.6 ALE Customizing (Basis Release 4.6D)

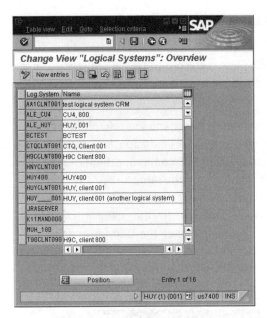

Figure 13.7 Defining the Logical Systems

The changes made are recorded in a Customizing request, which must be assigned by the user if the client in question is configured with the option for **Automatic recording of changes** (see Chapter 7). This request can be used to transport tested, basic settings to other systems. The settings are held in a cross-client table and must therefore be made only once for each SAP R/3 system.

Assigning clients

In the next step, the logical system names are assigned to the selected clients of the relevant SAP R/3 system. To do so, start at ▶ALE **Customizing** and branch to the activity **Sending and receiving systems · Logical systems · Assign client to logical system** or use ▶**Client maintenance** as discussed in Chapter 7 (see Figure 13.8).

With the definition of logical systems, the possible target points for ALE data distribution are set. In the next step, you must set the data flow in the system infrastructure.

Maintain distribution model

Using the logical system names, the *distribution model* describes the communication partners and the data to be sent. To ensure that there is just one active version of the model for all relevant systems, it is created and maintained in a single system. To do this, in ▶ALE **Customizing** select ▶**Modeling and Implementing Business Processes · Maintain Distribution Model and Distribute Views · Create Model View** or choose the direct approach, ▶**Maintenance of Distribution Model · Create Model**

View. Enter an appropriate short text and the technical name for the planned model view (see Figure 13.9).

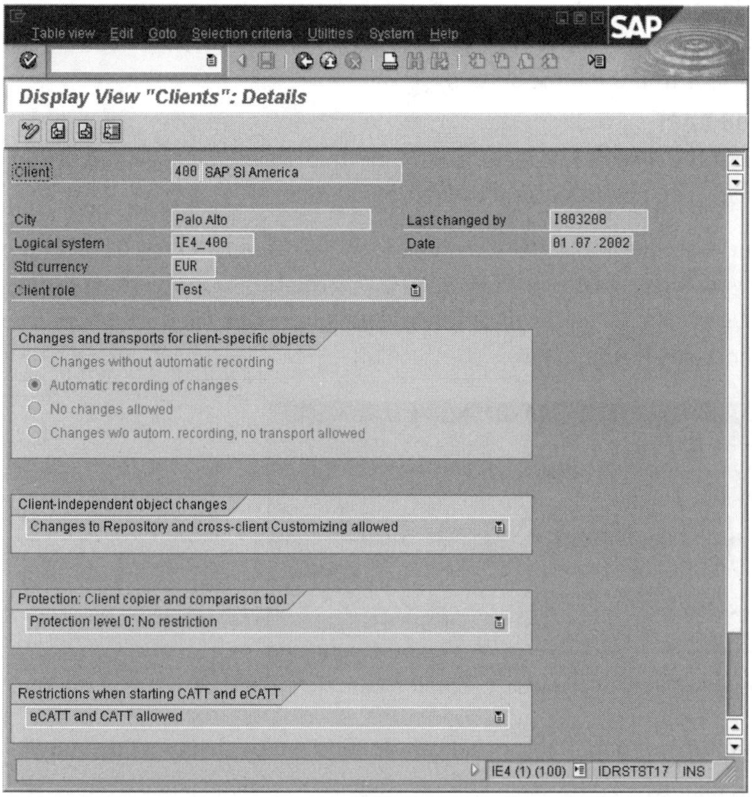

Figure 13.8 Assigning the Logical System to a Client

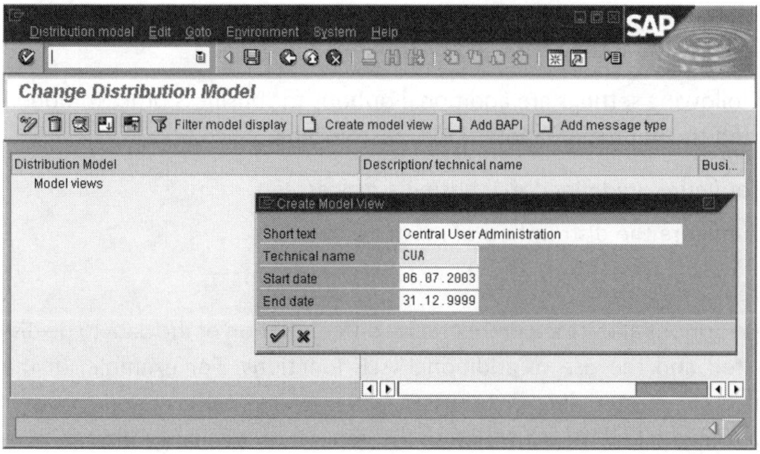

Figure 13.9 Creating a Model View for Central User Administration

BAPI/message type To define the sending and receiving logical system and the data type to be distributed, select from the following display of model views:

- **Add message type**
  With the new model view, an IDoc assigned to a message type should be sent to the remote system
- **Add BAPI**
  With the new model view, a BAPI method should be activated or supplied with parameters on the remote system.

In our example of CUA, the sending logical system is "EPA_001" and the receiving logical system is "EPACLNT001". The business object types *User* and *UserCompany* (company address) should each be filled with the *Clone* method (see Figure 13.10).

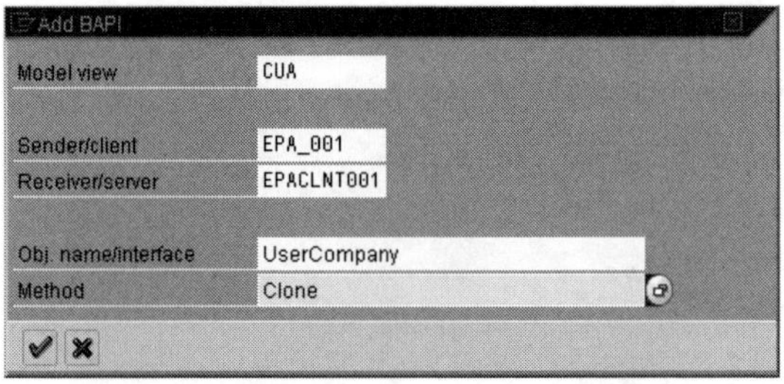

Figure 13.10 Distribution Model Descriptive Data

Filters The volume of data transmitted can be reduced by defining *filters*. By filtering message types, if you enter an object type/value pair, the IDoc segments and their subsegments are not transferred if they contain a field of the object type that does not have the defined value. Filtering BAPIs checks parameter/value pairs. Only if a parameter complies with the set value does the BAPI create and distribute an IDoc.

Special settings The following settings are additional options for business process modeling and the implementation of ALE customizing:

- Configure predefined ALE business processes
- Configure the distribution of master data
- Configure the synchronization of Customizing data

These options allow for a more precise differentiation of the data to be distributed and the use of additional ALE functions. For example, in the branch for master data distribution you can distribute material master data, triggered by the activation of the generation of change indicators. A change indicator shows where changes have been made to a master record and therefore allows the generation of a relevant IDoc, either manually or controlled by a report program.

A specific user must be created in all participating clients for communication between systems. For reasons of security, this should not be a dialog user but a *communication* type user (see Section 8.2.1).

Communication

In each system, an RFC connection (see Section 13.2) of connection type 3 (connection to an SAP R/3 system) must be created for communication between the partners in the ALE group. In the example of central user administration, RFC destinations must be created from the central system to all subsidiary systems and, depending on the settings of parameter changeability, also in the opposite direction (see Chapter 8).

If the name of the RFC destination corresponds to the name of the logical receiver system, additional settings can be generated automatically.

In the following ▶ **Partner profiles** in ALE Customizing, the parameters for inbound and outbound processing are described for the systems involved (see Section 13.11). By generating the partner profile, it is distributed to all selected partner systems, or, if only the model view is given without any explicit naming of partners, to all partners in the model view. By defining the partner profile in the central system in the example, the subsidiary systems are the partners.

Partner profiles

Packet size and output mode are set with output parameters. You can send every IDoc generated to the recipient immediately, or collect several IDocs into a group and send them once the group is complete. The disadvantage of several small packets is that you must establish a connection to the target system and follow the logon procedure for every packet. This approach can result in a degradation of performance. However, if you collect IDocs and then send them, the data pool in the sending and receiving system might differ over time. Transfer of a large number of IDocs also causes peak loads on the receiving system. Hence, there must be found a reasonable compromise between these approaches. In general, SAP recommends that you collect several IDocs and transmit them in one packet.

The settings to be maintained on the recipient pertain to the control of IDocs on the receiving side. IDocs can be processed immediately, or in the background. In typical cases, you can ensure better performance by not processing an incoming IDoc immediately, but by processing it later, when the system load is lighter. Postponing processing also means that you can parallelize incoming IDocs. After you have completed the definition, you must save and generate the partner profiles. The port and the resulting details of IDoc processing are created automatically as part of generating the partner profiles. The port must be specified manually with a port definition only in the case of a file interface. Partner profiles determine how to handle messages from ALE processing. They depend on the type of partner and on the various types of messages. Figure 13.12 shows the communication flow of data between the logical systems.

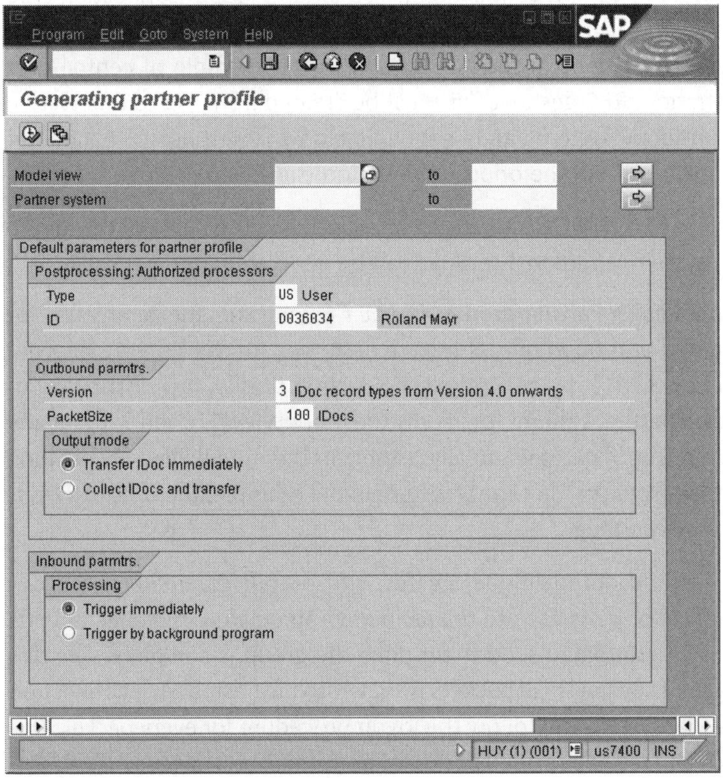

Figure 13.11 Generating the Partner Profile

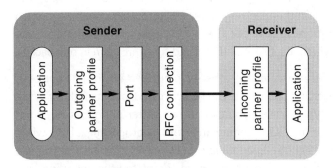

Figure 13.12 Technical Settings

A *port* defines the type of connection with a partner. Data can be trans-   Port
ferred over tRFC, with sequential files, with CPI-C to an SAP R/2 system,
or over the Internet. A unique port number is assigned for each port.

Partner profiles can be generated successfully only when the names of the
RFC connections agree with the names of the logical systems. If they do
not, you must maintain the partner profiles manually.

To ensure that the settings you have made and generated actually work,
you can run the **Check all partner profiles for consistency** function in
▶ **IDoc Check** to submit all partner profiles to a consistency check.

Distribution settings must be known to all partner systems. Accordingly,   Distributing model settings
the last step distributes the model settings: ▶ **Maintenance of distribution
model · Edit · Model view · Distribute**.

This step closes the definition of an ALE connection.

13.2.4 Monitoring and Analysis

If the ALE connection was set up so that the receiver transmits a message
to the sender about what has been executed, the sender can quickly check
the success of the transmission. The advantage of this procedure is that in
the event of an error, messages from the responsible party will be delivered immediately, so that the error can be dealt with there and the procedure can start again. Message type *ALEAUD* is available for this *auditing*:
you can use *ALEAUD* to transmit messages to the sender about IDocs
received by the recipient and their processing. As a precondition for the
use of this confirmation, you must define a message flow in the distribution model for this type of message and then periodically schedule a background job in the receiving system to return the audit data.

The ▶ **ALE status monitor** (see Figure 13.13) offers an overview of the processing status of IDocs that can be filtered according to several criteria.
You can branch to a detailed display from the overview. Once you have
determined and corrected the case of an error, you can also trigger the
reprocessing of IDocs that contain errors and have not been processed
completely.

To support various types of analyses, you can list the entries in the status
monitor and sort them according to different criteria. You can double-click
to view additional details, or click on an IDoc entry to display its definition
(see Figure 13.14).

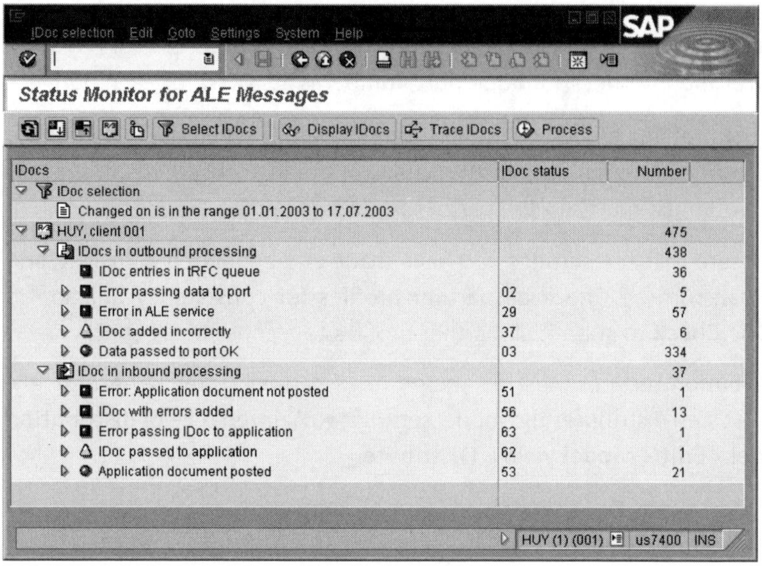

Figure 13.13 Status Monitor for ALE Messages

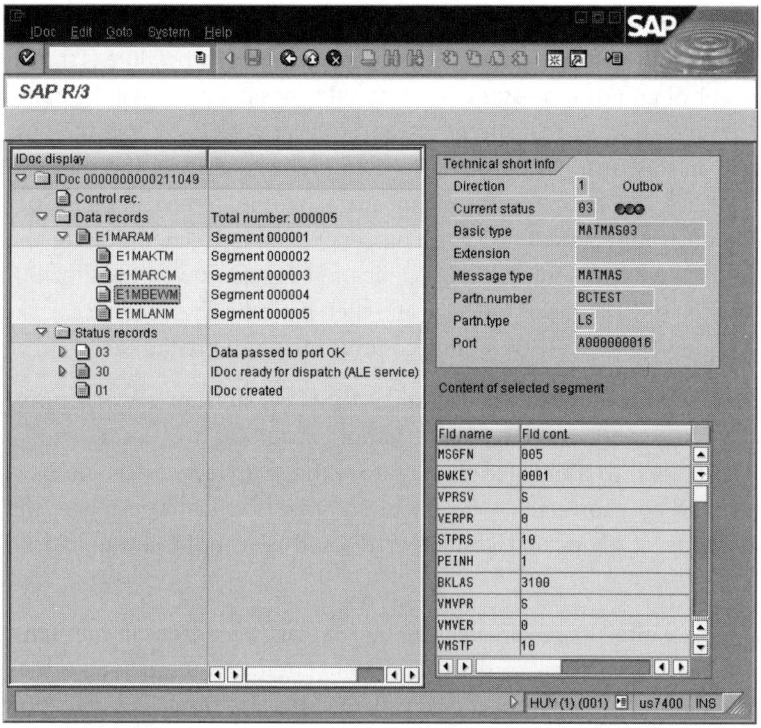

Figure 13.14 Individual Display of an IDoc from the ALE Monitor

The ►IDoc list also provides a detailed display of IDocs, but without a resend option.

The status monitor described here and additional analysis functions are integrated into the monitors for ALE administration. You can reach ALE administration from the SAP Menu via **Tools · ALE · ALE Administration**. No transaction exists to replace this path. Table 13.2 provides an overview of the functions available in ALE administration.

Menu	Submenu	Functions
Monitoring		Status monitor for ALE messages Monitor in the CCMS Display work items
Services	Change pointers	Process Reorganize
	ALE Audit	Send audit confirmations Reorganize audit database
	Customizing data	ALE Requests: Display outbound requests ALE Requests: Display inbound requests ALE Requests: Generate ALE Requests: Import ALE Requests: Consolidate
Serialization	Serialization using time stamps	Delete old time stamps
	Serialization using message types	Analyze Send Check Send
	Serialization using business objects	Display serialized IDocs Consistency check Outbound registry Inbound registry

Table 13.2 ALE Administration

Checking the processing of IDocs also includes controlling the work of scheduled background jobs to process the IDocs. Table 13.3 shows the programs involved.

Program	Description
RSEOUT00	ALE output processing
RBDAPP01	ALE input processing
RSNAST00	Generation of IDocs from message control
RBDMIDOC	Generation of IDocs from change pointers
RBDMOIND	Status conversion after successful tRFC communication
RBDCPCLR	Reorganization of the change pointer table
RSARFCEX	Processing terminated transmissions of IDocs

Table 13.3 Background Jobs for Monitoring

If IDoc processing terminates, you can use ▶ **IDoc error handling** to trigger manual reprocessing once you have corrected the error.

In addition to configurable confirmation with message type *ALEAUD*, you can also perform a synchronous status query for specific IDocs. To do so, you can click on the **Trace IDocs** button from the ALE status monitor or ▶ **IDoc Tracing**.

Dialog work processes handle received IDocs. Consequently, the processing of IDocs on the target system requires the presence not only of the usual dialog work processes for dialog users, but also of processes for ALE functions. The processing of received IDocs can be configured in parallel or sequentially. For parallel processing, you must create as many additional dialog processes as the average number of IDocs that are received in parallel. Sequential processing requires fewer dialog work processes, but only one IDoc can be processed at a time, so that congestion and degraded performance can occur on the receiving side. It also excludes a way of processing one IDoc ahead of another if you want to do so. The technical team must discuss the advantages and disadvantages of each method with the user departments and then create the appropriate technical support.

In addition to distributing the load between SAP R/3 instances by creating groups in the definition of the RFC connection, it can be advantageous in some situation to operate a separate SAP R/3 instance to process IDocs. Of course, such a solution demands a cost—benefits analysis, since implementing it would require additional hardware.

13.3 Data Transfer

If data from a legacy system is to be migrated to the new business solution as part of an implementation project, flexible and high-performance support is required for the following tasks:

▶ Conversion of highly-varied data formats into a format that SAP R/3 can read, once the data has been extracted with legacy-system tools

▶ Transporting the converted data into the new SAP R/3 system by determining which data should be mapped to which table fields and where adjustments are necessary, given the differing data structures in the new and legacy systems

▶ Ensuring a complete transfer

The type of transfer used to migrate external data into an SAP R/3 system depends on the application that receives it. Because different data is important for each application component, most applications contain their own data transfer programs that must be used. In addition to this factor, the selection of a specific technique for data transfer depends on important issues: the quantity of data involved and how frequently it is to be migrated (once or routinely).

SAP R/3 supports various techniques for data transfer: batch input, call transaction, direct input, and transfer via BAPIs. If the application does not have its own interface for transferring external data (this case is the exception), you can use the transaction recorder with batch input or call transaction to create the data that will be processed.

Techniques for data transfer

13.3.1 Batch Input

The batch input procedure is a standard approach that has long been used in the SAP environment to transfer data into an SAP R/3 system by simulating a user dialog. The consistency of the data is guaranteed because the procedure includes all transaction checks.

Data transfer occurs in two steps:

1. Creation of a batch input session that contains all the relevant data (transactions, screens, fields, and field values).

2. Processing the session in the system. Running the batch input session imports the data into the SAP R/3 system.

You can usually use predefined programs to format the external data and transfer it to a batch input session. In exceptional cases, you might have

Batch input sessions

to develop your own batch input program. The batch input program reads the data (which must be present in a form that SAP R/3 can process), formats it, and records it in the batch input session. A batch input session simulates the dialog entry of transaction codes and the associated data entry. In fact, the values that have been read are assigned to the screen fields of each transaction. The structure of the batch input session describes the fields involved, which result from the assigned transactions and the SAP structures used in them.

With this technique, the batch input procedure enables data transfer for every SAP R/3 dialog screen, including the integrity safeguards associated with it. This ability applies both to standard SAP R/3 programs and to customer-specific developments within the SAP R/3 system.

Automatic recording Automatic recording of transactions is particularly helpful. The corresponding structures of a batch input session and a batch input program can be generated automatically from the recorded transactions. Automatic recording is started with the ▶Transaction recorder. After it starts, the transaction recorder executes the transactions that will later be transferred with the batch input procedure. You can generate sessions from the recordings and adjust them as necessary. You can then generate and, if necessary, adjust the corresponding ABAP program in the next step. This approach reduces the manual programming work previously required to a minimum.

Once the screen fields of the assigned transactions of a batch input session have been filled, the batch input session is placed in the batch input queue. The session can be processed from the queue: the transactions it contains are executed in the background and the data is processed. The database uses table APQD to store the session; the table simultaneously realizes the batch input queue.

Two methods are available to run a batch input session:

▶ Manual start with ▶Batch Input; execution in dialog or in the background

▶ Automatic start by scheduling ABAP program **RSDBCSUB**

Figure 13.15 illustrates the basics of the batch input procedure.

For the system administrator, monitoring the batch input processes is of primary importance. During the batch input procedure, large amounts of data are imported into the SAP R/3 database in a relatively short time. Accordingly, the system administrator must pay close attention to the space required in the database, the increased number of writes, and the resulting increase in the amount of data contained in the database logs. If data transfer with batch input is planned, the system administrator must be included in the planning.

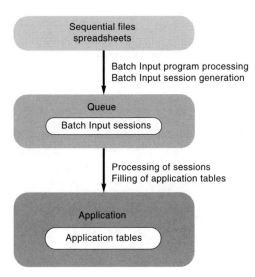

Figure 13.15 Principal Flow of the Batch Input Procedure

During development of a batch input program, you must note the length of the transaction. Because a batch input program runs in the background, no screen changes occur, therefore, from the viewpoint of the database, no *commit* occurs. Consequently, you must control the length of a transaction with explicit commits in the program.

You access the analysis of batch input flows and start a run with ▶ **Batch Input** (see Figure 13.16). Various views are available for analysis. Technical program issues and content problems can be resolved by close collaboration among the system administrator, user departments, and developers.

On occasion, successful sessions should be deleted from the database to save space. You can use report **RSBDCREO** for background processing to do so. This report should be scheduled daily as part of standard Basis jobs (see Chapter 9).

13.3.2 Direct Input

With direct input, the data in the data-transfer file is subject to all the checks that would occur in dialog entry; however, it is then transferred directly to the SAP R/3 system.

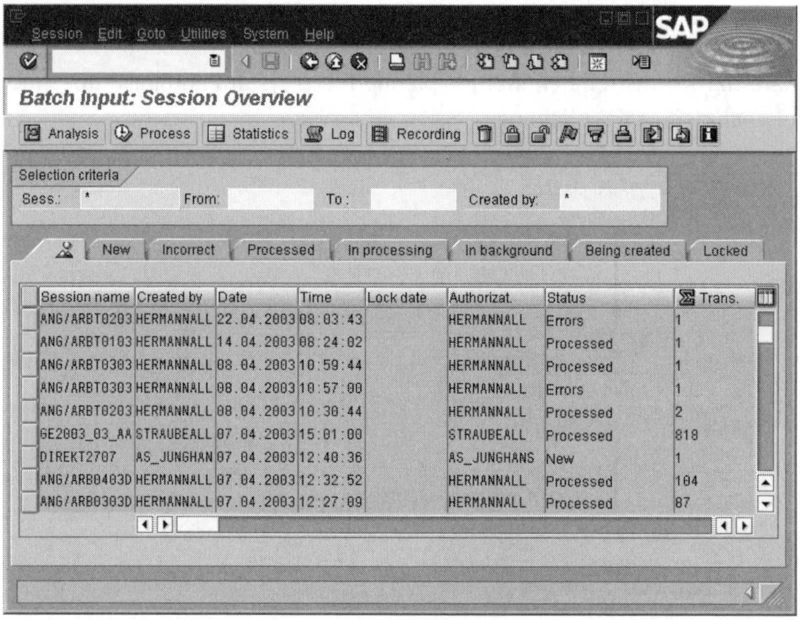

Figure 13.16 Access to Analysis of Batch Input

Strictly speaking, the direct input method is an enhancement of the batch input procedure. Batch input first transfers the data to a session, which assigns it to the corresponding screen fields; this step does not occur with direct input. Instead, the direct input method uses the function modules available in the system for data transfer. The developer must then call the appropriate function modules. During the batch input method, consistency checks of the data result from use of the screen technology; in the direct input procedure, these consistency checks are executed by the associated function modules.

Direct input programs can be started directly for testing purposes. In this case, no log is generated and a rerun in the event of errors cannot be performed. Accordingly, for use in production, data transfer with direct input should be controlled in the background with ▶**Direct input administration**.

The direct input procedure is faster; however, unlike the batch input procedure, it cannot be restarted automatically and offers less user-friendliness if an error occurs.

13.3.3 Fast Input/Call Transaction

The fast input method uses another technique to replace the initial transfer of data to a session. The data to be transferred is first written to an internal table. From there, it is processed via executing the selected transaction with an ABAP statement, CALL TRANSACTION. The structure of the internal table must therefore follow the data structure required for the transaction. With the fast input method, the developer is responsible for logging the flows. Because fast input requires less logging than does batch input, fast input is faster than batch input, but generally slower than direct input.

13.3.4 BAPI

You can also use BAPIs to transfer data. The data is processed via an ALE model by calling a BAPI of the receiving application. For this method to work, the source data must be present in IDoc format.

This process undergoes the same checks that occur during dialog entry.

13.3.5 Legacy System Migration Workbench

You can use the *Legacy System Migration Workbench* (LSMW) for one-time or periodic transfer of data from non-SAP systems. Migration occurs in the following steps:

1. Reading structured data from one or more files present on an application or presentation server.
2. Conversion of the files according to conversion rules, many of which are predefined. Conversion programs are generated from rules for special situations to migrate data objects that don't work at the level of tables or fields.
3. Importing the data into the target system over a standard interface (batch input, direct input, BAPI, or IDoc). During transfer, the data undergoes the same checks that occur during dialog entry.

The LSMW is completely integrated into the SAP R/3 system, but not in the standard delivery up to and including Basis Release 6.10. You can download the required transports from SAP Service Marketplace under Quicklink *lsmw*. As of Basis Release 6.10, you need Version 3; LSMW 4.0 is an integral component of the SAP Web Application Server.

As of SAP R/3 4.6C, the LSMW is integrated into the Data Transfer Workbench.

13.3.6 Data Transfer Workbench

You can use the ▶ **Data Transfer Workbench** to migrate large quantities of data into your SAP system. Data transfer is project-controlled: the Workbench handles administration of the projects, which consists of extraction, cleansing, conversion, loading, and checking.

Independently of the target application, the Data Transfer Workbench analyzes the required structure description and integrates the standard data-transfer programs, and, if necessary, supplemental tools that have been developed.

The conversion works with data in SAP format: you can use the integration of the LSMW to read data in external formats and convert it. It also supports loading the data via batch input, direct input, and BAPIs.

13.4 SAPconnect

SAPconnect has replaced the earlier SAPcomm interface. SAPconnect serves as a uniform interface to external services, such as the following:

▶ Internet (E-Mail)

▶ Fax

▶ Pager/Short Message Service (SMS)

▶ X.400

▶ Other SAP systems

Certifiable interfaces, BC-CON (fax) and BC-PAG (paging), are used to link external suppliers. In Basis Releases up to 4.6D, RFC establishes the e-mail connection, regardless of what the other side uses: Exchange Connector, Lotus Domino MTA, or SAP Internet Mail Gateway (sendmail). As of Basis Release 6.10, the Simple Mail Transfer Protocol (SMTP) is the standard protocol for an e-mail connection; an SMTP server can be addressed directly with the use of an SMTP plug-in. The documents are packed into e-mails and redirected to an internal fax server or an external supplier.

To use SMTP functions, the profile parameters of the SAP instance must be adjusted to enable loading the dynamic library realized over the SMTP plug-in. Additionally, a user of type *system* (see Chapter 8) with authorization profile S_A.SCON is required in every client that receives mails or status notifications.

You must create every external communications system to which you transfer messages as a *node*. The connection parameters are set independently of the connection type (SMTP or RFC). The SMTP plug in is part of the Internet Communication Manager (ICM: see Chapter 1).

The communications environment of SAPconnect is linked to the Alert Monitor (see Chapter 16) to monitor the external components. If nodes are to be displayed in the Alert Monitor, you must activate the flag that indicates that the node is to be monitored by the Alert Monitor when you define the node. You reach the administrative screen of SAPconnect via ▶ **SAPconnect Administration**.

▶ **SAPconnect Transmission jobs** provides an overview of the transmission jobs, which you can filter by a given period, the address type, the sender, and the status.

13.5 Tips

▶ **Renaming logical systems**
It is imperative that you avoid renaming logical systems, because the name of a logical system must be unique in an ALE landscape. However, if after a client or system copy with subsequent integration of the copied component into the ALE system, you determine that renaming a logical system is indeed necessary, you can use Transaction BDLS to implement the change.

▶ **Deleting IDocs**
IDocs that are no longer required can be deleted only with the standard archiving procedure (see Chapter 12) for object type IDOC.

13.6 Transactions and Menu Paths

ALE Customizing: SAP Menu • Tools • Administration • User maintenance • Central user administration • ALE Customizing (SALE)

ALE Status Monitor: SAP Menu • Tools • ALE • ALE Administration • Monitoring (BD87)

BAPI Explorer: SAP Menu • Tools • Business Framework • BAPI Browser • (BAPI)

Batch input: SAP Menu • Tools • Administration • Monitor • Batch input (SM35)

Client maintenance: SAP Menu • Tools • Administration • Administration • Client administration • Client maintenance (SCC4)

Data Transfer Workbench: SAP Menu • Tools • Data Transfer • Workbench • (SXDA)

Direct input administration: no standard menu entry (BMV0)

IDoc check: no standard menu entry (IDOC)

IDoc error handling: no standard menu entry (BD73)

IDoc list: SAP Menu • Tools • Business Communication • Idoc Basis • Idoc Idoc Lists • (WE05)

IDoc tracing: SAP Menu • Logistics • Logistics Execution • Master Data • Transportation • Shipment Costs • ALE Monitoring • Monitoring • Idoc • Trace • (BDM2)

Maintenance of distribution model: no standard menu entry (BD64)

Maintenance of server groups: no standard menu entry (RZ12)

Partner profile: ALE Customizing (SALE) • Model business processes • Maintain distribution model and distribute views (BD64) • Generate partner profile (BD82)

Port definition: SAP Menu • Tools • Business Communication • Idoc Basis Idoc • Port Definition • (WE21)

qRFC Monitor: no standard menu entry (SMQR)

qRFC Monitor input: no standard menu entry (SMQ1)

qRFC Monitor output: no standard menu entry (SMQ2)

RFC administration: SAP Menu • Administration • Administration • RFC destinations (SM59)

SAPconnect administration: SAP Menu • Tools • Business Communication • SAPconnect (SCOT)

SAPconnect transmission jobs: no standard menu entry (SOST)

Transaction recorder: no standard menu entry (SHDB)

tRFC Monitor: SAP Menu • Tools • Administration • Monitor • Transactional RFC (SM58)

Trusted system: no standard menu entry (SMT1)

13.7 Additional Documentation

Quicklinks

▶ SAP Service Marketplace: alias *ale*

▶ SAP Service Marketplace: alias *bapi*

▶ SAP Service Marketplace: alias *communication*

▶ SAP Service Marketplace: alias *connectors*

▶ SAP Service Marketplace: alias *dta*

▶ SAP Service Marketplace: alias *ibf*

▶ SAP Service Marketplace: alias *lsmw*

SAP Service Marketplace Notes

The following table provides an overview of important SAP Notes that pertain to data transfer and data distribution.

Content	Note
Meaning of input types in SMQS	484753
ALE: Transmission of IDocs and QOUT Scheduler	580869
Resource Management for tRFC and aRFC	74141
Problems with the names of logical systems	423184
Converting the names of logical systems	121163
ZBV: Tips for optimizing performance	399271
SXC: Version overview and history	122657

Table 13.4 SAP Notes on Data Transfer and Data Distribution

13.8 Questions

1. Which statement is correct?

   During data distribution based upon ALE:

   a. A fixed connection between the partner systems is set up.

   b. The partner systems are loosely coupled during data transfer.

   c. Functions of each RDBMS, such as SAPDBA, are used to transfer data.

2. **Which techniques can be used for data exchange?**

    a. CPI-C

    b. Sequential files

    c. tRFC

    d. Internet

    e. Telnet

3. **How can tRFCs interrupted by communications errors be repro-
   cessed?**

    a. Automatically, by activating the option for automatic repetition
       during definition of the tRFC connection

    b. Scheduling job **RSARFCE**

    c. Scheduling job **RSEOUT00**

    d. Correcting the error and re-executing the application transaction

4. **What's the purpose of the batch input procedure?**

    a. To transfer data from sequential files into the SAP R/3 database

    b. To process mass data in the background

    c. To import files with the Transport Control Program **tp**

14 Maintaining Instances

In the previous chapters, you frequently read about instance parameters, which have a profound effect on the configuration of the R/3 system and how user requests are processed in R/3. The profile management and parameter maintenance functions integrated in the R/3 system are far more reliable and easier to use than manually changing the profiles. This chapter describes how to use these maintenance functions, as well as possible configurations of the instance (operation modes) and how to configure their automatic, time-controlled switching.

14.1 Profile Maintenance

As you learned in Chapter 2, the system-wide or instance-specific configuration definitions for an R/3 system are saved in initialization files at the operating-system level. These *profiles* are generated and configured with default settings during installation by **R3setup** (up to R/3 Release 4.6C) or **SAPinst** (in Web Application Server 6.10 and later). During the lifetime of an R/3 system, changing circumstances—such as increasing numbers of users, R/3 release upgrades, or the installation of new modules and hardware—will make it necessary to readjust these system parameters.

You can optimize the system settings by changing the profile files manually **Manual Change** in a text editor; however, the settings are not checked for either syntax or semantics. If the system cannot interpret certain parameters during an instance startup, they are simply ignored. If you inadvertently defined the same profile values several times in one profile, the last read setting is valid.

Accordingly, the profile management functions within the R/3 system provide the following benefits:

▶ **Centralization**
You can manage and maintain all profiles of all instances centrally.

▶ **Version management**
Every saved change to a profile is stored as a version in the R/3 database. The versions are numbered consecutively.

▶ **Consistency checks**
The system checks the consistency of the profile after changes are made, verifying the logical relationships and basic rules for parameter configuration.

▶ **Comparison between the active profile and the profile saved in the database**
You can analyze variances between the currently active profile and the profile saved in the database. This analysis enables you to determine whether the R/3 system profile has been modified manually.

▶ **Immediate activation of parameter changes**
Some parameters can be activated immediately, without requiring a restart of the R/3 system.

Concurrently, the profile management functions within the R/3 system are a prerequisite for using system monitoring tools such as the control panel, as well as for defining and using operation modes.

▶ **Profile Maintenance** in R/3 enables you to maintain the standard profile of the system, *DEFAULT.PFL*, the start profiles, *Start_<instance_name>_ <server_name>*, and the instance profiles of all instances, *<SID>_ <instance_name>_<server_name>*, centrally. You already learned about the purpose and contents of the previous profiles in Chapter 2. To maintain these profiles with the R/3 tools, you first have to import them from the file system to the R/3 database. The installation programs merely save the profile files in the file system, but not in the database. To import the profiles, proceed as follows:

Step 1   Choose ▶ **Profile Maintenance**. The **Edit Profiles** screen opens (see Figure 14.1).

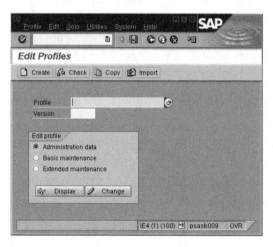

Figure 14.1 Initial Screen for Profile Maintenance

Step 2   Choose **Utilities · Import Profiles · Of Active Servers**. You can import the files of all instances and save them in the database through the central directory structure of the entire R/3 system. Listing 14.1 shows the import log for the central system, IE4. A consistency check of all contained parameters is also performed during the import. The logical profile names of the imported profiles are defined as the respective file names without path information.

Listing 14.1 Log of Profile Import with Subsequent Consistency Check

```
------------------------------------------------------------
|Importing start/instance profiles of all
|active servers
------------------------------------------------------------
|The following default profile will be imported:
------------------------------------------------------------
|psasb009_IE4_00:D:\usr\sap\IE4\SYS\profile\DEFAULT.PFL
|[Ok? Does this continue to another line?]
------------------------------------------------------------
|The following instance profiles will be imported:
------------------------------------------------------------
|psasb009_IE4_00:D:\usr\sap\IE4\SYS\profile\IE4_DVEBMGS
|00_psasb009
------------------------------------------------------------
|The following start profiles will be imported:
------------------------------------------------------------
|psasb009_IE4_00:D:\usr\sap\IE4\sys\profile\START_
|DVEBM|GS00_psasb009
------------------------------------------------------------
|Log for importing the profiles
------------------------------------------------------------
|Profiles were imported free of errors.
------------------------------------------------------------
|Overall check of instance profiles and a
|default profile
------------------------------------------------------------
|Log for the default profile, single check
|Profile name                  : DEFAULT
|Physical profile name  :
|D:\usr\sap\IE4\SYS\profile\DEFAULT.PFL
|Check on server         : psasb009_IE4_00
------------------------------------------------------------
|No errors found
------------------------------------------------------------
|Log for instance profile, single check
```

```
|Profile name                   : IE4_DVEBMGS00_PSASB009
|Physical profile name:
|D:\usr\sap\IE4\SYS\profile\IE4_DVEBMGS00_psasb009
- - - - - - - - - - - - - - - - - - - - - - - - - - - - - - - - - - - - - - - - - - - - - - - - -
|Unknown parameter em/reserve_mapping_window cannot
|be checked
|rtbb/buffer_length factor 10 greater than default 2000
- - - - - - - - - - - - - - - - - - - - - - - - - - - - - - - - - - - - - - - - - - - - - - - - -
|Log for the instance profile, overall check
|Profile name                   : IE4_DVEBMGS00_PSASB009
|Physical profile name:
|D:\usr\sap\IE4\SYS\profile\IE4_DVEBMGS00_psasb009
|Log for the overall check
- - - - - - - - - - - - - - - - - - - - - - - - - - - - - - - - - - - - - - - - - - - - - - - - -
|No errors found
- - - - - - - - - - - - - - - - - - - - - - - - - - - - - - - - - - - - - - - - - - - - - - - - -
|Overall check of start profiles
- - - - - - - - - - - - - - - - - - - - - - - - - - - - - - - - - - - - - - - - - - - - - - - - -
|Log for start profile, single check
|Profile name                   : START_DVEBMGS00_PSASB009
|Physical profile name:
|D:\usr\sap\IE4\sys\profile\START_DVEBMGS00_psasb00
- - - - - - - - - - - - - - - - - - - - - - - - - - - - - - - - - - - - - - - - - - - - - - - - -
|No errors found
- - - - - - - - - - - - - - - - - - - - - - - - - - - - - - - - - - - - - - - - - - - - - - - - -
|Log for start profile, overall check
|Profile name                   : START_DVEBMGS00_PSASB009
|Physical profile name:
|D:\usr\sap\IE4\sys\profile\START_DVEBMGS00_psasb00
|Log for start profile list
- - - - - - - - - - - - - - - - - - - - - - - - - - - - - - - - - - - - - - - - - - - - - - - - -
|No errors found
- - - - - - - - - - - - - - - - - - - - - - - - - - - - - - - - - - - - - - - - - - - - - - - - -
```

The log from Listing 14.1 shows the individual phases of the consistency check performed during the import. The log starts with the import of the default, instance, and start profiles. Because we are dealing with the central R/3 system, only one start profile and one instance profile exist. The parameters of each individual profile are then checked in their interactive contexts. No problems were diagnosed in the preceding log. After the single check, a system-wide overall check is performed for each profile class. During this check, the system verifies that the basic rules for configuring an R/3 system have been adhered to, such as the conditions introduced in Table 1.2 in Chapter 1. In the preceding example for the central R/3 system in Listing 14.1, this check also ran without problems.

The imported profiles form the basis for changing the contained parameters. You can also enter a profile name and the corresponding file to load individual profiles into the database (see Figure 14.1) using the **Import** button. This is necessary, for example, when you add additional R/3 instances to an existing R/3 system. You can save copies of existing profiles under different logical names (administrative names) in the database. The physical assignment of the profile is retained. You can freely select the administrative name of the profile in the database. The advantage of separating the freely definable administrative name and the actual profile name at file level is inherent in the administration: this method enables you to save different variants of a similar profile, which serve different purposes, under different administrative names. The following example deals with an instance profile that can be activated with or without the SNC option for encrypted data transfer. The procedure is as follows:

Click the **Copy** button in ▶**Profile Maintenance.** A dialog box is displayed, in which you enter the source and target. Any information that you entered in the initial screen for profile maintenance is proposed as the source. You can change these values if necessary.

Enter the name of the target. You can enter the same profile name if you want to create another version of an existing profile, or enter a new name (see Figure 14.2). **Step 3**

Figure 14.2 Copying a Profile

Click **Copy**. Version 1 of the new profile is generated. If you used the same name, a new version of the existing profile is generated. **Step 4**

You maintain the profiles in three ways:

▶ **Administration data**

In addition to an informative comment text, the administration data contains the type of profile (instance profile, standard profile, or start profile), the activation time, and the name of the user who activated it. It also contains the corresponding operating-system file and the application server where the operating-system-specific information in the profile will be checked. Figure 14.3 shows the administration data for profile HUY_D32_WITHOUT_SNC, which was created as a copy of instance profile HUY_D32_US7400.

▶ **Basic maintenance**

You use the basic maintenance function to maintain the most important parameters of the respective profile. Due to the different meanings and contents of the profiles, however, the appearance of basic profile maintenance depends on the specific profile type selected. Basic maintenance merely enables you to modify the most important parameters, and supports you via the use of logical names. In addition to the values for work processes and buffers shown in Figure 14.4, basic maintenance also includes information on the directories and languages used, as well as additional memory management information.

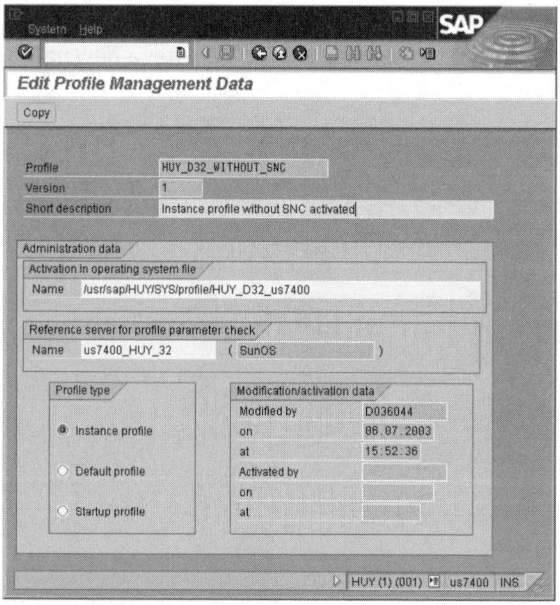

Figure 14.3 Changing the Administration Data of a Profile

The system then displays the required initial and maximum swap requirements for the instance, based on the defined settings. To ensure good performance, verify that this initial value does not exceed 150% of the total main memory on the server.

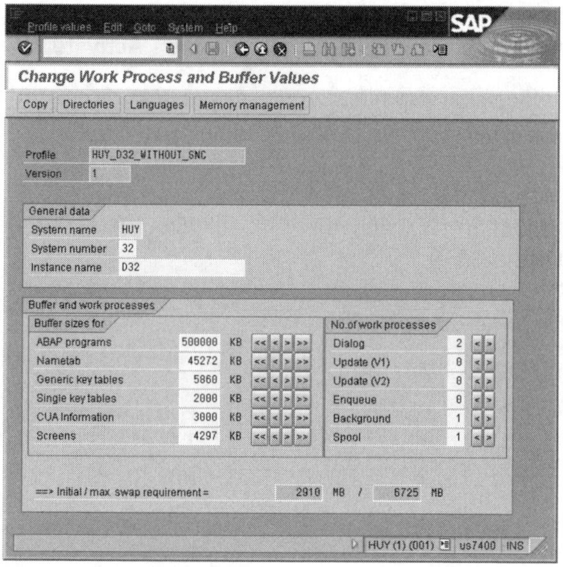

Figure 14.4 Basic Maintenance of a Profile

▶ **Extended maintenance**

The extended maintenance mode displays the contents of the respective profiles in unformatted form, which means the real names of the parameters are displayed. This mode is intended for expert users. In addition to changing parameters already contained in the profile, you can add new parameters at any time with **Parameter · Create**. You can also delete an existing parameter with **Parameter · Delete**.

If you want the changes to a profile to be permanent, click **Copy** to accept them temporarily at first. The profiles are saved permanently in the database when you choose **Save**. Do not forget to check the logical consistency of the profile by clicking **Check** first. When examining the check results, note that the check program may not recognize all the parameters that can be inserted and set—such as those parameters used for troubleshooting, special tuning measures, or functional enhancements. Therefore, the message

```
Unknown parameter em/reserve_mapping_window
```

from Listing 14.1 could indicate a typo, but it could also indicate an undocumented parameter that is actually required and queried in the system.

After you save the changes, the profile files have not been transferred to the operating-system level yet. To transfer your changes to the corresponding file at the operating-system level, choose **Profile · Activate**.

Activation   When you activate a profile, a backup file, *<profile_name>.BAK,* is created with the contents of the last valid profile file. You can only activate the latest version of a profile.

To help you track the change history, all parameter changes are recorded in the profile file (see Listing 14.2).

Listing 14.2 Modified Profile File (excerpt)

```
Directory  /usr/sap/HUY/SYS/profile
Name: HUY_D32_us7400
******************************************************
#.*        Instance profile HUY_D32_WITHOUT_SNC
#.*        Version              = 000002
#.*        Generated by user  = D036044
#.*        Generation date    = 07/06/2003,03:52:36 p.m.
#.******************************************************
#parameter created                        by: D024220
10/16/2002 11:02:06 a.m.
ssf/name = SAPSECULIB
#parameter created                        by: D024220
10/16/2002 11:00:22 a.m.
snc/accept_insecure_cpic = 1
#parameter created                        by: D024220
10/16/2002 11:04:21 a.m.
snc/gssapi_lib = /sapmnt/HUY/exe_64/libsapcrypto.so
#parameter created                        by: D024220
10/16/2002 11:03:02 a.m.
#old_value: 1                             changed:
D036044 07/06/2003 03:52:36 p.m.
snc/enable = 0
#parameter created                        by: D024220
10/16/2002 10:55:27 a.m.
......
```

The changes are not yet effective, however, for the relevant instance. The instance does not start using the new parameter values until the next restart. Only a small selection of parameters in the instance profile can be changed dynamically in an active system.

In ▶ **Profile Maintenance**, choose **Profile · Dyn. Switching · Execute** to switch to the instance parameters dynamically—individually or together— that are listed under ▶ **Profile Maintenance · Profile · Dyn. Switching · Display Parameters**. Dynamic changes to other parameters are possible in different ways, depending on the parameter type. You can temporarily adjust all dynamic parameters via ▶ **Maintain Profile Parameters**. Table 14.1 below provides an overview of the possible parameters.

Dynamic Parameter Changes

Parameter area	Parameters	Switching
Trace level	rdisp/TRACE	▶ **Process Overview**
tRFC/aRFC resources	rdisp/rfc_*	Implicitly with ▶ **RFC Server Group Maintenance**
Memory management	abap/swapreserve em/stat_log_* abap/heap_area_* ztta/roll_*	Report **RSMEMORY**
Gateway	gw/*	Implicitly with the ▶ **Gateway Monitor**
Dispatcher	rdisp/max_hold_time rdisp/max_sleep rdisp/max_priv_time rdisp/bufreftime rdisp/btctime rdisp/autoabaptime rdisp/keepalive* rdisp/gui_auto_logout rdisp/spooltime rdisp/wppriv_max_no	Report **RSMON000_ CHANGE_ PARAMETER** (a more user-friendly function is available in Web Application Server 6.20)
Task handler	rdisp/max_wprun_time rdisp/call_system rdisp/no_core_info rdisp/reinitialize_code_ page rdisp/no_rfc_commit_ in_update_task rdisp/async_dialog_ timeout	

Table 14.1 Profile Parameters That Can Be Changed Dynamically

Parameter area	Parameters	Switching
Task handler (cont.)	rdisp/wpdbug_max_no rdisp/wait_after_ deadlock rdisp/wp_auto_restart rdisp/wp_abap_restart rdisp/restartable_wp	
RFC/CPIC	rdisp/sna_gateway rdisp/sna_gw_service rdisp/accept_remote_ trace_level rdisp/rfc_pooling rdisp/rfc_pool_timeout	
Number range buffers	nobuf/max_attempts nobuf/server	
Update	rdisp/vbmail rdisp/auto_vb_stop rdisp/max_attempt_no rdisp/vb_stop_active rdisp/vb_auto_sync	
Message server	ms/http* ms/max_sleep ms/keepalive ms/suspend_time ms/conn* ms/max_queue ms/warn_queue ms/audit ms/cache_check ms/comment	Implicitly with the ▶ Message Server Monitor or Report RSM51000_CHANGE_ PARAMETER

Table 14.1 Profile Parameters That Can Be Changed Dynamically (cont.)

All profile parameters are described in detail individually in ▶ **Maintain Profile Parameters** (see Figure 14.5). The parameter-specific **Documentation** describes additional properties and examples for use. Click **Change value** to change the current parameter value dynamically.

Prior to now, one of the main focal points of this book has been the handling of the profile maintenance functions integrated in R/3. The corresponding chapters describe which parameters are available for configuring R/3 for the individual areas. Many more parameters exist, however, not all of them are relevant to the customer and therefore, should not be changed without consulting SAP first. The Glossary contains the most important parameters in the R/3 system, along with a brief description of each. In particular, the sizes of the main memory areas of an instance are critical to performance. For more information, refer to *SAP Performance Optimization*, a book by Thomas Schneider, which is also available from SAP PRESS.

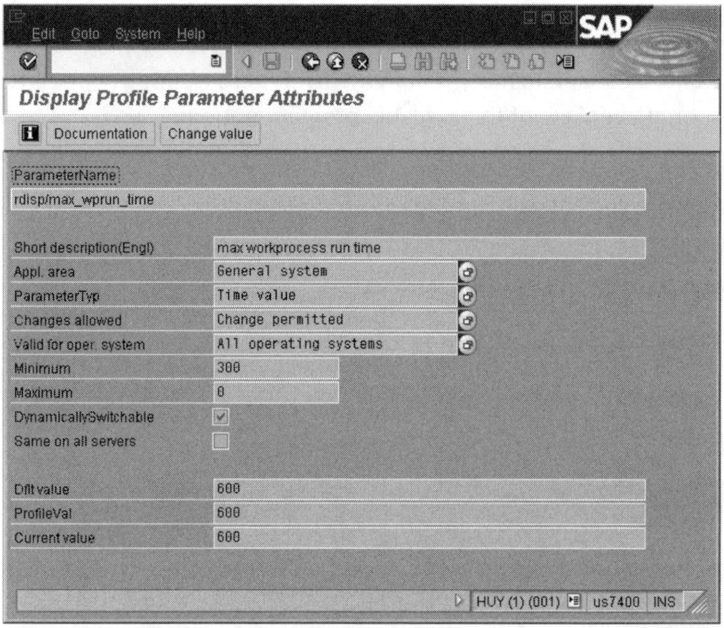

Figure 14.5 Maintaining Profile Parameters

If you must change a parameter that you only used in its default value (due to an SAP Note, for example), the parameter itself is not yet defined in the profiles. Instead, the value is extracted from the R/3 source coding (see Chapter 2). In ▶**Profile Maintenance**, choose the appropriate profile in which you want to create the parameter. Choose **Extended Maintenance · Change · Parameter · Create** to open the maintenance screen for the new parameter (see Figure 14.6).

When you enter the parameter name and value, the parameter value from the source coding is initially displayed for information. The substitution values refer to system parameters that may be evaluated, such as path names.

You can start report **RSPARAM** to discover which parameters are currently active in your R/3 system. Each R/3 parameter has a default setting that is implemented in the R/3 kernel. The custom settings in the profiles over-write these values. Report **RSPARAM** generates a list that shows you both values for each parameter. Furthermore, you can select individual parameters and view the available documentation in the report. Dynamic

Creating a New Parameter

RSPARAM

changes to parameters are valid until the next time the relevant profile file is read, that is, until the next time the instance is restarted. **RSPARAM** does not display these parameter values.

sappfpar User <sid>adm can use program **sappfpar** at the operating-system level. This program provides information on the parameter settings of an instance and the main memory requirements. Enter `sappfpar help` to display a brief overview of the available program options:

▶ `sappfpar <parameter name>`
Displays the current value of the selected parameter.

▶ `sappfpar all`
Displays a list of all defined parameters.

▶ `sappfpar check`
Checks the configured parameters, including configuration of the R/3 main memory areas. The resulting main memory requirements are also calculated.

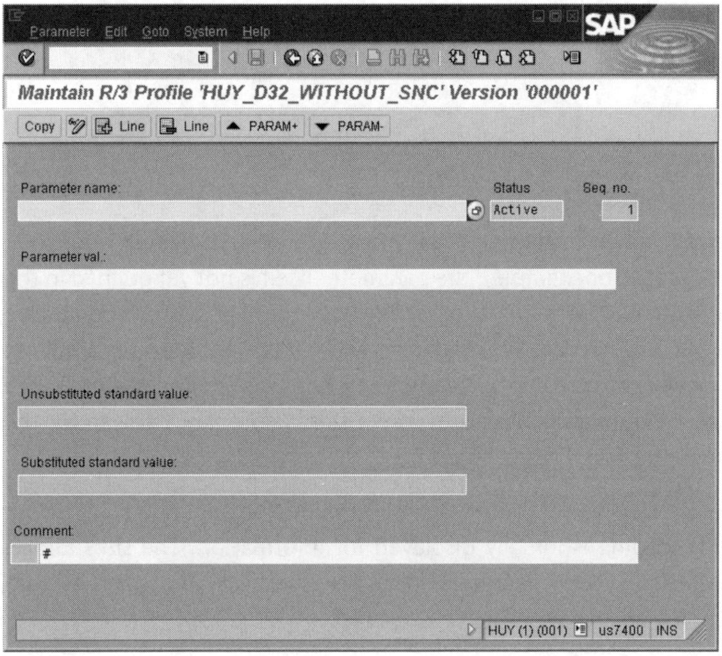

Figure 14.6 Creating a New Parameter

If needed, you can also specify an instance profile with pf=<instance_profile>, an instance number with nr= <instance_number>, or the R/3 system name with name=<SID>.

The **memlimits** program at the operating-system level might also be use- memlimits ful. This program is also available for user <sid>adm. It compares the main memory requirements of the R/3 system, which are calculated from the parameter settings, with the kernel parameters defined in the operating system. If the R/3 requirements exceed the limits defined in the operating system, serious problems can occur, such as not being able to start the R/3 system.

14.2 Operation Modes

An *operation mode* of one or more instances is defined as the number and type of configured work processes for a defined period. In order to optimize your available resources, you can define operation modes to modify the configuration of your R/3 system—to deal with periodic fluctuations in requirements during the day. For example, there are generally more dialog users on the system during the day, while background processing requirements increase at night. Accordingly, it makes sense to define one operation mode for day operations and another operation mode for night operations. As was previously noted, an operation mode defines a certain number of work processes and their types. The R/3 system can change the operation mode automatically, according to a defined schedule, without having to restart the instance.

In order to define operation modes, you first have to import the instance profiles into the system with the profile maintenance function. The parameters contained in the profile are the foundation for resource distribution on the instance.

To create operation modes, proceed as follows:

1. Choose ▶Operation Mode Maintenance.
2. Enter a name for the operation mode, along with a short description.
3. Define which monitoring properties variant you want to activate during an operation mode switch (see Chapter 15).
4. Save your entries.

The defined operation modes are displayed in an overview (see Figure 14.8).

To enable you to use system functions such as the control panel and background job scheduling, operation mode DUMMY already exists in the system—even if you haven't yet defined your own operation modes. However, you cannot use DUMMY for operation mode switching. Once you've defined your own operation modes, you can delete the DUMMY mode.

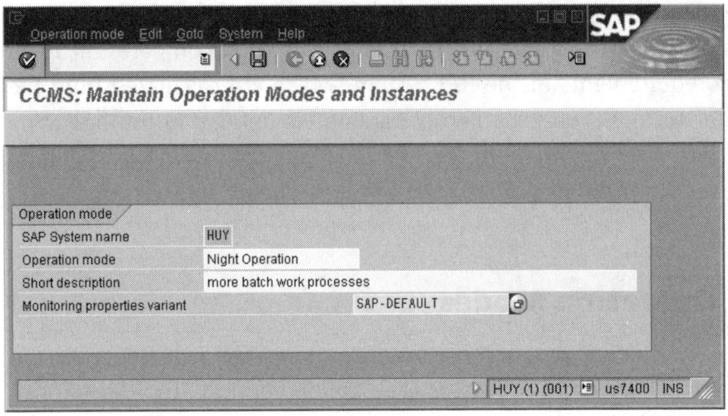

Figure 14.7 Defining an Operation Mode

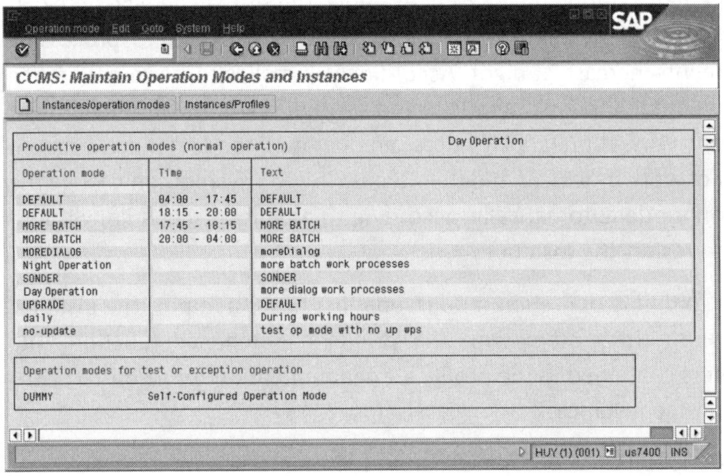

Figure 14.8 Overview of Defined Operation Modes

Now, enter all the instances in your system. To do so, proceed as follows:

1. Choose ▶**Operation Mode Maintenance** again, and then go to **Instances/Profiles**. The active standard profile is displayed (see Figure 14.9). If the mode hasn't been maintained, no application servers or instances are visible .

2. Select **Profile · Create New Instance** (see Figure 14.10).

3. Enter the name of the application server and the instance number.

4. Click **Current settings**. The current profile settings are used automatically, along with the number and type of work processes in the currently active configuration (see Figure 14.11).

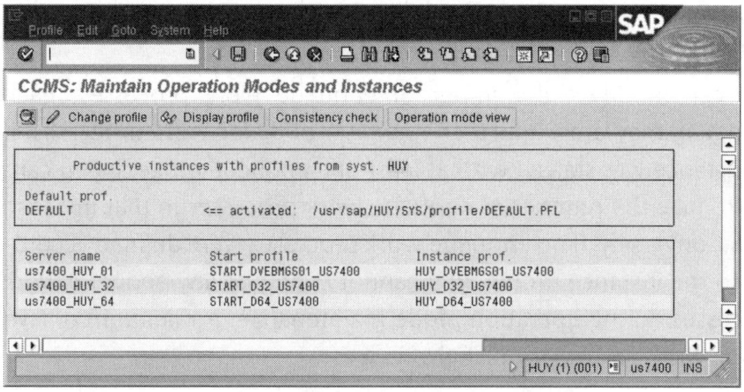

Figure 14.9 Profile View of Operation Modes and Instances

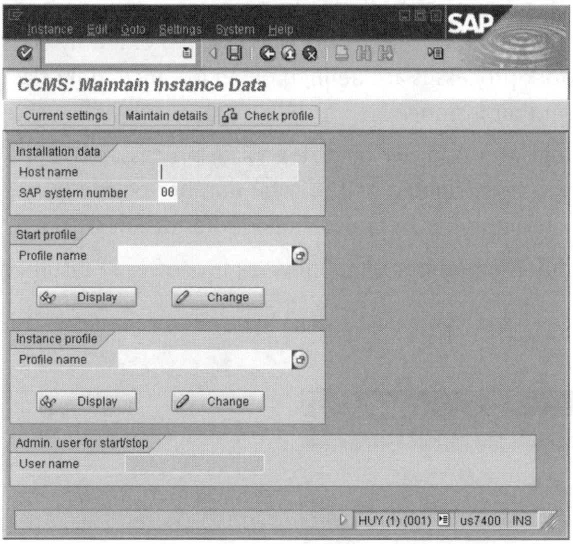

Figure 14.10 Maintenance of Instance Data

5. If you want to use the control panel to start and stop instances, choose **Instance · Maintain Start User** to enter the name and password of an operating-system user who is authorized to start and stop the instance. In the default settings, this is user <sid>adm.

To change a profile, select that profile and click **Change**. The profile maintenance function appears automatically.

6. In the displayed dialog box, you can now distribute the total number of work processes, which is extracted from the instance profile, to the various process types for an operation mode (see Figure 14.12). The information in the instance profile is the basis for distributing the work processes in the selected instance; the total number of configured

processes remains constant. The following changes are possible within operation mode switching:

- You can modify the number of enqueue work processes. Each change immediately affects the number of dialog work processes. If an instance was started with at least one enqueue process, you cannot reduce the number of enqueue work processes in that instance to 0. Conversely, if no enqueue work processes were defined according to the instance profile, you cannot configure any enqueue work processes during operation mode maintenance. A minimum of two dialog work processes must always exist.

- The same restrictions apply to the update and V2 update tasks.

- The upper limit for the number of class A background processes is equal to the total number of background processes. You can even reduce the number of background work processes to 0. If only class A background work processes are defined on an instance, only class A jobs can run on that instance.

- You cannot change the number of dialog work processes directly. Instead, this figure is calculated as the total number of configured processes minus the number of non-dialog work processes.

- You cannot modify the number of spool work processes in instance maintenance.

7. Save your entries.

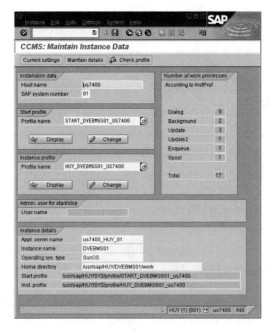

Figure 14.11 Copying the Current Settings

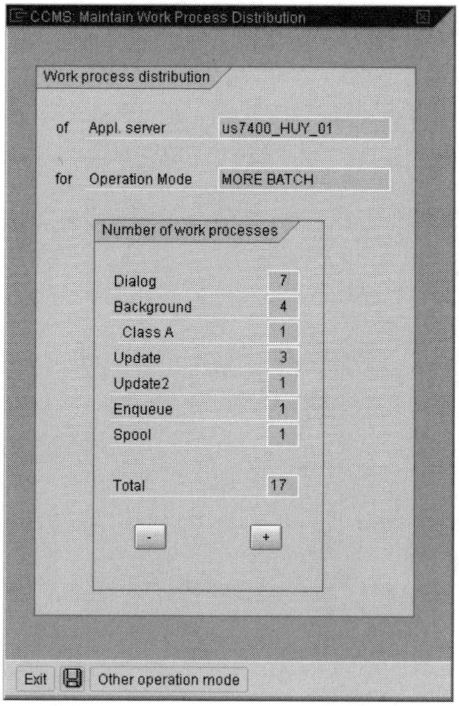

Figure 14.12 Distribution of Work Processes

You assign the other instances of an R/3 system to the defined instance profiles in a similar manner. To initially assign the instances after installation, you can create a collective instance definition for all servers with ▶Operation Mode Maintenance · Instances/Operation Modes · Settings · Based on Current Status · New Instances · Generate.

You can display the defined assignments between operation mode and instance definition in ▶Operation Mode Maintenance, with Instances/Operation Modes (see Figure 14.13).

Note

If you want to make changes, double-click on an operation mode to select it. The screen for distributing the work processes opens. You can also change the operation mode assignment by clicking on **Other operation mode** (see Figure 14.12). Save your settings. If necessary, you can also go to profile maintenance or instance maintenance directly in the menu.

The last step involves arranging the operation modes in the time table. Once again, you start in ▶Operation Mode Maintenance. Choose **Operation Mode · Time Table** to arrange the operation modes in the time table (see Figure 14.14).

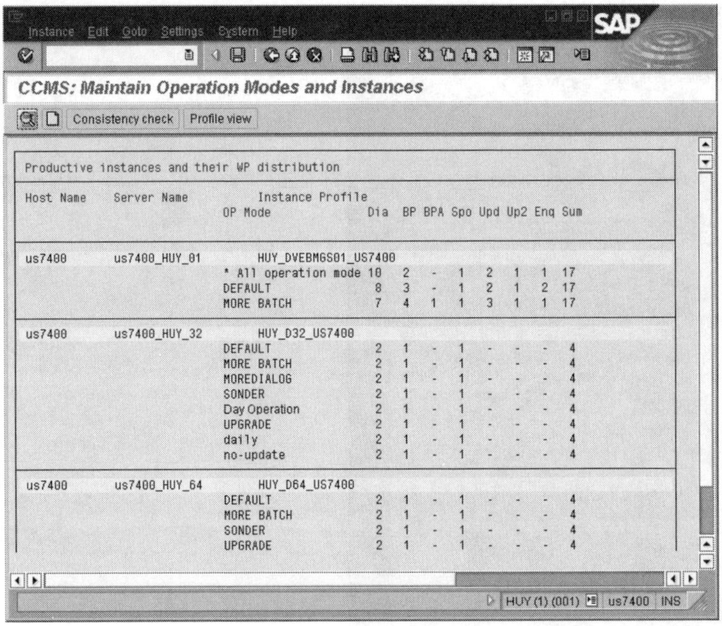

Figure 14.13 Overview of Operation Modes

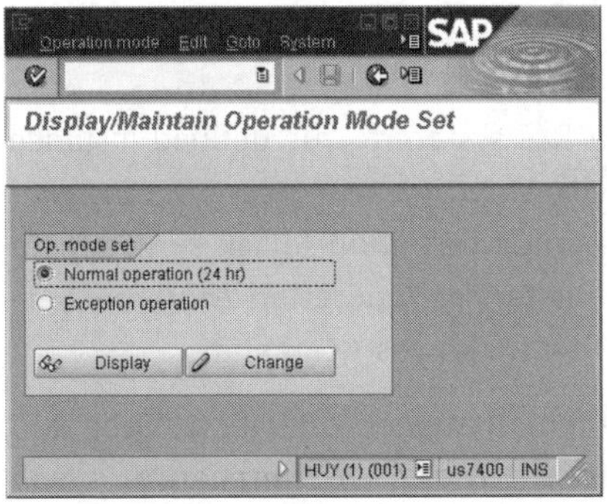

Figure 14.14 Maintaining the Time Table for Operation Modes

To activate a selected operation mode at a specific time, proceed as follows:

1. In the time table, choose **Normal operation (24hr) · Change**.

2. You can change the granularity of the time period by selecting **Edit · Time Period**. You can choose between intervals of 15, 30, and 60 minutes.

To select the beginning of the required time period, click on the start time that you want and choose ▶**Operation Mode · Select Interval** (or the shortcut, F2). Select the end of the required time interval in the same manner.

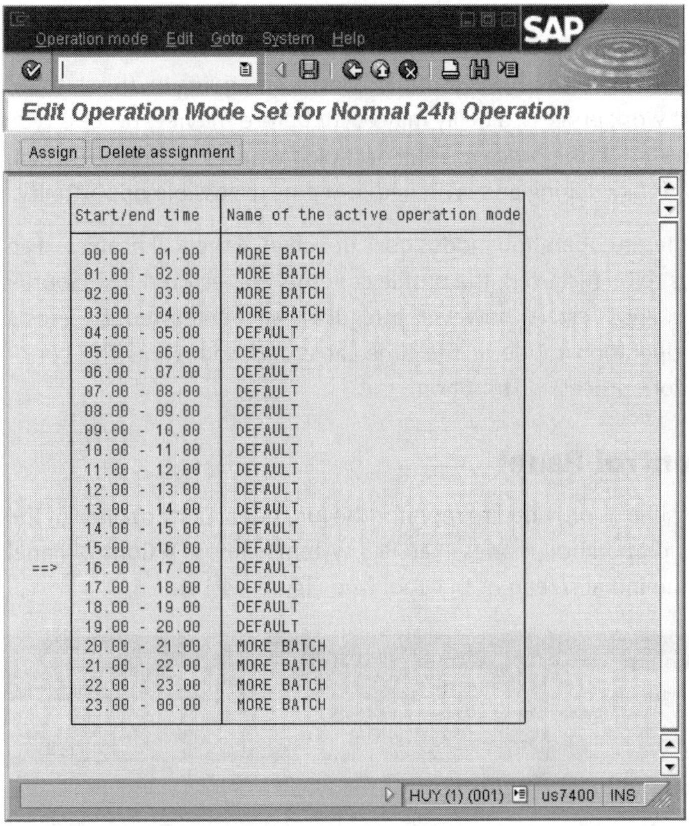

Figure 14.15 Time Table of Operation Modes

3. Click **Assign** to assign an operation mode, by entering its name.

4. Repeat step 3 until the time table is filled completely.

5. Save your entries (see Figure 14.15).

You can delete existing assignments by clicking on the **Delete assignment** button. The arrow in the screen indicates the current time in the time table.

In addition to the generally valid time table, you can define an exception mode for individual days and times with ▶ **Operation Mode Maintenance · Operation Mode · Time Table · Specify Exception Operation**. This can be necessary for routine maintenance work, for example, or for special settlement runs.

Exception Rules

The configuration of automatic operation mode switching is now complete.

When the operation mode is switched, only the work process types change. For example, a work process that was used as a dialog work process can be switched to a background process. Depending on the status of the relevant work process, a delay may occur before the new process type can be activated. If the process is still occupied when it is to be switched, it is flagged for switching and switched at the next possible opportunity.

Defining different operation modes does not change the R/3 profiles. If an instance has to be restarted, the profile contents are restored first. Shortly after the instance restart, however, a regularly scheduled report detects the active operation mode in the time table and configures the corresponding work process distribution.

14.3 Control Panel

The *control panel* is provided to monitor the functional performance of the instances and operation modes in an R/3 system. Choose ▶ **Control Panel** to display the initial screen of this tool (see Figure 14.16).

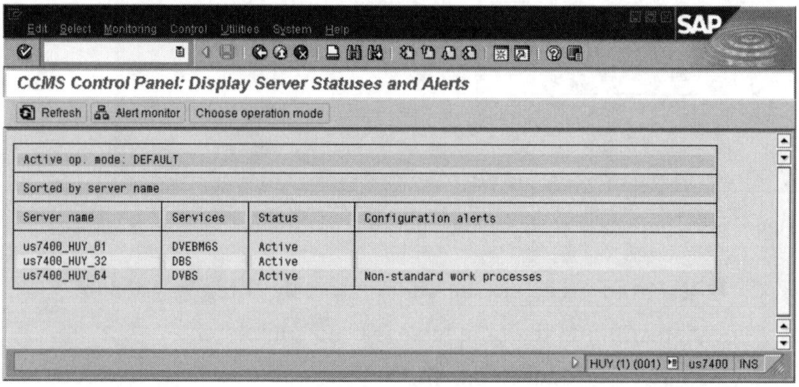

Figure 14.16 Control Panel-Initial Screen

The functions integrated in the control panel enable you to do the following:

▶ Check the status of all the instances in the R/3 system, including the operation modes

▶ Start and stop instances

▶ Change operation modes manually, independently of the defined schedule

- ▶ Display overviews, such as number and type of work processes and background work processes
- ▶ Go to the alert monitors
- ▶ Display the most important trace files

The main function of the control panel is to give the user the option of starting and stopping individual instances centrally. Some restrictions apply, however, depending on the operating system of the relevant instance:

- ▶ **UNIX platforms**

  The `rexec` command is used to execute commands on the remote UNIX server. The administration user on the local system that will use `rexec` to start or stop the instance must have a suitable entry (user name and password) in the *.netrc* configuration file on the target system.

- ▶ **NT and Windows 2000 platforms**

  An R/3 instance on an NT or Windows 2000 server is stopped and started through a message to the SAP Service Manager on the remote system.

- ▶ **AS/400 platforms**

  An internal AS/400 mechanism is used to start and stop the instance on an AS/400 platform.

14.4 Dynamic User Distribution

In R/3 systems with multiple application servers, it is advisable to distribute the load equally among all the servers, or even to assign users with particularly time-critical applications to the application servers with the best performance values. You can define *logon groups* for this purpose. A *logon group* is a subset of all application servers within an R/3 system. A user selects the assigned logon group to log on to the R/3 system. From this group, the R/3 system assigns the user to the application server that currently has the lightest load (according to response times). This process is also called *load distribution* (*logon load balancing*) between the instances.

Load Distribution

When creating logon groups, you must consider which groups of users exist in the application areas. Each instance has its own main memory area. Ideally, all the programs employed by the users of an instance, along with a majority of the data, will already be available in the main memory. The best way to attain this ideal occurs when the users of an instance all have similar responsibilities. You then define a logon group for this group of users. To do so, proceed as follows:

1. Choose ▶ **Logon Group Maintenance**.
2. Choose **Edit · Create Assignment**.
3. Enter the name of a logon group and assign the required instances.
4. Save the data.

Figure 14.17 shows the definition/overview screen for the logon groups.

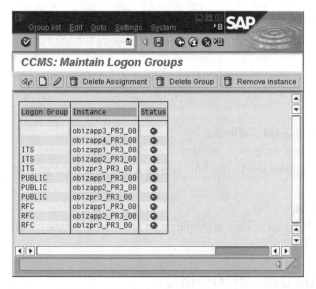

Figure 14.17 Defined Logon Groups

Load Limits You can also define a *load limit* for each instance, as an upper limit for the average response time and maximum number of users. These values are not absolute limits, however; they are thresholds used to calculate the current logon server for the group. The load limits defined for one instance are valid in all logon groups containing that instance.

IP Address of the Application Server In addition, one instance can be assigned a specific IP address to use for logging on the frontends. This is necessary when separate local networks are used within the R/3 system. Often, a particularly fast network is used to connect application servers with the database server, in order to deal with the large amounts of data. The computers in the presentation layer, however, are usually connected in the general network. Here, the application servers have two network cards and therefore, two IP addresses. You must define which IP address is valid for the frontends.

To define the load limits for an instance in the logon groups, as well as the IP address assignment, proceed as follows:

1. Select the required instance in ▶Logon Group Maintenance.

2. Double-click on the instance to select it and enter the required values.

3. Save your defined settings.

You can choose to allow or block access to the logon group via Remote Function Controller (RFC) queries (see Figure 14.18). Use the **Assignment** tab page to assign the selected instance to a different logon group.

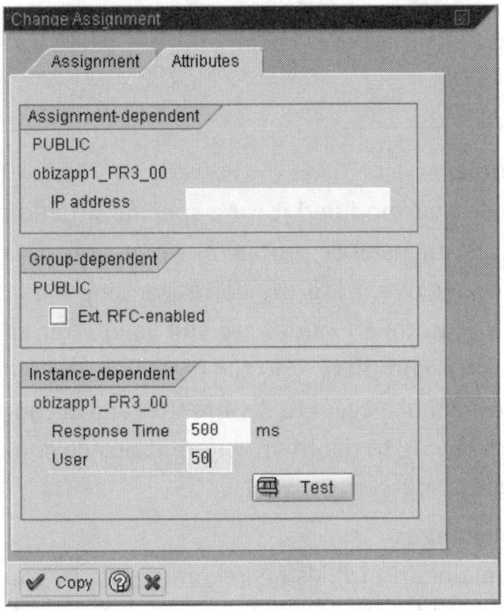

Figure 14.18 Attributes of a Logon Group

To display an overview of the current system's utilization, select **Goto · User List** in ▶**Logon Group Maintenance** to display the current list of active users, and **Goto · Load Distribution** to display the current distribution to instances in the logon group (see Figure 14.19).

The defined logon groups can be used together with the **SAPLOGON** program or, up to R/3 Release 4.6C, with the SAP Session Manager. A SAP GUI must always be called directly for an instance of an R/3 system. Automatic load distribution between the instances of a logon group cannot be used in this case. The required information in **SAPLOGON** was already described within the framework of the post-installation activities in Chapter 4.

SAPLOGON

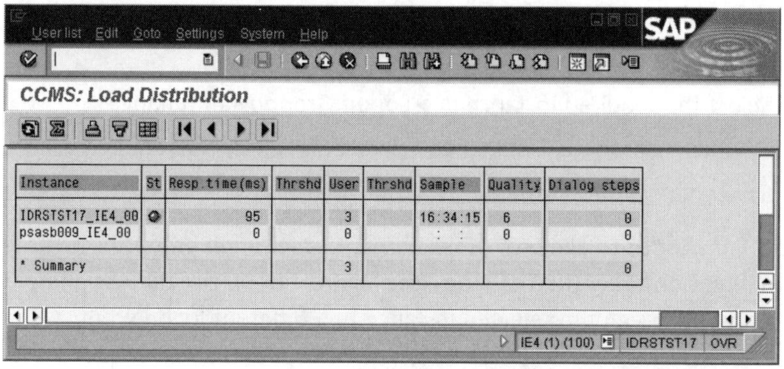

Figure 14.19 Current Load Distribution Within a Logon Group

14.5 Tips

▶ **Activating a special case profile**

If you copied a standard profile and modified it for a specific situation as described above (for example, an instance profile for a one-time data migration), the special case values overwrite the corresponding file at the operating-system level. The modified values are still valid after an instance restart. Once the action is complete, you can reactivate the old instance profile and restart the instance again to restore the typical configuration. This saves you from having to maintain different profile configurations manually at the operating-system level.

▶ **Determining manual profile changes**

If you use the R/3 system to maintain profiles (as recommended), you can determine any manual modifications to the profile files with ▶ **Profile Maintenance · Profile · Comparisons · Profile in Database · Against Active Profile.**

▶ **Automatic adjustment of the shared memory pool**

You no longer have to configure the sizes of the R/3 pool buffer (for communication between the work processes within an R/3 instance) manually in the instance profile. These values are calculated automatically. If the system detects a variance during a profile check, you can continue using the active parameter set. This situation does not represent an error.

▶ **Parameter changes**

If you have to change a profile parameter, make sure you only do so in the suitable profile.

  ▶ Cross-instance: *DEFAULT.PFL*

  ▶ Instance-specific: Instance profile

If a parameter is defined in both profiles, the entry in the instance pro-file has priority. If a parameter is set several times in the same profile, the last entry has priority.

▶ **Defining logon groups**
If only two application servers are available, it is not advisable to dis-tribute the various user groups to these two instances. To ensure sys-tem availability, a logon group must always consist of at least two instances on different servers.

▶ **Using logon groups to service application servers**
If you want to prevent logons to an application server for a certain amount of time, in order to service the computer, you can temporarily remove the respective instance from the logon group and reintegrate it once the servicing activities are complete. This process is completely transparent to end users.

14.6 Transactions and Menu Paths

Control panel: SAP menu • Tools • CCMS • Control/Monitoring • Control Panel (RZ03)

Gateway monitor: SAP menu • Tools • Administration • Monitor • System Monitoring • Gateway Monitor (SMGW)

Logon group maintenance: SAP menu • Tools • CCMS • Configuration • Logon Groups (SMLG)

Operation mode maintenance: SAP menu • Tools • CCMS • Configura-tion • Operation Modes/Instances (RZ04)

Maintain profile parameters: Not available in the SAP standard menu (RZ11)

Message server monitor: Not available in the SAP standard menu (SMMS)

Operation mode calendar: SAP Menu • Tools • CCMS • Configuration • Operation Mode Calendar (SM63)

Process overview: SAP Menu • Tools • Administration • Monitor • System Monitoring • Process Overview (SM50)

Profile maintenance: SAP Menu • Tools • CCMS • Configuration • Profile Maintenance (RZ10)

RFC server group maintenance: Not available in the SAP standard menu (RZ12)

14.7 Additional Documentation

SAP Service Marketplace Notes

The table below provides an overview of important SAP Notes from the SAP Service Marketplace that pertain to profile maintenance, dynamic user distribution, and the control panel.

Contents	Note
Set up for Logon group for automatic load balancing	26317
Test tool for message servers: lgtst	64015
Logon workload balancing verification test	27044

Table 14.2 SAP Notes for Maintaining Instances

14.8 Questions

1. What is meant by "operation mode"?

   a. An operation mode describes the number and type of work processes on one or more instances.

   b. An operation mode also includes all settings for the R/3 main memory areas.

   c. An operation mode describes the status of the R/3 system: "active" means operational; "DB active" means only the R/3 database is available and the R/3 system is shut down.

2. What is a logon group?

   a. All users who are assigned to the same user group form a logon group.

   b. A logon group is a logical unit and a subset of all application servers within an R/3 system.

   c. All users who have the same responsibilities form a logon group.

15   System Monitoring

A system administrator's routine activities include the monitoring and supervision of the individual R/3 systems. These activities are just as important as the configuring of the system settings; their preventive and proactive nature makes them essential to ensure problem-free operations. This chapter introduces the system monitoring tools and describes their use. It also describes the list of administrative tasks that are performed regularly and repeatedly by the system administrator.

The SAP system supplies a multitude of functions for monitoring and configuring the technical system status. System administrators use many of these transactions daily.

15.1   Server and Process Overviews

You can get a detailed overview of the status of the instances of R/3 systems and the functionality of the R/3 work processes by looking at the server overview, the process overview (which was described briefly in Chapter 2), and the Control Panel (see Chapter 14). In this chapter, the descriptions from previous chapters are supplemented with several important details for system administrators.

The ▶ **Server Overview** displays all the available instances of an R/3 System (see Figure 15.1), with information regarding the used server and type of configured work processes. In the Web Application Server, the status of the instance is also indicated:

Server Overview

▶ **initial**
The application server has logged on to the message server but cannot be addressed yet.

▶ **starting**
The configured work processes of the application server are being started; however, they cannot process any requests yet.

▶ **active**
The application server works in regular operation mode and is processing its requests.

▶ **passive**
The application server will be deactivated. It will complete processing its tasks, but it will not accept any new tasks.

► **shutdown**

The application server is being shut down and will not process any more tasks.

► **stop**

The application server no longer has a connection to the message server and is therefore unreachable.

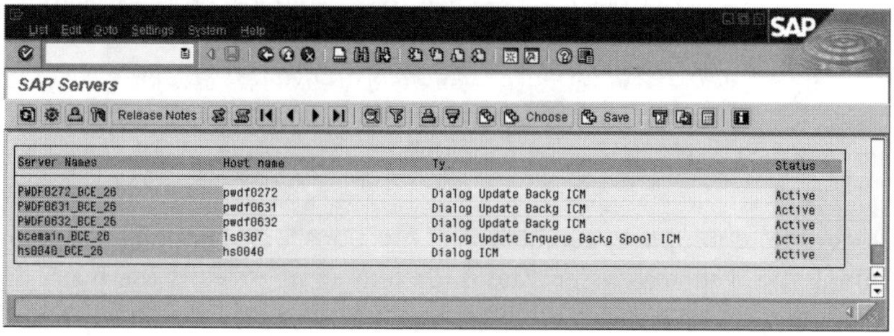

Figure 15.1 Server Overview in an R/3 Enterprise System

You can use icons or the **Goto** menu to display more detailed information or start actions for each list entry. These functions are listed in Table 15.1.

Menu item Goto	Icon	Activity
Processes	⚙	Go to the process overview for the selected instance (see Figure 15.1)
User	👤	Go to the user overview for the selected instance (see Figure 15.2)
SNC Status	📟	Information about the SNC status, such as SNC activation, path to the GSS library, how to deal with non-secure connections
Release Info	Release information	Detailed release information (R/3 kernel, database, operating system); additional information on the message server in Web AS 6.10 and later
Environment		Server environment variables; integrated in the selection of server information in Web AS 6.10 and later
Remote Logon	📇	Log on to the selected instance (the current server is displayed in the status bar)
System Log	📇	Go to the system log for the selected instance (see Figure 15.3)

Table 15.1 Options in the Server Overview

Menu item Goto	Icon	Activity
SAP Directories		Go to the display of the SAP directories for the selected instance (see Figure 15.5)
OS Monitor		Go to the ▶ OS Monitor for the selected instance (see Figure 15.7)
Communication table		Display all CPI-C connections (client and server)
Queue Information		Information on the request queue: number of configured processes for each request type and statistics data on their use; integrated in the selection of server information in Web AS 6.10 and later
Host Name Buffer		Entries in the network configuration files, *hosts* and *services*, can be activated without restarting the instances
Gateway Monitor		Go to the ▶ Gateway Monitor for the selected instance (see Chapter 13)
Server Information		In Web AS 6.10 and later, the items Environment, Queue Info, and Comm. Table described above are consolidated here. You can also log on to the application server (Logon Data) and conduct a connection test (Connection Test). The trace search function enables you to search for a specified string in all the developer traces on the selected instance (see Section 15.5).

Table 15.1 Options in the Server Overview (cont.)

The Web Application Server also includes a ▶ **Message Server Overview**, which is similar to the server overview. To analyze the message server, you can select from the **Goto** menu options. In addition to the information available in the server overview, this new overview also includes the following data and actions:

▶ Display hardware key (see Chapter 4)

▶ Display all (and change some) message server-specific system parameters.

▶ Display statistics data such as the number of logons, queries received, and bytes written/read.

▶ Display the developer trace file of the message server, *dev_ms*, and change the current trace level without restarting the instance.

Message Server Overview

▶ Stop application servers, with or without completing processing of requests still present in the dispatcher queue; the target status is *shutdown*.

▶ Deactivate application servers and complete processing of requests still present in the dispatcher queue; the target status is *passive*.

▶ Reactivate deactivated application servers.

Process Overview   To display the comprehensive process overview of a single instance (aside from the corresponding function call in the server overview), choose ▶ **Process Overview**. The following information is displayed in tabular form:

▶ **Internal process number**
The system uses this number internally, for example, to assign messages to processes. The process number is contained in the name of the corresponding developer trace.

▶ **Process type**

  ▶ DIA: Dialog work process

  ▶ UPD: Update process for time-critical changes in the database (V1 update, see Chapter 10)

  ▶ UPD2: Update process for non-time-critical changes in the database (V2 update, see Chapter 10)

  ▶ ENQ: Enqueue work process for handling SAP locks

  ▶ BTC: Background work process

  ▶ SPO: Spool work process

▶ **Process number at operating-system level (PID)**
If necessary, you can specify this process number to terminate the process at operating-system level.

▶ **Status of the process**

  ▶ *running*: The process is currently processing a request.

  ▶ *waiting*: The process is available and waiting for new requests.

  ▶ *hold*: The process is currently assigned to a single user. This status occurs during regular system operations, but can cause performance problems if too many processes have it.

  ▶ *killed*: The process was terminated due to an error and has not been restarted.

► **Reason for hold**

When processes have status *hold*, the reason for holding the process appears here. Common reasons for hold include:

- ► CPIC: Work process is waiting for a CPI-C message.
- ► DEBUG: Work process is currently in debugging mode.
- ► LOCK: Work process has been assigned to one user exclusively for system analysis.
- ► NUM: Work process is waiting for a response from a number range server.
- ► OS: Work process is waiting for an operating-system command to be processed.
- ► PRIV: Work process is working exclusively for one user.
- ► SLEEP: Work process is waiting due to a resource bottleneck.
- ► VB: Work process is waiting for a synchronous update request to be processed.

► **Startup method**

If a work process fails, the dispatcher of the instance immediately tries to start a new work process to replace it. If the new work process terminates again during the start phase as the result of a serious problem, the system sets the restart value to *no* to avoid an endless loop of failed process starts.

► **Number of terminations**

The *Err* column specifies the number of times the work process has terminated since the instance was last started.

► **Semaphores**

If a work process is on hold because it is waiting for a semaphore to be released, the number of the semaphore is displayed in this column, highlighted in red. You can use this information to analyze situations that cause extreme delays for work processes. If the semaphore number is highlighted in green, the work process itself is holding it. Work processes use the semaphore mechanism to reserve resources.

► **Accumulated runtime of the current action in seconds**

► **Current report**

► **Currently assigned user with client**

► **Current action and table being processed**

You can use the **List · CPU** function in the ▶ **Process Overview** to display additional information on the CPU load posed by the processes. Figure 15.2 shows a section of the process overview.

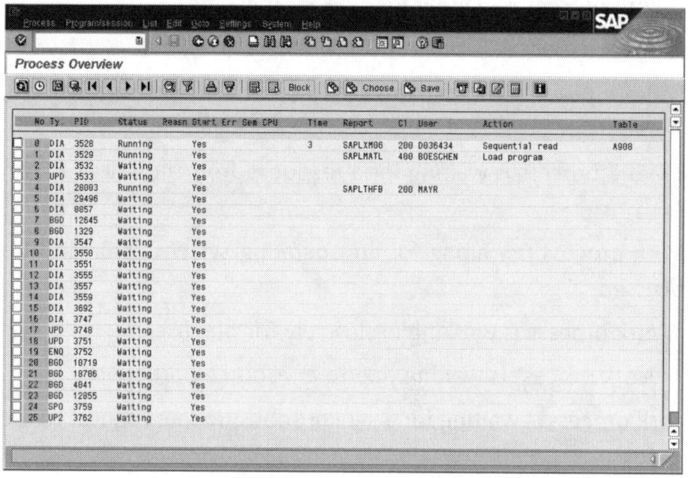

Figure 15.2 Process Overview

The process overview enables you to identify especially long-running reports, for example. You can also choose **Process · Details** (or double-click on the corresponding line) to display detailed information for a processing step. The table that is currently being processed and the resources used so far are displayed.

Debugging Mode   Experts may also find the debugging mode helpful and informative for running an ABAP program. To activate this mode for the selected process, choose **Program/Session · Program · Debugging**. The step-by-step execution of the corresponding program is displayed. The user receives full control over the program flow. Because running a program in debugging mode is extremely resource-intensive, you should only use it in test and development systems.

If you encounter serious problems, you can also cancel or restart a dialog or background work process (**Process · Cancel with Core, Process · Cancel w/o Core, Restart after Error · Yes**). The relevant transaction is rolled back. The user is usually sent a message indicating that the system administrator canceled his or her process. You should never cancel update and enqueue processes manually, however, as this could create logical inconsistencies in the database.

Each work process writes a separate error log file (see Section 15.5). You can configure the degree of detail in the error log by using various criteria—such as manual selection or work process type—by setting a system parameter, or via **Process · Trace** from the ▶**Process Overview**. You can restrict the loading components to limit the recorded trace information to defined subareas. The display components are a subset of the selected load components and describe the trace information that is actually displayed from the collected information. Work processes that run with a trace level greater than 1 are highlighted in yellow in the process list.

A ▶**Global Work Process Overview** is available in addition to the local process overview described above. You can use this transaction to monitor the load of work processes on all active instances. A wide variety of selection criteria is available for formatting, filtering, and sorting the display.

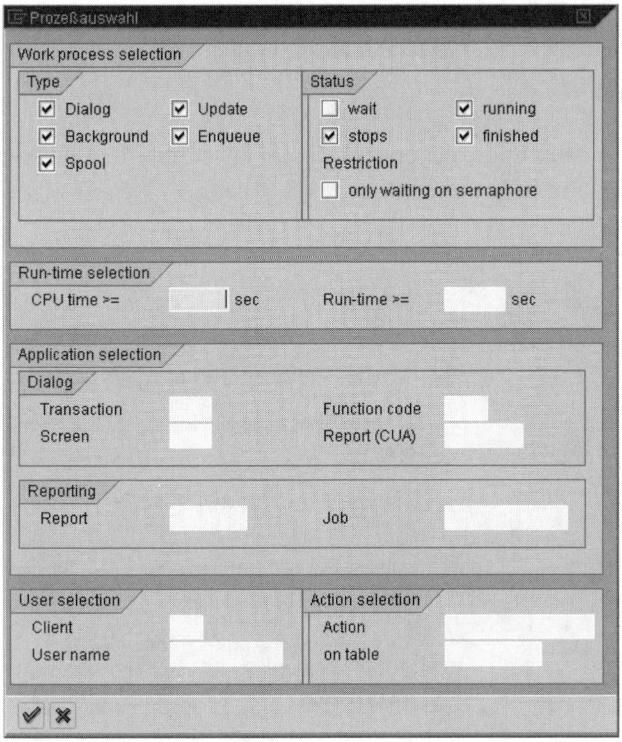

Global Work Process Overview

Figure 15.3 Process Selection in the Global Work Process

You administer and monitor the Internet Communication Manager (ICM, see Chapter 1) in the ▶**ICM Monitor**. Like the process overview, the ICM Monitor (see Figure 15.4) displays a list of the configured worker threads and their current status, along with additional information and possible actions.

ICM Monitor

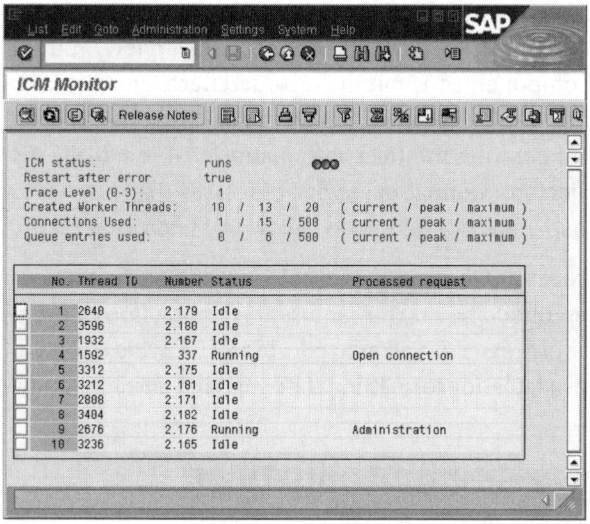

Figure 15.4 ICM Monitor

The **Goto** menu contains the select options described in Table 15.2 below, some of which can also be accessed directly via clicking on the respective icon.

Menu item Goto	Icon	Activity
Trace Level		Set the trace level to a value from 0-3
Trace File		Display/reset trace file *dev_icm* (see Section 15.5)
Parameters		Display/change the profile parameter set for the ICM
Memory Pipes		Display status information for the memory pipes
Host Name Buffer		Display/reset the buffered mapping of server names to IP addresses and service names to port numbers
Release Notes	Release Info	Display information on the kernel release and patch level
Services		Display the services configured in the ICM: log, port, timeout, status
Statistics		Information on ICM use since the process was started

Table 15.2 Options from the Worker Thread Overview

You can use the **Administration** menu to terminate or restart the ICM, as well as administer the J2EE engine.

If necessary, several of the ICM Monitor functions can also be executed at operating-system level with program **icmon**:

icmon

```
icmon [-gs -c <cmdfile> -f <tracefile> -t <trclevel>]
   -u <user> -p <password> pf=<profile>
```

Similar to the utility **dpmon** (see Chapter 2), **icmon** provides statistical data on the ICM status and enables you to modify the trace level of the worker threads, for example.

Listing 15.1 Output of icmon

```
ICM's Statistics
================

Server started at: Wed Oct 16 10:04:11 2002
Status: ICM_STATUS_RUN (pid: 956), DP port: 65000
Current number of threads: 10, peak: 10, max: 50
Current number of open connections: 0, peak: 4, max: 300
Current number of requests in queue: 0, peak: 2, max: 100
Floating average of requests in queue: 0
Statistics level:   1
Bytes read(MB):     0
Bytes read:         123425
Bytes written(MB): 1
Bytes written:      495546
No. of requests:    281
No. of rollouts:    81
No. of rollins:     81
No. of timeouts:    0
No. of errors:      23
Overall time:       0:33:17:929851
Min req time(sec):  0.019779
Max req time(sec):  154.859192
+--+----+----+---+--------------------+----------------+
|No|thid|#req|cid|   Thread Status    | Request type   |
+--+----+----+---+--------------------+----------------+
| 0|  0 | 29 |-1 |ICM_THR_STATUS_IDLE|            NOP |
| 1|  0 | 38 |-1 |ICM_THR_STATUS_IDLE|            NOP |
| 2|  0 | 28 |-1 |ICM_THR_STATUS_IDLE|            NOP |
| 3|  0 | 31 |-1 |ICM_THR_STATUS_IDLE|            NOP |
```

```
| 4|  0 | 36 |-1 |ICM_THR_STATUS_IDLE|                NOP |
| 5|  0 | 26 |-1 |ICM_THR_STATUS_IDLE|                NOP |
| 6|  0 | 31 |-1 |ICM_THR_STATUS_IDLE|                NOP |
| 7|  0 | 28 |-1 |ICM_THR_STATUS_IDLE|                NOP |
| 8|  0 | 33 |-1 |ICM_THR_STATUS_IDLE|                NOP |
| 9|  0 | 36 |-1 |ICM_THR_STATUS_IDLE|                NOP |
+--+----+----+---+--------------------+----------------+
    + - increase trace level by one
    - - decrease trace level by one
    S - increase statistic level by one
    s - decrease statistic level by one
    q - quit
    m - menu
```

Figure 15.5 shows the ICM server cache statistics with statistics level 1 (default setting).

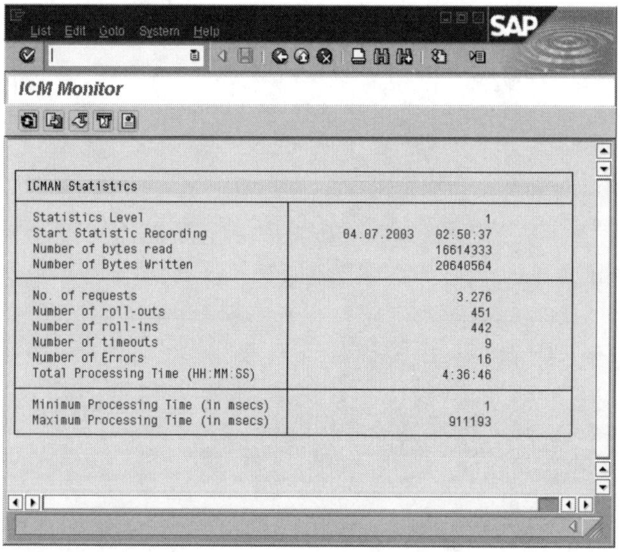

Figure 15.5 ICM Statistics

15.2 User Overviews

For further analysis, you can choose function **Goto · User** in the ▶**Server Overview** to display the ▶**User Overview**, or call the action directly.

User Activities on the Local Instance This overview (see Figure 15.6) gives you an idea of the current user activity on the local instance. The system displays the following information for each active user: terminal used to log on, current transaction, number of open sessions, and time of last performed dialog step. You can activate a user trace (**User · Trace · Activate**) for selected users, which logs all actions performed by these users. You can analyze and deactivate the user trace in a similar manner. Activating the user trace is recommended when you must analyze problematic situations that only arise for individual users. If necessary, you can also delete user sessions and force users to log off from within the user overview.

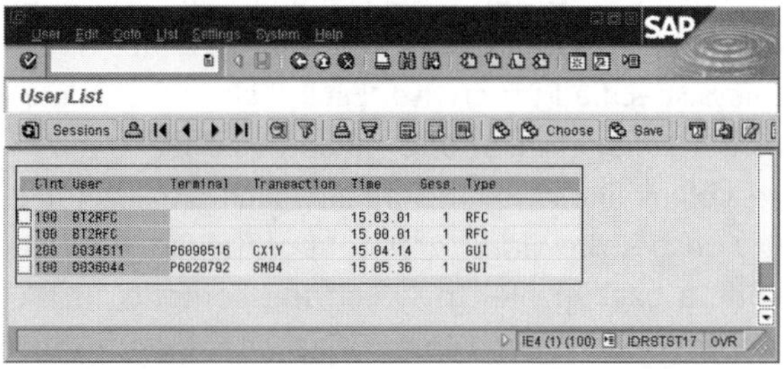

Figure 15.6 Local User Overview

The ▶**Global User Overview** displays all active users in any of the active instances, with detailed information on type, logon client, executed transaction, and time of the last dialog step (see Figure 15.7).

Global User Overview

This monitor always appears in English, regardless of your logon language.

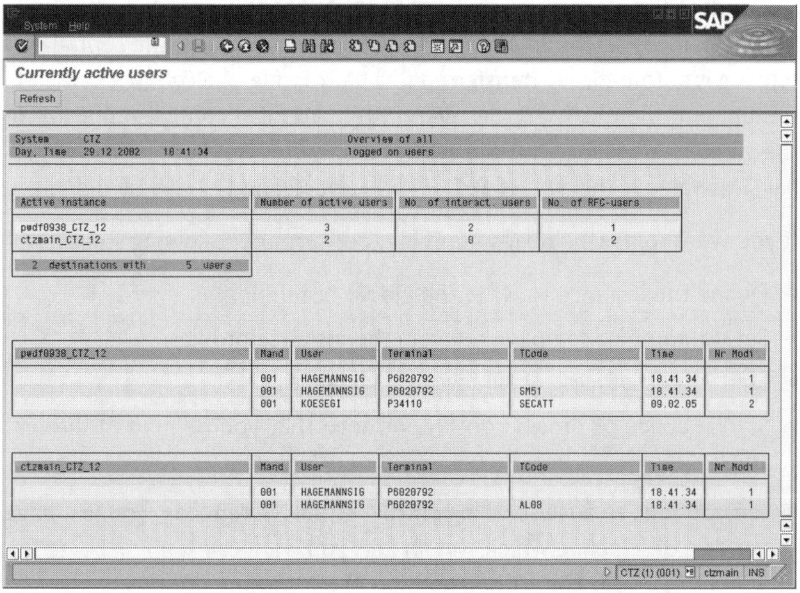

Figure 15.7 Global User Overview

15.3 System Log

The *system log* is the most important log in the normal operation of an R/3 system; it represents your starting point for all problem analysis. The system log records system information messages, warnings, and error messages, each highlighted in a different color.

Accordingly, checking the ▶ **System Log** is a daily activity for every system administrator. A local system log is written for each application server, to file *SLOG<instance_number>.log* in subdirectory *log* of the instance directory (see Chapter 1), unless specified otherwise. Each log entry occupies 192 bytes, which means the default size of 500 KB corresponds to 2,065 log entries. Starting from a blank file, when the log file reaches the defined size limit, each new entry pushes the oldest entry out of the file. Alternatively, you can also define a backup file, to which the contents of the actual log file are transferred once the maximum size is reached. In this case, the log file starts over with a blank file.

The relevant parameters are *rslg/max_diskspace/local* for the size of the log file and *rslg/local/file* and *rslg/local/old_file* for the names of the log and backup files.

Global System Log | A *global system log* is also available in UNIX systems. The entries of all local system logs of the configured instances can be merged in this log. The corresponding file is saved in subdirectory *global* of the system directory; its default name is *SLOGJ*. In contrast to the local system log, the central system log is automatically transferred to a backup file, *SLOGJO*, when the file fills up, and the old *SLOGJO* is overwritten. You can configure the size of the global system log with the system parameter *rslg/max_diskspace/global*. This value is the sum of *SLOGJ* and *SLOGJO* and is 2 MB by default.

If you want to use a global system log, perform the following steps:

- ▶ Define the instance to write the global system log.
- ▶ Set the required log parameters in the instance profiles.
- ▶ Start a send process on all involved instances.
- ▶ Start a collector process on the instance that you defined in the first step.

Selecting the System Logs | When you start an analysis of log entries with ▶ **System Log**, you first have the option of selecting which system logs you want to examine. Using the menu path **System Log · Choose** offers the following options:

- ► **Local SysLog**

  Default setting; the system log entries on the local instance are displayed.

- ► **Remote SysLog**

  The system log entries of the instance in the **Instance Name** field are displayed.

- ► **All Remote SysLogs**

  The system log entries of all reachable instances are displayed.

- ► **Central SysLog**

  The entries in the central system log are displayed. This item is only active when a central system log has been configured. The entries in the local system log are always current. Because the entries in the central system log are transferred at regular intervals, they may be slightly outdated.

A multitude of selection criteria is available for analyzing the ►**System Log**. The expert mode (**Edit · Expert Mode**) offers an even wider range of options. You can optionally restrict selection by:

Analyzing the System Logs

- ► Time frame
- ► User
- ► Transaction code
- ► Process type
- ► Problem class
- ► Additional criteria in expert mode

The system log is read and all messages that meet the defined criteria are displayed in list form.

Figure 15.8 shows an excerpt from a local system log for system "HUY". The system log contains the last actions of the instance startup, along with related actions such as starting send process *rslgsend* for the global system log. At 13:06, an update process was switched dynamically to a work process for background processing (operation mode switching, see Chapter 14). Afterwards rollbacks occured in several transactions. You can display the cause of the problems by double-clicking on the entry or by choosing **Edit · Details** in the list. The standard list layout displays time stamp, the relevant work process, client, user, transaction code, message number, and a short text. You can also supplement this display with other information if you want, such as the program name as shown in the example.

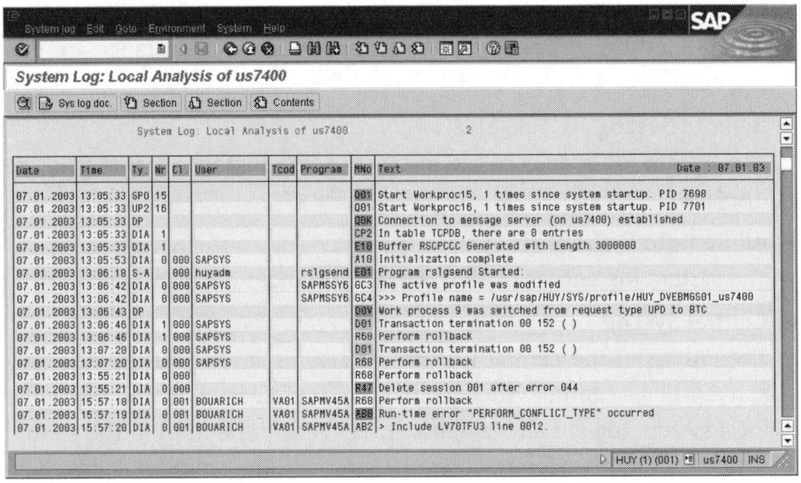

Figure 15.8 Excerpt from a Local System Log

15.4 Analyzing Runtime Errors

Short Dump
If a termination occurs during the execution of an ABAP program, a *short dump* is generated per problem and saved for further analysis. In development systems, the dump is an important utility for programming; the developer is primarily responsible for analyzing and correcting the errors. Runtime errors, however, should never occur in production systems where no developments take place. Therefore, the system administrator must check daily to see whether program terminations occurred and, if so, determine why they did. If you want to do so, use the ▶ **Dump Analysis**. All important background information, in addition to the termination point and time of error, is saved for each program termination. This information includes the time of the termination, information on the R/3 release, RDBMS and operating system used, as well as variable values. Users are also offered troubleshooting tools (see Figure 15.9).

You should schedule report **RSSNAPDL** (see Section 9.6) regularly in order to delete runtime error reports that are outdated or have already been analyzed. If you want to prevent short dumps from being deleted because you have not analyzed them yet, you can do so via **Short Dump · Keep/Release**.

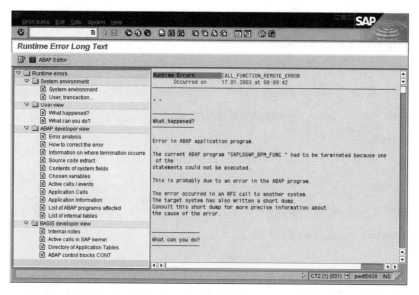

Figure 15.9 Dump Analysis, Web AS Layout

15.5 Trace Files

To enable a detailed analysis of error situations, many components in the runtime environment write their own dedicated log and trace files. Depending on the specific problem, system administrators may find additional information here that can be accessed even if the database or R/3 system is not running.

While the application-specific interpretation of trace files is often the application specialists' responsibility, system administrators are responsible for managing the necessary system settings and resources, which means:

▶ Providing enough disk space for the output files

▶ Cleaning up the trace files after the analysis is complete

▶ Adjusting the trace levels—in particular, resetting the trace level (or deactivating the trace completely) after the analysis is complete

An error log file, the *developer trace*, is written for any of the processes of each application server. These are the *dev_<xx>* files in the *work* subdirectory of the instance directory (see Chapter 1). The most important traces are listed in Table 15.3.

Developer Traces

The number of the work process is identical to the number shown in the ▶ **Process Overview**.

File name	Associated process
dev_disp	Dispatcher
dev_icm	Internet Communication Manager (ICM)
dev_ms	Message server
dev_rd	Gateway reader process
dev_rfc	RFC calls of external functions
dev_rfc<n>	RFC calls of work process number *n*
dev_tp	**tp** and **R3trans**
dev_w<n>	Work process number *n*

Table 15.3 Developer Traces

This data is particularly important when an instance cannot be started or processes terminate in active systems. You can set the trace level for each instance with parameter *rdisp/TRACE*. You can also adjust the trace levels dynamically for individual processes in the process overview of the R/3 system (see Section 15.1), or by using the command line.

Trace Levels | You can configure the following detail depths:

▶ **Trace level 0**
Tracing is deactivated.

▶ **Trace level 1 (default setting)**
Error messages are recorded in the trace files.

▶ **Trace level 2**
Full trace.

▶ **Trace level 3**
In addition to error and action messages, the contents of data blocks are also written to the trace files.

You should only increase the trace level if you want to analyze specific errors, as this also increases the write load on the files. In production systems, the trace level in normal operations is not greater than 1.

When you restart the R/3 system, new versions of the *dev_<xx>* developer traces are created; the last version is saved to *dev_<xx>.old* backup files.

You can analyze developer traces at operating-system level and, if possible, from within the R/3 system with ▶Trace Files, ▶Process Overview, or ▶SAP Directories. Selecting ▶SAP Directories lets you display files within the SAP frontend. All files in the R/3 directories can be accessed under the default settings; you can use the **Configure** icon (see Figure 15.10) to make additional directories accessible under a logical name.

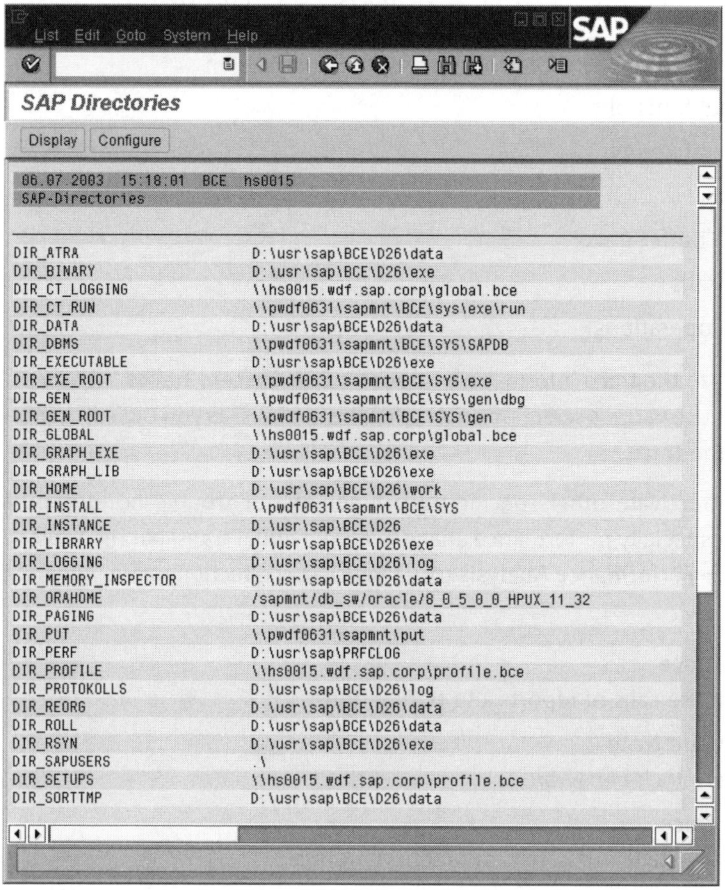

Figure 15.10 Initial Screen of SAP Directories

As already described in Chapter 4, you can activate multi-level tracing for the frontend under the selection options in **SAPLOGON**. The trace files are saved in the work directory on the frontend. To display the current setting for this directory in **SAPLOGON**, choose **SAPLOGON · System Information · Additional Information**. You can use any text editor to open and analyze the defined trace files.

Frontend Trace

You can use the ▶**SAP system traces** to record detailed process flows within the R/3 system. You should use the SAP system trace carefully and only together with SAP, as the recorded information is extremely compre-

SAP System Trace

hensive and difficult to interpret. The SAP system trace is not suitable for live systems.

The available trace components are release-specific. The following components, at least, are available in both R/3 4.6 and the Web AS:

- ▶ Authorization check
- ▶ Kernel functions
- ▶ General kernel
- ▶ DB access (SQL trace)
- ▶ Table buffer trace
- ▶ RFC calls
- ▶ Lock operations

To analyze the trace information, choose ▶ **SAP System Traces · Analysis**. You can use various selection criteria for the analysis, as you did when activating the trace.

Performance Trace You can activate other specific trace functions for troubleshooting purposes, especially performance analyses of individual transactions. You can use the ▶ **Performance Analysis** to activate data collection in the following areas:

- ▶ **SQL trace**
  Database calls of reports and transactions

- ▶ **Enqueue trace**
  System lock behavior

- ▶ **RFC trace**
  Cross-instance RFC calls of function modules

- ▶ **Buffer trace**
  Table buffer trace

In this case, all SQL commands that are created by user actions are recorded, together with duration, results, and data. You can use ▶ Performance Analysis · Deactivate Trace · Display Trace (or ▶ Performance Analysis · Performance Trace · Display Trace or Deactivate First) to filter the data by various criteria first, and then analyze it.

Figure 15.12 shows an excerpt from a SQL trace. For example, the execution time of statement

```
SELECT WHERE "MANDT" = 'EXP' AND "SOURCEMAND" = '001'
OR "MANDT" = '001' ORDER BY "TSTAMP"
```

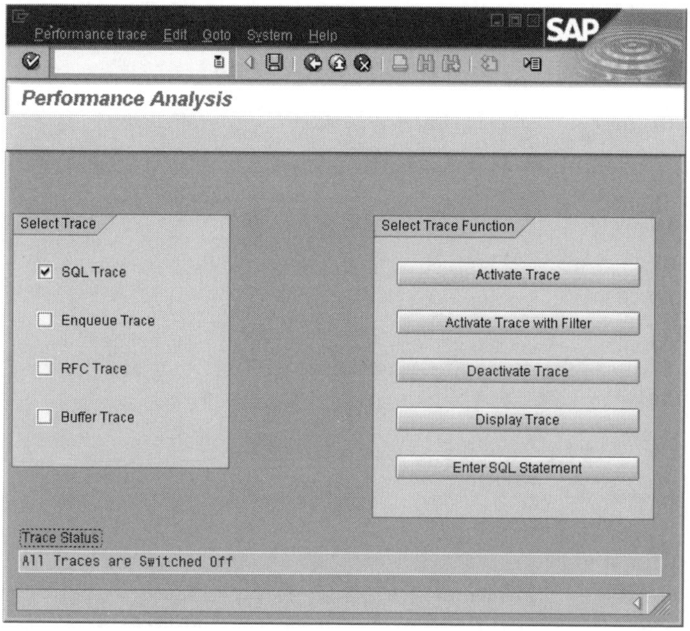

Figure 15.11 Activating the SQL Traces

was 59 milliseconds (ms) in this case, the search took place in table CCC-FLOW (the tracked operation was the display of client copy logs). The duration of an operation is always specified in milliseconds. Commands that exceed a defined runtime and therefore may be critical are highlighted in red.

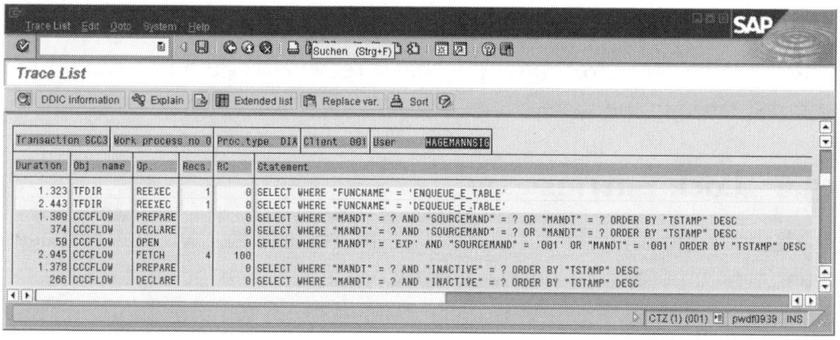

Figure 15.12 Excerpt from a SQL Trace

Choose **Edit · Explain for an SQL statement** to call the execution plan calculated by the optimizer for this command. Choose **Goto · ABAP Display** to go to the ABAP program where the SQL statement was generated.

The table columns have slightly different meanings, depending on which trace is used (see Table 15.4).

Column	SQL trace	Enqueue trace	RFC trace	Buffer trace
Duration	Execution time of the statement	Execution time of the statement	Execution time of the statement	Execution time of the statement
Object Name	Table or DB procedure	Lock object	Instance name	Table name
Operation	Operation performed on the DB	Lock operation	Role (client or server)	Function performed for the object in the buffer
Records	Number of records processed	Number of granulates	Type of record	Number of records read
RC	Return code from the RDBMS	0: Correct 2: Collision 8: Internal error	0: Correct	0: Correct 64: No record found 256: Record not available 1024: Loading buffer
Statement	SQL command	Granulates	Source and target server function module	Buffering type Key value

Table 15.4 Performance Traces

Database Logs   All the database systems used in the SAP environment write their own log files that are independent from the SAP system. You can display these files at operating-system level or with the ▶**Database Monitor** within the R/3 system. Important error messages that directly affect the R/3 system are also displayed in the system log.

15.6 Lock Entries

As described in Chapter 1, the R/3 system features its own lock management, which utilizes the enqueue work processes. The lock entries are set by the active programs and usually deleted again without requiring any manual intervention. If problems occur in the R/3 system, however—for example, if the dispatcher of an instance or the entire application server suddenly fails—outdated lock entries can persist. Therefore, you must check the lock entries daily and delete them manually as necessary. To do so, proceed as follows:

1. Use the ►**Lock Monitor** to reach the screen for selecting the lock entries to display. You can restrict the selection by table name, lock argument, client, or user.

2. Choose **List**. A list of all the current locks in the system is displayed (see Figure 15.13).

In addition to the user and client that set the lock, the system also displays the time when the lock was generated and the table affected. The lock argument (*lock key*) is particularly important. The **Shared** column indicates whether the lock is used by several users. To sort the list by various criteria, you can use **Edit · Sort by.**

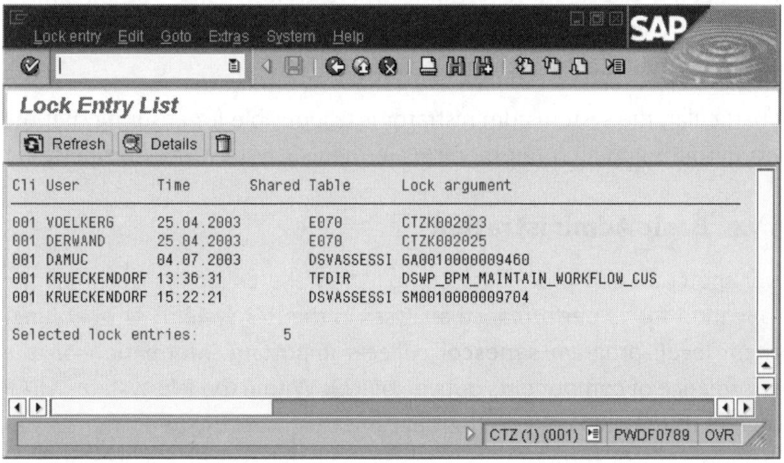

Figure 15.13 Lock Entries

3. Check the times when the lock entries were generated. Lock entries that have been held for a long time must be analyzed. Double-click on the lock key of an entry to display more detailed information on that entry, such as the transaction code that caused the lock.

4. If open update requests still exist for the lock entries, first check and clean up these update transactions.

5. Check whether the user who belongs to the lock entry is still active in the system.

Problems in lock management are often symptoms of other problems. Therefore, if you detect outdated lock entries, you first have to check the application area that is involved. If your analysis reveals that a lock entry is unnecessary, you can remove it by selecting it in the ►**Lock Monitor** and then calling function **Lock Entry · Delete**. The deletion of lock entries is recorded in the system log of the instance.

To display statistics data on lock behavior, especially the use of the shared memory area where the locks are held, choose **Extras · Statistics**. To ensure that lock management is functioning properly, choose **Extras · Diagnosis**. To check the interaction between lock management and update task, choose **Extras · Diagnosis in Update**.

15.7 Performance Monitoring

The foundation of all tuning activities for improving performance in an R/3 system is the regular monitoring of all relevant indicators, only some of which can be automated. Experienced system administrators can interpret the collected values and determine where to intervene. The integrated alert monitor is a useful tool. Its basic principles and instructions for using and configuring it are described in Chapter 16.

In particular, the system administrator is responsible for ensuring that the alert monitor and all other monitors in the R/3 system work properly.

15.7.1 Basic Administration

Over the course of time, data compiled by the collectors becomes the foundation for all performance analyses in the R/3 system. At operating-system level, program **saposcol** collects important information on the performance of components outside of R/3. Within the R/3 system, ABAP program **RSCOLL00** collects this data and calculates the performance values for other R/3 components, such as the database and the R/3 buffers. You should schedule **RSCOLL00** to run hourly as a background process under the standard name **SAP_COLLECTOR_FOR_PERFMONITOR**. The summarized data is written to table MONI, also called the *performance database*. To configure the performance database in systems up to R/3 4.6C, choose ▶ **Workload Analysis · Goto · Parameters · Performance Database**; in 4.6D and later, choose ▶ **Load Analysis · Collector · Workload Collector · Data**. Additional configuration options are:

▶ Retention duration of the collected statistical data

▶ Summarization of the data

▶ Reorganization rules

The performance data is reorganized automatically by background job **SAP_COLLECTOR_FOR_PERFMONITOR** based on these settings.

15.7.2 Monitors

The SAP system provides several different monitors to enable precise analysis of system performance. They involve the following areas:

Workload Analysis

▶ **Workload analysis** (up to R/3 4.6C)
Predecessor to the load analysis

▶ **Load analysis**
Displays the system load per instance, distribution to work processes, user statistics, distribution of response times, history data, and hit lists (see Figure 15.14)

▶ **Business process analysis**
Analysis of single statistics records

▶ **Application monitor**
Display user distribution

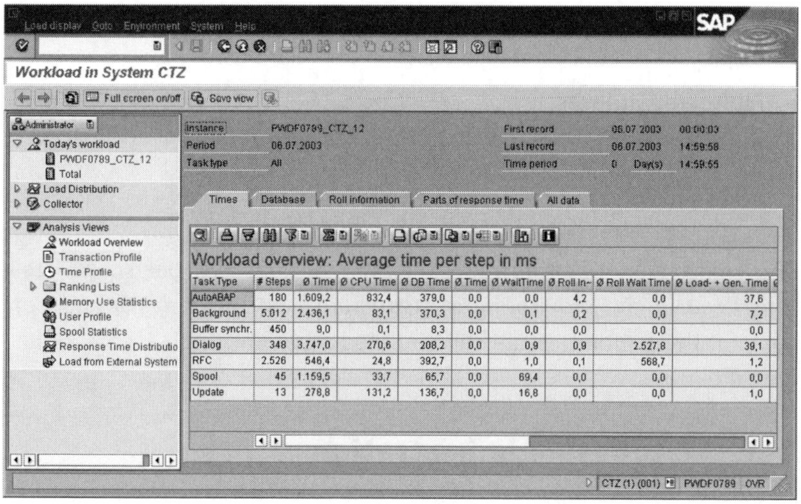

Figure 15.14 Load Analysis

Buffers

▶ **Buffer load**
Displays the quality and size of the most important SAP buffers, including information about memory use.

▶ **Table calls**
Displays the table call statistics.

► **Profile parameter changes**
Displays the change history for the profile parameters.

Operating System

► **OS monitor**
Monitors operating-system resources such as memory, CPU, file system, hard disks.

► **OS system configuration**
Displays the current operating-system parameters.

► **OS parameter changes**
Displays the change history for the operating-system parameters.

Database

► **Database monitor**
Displays the most important statistics for analyzing database activity and allows access to the database log.

► **Lock waits**
Displays the number of lock waits and escalations.

► **Tables and indexes**
Displays the resource statistics, table analysis, and index analysis.

► **DB parameter changes**
Displays the change history for the database parameters.

The familiar alert monitors from earlier R/3 versions have been completely integrated in the monitoring infrastructure (see Chapter 16) and only some of these monitors can still be called separately in R/3 4.6C for historical reasons.

15.8 Database Administration

The database administrator is responsible for managing the deployed RDBMS and database. Because the associated tasks are RDBMS-specific, they can only be described in general here.

The system administrator's most important activities involving database monitoring and administration are:

► Scheduling, executing, and monitoring the database backup

► Scheduling, executing, and monitoring the backup of the transaction logs

- ▶ Scheduling, executing, and monitoring the verification of tape contents (database backup) and database consistency

- ▶ Scheduling, executing, and monitoring the generation of statistics for the cost-based optimizer

- ▶ Capacity planning and resource monitoring (at operating system and database level)

- ▶ Configuring and monitoring the database parameters

Similar tools are available for every RDBMS used with the R/3 system; however, their appearance and names may vary in detail.

15.8.1 Regularly Scheduled Tasks

The database performs an extremely important role within the R/3 system. It is the center for data storage and retention. Therefore, it is imperative that you back up the database data regularly, in order to be able to restore the data in case of error. A ▶DBA **Planning Calendar** is integrated in the R/3 system for this and other regularly required tasks.

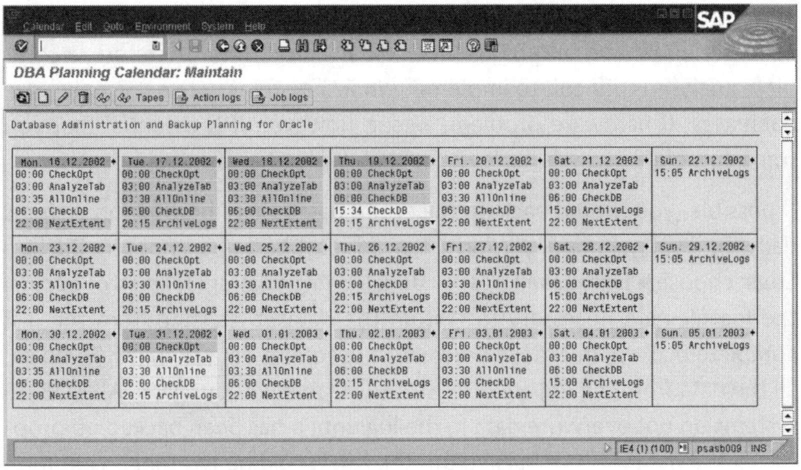

Figure 15.15 Weekly Planning in the DBA Planning Calendar

You can schedule the most important database administration tasks for background processing here (see Figure 15.15). They include:

- ▶ Backing up the database on-the-fly (online) or stopped (offline)
- ▶ Incremental data backup
- ▶ Backup of log areas
- ▶ Backup of individual data areas

- ▶ Update optimizer statistics
- ▶ Analysis of database structures
- ▶ Analysis of database status

Cost-Based Optimizer
All Relational Database Management Systems currently used with the R/3 systems use a cost-based optimizer to calculate the execution strategy for the SQL commands. If several execution plans are available, the *cost-based optimizer* determines the most cost-saving strategy. Costs are calculated as the total number of data blocks to be processed, that is, the actual data records and any index information used. The strategy is based on statistics of the data in a table, such as the number of records and the number of different values within an indexed column. The statistics used by the optimizers are not updated automatically. The database administrator must update them depending on the dynamism of the database—at least weekly and after major changes. Outdated statistical information is worse than having no information, as it can have a major impact on access speed.

Verification
Analyzing and verifying the entire dataset is the only reliable, defined method for excluding corrupt blocks in the dataset caused by hardware errors. This transaction is extremely time—intensive, however, and causes increased input and output activities on all hard drives. Therefore, a complete analysis is difficult to implement in R/3 systems with extremely large databases. If hardware problems occur, however, it is essential that you run a complete analysis, at least for the involved areas.

Backup
If possible, you should back up the entire database of production systems daily. To display summary information for past backups, choose ▶ **Backup Logs;** choose ▶ **Database Logs** for detailed information. If an error occurs, the log files are necessary to restore the dataset, starting from the last complete backup, in order to recover subsequent data changes. To do so, all the data from the log areas must be available without gaps. All RDBMS systems do not overwrite data in the log until it has been backed up properly. If the data was not backed up, the risk would be twofold: in addition to the potential for data loss, the log area might fill up completely. In this case, the database—and therefore the R/3 system as well—would no longer be operational. You can use RDBMS-specific tools or those tools provided by SAP for database-specific administration outside of the SAP system. The most widely used administration tool for Oracle databases used in SAP installations is **sapdba**.

15.8.2 Database Fill Level and Objects

Database administrators have to keep a constant eye on database growth. If the database does not have enough space to store the data, it could render the R/3 system inoperable. Therefore, you must check the database fill level regularly and enlarge the database if necessary. To display information on the size of the database and the objects it contains, choose ▶Tables and Indexes. This monitor provides information on the current fill level and its development, along with the size of individual objects such as tablespaces, tables, and indices. Figure 15.16 shows the development of the database fill level in graphical form for an SAP DB. A forecast is calculated at the same time to help administrators spot potential bottlenecks.

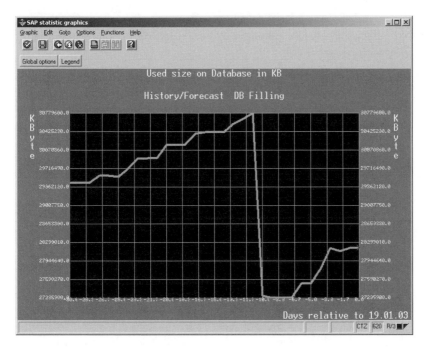

Figure 15.16 Database Fill Level

In addition to the space requirements of individual objects, the R/3 system regularly checks the objects defined in the R/3 Data Dictionary and in the database. System administrators must ensure that no inconsistencies arise between R/3 and the database. Missing indices can result in an enormous loss of performance. After upgrades, in particular, you should always use this monitor to verify the consistency of the objects and create any missing objects.

Dictionary Consistency

15.9 Overview of Regular Tasks

Table 15.5 summarizes all regularly repeated administration tasks in a live R/3 system. The system monitoring tasks can be reduced accordingly for development and consolidation systems, whose availability usually doesn't have to be as high.

Activity	Paths and transaction codes	Schedule	Details
Observe alert monitor	▶ Alert Monitor	Several times a day	Chapter 16
Check system log	▶ System Log	Several times a day	Section 15.3
Check runtime errors	▶ Dump Analysis	Daily	Section 15.4
Status of instances and operation modes	▶ Control Panel	Weekly	Chapter 14
Status of application servers and work processes	▶ Server Overview ▶ Process Overview	Daily	Section 15.1
Check update service	▶ Update Administration	Daily	Chapter 10
Check updates	▶ Update Monitor	Daily	Chapter 10
Check spool service	▶ Output Control	Daily	Chapter 11
Check spool service	▶ Output Control	Daily	Chapter 11
Check lock entries	▶ Lock Monitor	Daily	Section 15.6
Check background processing logs	▶ Job Selection	Daily	Chapter 9
Check regular maintenance jobs	▶ Job Selection	Monthly	Section 9.6
Maintain optimizer statistics	▶ DBA Planning Calendar	Weekly and as needed	Section 15.8
Carry out and check backups	▶ DBA Planning Calendar ▶ Backup Logs ▶ Database Logs	Daily	Section 15.8
Check database administration logs	▶ Database Logs	Daily	Section 15.8

Table 15.5 Regular Administrative Tasks

Activity	Paths and transaction codes	Schedule	Details
Check database consistency	▶ DBA Planning Calendar	Once per backup cycle	Section 15.8
Check database consistency	▶ DBA Planning Calendar	Once per backup cycle	Section 15.8
Check database fill level	▶ Tables and Indices	Weekly	Section 15.8
Check file system fill levels	Operating system command	Regularly and as needed	
Check consistency of database objects	▶ Tables and Indexes	At least after upgrades	Section 15.8
Performance analysis	▶ Load Analysis	As needed	Section 15.7
Check batch input sessions	▶ Batch Input	Regularly if batch input procedures are used	Chapter 13
Check gateway functionality	▶ Gateway Monitor	Regularly if gateways are used	Chapter 13
Check ALE flows on sender and receiver side	▶ ALE Status Monitor	Regularly if ALE is used	Chapter 13
RFC communication	▶ Transactional RFC ▶ qRFC Monitor Inbox ▶ qRFC Monitor Outbox	Regularly if RFC connections are used	Chapter 13

Table 15.5 Regular Administrative Tasks (cont.)

The ▶ **System Administration Assistant** was created to support system administrators as part of SAP's Ready-to-Run initiative. The most important issues for system administration are listed in the System Administration Assistant in a tree structure, assorted by daily, weekly, annually, and sporadically required tasks. In addition to detailed documentation on the individual items, which you can display from within the structure, you can also start the required activities directly and mark them as complete.

System Administration Assistant

You can adapt the structure to your specific requirements, hiding irrelevant activities to improve clarity and usability.

Figure 15.17 shows the administrative tasks that have to be performed daily to support a production system with an Oracle database; the first few steps have already been completed.

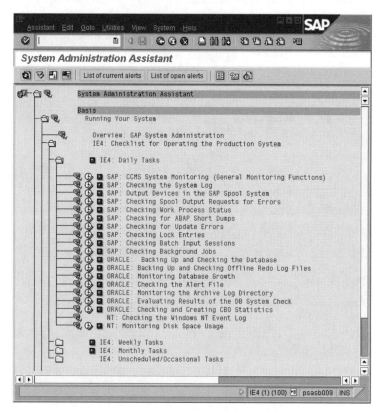

Figure 15.17 Daily Tasks in the System Administration Assistant

15.10 Tips

▶ **Developer trace and trace level of the dispatcher process**
You can set the dispatcher trace level and display the trace file with ▶**Process Overview · Process · Trace · Dispatcher**, although the process itself is not listed in the process overview.

▶ **Trace logging–Automatic reset of the trace level**
Starting in the SAP Web Application Server release, you can define the maximum size of a trace file. To search for a sporadic error, you can increase the trace level of the corresponding work process to 2 or 3; the trace file is then searched for a predefined word pattern automatically at regular intervals. If this pattern is found, the trace level is automatically reset to 1. If the trace file reaches the defined maximum size, it is

saved to a backup file, *<trace_file_name>.old*, and a new trace file is created.

▶ **Repairing a local system log**
If you accidentally deleted the file of the local system log, but did not delete the corresponding shared memory segment (SCSA), you can run report **RSLG0020** to restore the system log.

▶ **Global performance analysis**
The need to analyze performance in an entire mySAP system landscape makes it necessary to create and evaluate trace files and statistical analyses along a business process even across system boundaries. In addition, automated test cases and test configurations have to run on remote systems. You can use the ▶**Global Performance Analysis** for this purpose starting in SAP R/3 4.6C.

▶ **Lock table**
The lock table is actually a shared memory area, not a table. To change its size, modify instance parameter *enque/table_size*.

▶ **Enqueue in the central system**
In a central system, the dialog processes access the log table directly, without utilizing the enqueue process. Therefore, you will not be able to detect any activity by the enqueue process in the process overview.

▶ **File system cleanup**
In addition to monitoring the fill level of the file systems that contain the database and log files, it also helps to regularly clean up the other SAP directories. Full transport or instance directories can also cause system terminations, for example, because the system can no longer write required logs.

15.11 Transactions and Menu Paths

Alert monitor: SAP Menu • Tools • CCMS • Control/Monitoring • Alert Monitor (RZ20)

ALE status monitor: SAP Menu • Tools • ALE • ALE Administration • Monitoring • Status Monitor for ALE messages (BD87)

Application monitor: SAP Menu • Tools • Administration • Monitor • Performance • Workload • Application Monitor (ST07)

Backup logs: SAP Menu • Tools • CCMS • DB Administration • Backup Logs (DB12)

Batch input: SAP Menu • Tools • Administration • Monitor • Batch Input (SM35)

Buffer load: SAP Menu • Tools • Administration • Monitor • Performance • Setup/Buffers Buffers (ST02)

Business process analysis: SAP Menu • Tools • Administration • Monitor • Performance • Workload • Bus. Trans. (STAD)

Control panel: SAP Menu • Tools • CCMS • Control/Monitoring • Control Panel (RZ03)

Database logs: SAP Menu • Tools • CCMS • DB Administration • Operations Monitor (DB24)

Database monitor: SAP Menu • Tools • Administration • Monitor • Performance • Database Activity (ST04)

DBA Planning Calendar: SAP Menu • Tools • CCMS • DB Administration • DBA Planning Calendar (DB13)

DB parameter changes: SAP Menu • Tools • Administration • Monitor • Performance • Database • Parameter Changes (DB03)

Dump analysis: SAP Menu • Tools • Administration • Monitor • Dump Analysis (ST22)

Trace files: SAP Menu • Tools • Administration • Monitor • Traces • Developer Traces (ST11)

Gateway Monitor: SAP Menu • Tools • Administration • • Monitor • System Monitoring • Gateway Monitor (SMGW)

Global performance analysis: No standard menu path (ST30)

Global user overview: SAP Menu • Tools • Administration • Monitor • Performance • Exceptions/Users • Active users • Users global (AL08)

Global work process overview: SAP Menu • Tools • CCMS • Control/Monitoring • Work Process Overview (SM66)

ICM monitor: SAP Menu • Tools Administration • • Monitor • System Monitoring • Internet Communication Manager (SMICM)

Job selection: SAP Menu • Tools • CCMS • Jobs • Maintenance (SM37)

Load analysis: SAP Menu • Tools • Administration • Monitor • Performance • Workload Analysis (ST03N)

Lock monitor: SAP Menu • Tools • Administration • Monitor • Lock Entries (SM12)

Lock waits: SAP Menu • Tools • Administration • Monitor • Performance • Database • Exclusive Lock Waits (DB01)

Message server overview: No standard menu path (SMMS)

OS monitor: SAP Menu • Tools Administration • • Monitor • Performance • Operating System • Local • Activity (ST06, OS06)

OS parameter changes: SAP Menu • Tools • Administration • Monitor • Performance • Operating System • Local/Remote • Parameter Changes (OS03)

OS system configuration: SAP Menu • Tools • Administration • Monitor • Performance • Operating System • Remote • Activity (OS07)

Output control: SAP Menu • Tools • CCMS • Spool • Output Controller (SP01)

Performance analysis: SAP Menu • Tools • ABAP Workbench • Test • SQL Trace (ST05)

Process overview: SAP Menu • Tools • Administration • Monitor • System Monitoring • Process Overview (SM50)

Profile parameter changes: SAP Menu • Tools • Administration • Monitor • Performance • Setup/Buffers Parameter Changes (TU02)

qRFC monitor inbox: Not available in the SAP standard menu (SMQ2)

qRFC monitor outbox: Not available in the SAP standard menu (SMQ1)

SAP directories: SAP Menu • Tools Administration • • Monitor • Performance • Exceptions/Users • Exceptions • SAP Directories (AL11)

SAP system trace: SAP Menu • Tools • Administration • Monitor • Traces • System Trace (ST01)

Server overview: SAP Menu • Tools • Administration • Monitor • System Monitoring • Servers (SM51)

System administration assistant: SAP Menu • Tools • Administration • Monitor • System Administration Assistant (SSAA)

System log: SAP Menu • Tools Administration Monitor System Log (SM21)

Table calls: SAP Menu • Tools • Administration • Monitor • Performance • Setup/Buffers Table Calls • Calls (ST10)

Tables and indexes: SAP Menu • Tools • Administration • Monitor • Performance • Database • Tables/Indexes(DB02)

Transactional RFC: SAP Menu • Tools • Business Documents • Environment • Transactional RFC (SM58)

Update monitor: SAP Menu • Tools • Administration • Monitor • Update (SM13)

Update program administration: Not available in the SAP standard menu (SM14)

User overview: SAP Menu • Tools • Administration • Monitor • System Monitoring • User Overview (SM04)

Workload analysis: SAP Menu • Tools • Administration • System Monitoring • Monitor • Performance • Workload Analysis (ST03)

15.12 Additional Documentation

Quicklinks

▶ SAP Service Marketplace, alias *systemmanagement*
▶ SAP Service Marketplace, alias *performance*

SAP Service Marketplace Notes

Table 15.6 provides an overview of important notes from the SAP Service Marketplace related to system monitoring issues:

Contents	Note
FAQ: Lock management R/3	552289
Several enqueue work processes	127773
System error in the block handler, overflow lock table	13907
Contents of table TCOLL	12103
Get the latest **saposcol**	19227
saposcol: monitoring processes	451166

Table 15.6 SAP Notes for System Monitoring

15.13 Questions

1. In which directory are the developer traces written?

    a. \users\<sid>adm

    b. \usr\sap\<SID>\<instance>\work

    c. \usr\sap\<SID>\SYS\global

2. A user informs you that his session terminated with an error. Unfortunately, he didn't write down any of the termination details. Where is the best place to start your analysis?

    a. Nowhere. If I can't get more information, there is no way to find the cause of the termination.

    b. Check all the runtime errors in the R/3 system.

    c. Check the system log.

    d. Check the backup log.

16 Monitoring Architecture

The monitoring architecture is an integral component of the mySAP technology. It provides system administrators with a centralized monitoring platform for the mySAP system landscape.

In addition to the manual monitoring and analysis options described in Chapter 15, using the automatic features in the monitoring architecture will increase both the quality and the reliability of your system administration activities.

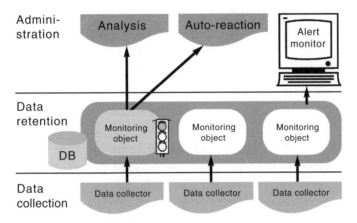

Figure 16.1 Monitoring Architecture

In an extensible infrastructure, specialized collection programs accumulate and save data and key figures for predefined objects in the shared memory areas and in database tables of mySAP systems. You can analyze this data with various criteria, using third-party products and the Alert Monitor integrated in the Computing Center Management System (CCMS). In addition to local analyses of the monitored systems themselves, you can also configure a central mySAP Basis system, where all the data of the monitored SAP and non-SAP systems comes together. The three layers are:

▶ Data collection

▶ Data retention

▶ Data administration and analysis

The way in which these three layers interact is illustrated in Figure 16.1.

16.1 Alert Monitor

16.1.1 Basics

In addition to local monitoring of individual systems, the monitoring architecture centrally monitors multiple mySAP systems—their critical components, statistics, and performance in the system landscape. Related external, non—SAP systems can also be connected and monitored. The Alert Monitor (see Section 16.1.2) displays the values that are collected and analyzed, according to various criteria within the monitoring architecture. As system administrator, you can configure system-specific threshold values for incoming information. When incoming information exceeds or falls below these threshold values, you can flag this situation as a malfunction (an *alert*) by changing the traffic signal color in the Alert Monitor (see Figure 16.3). You can also define analysis methods and auto-reaction methods; assign these methods to tree elements for detailed problem analysis; inform the system administrator; and trigger automatic corrective actions.

The Alert Monitor's primary benefit is that it independently notifies system administrators of disturbances, without requiring them to send an explicit request or log to the relevant system. As you discovered in Chapter 15, mySAP systems feature a variety of analysis tools for their assorted components; however, administrators must initiate these analyses themselves. In addition, the Alert Monitor developed by SAP can analyze the system landscape independently—based on selected parameters and specifically configured threshold values—and generate alerts if necessary. The system administrator can then use the specific tools integrated in the mySAP software to start a detailed analysis based on the information in the Alert Monitor, or, he or she can begin correcting the indicated problem immediately.

SAP provides alert monitors with every software product in the mySAP family. These alert monitors include all critical areas of system, database, and operating-system administration required to operate the software components.

Monitor Set   The alert monitors are grouped together for specific target groups in so-called *monitor sets* and are shipped with default settings that enable you to begin using their basic functions immediately after system installation. The predefined monitors (with their minor, release-specific differences) are located in the CCMS under ▶**Alert Monitor**:

► **SAP CCMS Monitor Templates**
Monitors for regular SAP system administration

► **SAP CCMS Technical Experts Monitors**
Monitors for troubleshooting and for supervising the monitoring architecture itself

► **SAP CCMS Monitors for Optional Components**
Monitors for observing specific components such as logon load distribution, selected transactions or clients, and predefined log files

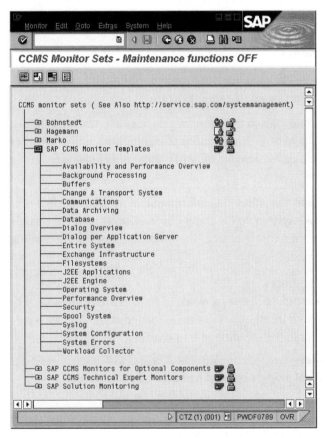

Figure 16.2 Preconfigured Monitor Sets (Release 6.20)

Based on these monitor sets (see Figure 16.2), customers can create their own monitors with special views of selected areas, defining their own data collectors and objects to add more alerts (see Section 16.1.3), and modify the standard settings. External tools can also be integrated. The specific customer requirements determine the extent to which changes to the default settings and monitor sets are necessary and desirable. In smaller system landscapes and during the implementation phase of a system, the monitors provided by SAP are usually sufficient with only minor customer-specific modifications. The analysis of an alert monitor is relatively simple and self-explanatory. What is far more difficult is the definition of custom alert monitors and the integration of custom alerts. The following sections, therefore, can only describe the basics. You will learn about the terminology of the alert monitor concept, which is the basis for all potential changes. You will then learn how to implement the Customizing—that is, adapt the predefined monitors to the customer-specific instantiation of a system and a landscape.

16.1.2 Components

A *monitor set* is a logical grouping of any number of monitors; the monitors themselves are arranged in a tree structure.

Monitoring Tree Elements

The nodes of the branches in the monitor tree are called *monitoring tree elements* (MTE). An MTE logically groups the underlying nodes or other MTEs. They are also called *monitor summary nodes* or simply *nodes*.

Monitoring Attributes

The leaves in the monitoring tree are formed via *monitoring attributes*. A monitoring attribute describes the information type of individual elements of the mySAP system that is under observation. It refers to a single characteristic of a monitoring object. The following types of monitoring attributes are defined:

▶ **Performance attributes**
A *performance attribute* defines a measure for the size or frequency of an event. If defined threshold values are exceeded, the color of the corresponding entry in the monitoring tree changes.

▶ **Status attributes**
The occurrence of a single defined message triggers an alert.

▶ **Log attributes**
The messages in a log file are searched for predefined patterns. If one of these strings occurs, an alert is triggered.

▶ **Heartbeat**
Activities in defined elements of the system, such as R/3 Services, are observed. If the monitored element fails, an alert is triggered.

▶ **Text attributes**
In contrast to the other monitoring attributes, *text attributes* are used to describe the values of certain MTEs. They merely provide information; they don't trigger any alerts.

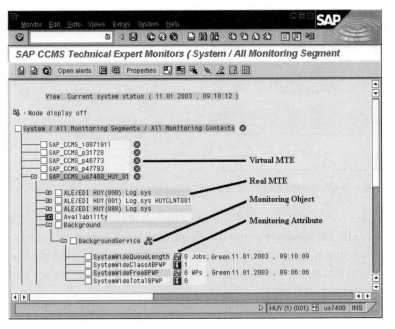

Figure 16.3 Elements of a Monitor

All monitoring attributes that refer to a common object or situation are grouped together in a logical unit—the *monitoring object*. The incoming data for a monitor object is physically stored in a *monitor segment* in the memory area. Examples of monitor objects are:

Monitoring Object

▶ *Dialog*, which includes the monitoring attributes *ResponseTime*, *ProgramErrors*, and *UsersLoggedIn*

▶ *R3Syslog*, which includes the monitoring attributes *BasisSystem*, *Database*, and *Applications*

▶ *Server Configuration*, which includes the monitoring attributes *R/3 Kernel Release*, *Machine Type*, and *Host*

A monitor object is also an MTE, the smallest monitor summary node. Several MTEs can be grouped together to form yet another MTE, to improve the clarity of the display. If an alert is generated by a monitoring attribute—for example, because incoming data exceeds or falls below a configured threshold value—the corresponding attribute and all higher-level nodes are highlighted in red in the display. Consequently, a glance at the top-level node shows administrators when a problem has occurred with at least one of the subordinate attributes in the hierarchy tree. A yellow background indicates a warning; a green background indicates a normal system status (see Figure 16.4).

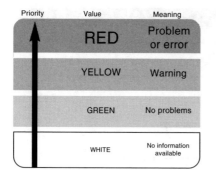

Figure 16.4 Display of the Node Status with Traffic Light Colors

Real and Virtual MTEs

If the data for an MTE is saved in a separate monitor segment, that MTE is *real*. MTEs that merely improve the clarity of the display and do not have their own monitor segments are called *virtual*. Various icons can help you to visualize and better understand the meanings of the monitor nodes and their respective attributes.

The highest monitor summary node forms the *monitor context*.

16.1.3 Technical Implementation

To ensure that current values and (if necessary) alerts can be displayed, the relevant characteristics have to be collected and made available regularly.

Data Collectors

Data collectors (see Figure 16.1) perform these tasks. These programs—which are written in C, ABAP, or Java—collect the required data and save it in defined memory segments (*monitor segments*) on the server. In addition to the collected data, the user-defined threshold values are also saved in the memory segment. By merely analyzing the memory, the system can detect deviances from threshold values. You can add your own data collectors if you want to collect and monitor additional data. These collectors can be integrated in the monitoring architecture via the defined program interface.

One example of an important collector is the operating-system data collector **saposcol**, which you learned about in Chapter 15. **saposcol** is an independent program that runs once on each server, independently of the SAP instance, and determines the relevant operating-system data. Examples include:

▶ Memory usage (virtual and physical)

▶ CPU load, divided into percentages for system time, user time, and idle time

- ▶ Utilization of physical disk space and file systems
- ▶ Resource usage by the current processes

The data, which is collected every ten seconds under the default configuration, is provided in a defined shared memory area on the server. **saposcol** also uses this area to save average values calculated hourly for many of the objects it monitors. The data is transferred from the shared memory segment to database tables for further summarization.

Because **saposcol** is operating system-specific, slightly different data is determined for each operating system.

Examples of other data collectors include report **RSDSLAN1**, which collects data on the LAN for method CCMS_OS_LAN, and function module **RSDS_BP_CLASSAWP**, which counts the number of background processes reserved for class A requests for method CCMS_BP_CLASSA_WP.

SAP components without an R/3 kernel or external systems play a special role. SAP provides so-called *agents* for these components. The agents are installed on the appropriate servers and monitor the required component. Agents have their own memory segments on the server where they store their collected data. From here, the data can be sent to an assigned central monitoring instance via the Remote Function Call (RFC) interface.

Agents

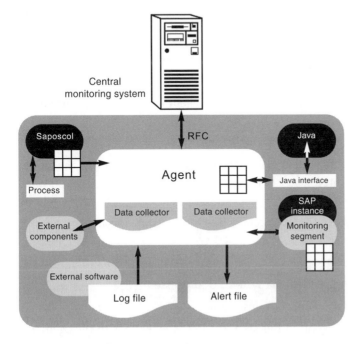

Figure 16.5 Using Agents

SAP provides the following agents for the various systems:

▶ **SAPCCMSR**

This agent works together with the operating-system data collector, **saposcol**. The agent manages this data in a corresponding shared memory area and sends it to a selected R/3 instance. This technique can be used for any SAP component, as well as for non-SAP systems. In addition to analyzing the data in the ▶ **Alert Monitor**, you can also evaluate it from within the ▶ **OS System Configuration**.

▶ **SAPCCM4X**

The SAPCCM4X agent improves the connection between an SAP system with a 4.x Basis and a central monitoring system with Release 4.6C or later. No dialog work process is needed on the central server to transfer the collected data.

▶ **SAPCM3X**

You must install the SAPCM3X agent to monitor mySAP systems with a Basis Release 3.x. This agent establishes an independent shared memory segment for data management.

In addition to executing function modules, the agents can check log files and report problems in the monitor architecture, access the data collected by **saposcol**, and integrate additional data collectors through a dynamic library interface. Example configurations of agents are described in Section 16.4.

Installing and Registering Agents

If you want to use agents to supplement your system monitoring, proceed as follows:

1. Download the current version of the agent from the SAP Service Marketplace.

2. Copy the agent to its work directory.

3. Create a configuration file for the dialog-free installation of the agent. Once generated, you can reuse this file on all servers where you want to run the agent.

4. Create additional configuration files to configure specific agent tasks, such as

   ▶ Monitoring log files

   ▶ Monitoring certain file systems or processes

   ▶ Monitoring clients or transactions

5. Register the agent. In this step, the RFC connections to the agent are created automatically in the central monitoring system.

All agents are downward-compatible with regard to the SAP release. This means a CCMS agent can work together in any SAP system with a release that is less than or equal to its own release. Therefore, you should always use the latest available release of the CCMS agents. Because the instantiation of the agents is operating system-specific, the SAP Service Marketplace features appropriate agents for the different operating systems and their releases. Generally, all available **SAPCCMSR**, **SAPCCM4X**, and **SAPCM3X** agents are archived in a shared file, *CCMAGENT.SAR*. Download the appropriate archive for your hardware environment from the SAP Service Marketplace under the alias */patches* or from the SAP service host *sapserv3* (see Chapter 3). Use the **SAPCAR** tool, which is available in every SAP installation, to unpack the archive.

The agents need a work directory to store the configuration and log files (see Table 16.1):

CCMS agent	UNIX directory	NT directory
SAPCCMSR	*/usr/sap/tmp/sapccmsr* Alternative: *$DIR_PERF/sapccmsr*	*\\<host>\saploc\prfclog\sapccmsr*
SAPCCM4X	*$DIR_LOGGING/ sapccm4x*	*%DIR_LOGGING\sapccm4x*
SAPCM3X	*$DIR_PERF/sapcm3x*	*%DIR_PERF\sapcm3x*

Table 16.1 Work Directories of the Monitoring Agents

Enter the following commands to install and register the agents:

```
sapccmsr -r [ -f <name_of_installation_file> ]
            [ pf=<profile_path> ]
sapccm4x -r [ -f <name_of_installation_file> ]
            [ pf=<profile_path> ]
sapcm3x  -r [ -f <name_of_installation_file> ]
            [ pf=<profile_path> ]
```

If you install the agents in dialog mode, the system prompts you to enter all the parameters required to describe the central monitoring system with which the agents will communicate. If you want to install the agents in a larger system landscape with multiple servers, you should create a file with the necessary installation data.

The meaning of the profile path differs among the agents. You must specify this profile path for **SAPCCM4X**; the profile is that of the monitored

SAP instance. If you use the other two agents, you will learn that either no SAP instance exists (**SAPCCMSR**), or the SAP release does not have an operative monitoring architecture (**SAPCM3X**). Here, you can use a profile file to control the following settings (optional):

▶ Size of the monitor segment in bytes of shared memory as *alert/MONI_SEGM_SIZE* (only **SAPCCMSR**)

▶ The work directory of the agent and the local **saposcol**, *DIR_PERF*

▶ The complete path of the data collector for operating-system data, *exe/saposcol*

Agent Log Files When you start an agent, a log file *<name_of_agent><processID>.log* is created in that agent's work directory. This file is used to record all initialization steps and error messages caused by running the agent. Any problems with the configuration or control files are also recorded.

The agents are run as services in Windows systems and as processes under UNIX. Therefore, the agents start and stop together with the operating system under Windows. Under UNIX, use the following explicit commands

```
sapccmsr -DCCMS [ pf=<profile_path> ]
sapccm4x -DCCMS [ pf=<profile_path> ]
sapcm3x -DCCMS [ pf=<profile_path> ]
```

to start the agents, and the same commands with option -stop to stop the agents.

As soon as the agents are started, their collected information appears in the monitor set. The data of the **SAPCCMSR** agents is located in the ▶**Alert Monitor** in monitor set **SAP CCMS Technical Experts Monitors**, under **System/All Monitoring Segments/All Monitoring Contexts** as virtual node *SAP_CCMS_<host_name>*, contexts with name *SAP_CCMS_<host_name>_local* belong to agent **SAPCM3X**. The contexts of the data supplied by the **SAPCCM4X** is located in the same place; the only difference is the type of communication with the SAP instances. If the supply of information from the agent is interrupted, you can display an overview of all memory segments that report to the central monitoring instance under ▶**Monitoring: Properties and Methods · Technical Infrastructure · Overview of Segments** (to Basis Release 4.6D) or ▶**Monitoring: Properties and Methods · Technical Infrastructure · Display Topology** (in Basis Release 6.10 and later). **Segment type Agent** lists the required segments, which you can analyze further by double-clicking.

16.2 Customizing the Alert Monitor

The Alert Monitor serves to visually indicate critical situations. The colors of the MTEs as displayed in the monitoring tree change from green to yellow to red, depending on the defined threshold values and their level of severity. The definition of a critical situation differs from system to system. Therefore, you should adjust the default values that SAP provides with the monitor sets.

16.2.1 Integrating Remote Systems

To enable the monitoring of multiple components from a central SAP system, you must register the non-local components that you want to monitor as new contexts in the ▶ **Monitoring: Properties and Methods**. First, you must define two RFC connections (see Chapter 13). We recommend defining the RFC connections as follows:

Defining RFC Connections

▶ **Data retrieval**
Read access to the shared memory segments that contain the data must be possible in order to retrieve the data collected on the remote systems. Therefore, you should configure a user with type "CPIC" (to Basis Release 4.6D) or "Communication" (in Basis Release 6.10 and later) for this purpose.

▶ **Analysis functions**
Because further operations are required to execute the analysis functions when an alert is received, you should define the necessary RFC connection under your own user name (settings for current user, see Chapter 13).

You can then add another system under **Technical Infrastructure · Create Entry for Remote Monitoring**.

16.2.2 Creating Customer-Specific Monitors and Monitor Sets

Starting from the standard monitor sets, you can create your own specific monitor sets and define specific, summarized monitors within them. The advantage of defining your own monitor is that it focuses on your customer-specific requirements and the specific aspects of the underlying system landscape. You can use the monitors provided by SAP as copy templates; however, you cannot change the standard monitors themselves. If your interface administrator wants to restrict his or her view of the system landscape to the interfaces, for example, you will need to define a specific monitor to enable this functionality.

To create your own monitor with the required MTEs, proceed as follows:

1. Call the maintenance function within the ▶**Alert Monitor** display via **Extras · Activate Maintenance Functions**. The active change functions appear in the menus.

2. Select **Monitor (Set) · Create**.

3. Enter a name for the monitor set and define who is allowed to maintain and view it. Please note that the name cannot start with "SAP."

4. Save your entries; this creates an empty monitor set as a container for the customer-specific monitors.

5. To create a static monitor within this new monitor set, select **Monitor (Set) · Create** again within your new monitor set; all available MTEs are displayed.

6. Select all the MTEs that you want to include in your monitor, and save the monitor with a mnemonic name.

Making Changes   The MTEs that you selected are now integrated in the new monitor. If you want to make changes, select **Monitor (Set) · Change**. In particular, if you add a new system and want to make it visible in the central monitor, you must add the relevant parameters of the additional system as previously described. It therefore makes sense to use a rule-based addition of existing monitors in large, dynamic system landscapes. First, either select an existing monitor, which you will update with rules, or create a new monitor as described above. Then, proceed as follows:

1. In the existing structure, select the node that is located where you want to add the dynamic values.

2. When you select **Edit · Create Node · Rule node**, the available rules that you can use—to dynamically enhance the monitor structure during startup—are displayed.

Figure 16.6 shows the addition of a monitor with rule CCMS_GET_MTE_BY_CLASS regarding all reachable systems and MTE class CPU_Utilization. When you call the monitor, current data on CPU utilization is displayed for all systems that are registered and reachable via RFC.

If necessary, you can transport monitor sets to other systems. This means that you can create your own monitor sets in a development system first, test them, and then distribute them to the system landscape. To transport monitor sets to other systems, use the function ▶**Alert Monitor · Monitor (Set) · Transport Monitor Set**.

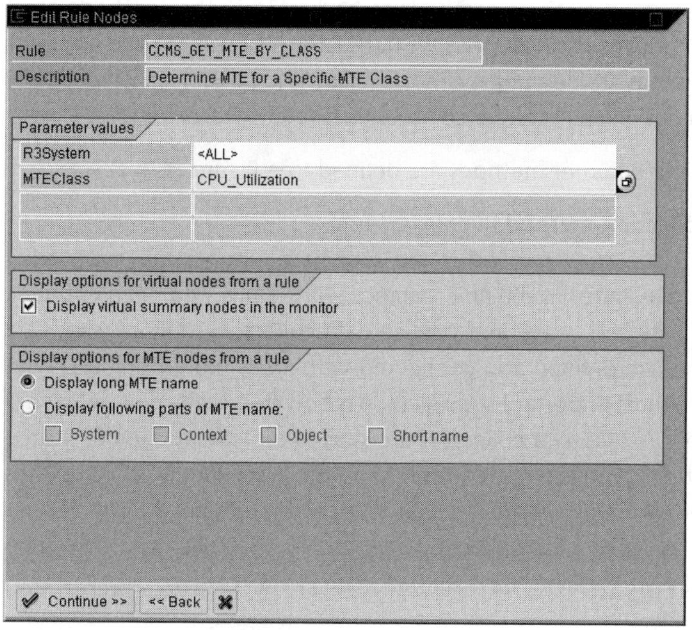

Figure 16.6 Rule-Based Monitor

16.2.3 Specific Adjustment of Properties

In the next Customizing step, you have to adjust the predefined object and attribute properties to reflect your specific system requirements. The optimal way to do this is to fine-tune the monitors that you defined yourself; if you want to use the standard monitors provided, you can also implement the customer-specific settings.

The MTE **Properties** are divided into the following areas, which have different values depending on the type of MTE involved:

You can define the following properties in the **General** area:

General Properties

▶ Description and display of text to be displayed in the monitor when an alert occurs, as a combination of message class and message number.

▶ Visibility for user groups dependent on the user authorization (to Basis Release 4.6B).
   You can define various levels of areas for monitoring, detailed analysis, and developer view.

▶ Settings for monitor properties
   These settings include the weight or importance of the setting, the maximum number of alerts of a respective type to retain, and the restrictions for triggering an alert.

You can assign up to three methods to each MTE in the **Methods** area. Function modules, reports, URLs, or transactions can all be used as methods. Commands at operating-system level are also possible, provided they have been defined as external commands (see Chapter 9).

The following different methods are defined (see Figure 16.7):

▶ **Data collection method**
The *data collection method* is the tool that supplies the monitoring attributes assigned in the final instance with values. You need to differentiate between active and passive data collectors; only passive data collectors are defined and configured within the monitoring architecture. The most important specification is how frequently new values are collected. Active data collectors are started directly by the monitored applications, and are not controlled by the Alert Monitor. The data is reported at irregular intervals that you cannot influence. All MTEs are already assigned data collection methods by default. Data collection method *<No Method>* describes an active data collector that you cannot modify.

▶ **Analysis method**
The *analysis method* defines which action will be triggered to investigate a problem that is displayed in the monitor in more detail. The action for the MTE for monitoring buffer quality, *R3BufferSpaceUsed*, for example, is to display the analysis of the ▶ **Buffer Load**.

▶ **Auto-reaction method**
These tools can respond to a triggered alert, for example, by sending a message. No *auto-reaction methods* are defined in the standard monitor sets. If you want to use auto-reaction methods, you must define them yourself.

Before you can use a report, a function module, a URL, or a transaction as a method, you must register the respective object as a method and assign it a method name. To do so, start ▶ **Monitoring: Properties and Methods** and select **Methods · Create New Method**. During method definition, you define which method type is involved (data collection, analysis, auto-reaction), how it will be executed (manually, in dialog, or in the background), and where it will be executed (local host, any other server). You can also assign parameters. The overview **Methods · Definitions** contains all the available methods in the system, including preconfigured auto-reaction methods, which you can use as necessary. Templates for sending messages, for example, are already provided by SAP. As system administrator, you can create new tools and integrate them in mySAP systems at any time. For example, you could write an ABAP program that triggers a defined action in the system when a specific problem occurs.

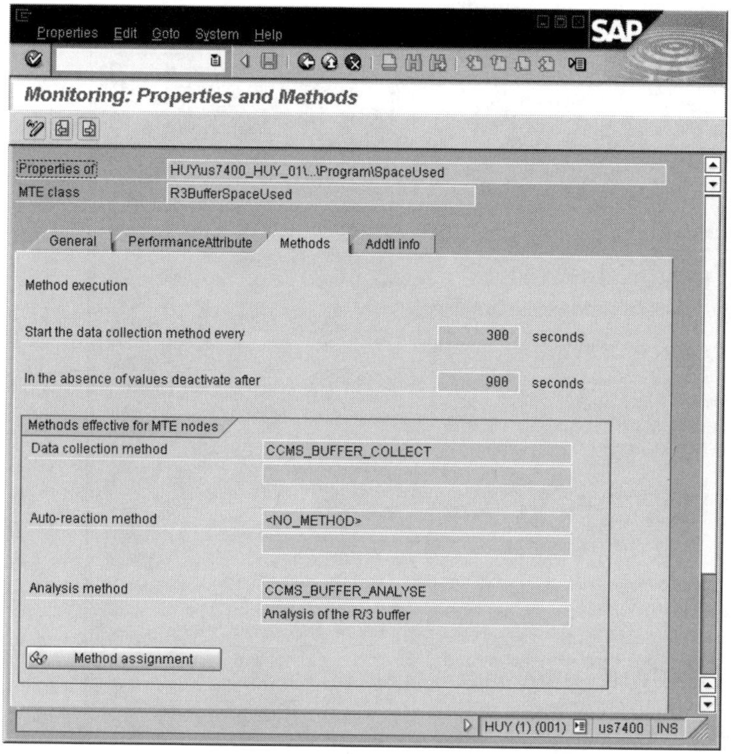

Figure 16.7 Method Assignment

The lowest level in the monitoring tree contains the monitoring attributes. These monitoring attributes are assigned additional threshold values (in the widest possible definition) under **Properties**. The threshold definition differs depending on the type of monitor property involved:

Performance, Status, and Log Properties

▶ **Performance attributes**
The alert is triggered as soon as the data exceeds or falls below the configured threshold value. Threshold values are used heavily in performance measurements, such as they are here, that is, in monitoring of the *ResponseTime* in MTE *Dialog* (see Figure 16.8).

▶ **Status attributes**
One example for using a status attribute to generate an alert is the occurrence of an error message in a specific component, such as the update task as shown in Figure 16.9.

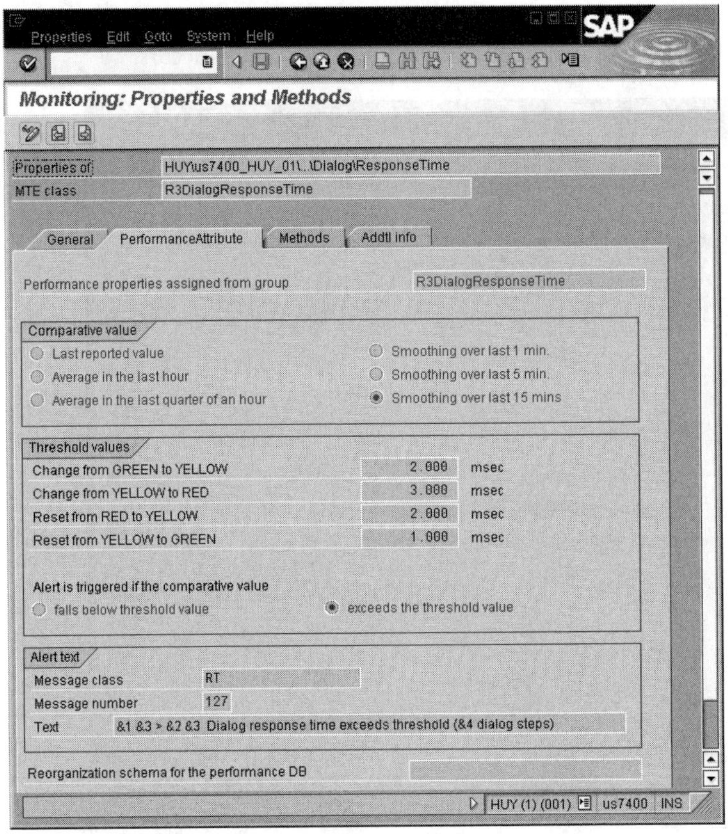

Figure 16.8 Threshold Value Definition

▶ **Log attribute**

If you search the log file of a system component for a string, an occurrence of this text can also trigger an alert. You can use filters to define additional restrictions.

You must pay special attention when configuring threshold values. If your threshold values are configured too low and are exceeded during the regular operation of a mySAP system, red alerts will be triggered constantly. The system will trigger an alert for a state that is actually normal. Alternatively, threshold values that are configured so high as to never be exceeded also falsify the signals from the Alert Monitor; even if the situation reaches a critical level, the monitor color will not change to indicate a problem. Therefore, if possible, you should configure the threshold values such that all the traffic signals are set to green in a normal system. Highlight only those states that deviate from the norm. Because it can prove difficult to determine the appropriate threshold values during the initial implementation phase of a mySAP system, it's a good idea to first use the default values provided by SAP, or estimate your own values. Then, you must adapt these values iteratively, based on your experiences.

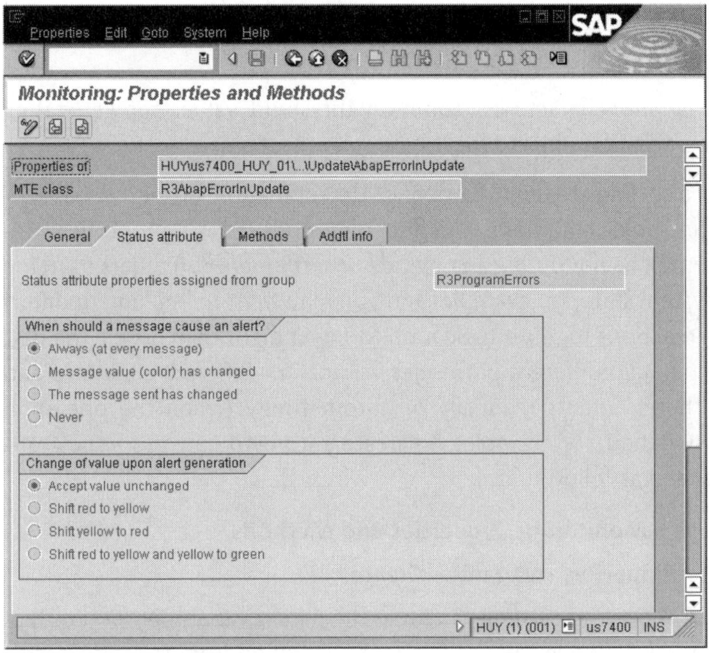

Figure 16.9 Status Attribute Property

The last person who changed the object is recorded in the **Additional Information** property.

Additional Information

You can configure the settings of both the attributes themselves and (more simply) their higher-level structures. To change the threshold value of a specific attribute, proceed as follows:

1. Select the required attribute in the ▶**Alert Monitor** and choose **Properties**.

2. Switch from display to change mode and modify the required properties.

3. Choose **Edit · Properties · Use for individual MTE** to save the changed properties only for the selected element.

Because many monitoring tree elements have similar properties, you will note that when fine-tuning your MTEs, the default setting for maintaining properties is the entire MTE class or attribute group.

MTE Classes   To simplify administration, monitoring tree elements with similar physical and logical properties are grouped together in *MTE classes*. MTE class *R3BufferHitRatio*, for example, groups together all the MTEs that describe a buffer quality. Therefore, instead of assigning analysis method ▶**Buffer Load** to every MTE, you can select an attribute of the class to implement the change in all MTEs of that class.

Attribute Groups   *Attribute groups* characterize common threshold values for generating alerts for a selected object type.

Properties Variants   You may also find it useful to define a combination of method assignments, threshold definitions, and general properties as a properties variant. System behavior during an upgrade or settlement run differs from the normal system state, for example, and you may want to implement different auto-reactions for automatic monitoring at night than during the day. You can maintain different properties variants for different situations and activate these variants manually or automatically (when the operation mode is switched, for example). To create your own new properties variants, proceed as follows:

1. Start the ▶**Monitoring: Properties and Methods**.
2. Choose **Properties · Variants · Create**.
3. You can choose an existing variant as the parent variant; properties that you do not define in the child variant are copied from the parent variant.
4. Enter a name for the variant.

You can also copy and modify one of the existing variants:

1. Start the ▶**Monitoring: Properties and Methods**.
2. Choose **Properties · Variants · Copy**.
3. A selection of properties you can copy is displayed.
4. Enter a name for the variant.

Activate the new variant by using **Variant · Activate**. The new variant is now generated and active. All the Customizing settings that you subsequently define will be automatically assigned to this properties variant. You can easily return to the SAP defaults by switching back to properties variant SAP-DEFAULT. You can maintain several properties variants to adapt your monitors to special situations quickly and easily. You can also transport properties variants: if you created and tested a satisfactory properties variant in one mySAP system, you can transport this variant into any other mySAP system. To do so, choose ▶**Monitoring: Properties and**

Methods · **Properties Variants** · **Variant Overview**. Select the required variant and choose **Variant** · **Transport**.

To assign a properties variant to an operation mode, choose ▶**Maintain Operation Mode** · **Operation Mode** · **Change** and enter the properties variant.

16.3 Analyzing the Alert Monitors

To ensure that the mySAP system and landscape remain operational, it is imperative that you analyze the alerts. Two views of monitor events are available. The initial screen shows all the alerts that are currently valid, and is called **Current Status**. You can press the **Open Alerts** button to go to the view of all collected alerts. Double-click on an MTE to display the corresponding alerts, which are sorted by level of severity, in a table. You can use the **Properties** button to determine which alerts you want to retain for each monitor: all, oldest, most recent, or only those that represent the current status.

To remove known alerts from the display, click on **Complete** · **Alerts** in this display (or directly from the alert monitor). The selected values are saved in the alert database, but are not used to rate the current situation; only new values are used. Note that you should only use this function after an analysis, if you have eliminated the cause of the problem or can diagnose it as non-critical. Click on **Show Alert History** to display a history of all the alerts triggered to date. This enables you to rate the level of severity of the current situation with past situations. Select **Goto** · **Display Details** to list the details of the selected monitor attribute. If a more precise analysis of the problem is required, you can click the **Start Analysis Method** icon or double-click on the MTE to go directly to the transaction that has been designated as the analysis method.

Closing an alert removes it from the list of active alerts and the monitor segment; however, it is retained in the database. Therefore, you should also periodically clean up these entries in the database. You can do this with the analysis method for monitoring object *AlertsInDB* in Monitor **CCMS Self-monitoring** of collection **SAP CCMS Technical Experts Monitor**, or configure an automatic reorganization that deletes alerts from the database when the monitor segment reaches a defined fill level or after a defined number of days. You do this by modifying parameters *CMPL_ALERT_AFTER_DAY* and *CMPL_ALERT_IF_QUOTA* for method *CCMS_Segment_Space_Collect* with ▶**Monitoring: Properties and Methods** · **Methods** · **Definitions**.

16.4 Example Customizing

This section describes several examples of possible uses of system monitoring using the alert monitors. The information should help you learn how to deal with similar situations and issues.

Alert monitors are available for all SAP system components. The initial primary task for you, as system administrator, is to adjust the threshold values and maintain the reaction methods. You can also configure the agents (see Section 16.1.3), which provide additional monitoring options.

16.4.1 Analyzing a Log File

You can use agents **SAPCCMSR**, **SAPCCM4X**, or **SAPCM3X** to analyze the contents of any text files. The agent searches the files for the specified text strings and displays the results in the alert monitor. To configure the log adapter, perform the following steps:

▶ Specify the log file(s) to search
  Logfile entries in configuration file *sapccmsr.ini*

▶ Specify the target text string
  Pattern entry in the corresponding control file for the log file

▶ Configure the appearance of the alert in the central alert monitor
  Entries in the corresponding control file for the log file

Configuration File
sapccmsr.ini

First, modify configuration file *sapccmsr.ini* in the agent's work directory (the configuration file name is always *sapccmsr.ini*, regardless of the type of agent). This file primarily consists of path information for controlling the agent functions. This path information refers to additional, specific configuration files using a keyword mechanism. Example path entries in *sapccmsr.ini* are listed in Table 16.2.

Parameter	Value	Description
PlugIn	<path_name>	Name of a library to be loaded by the agent
Logfile	<path_name>	Configuration file for the log adapter
LogfileParam	DelTree	Obsolete elements are removed from shared memory
OsColFile	<path_name>	Name of a file for filtering subtrees within the scope of operating-system monitoring
Alertlog	<path_name>	Name of a file for storing reported alerts

Table 16.2 Configuration Entries in File sapccmsr.ini

Listing 16.1 shows an example configuration file. File *c:\saploc\PRF-CLOG\sapccmsr\ccmsini.ini* was specified as the control file for analyzing a log file.

Listing 16.1 Configuration File for CCMS Agents

```
#### Configuration file for CCMS agents SAPCCMSR,
#### SAPCM3X and SAPCCM4X
####
#### Format of entries for plugins:
#    PlugIn <full path of shared library to load>
####
#### Format of entries for logfile monitoring:
     Logfile c:\saploc\PRFCLOG\sapccmsr\ccmsini.ini
####
#### Format of entries for the option to delete trees if
#### no corresponding logfile exists:
#### This Parameter is optional, if not specified the
#### tree still remains
#    LogFileParam DelTree
####
#### Format of entries for mechanism to filter out
#### SAPOSCOL values:
#    OsColFile <full path of oscolfile template>
#
```

Listing 16.2 shows the content of the control file used, *ccmsini.ini*.

Listing 16.2 Control File ccmsini.ini (Monitoring of SAP DB Log File)

```
LOGFILE_TEMPLATE
DIRECTORY="c:\sapdb\LVC\db"
FILENAME="knldiag"
MTE_CLASS="SAPDB_LOG"
SHOWNEWLINES=1
MONITOR_FILESIZE_KB=5
PATTERN_0="cannot"
VALUE_0=RED
SEVERITY_0=51
MESSAGEID_0="RT-013"
```

The settings in this control file mean that file *knldiag* in directory *c:\sapdb\LVC\db* is analyzed automatically. All the monitors that the agent can generate to monitor the file are assigned to monitoring tree class

SAPDB_LOG (parameter *MTE_CLASS*). The advantage of this approach is that all settings and changes to general properties and methods affect this MTE class in general.

SHOWNEWLINES causes the number of new entries, which were added to this file in the last minute, to be displayed in a monitor. The file size will also be monitored. If the file size exceeds the defined value of 5 KB, an alert will be triggered (parameter *MONITOR_FILESIZE_KB*). You can use *PATTERN_<x>* to define the character strings that will trigger an alert. In the preceding example, a red alert is triggered when the word "cannot" is found (*VALUE_<x>*). The severity of the alert (*SEVERITY_<x>*) is set to 51. Message *013* of message class *RT* (*MESSAGEID_<x>*) is output. At this point in the analysis of this file, you can use all messages that have been defined in ▶ **Message Maintenance** and are available. *RT-013* means "No detailed description available." The control file is concluded by a period "." in the last line of the file.

16.4.2 Auto-Reaction Method: Send Mail

One important decision that is integral to configuring a monitor is the type of auto-reaction method. In general, every function module and report can be used as an auto-reaction method. An auto-reaction could also involve sending an e-mail; however, you would first have to configure SAPconnect to enable the SAP system to send e-mail (see Chapter 13).

You then have to maintain and assign an appropriate auto-reaction method for sending an e-mail in case of a red alert. The standard system already contains a corresponding auto-reaction method that is called *CCMS_OnAlert_Email*.

1. Start the ▶ **Monitoring: Properties and Methods** in client 000 of the system.

2. Choose **Methods · Definitions**.

3. Double-click to select method *CCMS_OnAlert_Email*.

4. Maintain the properties of the method, especially the parameters (**Parameters**). You can specify the sender as an existing SAP user in client 000, or any SAP user with the notation *<SID>:<client>:<name>* starting in Basis Release 6.10. The defined user is recorded as the sender of the alert mails generated by the monitor. You must select a valid e-mail address as the *Recipient*. Parameter *Recipient Type* determines the type of address. "U" stands for Internet e-mail. The generated e-mails are sent to this address. You can also use a distribution list.

You assign the auto-reaction methods either with ▶Monitoring: Properties and Methods · Properties · Assigned MTE Classes, Properties · Single MTEs, or directly in the ▶Alert Monitor.

If you want to send e-mails to different users for each alert monitor, copy method *CCMS_OnAlert_Email* under a different name and adjust the parameters as necessary.

16.4.3 Filtering the System Logs

As another example for using alert monitors, this section illustrates how to filter specific messages from the system log of an SAP system and respond to them. You could, for example, send e-mail when a critical database error occurs. A separate monitor set is provided for analyzing system logs of mySAP instances. These monitors are located in the ▶Alert Monitor under SAP CCMS Technical Expert Monitors · System / All Monitoring Segments / All Monitoring Context. A node is defined for each instance that reports to the SAP system and has the following name structure: *<host_name>_<SID>_<instance_number>*. The *R3Syslog* node appears below the instance node. The system log is differentiated further, depending on the system function. All monitors in the *R3Syslog* node are supplied by active collectors (see Section 16.2.3), which means you cannot configure them directly within the monitoring architecture.

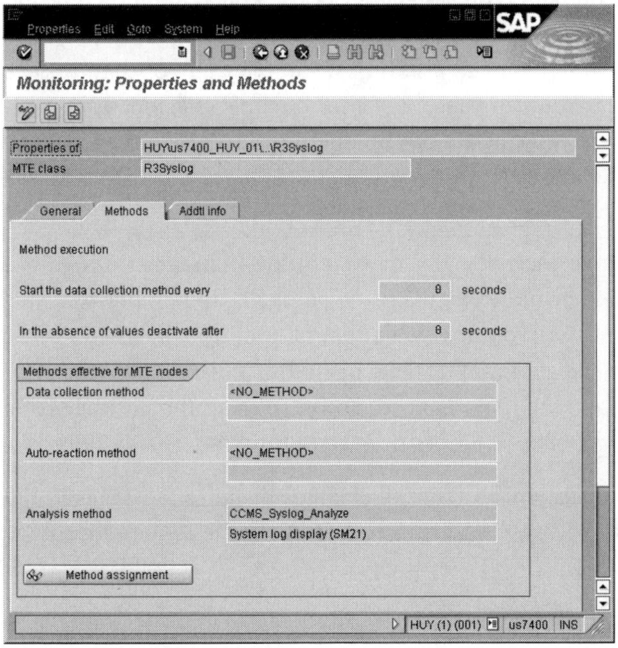

Figure 16.10 Methods in the System Log Monitors

You can filter messages in the system log indirectly by redefining the criticality of a message. Typically, standard messages in the system log are rated with a maximum criticality of 50; however, you can set the criticality to any value between 0 and 250.

If you only want to trigger a red alert in the event of specific selected messages in the system log, change the threshold values for the system log monitors.

Because all system log monitors read from the same monitoring segment and are supplied by the same SAP kernel data collector, changes to one system log monitor affect all other system log monitors.

Select a system log monitor, such as **BasisSystem**. Go to the **Properties** area and adjust the alert settings in the **Log Attribute** section. Set the threshold value for a red alert to a value greater than 50. Next, increase the criticality of the selected messages (to a value greater than 50). Consequently, only these messages will exceed the threshold value for a red alert. There are two ways to adjust the criticality of messages:

Maintaining
System Log
Messages
Choose ▶ **System Log Messages · Edit · List All Numbers** to display a list of all available system log messages available in the system. Select the required number, such as *BY2 – Database error* &6 *occurred at* &3. You automatically go to the initial screen for ▶ **System Log Messages**; the selected message number is preassigned. Choose **Edit · Maintain**. In addition to defining the category where the system log message is displayed in the alert monitor tree, you can also adjust the criticality of the message (see Figure 16.11). You can therefore filter out the selected system log messages and trigger specific actions for them by increasing their criticality. In the example above, increasing the criticality for message BY2 will trigger a red alert in case of database errors.

Modification in
the Alert Monitor
You can also change the criticality of system log messages through the monitor properties in node *R3Syslog*. Once again, remember that any changes to one of the monitors will affect all monitors in the *R3Syslog* node. Changes in the alert monitor will overwrite any existing definitions configured in system log maintenance. To reconfigure the criticality of a system log message, choose **Filters** from the properties of a monitor.

This approach enables you to track all changes made to messages in the relevant monitor. However, you do need to know the required message numbers.

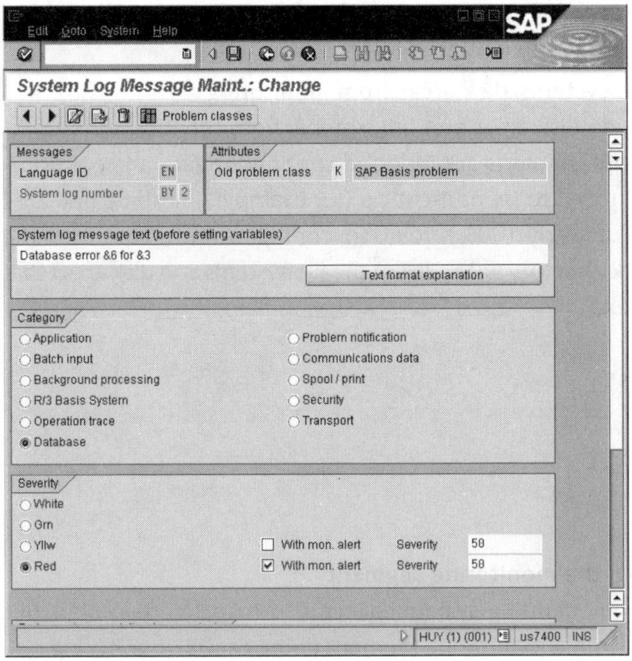

Figure 16.11 System Log Maintenance

16.5 Tips

▶ **Using saposcol in dialog mode**

The operating-system data collector, **saposcol**, can also be used in dialog mode at operating-system level. The command:

```
saposcol -d
```

starts the dialog interface. You can enter

```
Collector> dump <parameter> <option>
```

to display the data that **saposcol** has written to its shared memory segment. Enter `quit` or `exit` to exit the dialog mode.

▶ **Activating saposcol process monitoring**

If you want **saposcol** to monitor processes of a specific user or with a certain name, you have to make the necessary information available in a configuration file, *dev_proc*, in directory *DIR_PERF*. The list of processes to monitor has the following structure:

```
$PROC
<process_name> <user_name>
<process_name> <user_name>
...
$
```

You can replace name segments with "*". You must restart **saposcol** to activate the new configuration

▶ **Excluding file systems/disk areas from monitoring**
You can exclude disk areas and file systems from the monitoring process, for example, if alerts are reported continuously for a known situation that is judged to be non-critical (for example, if a static disk area has a fill level of nearly 100%). To do so, configure a *dev_filter* file in the **saposcol** work directory with a list of the file systems and disk areas that you want to exclude:

```
$DISK
<disk_name>
...
$FSYS
<file_system_name>
...
```

▶ **Hiding data in the monitoring segment**
If you want the operating-system collector to collect certain data, but not transfer it to the monitoring segment of the central monitoring system, you can implement this condition with an entry in the configuration file, *sapccmsr.ini*. Enter the path name of a control file under key entry *OsColFile*; define the values that you want to suppress in this control file.

▶ **Sorting the alerts in the alert list**
The alerts within a color group are sorted by level of severity within a color group. If you want an alert to always appear at the top of the list, you can change its weight (that is, its level of severity) accordingly.

▶ **Central auto-reaction method**
You can define auto-reaction methods to enable automatic responses to an alert. Under the default settings, this method is started on the system where the alert occurs. Starting in Basis Release 6.10, you can configure a central auto-reaction method that runs on the central monitoring system when an alert occurs in one of the monitored systems. You configure this method under ▶ **Monitoring: Properties and Methods · Technical Infrastructure · Assign Central Auto-Reactions**.

▶ **Access privileges for agent SAPPCCM4X**
Because **SAPCCM4X** accesses the local shared memory segments of the monitoring architecture in the monitored SAP system, it must possess the necessary read privileges. You must grant the privileges of <sid>adm (UNIX) or SAPService<SID> (NT).

▶ Retaining the saposcol data of a remote system for 30 days

If you want the data that saposcol has collected and sent to a central monitoring system to be retained longer than the default period of 24 hours, you must activate selection **save last 30 days** for the existing destination under ▶ **SAPOSCOL · Destination**.

16.6 Transactions and Menu Paths

Alert monitor: SAP Menu • Tools • CCMS • Control/Monitoring • Alert Monitor (RZ20)

Buffer load: SAP Menu • Tools • Administration • Monitor • Performance • Setup/Buffers Buffers (ST02)

Maintain operation modes: SAP Menu • Tools • CCMS • Configuration • Operation Modes/Instances (RZ04)

Message maintenance: SAP Menu • Tools • ABAP Workbench • Development • Programming Environment • Messages (SE91)

Monitoring: Properties and Methods: SAP Menu • Tools • CCMS • Configuration • Alert Monitor (RZ21)

OS system configuration: SAP Menu • Tools • Administration • Monitor • Performance • Operating System • Remote • Activity (OS07)

SAPOSCOL destination: SAP Menu • Tools • Administration • Monitor • Performance • Operating System • SAPOSCOL Destination (AL15)

System log: SAP Menu • Tools • Administration Monitor • System Log (SM21)

System log messages: SAP Menu • Tools • ABAP Workbench • Development • Programming Environment • System Log Messages (SE92)

16.7 Additional Documentation

Quicklinks

▶ SAP Service Marketplace, alias *systemmanagement*
▶ SAP Service Marketplace, alias *monitoring*

SAP Service Marketplace Notes

Table 16.3 provides an overview of important SAP notes about alert monitors and agents from the SAP Service Marketplace:

Contents	Note
FAQ-CCMS monitoring infrastructure	110368
FAQ-CCMS monitor architecture: meaning of profile parameters	135503
Composite SAP note: Central monitoring of mySAP	420213
Get the latest **saposcol**	19227
SAPOSCOL: monitoring processes	451166
SAPOSCOL: Disk and file system filter	498112
RZ20: Monitoring operating system data	522453, 371023
CCMS agent technology (composite SAP note)	209834
SAPCM3X (CCMS monitor architecture: monitor 3x systems)	308061
RZ20: Availability of R/3 systems	381156
CCMS monitor architecture: Service level agreements	308048
RZ20: Monitoring background jobs	553953
CCMS agents: Monitoring log files	535199
Setting up tRFC and qRFC monitoring in the Alert Monitor	441269
Enable Monitoring of InQMy/SAP J2EE Engine	498179
CRM: CCMS Agent Plug-In for IPC/IMS	502461, 502463
Installation of the ITS-Plug-In for the CCMS Agent	418285
Alerts for Oracle database monitoring	483856, 426781
Auto-reactions	176492, 502959, 536535, 429265
RZ20: Automatic reorganization of alerts	414029

Table 16.3 Important SAP Notes Regarding Alert Monitoring

16.8 Questions

1. Which systems, and how many of them, can be monitored with CCMS?

   a. Only the local R/3 system

   b. Multiple R/3 systems, but no non-R/3 systems

c. Multiple R/3 systems, as well as non-R/3 systems that have installed the appropriate data collectors

2. You discovered that an alert is triggered too often for an MTE; therefore, you change the threshold values. Which statement is correct?

a. The changed threshold definition only applies to the currently selected MTE.

b. The changed threshold definition applies to the entire MTE class.

c. Generally, changes affect the entire MTE class. You can change this setting, however, to maintain individual MTEs as well.

d. You can never change the threshold values of an MTE.

A   Questions and Answers

Chapter 1: Technical Realization of Client/Server Architecture in SAP R/3

1. Which services does the application layer provide?

    a. Communication service

    b. Dialog service

    c. Spool service

    d. Update service

    e. Message service

    f. Transport service

    g. Gateway service

    h. Network service

    i. Enqueue service

    j. Batch service

    k. Change service

    Answer: b, c, d, e, g, i, j

2. Which of the following recommendations is correct?

    a. The dispatcher and dialog processes should not run on the same instance.

    b. The enqueue and message servers work closely together and therefore, should run on one instance.

    c. The batch service and update service work closely together and therefore, should never run on different instances.

    Answer: b

3. What does the gateway service manage?

    a. Communication between SAP R/3 processes

    b. Communication between SAP R/3 systems and instances of another SAP R/3 system

    c. Communication with the operating system spool process

    d. Connections to external programs, such as MAPI, EDI, and telex service

    e. Communication with SAP R/3 systems

    Answer: b, d, e

4. How many message servers are active in an R/3 System?

   a. 0

   b. 1

   c. 2

   Answer: b

5. How many update tasks can be active per instance?

   a. 1

   b. 2

   c. The SAP R/3 system regulates the number automatically, depending on the need.

   d. As many as requested, depending on the available resources. The administrator must set the number of tasks in advance.

   Answer: d

Chapter 2: Getting Started

1. Which profiles are used to configure the SAP R/3 system?

   a. R/3 profile

   b. Instance profile

   c. Application server profile

   d. *DEFAULT.PFL*

   e. Start profile

   f. Stop profile

   Answer: b, d, e

2. Your SAP R/3 system will not start. Where can you find information on the cause of the problem?

   a. *startdb.log*

   b. *startsap_<host_name>_<instance_number>.log*

   c. *startsap.log*

   d. Developer traces

   e. System log

   f. SQL trace

   Answer: a, b, d

3. Which of the following statements is correct?

    a. The **SAPLOGON** program enables you to define accesses to various SAP R/3 systems.

    b. If you use **SAPlogon**, you no longer need an SAP GUI.

    c. The names of the entries in SAPlogon must be identical to the SID of the SAP R/3 system.

Answer: a

Chapter 3: Service and Support

1. What is SAProuter used for?

    a. It replaces a firewall.

    b. It controls the setup of remote connections to the application server of an SAP R/3 system.

    c. It sets up connections between the frontends and the application servers of an SAP R/3 system in the local network.

Answer: b

2. Which file is used as a default to maintain the routing data of SAProuter?

    a. saprouttab

    b. *DEFAULT.PFL*

    c. *autoexec.bat*

Answer: a

3. Which preconditions must be met in order for SAP to set up a service connection to a customer's SAP R/3 system?

    a. The SAP R/3 system must be registered in the OSS.

    b. The connection data of the application server and SAProuter must be maintained on the customer side.

    c. The customer must open the connection.

Answer: a, b, c

Chapter 4: Installation Concepts

1. Which statement is true?

For a minimal installation of SAP R/3:

    a. Installation of the RDBMS is sufficient.

b. Installation of a database instance and a central instance is required.

c. The database instance and the central instance can reside on one system.

d. A database instance, a central instance, and at least one application server must be installed.

Answer: b, c

2. Which statement is true?

a. SAP R/3 naming conventions can be changed at any time with tools available at the operating-system level.

b. SAP R/3 naming conventions are a fixed component of various SAP R/3 tools and cannot be changed at will.

c. SAP R/3 naming conventions help users to find logs and messages quickly.

Answer: b, c

3. Which statement is correct?

a. Use of RAID systems increases the reliability of SAP R/3 systems.

b. Running the R/3 database on a RAID system is not recommended, because it results in poor performance.

c. RAID systems are only recommended for the data area of the SAP R/3 database. For performance reasons, they are not recommended for log areas.

Answer: a

Chapter 5: Setting Up the System Landscape

1. Which of the following statements about TMS configuration is accurate?

a. Several transport groups can exist in a transport domain.

b. All systems that access a common transport directory, /usr/sap/trans, are assigned to one transport group.

c. At any one time, only one transport layer can be defined.

d. The transport layer indirectly determines the route to the target system.

Answer: a, b, d

2. Which of the following statements is true?

In a multisystem landscape, transports:

a. Can only be controlled by the active import or export system.

b. Can be controlled centrally by the Domain Controller of the transport domain.

c. Can only be controlled at the operating-system level with the **tp** program.

d. Can be controlled by each SAP R/3 system in a transport domain.

Answer: b, d

3. Which transport routes are differentiated?

a. Direct transport route

b. Indirect transport route

c. Consolidation route

d. Delivery route

e. Detour

Answer: c, d

4. Which program is responsible for executing transports at the operating-system level?

a. R3load

b. R3inst

c. tp

d. dpmon

e. sapdba

Answer: c

Chapter 6: Software Logistics

1. Which statement is correct?

a. The SAP R/3 transport system is equivalent to copying clients.

b. The SAP R/3 transport system helps exchange development and Customizing data between different SAP R/3 systems.

c. The SAP R/3 transport system is used to exhange data between various clients of a single SAP R/3 system.

Answer: b

2. Which statement is correct?

A development class is:

a. A defined group of developers

b. Client-independent

c. To be assigned when modifying an original SAP object

d. Is assigned to a transport layer

Answer: b, d

3. Which statement is correct?

Modifications of SAP objects

a. Must be registered in the OSS

b. Are not permitted

c. Are highly recommended to realize company-specific processes

Answer: a

4. Which statement is correct?

A Repository object of an SAP R/3 system:

a. Is automatically locked while a developer modifies it. The lock is removed automatically when the modifications are saved.

b. Can only be changed when it has been assigned to an appropriate change request. This approach ensures that other users are automatically blocked from modifying the objects until the developer releases the assigned task and the change request.

c. Can only be changed when it has been assigned to an appropriate change request; only users who are involved in the change request can modify the object.

Answer: c

Chapter 7: Client Administration

1. Which of the following statements regarding the R/3 client concept are true?

a. Customizing settings are basically client-independent.

b. A client is a commercially self-contained unit in an R/3 system.

c. Each client has its own application data.

d. Each client has its own technical data that is independent of other clients.

e. Each client has its own application tables.

Answer: b, c

2. **What methods does R/3 offer for copying clients?**

    a. Local copy

    b. Remote copy

    c. Data exhange procedure

    d. Client export

    e. Data backup

    Answer: a, b, d

3. **What data can be transferred in a remote client copy?**

    a. Client-specific application data

    b. Client-specific table definitions

    c. Client-independent data

    d. All data in the R/3 system

    Answer: a, c

Chapter 8: R/3 Users and Authorizations

1. **Which statement is correct?**

    A user with type "System":

    a. Can log on without a password via RFC interface

    b. Has a password, but the settings for the validity period do not apply

    c. Cannot log on in dialog

    Answer: b, c

2. **Which statement is correct?**

    a. A user can only be assigned one role.

    b. A user can be assigned several roles.

    Answer: b

3. **Which information is transported when roles are transported?**

    a. The authorization profiles for the role

b. The definition of the users

c. The assignment of roles to users

Answer: a, c

4. The authorizations of a role are extended. From which point can a user who has been assigned this role, and who is already logged on to the system, start using the changed authorizations?

   a. The user can start using the changed authorizations instantly.

   b. The user can use the change authorizations after a user comparison.

   c. The user has to log on again and can then start using the changed authorizations.

   d. A user comparison has to be performed first. The user then has to log on again. The user can then start using the changed authorizations.

   Answer: d

Chapter 9: Background processing

1. Which transaction can you use to analyze the job logs?

   a. SE38

   b. SM37

   c. S000

   Answer: b

2. Which external program can you use to trigger events in the R/3 system?

   a. sapevt

   b. sapxpg

   c. sapstart

   d. spmon

   Answer: a

3. What does status *Ready* mean for a background job?

   a. Job scheduling was completed and saved.

   b. The job was executed and is ready to print the log.

   c. The job is waiting for system resources to become available to start execution.

   Answer: c

Chapter 10: Update

1. Update was deactivated due to a tablespace overflow. Which actions are required after you extend the tablespace?

   a. No actions are required; the update task is reactivated automatically.

   b. You must activate the update task.

   c. You must repost all the update records manually.

   Answer: b

2. Which status does an update record have when it is waiting to be updated?

   a. Active

   b. Released

   c. init

   d. start

   Answer: c

3. Which R/3 profile parameters can you use to control whether an R/3 user receives a notification when his or her update task is canceled?

   a. rdisp/vbmail

   b. A message is always sent to the user.

   c. rdisp/rbdelete

   Answer: a

Chapter 11: Output Configuration and Management

1. Which access methods are differentiated?

   a. Local access methods

   b. Remote access methods

   c. Special access methods

   d. Access methods with formatting

   e. Access methods without formatting

   f. Internal access methods

   g. External access methods

   Answer: a, b, c

2. For which authorizations does SAP R/3 provide authorization objects?

 a. Device authorizations

 b. Display authorizations for spool requests

 c. TemSe management authorization

 d. Authorizations for operations with spool requests

 Answer: a, b, c, d

3. Which of the following statements is correct?

 An output request:

 a. Is generated by a spool work process from a spool request

 b. Can be printed multiple times

 c. Can be output to any printer

 Answer: a, b

4. Which access methods are recommended for mass printing?

 a. Local access method L for transfer to the host spool, using the appropriate command interface

 b. Local access method C for direct transfer to the print manager of the host spool, using the appropriate command interface

 c. Local access method F for front-end printing

 d. Remote access method S for desktop printing with SAPLPD

 e. Remote access method U, based on the Berkeley protocol

 Answer: a, b

5. What is a dedicated spool server?

 A dedicated spool server is:

 a. A selected application server of the SAP R/3 system that is used for centralized spool administration.

 b. An application server assigned to an output device defined in the SAP R/3 system. The spool service of a dedicated spool server formats and manages the spool requests sent to this device.

 c. The front-end computer (desktop) that currently processes front-end printing.

 d. An application server of the SAP R/3 system that is explicitly assigned to a user as a explicit spool server.

 Answer: b

Chapter 12: Data Archiving

1. What is an archiving object?

   a. CD-ROM or WORM

   b. The archive files created by the archiving session

   c. A logical unit of related data and the programs needed to archive it

Answer: c

2. What is meant by "data archiving"?

   a. Saving archive logs

   b. Archiving any documents, such as incoming and outgoing print lists, invoices, or documents from application components

   c. Removing data from the database and storing it in an archive system or on other data media

Answer: c

3. Which R/3 tool is used for transferring data to an archive during data archiving?

   a. SAP ArchiveLink

   b. HSM (Hierarchical Storage Management)

   c ADK (Archive Development Kit)

   d. RFC

Answer: c

4. Which of the following statements is true?

   a. The entire archiving process can be performed while the SAP R/3 system is running.

   b. The R/3 system must be stopped during the entire archiving process.

   c. The R/3 system cannot be used while the archive files are being generated.

Answer: a

Chapter 13: Data Distribution and Transfer

1. Which statement is correct?

When data is distributed via ALE

   a. A fixed connection is established between the partner systems

b. The partner systems are loosely connected during the data transfer

c. Functions of the respective RBDMS, such as SAPDBA, are used to exchange the data

Answer: b

2. Which techniques can be used for data exchange?

    a. CPI-C

    b. Sequential files

    c. tRFC

    d. Internet

    e. Telnet

Answer: a, b, c, d

3. How can tRFCs that were cancelled due to communication errors be processed again?

    a. Automatically, by activating the option for automatic repeat when you define the tRFC connection

    b. By scheduling job RSARFCE

    c By scheduling job RSEOUT00

    d. By correcting the error and repeating the application transaction

Answer: a, b

4. What is the batch input process used for?

    a. To transfer data from sequential files to the R/3 database

    b. For processing mass data in the background

    c. For importing data with the transport control program, tp

Answer: a

Chapter 14: Maintaining Instances

1. What is meant by "operation mode"?

    a. An operation mode describes the number and type of work processes on one or more instances.

    b. An operation mode also includes all settings for the R/3 main memory areas.

c. An operation mode describes the status of the R/3 system: "active" means operational; "DB active" means only the R/3 database is available and the R/3 system is shut down.

Answer: a

2. What is a logon group?

a. All users who are assigned to the same user group form a logon group.

b. A logon group is a logical unit and a subset of all application servers within an R/3 system.

c. All users who have the same responsibilities form a logon group.

Answer: b

Chapter 15: System Monitoring

1. In which directory are the developer traces written?

a. \users\<sid>adm

b. \usr\sap\<SID>\<instance>\work

c. \usr\sap\<SID>\SYS\global

Answer: b

2. A user informs you that his session terminated with an error. Unfortunately, he didn't write down any of the termination details. Where is the best place to start your analysis?

a. Nowhere. If I can't get more information, there is no way to find the cause of the termination.

b. Check all the runtime errors in the R/3 system

c. Check the system log

d. Check the backup log

Answer: c

Chapter 16: Monitoring Architecture

1. Which systems, and how many, can be monitored with CCMS?

a. Only the local R/3 system

b. Multiple R/3 systems, but no non-R/3 systems

c. Multiple R/3 systems, as well as non-R/3 systems that have installed the appropriate data collectors

Answer: c

2. You discovered that an alert is triggered too often for an MTE; therefore, you change the threshold values. Which statement is correct?

a. The changed threshold definition only applies to the currently selected MTE.

b. The changed threshold definition applies to the entire MTE class.

c. Generally, changes affect the entire MTE class. You can change this setting, however, to maintain individual MTEs as well.

d. You cannot change the threshold values of an MTE.

Answer: c

B Important Transaction Codes

The following table lists the most important transaction codes for R/3 system administration. You can enter R/3 transaction codes in the SAP GUI command field. The following options are available:

▶ /n<transaction_code>
Exits the currently active R/3 transaction and starts the requested new transaction in the same session.

▶ /o<transaction_code>
Starts the new transaction code in a new session.

▶ /h<transaction_code>
Starts the new transaction in debugging mode in the current session.

If you enter /h in the command field without a transaction code, and press the **Enter** key to confirm, the current transaction is run in debugging mode from that point forward.

AL08	Global user overview
AL11	Display CCMS operating-system files
AL12	Buffer synchronization
DB02	Missing database objects and space requirements
DB12	SAPDBA logs
DB13	Weekly scheduling
FILE	Archiving: Assignment between logical and physical file names – cross-client
OSS1	SAP Service Marketplace logon
PFCG	Role maintenance
RZ01	Graphical background job Scheduling Monitor
RZ02	Network graphic of the instances
RZ03	Control panel: Operation mode and server states
RZ04	Maintain instances
RZ06	Maintain thresholds for alert monitors
RZ08	SAP alert monitor
RZ10	Maintain profile parameters
RZ20	Alert monitor

RZ21	Alert monitor Customizing
S000	Short message
SA38	ABAP reporting
SADC	Addresses: Maintain communication types
SALE	IMG Application Link Enabling
SAR	Archive administration: Generate archive files
SAR0	Display standard report tree
SAR1	Structure of an archiving object
SAR2	Define archiving object
SAR3	Customize archiving
SAR4	Define archiving classes
SAR5	Assign archiving classes
SAR6	Archiving time-spot generating program
SARA	Archive administration
SARL	Call ArchiveLink monitor
SC38	Start remote report
SC80	CATT utilities
SCAM	CATT management
SCAT	Computer-Aided Test Tool
SCC1	Copy client via transport request
SCC3	Client copy log
SCC4	Client administration
SCC5	Delete client
SCC6	Client import
SCC7	Client import-postprocessing
SCC8	Client export
SCC9	Remote client copy
SCCL	Local client copy
SCMP	View/table comparison
SCPF	Generate Enterprise IMG
SCPR1	Customizing profiles: maintenance tool

SCPR2	Compare Customizing profiles
SCU0	Customizing comparison
SDBE	Explain a SQL statement
SDW0	Start ABAP Workbench
SE01	Transport Organizer
SE03	Workbench Organizer: Tools
SE06	Set up Workbench Organizer
SE07	Display status of transport system
SE09	Workbench Organizer
SE10	Customizing Organizer
SE11	Maintain R/3 Data Dictionary
SE12	Display R/3 Data Dictionary
SE14	Tool for converting Data Dictionary tables at database level
SE15	R/3 Repository Information System
SE16	Display table contents
SE17	General table display
SE93	Maintain transaction codes
SEU	Repository Browser
SF01	Archiving: Assignment between logical and physical file names— client-specific
SFT2	Maintain holiday calendar
SFT3	Maintain factor calendar
SHDB	Record batch input
SICK	Installation check
SM01	Lock transactions
SM02	System messages
SM04	Local user list
SM12	Display and delete locks
SM13	Display update records
SM21	System log
SM28	Installation check

SM30	Call view maintenance
SM31	Table maintenance
SM35	Batch input monitoring
SM36	Schedule background jobs
SM37	Overview of background jobs
SM39	Job analysis
SM49	Execute external commands
SM50	Overview of work processes
SM51	Overview of instances
SM56	Number range buffers
SM58	Asynchronous RFC error log
SM59	RFC connections (display and maintain)
SM63	Display/maintain operation modes
SM64	Trigger an event
SM65	Analysis tool for background processing
SM66	Global work process overview
SM69	Maintain external operating-system commands
SMLG	Maintain assignment to logon group instance
SMLI	Language import
SMLT	Language administration
SO00	SAPoffice short message
SO01	SAPoffice inbox
SO02	SAPoffice outbox
SO03	SAPoffice private folders
SO04	SAPoffice shared folders
SO21	Maintain PC work directory
SO99	Upgrade information system
SOA0	ArchiveLink: workflow document types
SOA1	ArchiveLink: early archiving
SOA2	ArchiveLink: late archiving
SOA3	ArchiveLink: default settings for early archiving

SOA4	ArchiveLink: default settings for late archiving
SOA5	ArchiveLink: store and enter
SOA6	ArchiveLink: default settings for store and enter
SP00	Spool and related areas
SP01	Spool control
SP02	Display output requests
SP11	TemSe table of contents
SP12	TemSe administration
SPAD	Spool administration
SPAM	SAP Support Package Manager
SPAU	Display modified objects in the runtime environment
SPCC	Spool consistency check
SPDD	Display modified DDIC objects
SPIC	Spool: installation check
SPRO	Customizing: initial screen
SPRP	Direct entry to project management
ST01	SAP system trace
ST02	Statistics of R/3 buffers
ST03	Workload analysis
ST04	Statistics of RDBMS activities
ST05	SQL trace
ST06	Operating-system monitor
ST07	Application monitor
ST08	Network monitor
ST09	Network alert monitor
ST10	Table call statistics
ST11	Display developer traces
ST12	Application monitor
ST14	Application analysis
ST22	ABAP runtime error analysis
ST4A	Oracle: analyze shared cursor cache

STAT	Local transaction statistics
STMS	Transport Management System
STUN	R/3 performance menu
SU01	User maintenance
SU01D	User display
SU02	Maintain authorization profiles
SU03	Maintain authorizations
SU05	Maintain Internet users
SU10	Mass changes to user masters
SU12	Mass changes to user masters-delete all users
SU2	Maintain user parameters
SU20	Maintain authorization fields
SU21	Maintain authorization objects
SU22	Authorization object usage in transactions
SU24	Modify SAP check indicators
SU25	Transfer SAP proposals to customer tables
SU26	Compare authorization checks
SU3	Maintain user-specific data
SU30	Overall authorization checks
SU52	Maintain own user parameters
SU53	Display test values
SU56	Analyze user buffers
SUPC	Profiles for activity groups
SUPF	Integrated user maintenance
SUPO	Maintain organizational levels
SWDC	Workflow definition: administration
SWUE	Trigger an event
TU02	Display active parameters

C   Profile Parameters

The R/3 system contains a variety of profile parameters. Default settings for all profile parameters are included with the standard R/3 system. While you can theoretically modify all these parameters, you should exercise caution when doing so. Only very few of the parameters actually have to be adjusted for your specific system. All other parameters should only be adjusted after consulting with or upon recommendation of SAP. Any specific settings that you configure will overwrite these default values.

The most important R/3 parameters are summarized in the following tables.

The parameters that are used exclusively in the R/3 default profile, *DEFAULT.PFL*, and are therefore effective system-wide, are listed in Table C.1.

Parameter	Description
SAPSYSTEMNAME	Three-place identifier (SID) of the R/3 system
SAPDBHOST	Name of the database server
sna_gateway	Host name where the SNA gateway runs
sna_gwservice	Port of the SNA gateway
rdisp/mshost	Host name of the message server
rdisp/vbname	Instance whose update service acts as the dispatcher for all update tasks
rdisp/enqname	Instance that provides the enqueue service
rdisp/btcname	Instance that provides the event scheduler
rdisp/bufrefmode	Parameters for synchronizing buffers in distributed systems For a central instance: sendoff/exeauto In distributed systems: sendon/exeauto
rdisp/bufreftime	Interval between two buffer synchronizations in seconds Default: 60

Table C.1 Parameters in the Default Profile

Parameter	Description
auth/no_check_in_ some_cases	Activation of the Profile Generator N: inactive Y: active (default)
dbs/ora/tnsname	Logical name of an Oracle database Identifies the Oracle database if SQL*Net V2 is used. The corresponding name must be defined in the configuration file, tnsname.ora. Default: $(SAPSYSTEMNAME)

Table C.1 Parameters in the Default Profile (cont.)

The parameters in Table C.2 are typical parameters in the instance profile. They can also be used in the standard profile, *DEFAULT.PFL*. The parameter values entered in the standard profile are valid throughout the R/3 system, as long as they are not set to different values in the respective instance profile.

Area	Parameter	Description
Dialog	rdisp/wp_no_dia	Number of dialog work processes
Spool	rdisp/wp_no_spo	Number of spool work processes
	rspo/store_location	Storage location of the TemSe db in the database G: in the global R/3 directory /usr/sap/<SID>/SYS/global L: in a local file of the instance /usr/sap/<SID>/<instance>/ data T: local in the /tmp (Unix) or \TEMP (Windows NT) directory
	rspo/host_spool/print	Operating-system print command, including options
	rspo/tcp/retries	Number of attempts to establish a connection to a remote output device (access method U) Default: 3
	rspo/tcp/retrytime	Time in seconds between two attempts to establish a connection to a remote output device Default: 300

Table C.2 Parameters and their Default Settings in the Instance Profiles-Part 1

Area	Parameter	Description
	rspo/tcp/timeout/connect	Allowed time to wait for establishing a connection to a remote printer in seconds Default: 10
Update	rdisp/wp_no_vb	Number of update work processes
	rdisp/wp_no_vb2	Number of update work processes for V2 updates
	rdisp/vbreorg	Delete incomplete update requests when restarting the instance 1 (default): Active 0: inactive
	rdisp/vbmail	Notify a user when an update termination occurs 1 (default): Active 0: inactive
	rdisp/vbdelete	Number of days after which terminated update requests will be deleted Default: 50
Back-ground	rdisp/wp_no_btc	Number of background work processes
	rdisp/btctime	Time period between two batch scheduler runs in seconds Default: 60
Enqueue	rdisp/wp_no_enq	Number of enqueue work processes
R/3 memory	rsdb/ntab/entrycount	Maximum number of buffer entries in the TTAB buffer Recommendation: 30,000
	rsdb/ntab/entrycount	Size of the FTAB buffer (in KB) Recommendation: 30,000
	rsdb/ntab/irbdsize	Size of the IRDB buffer (in KB) Recommendation: 4,000
	rsdb/ntab/sntabsize	Size of the STAB buffer (in KB) Recommendation: 2,500
	rsdb/cua/buffersize	Size of the FTAB buffer (in KB) Recommendation: 5,000

Table C.2 Parameters and their Default Settings in the Instance Profiles-Part 1 (cont.)

Area	Parameter	Description
	zcsa/presentation_buffer_area	Size of the screen buffer * 2 (in bytes) Recommendation: 20,000,000
	sap/bufdir_entries	Maximum number of buffer entries in the screen buffer Recommendation: 4,500
	zcsa/table_buffer_area	Size of the generic table buffer (in bytes)
	zcsa/db_max_buftab	Maximum number of entries in the generic table buffer
	rtbb/buffer_length	Size of the single record table buffer (in KB)
	rtbb/max_tables	Maximum number of entries in the single record table buffer
	abap/buffersize	Size of the ABAP program buffer
	rsdb/obj/buffersize	Size of the import/export buffer (in KB)
	rsdb/obj/max_objects	Maximum number of buffer entries in the import/export buffer
	rsdb/obj/large_object_size	Estimated size of the largest object in the import/export buffer (in bytes)
	rdisp/ROLL_MAXFS	Size of the roll area—that is, roll buffer plus roll file (in 8KB blocks) Recommendation: optimal: 32,000, minimum: 16,000
	rdisp/PG_MAXFS	Size of the R/3 paging area—that is, paging buffer plus paging file (in 8KB blocks) Recommendation: optimal: 32,000, minimum: 16,000
	rdisp/ROLL_SHM*	Size of the roll buffer (in 8KB blocks)
	rdisp/PG_SHM*	Size of the R/3 paging buffer (in 8KB blocks)
	em/initial_size_MB*	Initial size of extended memory (in MB)
	em/max_size_MB*	Maximum size of extended memory (in MB) (only under Windows NT)
	em/address_space_MB*	Address space reserved for extended memory (in MB) (only under Windows NT)

Table C.2 Parameters and their Default Settings in the Instance Profiles-Part 1 (cont.)

Area	Parameter	Description
	ztta/roll_first*	Size of first memory area allocated from the roll area (in bytes) Recommendation: 1
	ztta/roll_area*	Size of the roll area in bytes Recommendation: 2,000,000 (Windows NT) 6,500,000 (other)
	ztta/roll_extension*	Amount of memory that the work process can request in extended memory (in bytes) Recommendation: 2,000,000,000 (Windows NT) $1/3$ of the size of extended memory (other)
	abap/heap_area_dia*	Size of local process memory (heap) that a dialog process can use (in bytes) Recommendation: Default: 2,000,000,000
	abap/heap_area_nondia*	Size of local process memory (heap) that non-dialog processes can use (in bytes) Default: 400,000,000
	abap/heap_area_total*	Maximum heap memory for all work processes (in bytes)
	abap/heaplimit*	If a work process occupies more memory than defined by this parameter (in bytes), the work process is automatically restarted after the processing step is complete, in order to release the annexed memory. Recommendation: 20,000,000

Table C.2 Parameters and their Default Settings in the Instance Profiles-Part 1 (cont.)

The parameters marked with asterisks (*) in Table C.2 are set automatically for R/3 4.0 by "Zero Administration Memory Manager" under Windows NT. If you run R/3 4.0 with Windows NT, you should delete these parameters from the profiles. The preceding recommendations only apply to R/3 in UNIX environments.

All recommendations apply to hosts with main memory of at least 500 MB for an R/3 instance and 750 MB for a central R/3 system. For more recommendations, refer to the book *SAP Performance Optimization* in this series of books.

Area	Parameter	Description
Alert monitor	alert/ALERTS	File name for saving alerts in the CCMS monitor architecture
Registration	login/fails_to_session_end	Number of failed logon attempts allowed before the SAP GUI is closed Default: 3
	login/fails_to_user_lock	Number of failed logon attempts allowed before the user is locked Default: 12
	login/failed_user_auto_unlock	Unlock locked users the next day 1: users are unlocked 0: users remain locked
	login/min_password_lng	Required minimum length of passwords Default: 3
	login/password_expiration_time	Maximum validity period of a password Default: 0: no restriction
	login/no_automatic_user_sapstar	0: If user SAP* is deleted, user SAP* is available automatically with password PASS 1: No automatic user SAP*
	login/system_client	Default logon client
	rdisp/gui_auto_logout	Automatic logout after a defined period of inactivity (in seconds) 0: inactive
System log	rslg/max_diskspace/local	Maximum size of file for the local system log
	rslg/max_diskspace/central	Maximum size of file for the global system log (UNIX only)
Trace	rdisp/TRACE	Logging level in developer traces 0: Trace off 1 (default): Errors only 2, 3: Extended trace
Batch input	bdc/altlogfile	Directory for reorganizing the batch input log file (RSBDCREO)

Table C.3 Parameters and their Default Settings in the Instance Profiles-Part 2

D   Menu Structures

The menu trees below show the structure of menu item "Tools" from the standard start screen of the R/3 system, along with menu items "System" and "Help," which are available in every R/3 menu.

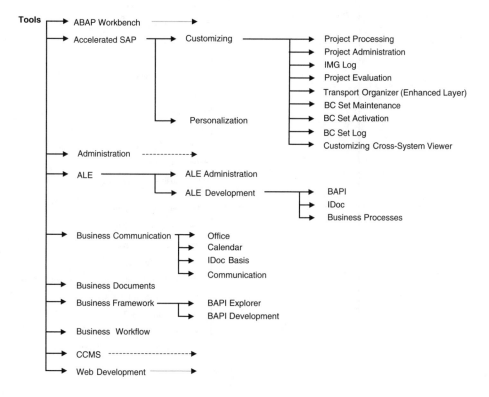

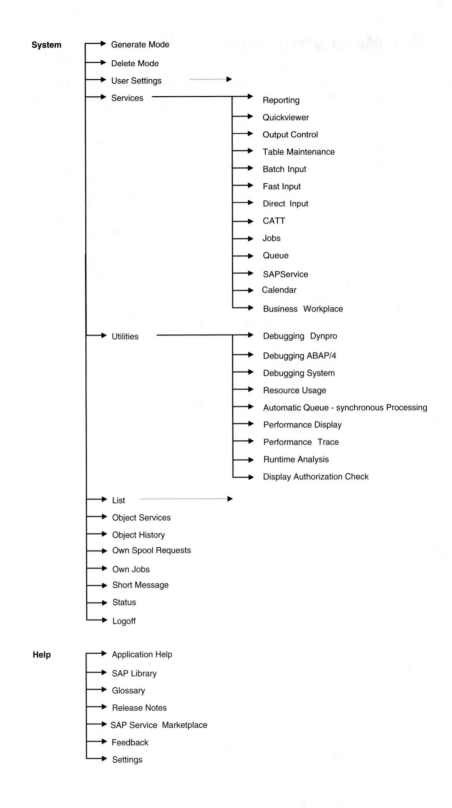

System → Generate Mode
→ Delete Mode
→ User Settings
→ Services → Reporting
→ Quickviewer
→ Output Control
→ Table Maintenance
→ Batch Input
→ Fast Input
→ Direct Input
→ CATT
→ Jobs
→ Queue
→ SAPService
→ Calendar
→ Business Workplace
→ Utilities → Debugging Dynpro
→ Debugging ABAP/4
→ Debugging System
→ Resource Usage
→ Automatic Queue - synchronous Processing
→ Performance Display
→ Performance Trace
→ Runtime Analysis
→ Display Authorization Check
→ List
→ Object Services
→ Object History
→ Own Spool Requests
→ Own Jobs
→ Short Message
→ Status
→ Logoff

Help → Application Help
→ SAP Library
→ Glossary
→ Release Notes
→ SAP Service Marketplace
→ Feedback
→ Settings

The following menu tree shows the activities assigned to menu item "Administration."

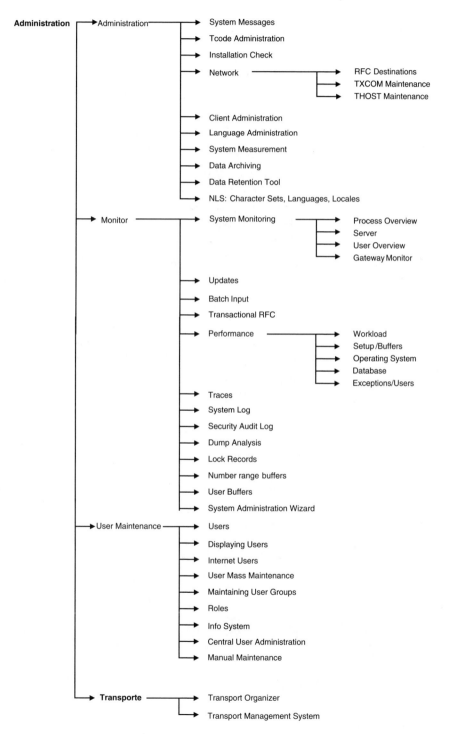

The following menu tree shows the structure of the Computing Center Management System (transaction CCMS).

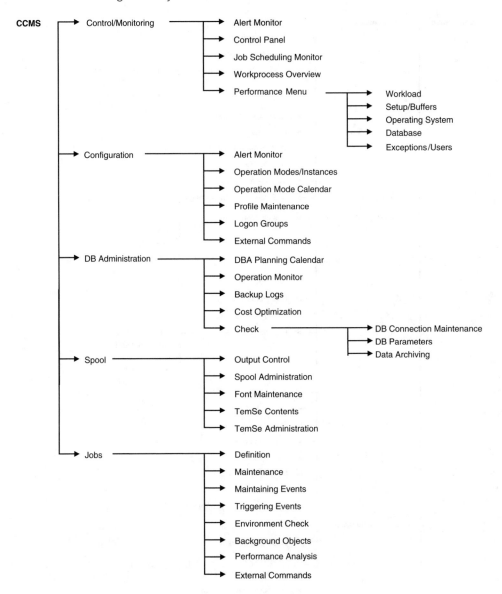

E   Glossary

ABAP
Advanced Business Application Programming. The programming language used in the R/3 system for developing applications.

ABAP Dictionary
Central metadata of all objects in the R/3 system.

ACID
Describes the basic principles of transaction management in the database area and in R/3: stands for Atomic, Consistent, Isolated, Durable.

ADK
Archive Development Kit. Contains tools for defining commercially related data as a logical archiving unit (archiving object), methods for transferring the data to be archived to an archive file in the form of function modules, example programs, documentation, archive administration for starting programs, control of data transfer, network graphics for illustrating the dependencies between archivable data.

ADO
Active Data Object. Application-defined object

ALE
Application Link Enabling. ALE is a technology for creating and operating distributed applications. The main idea behind ALE is to ensure a distributed but integrated R/3 installation. This includes a commercially controlled message exchange with consistent data across loosely linked SAP applications.
Applications are not integrated via a central database, but via synchronous and asynchronous communication. Business objects can be distributed between the systems in an SAP infra-

structure, thanks to the ALE distribution model.
ALE is made up of three layers: application services, distribution services, and communication services.

Alert Monitor
Graphic screen for analyzing system states and events.

ANSI
American National Standards Institute.

API
Application Programming Interface. An API is a logical, closely related set of interfaces (functions or services) for using a range of functions predefined by an application.

APPC
Advanced Program-to-Program Communication. Program-to-program communication within the world of IBM and based on the LU6.2 protocol.

Application server
Synonym: application server. Server on which at least one SAP instance is located.

ArchiveLink
One of the communication interfaces between the mySAP components and external components. One of the basic components of the R/3 system. The SAP ArchiveLink includes the following interfaces:

▶ User interface: Interface to R/3 applications

▶ Interface to external components: archive systems, viewer systems, scan systems

Archiving object
Logical object of commercially related data that can be read from the database with an archiving program. After successful archiving, it can be deleted

from the database using the appropriate delete program.

ASAP
AcceleratedSAP. Standardized process model for implementing R/3 and other SAP solutions.

Background processing
Processing that is not run on the screen. With this procedure, data is processed in the background while other functions can be executed in parallel on the screen. Although the user cannot see the processes in background processing, or have any direct influence over them (dialog mode is not possible), they have the same priority as online processing.

BAPI
Business Application Programming Interface. Standard programming interface that offers external access to the business processes and data in the R/3 system.

Batch input
Methods and tools that allow you to quickly import data from sequential files or spreadsheets to the R/3 database.

CATT
Computer-Aided Test Tool. You can use this tool to create test data and to automate and test business processes.

CCMS
Computing Center Management System. Tool for monitoring, controlling, and configuring the R/3 system. The Computing Center Management System (CCMS) supports 24-hour system administration functions. You can analyze and distribute the system load and monitor the resource requirements of the different system components.

Client
In commercial, organizational and technical terms, a self-contained unit within an SAP system with separate master records within a table.

Control panel
Central tool for monitoring the R/3 system and its instances.

CPI-C
Common Programming Interface Communication. Basic programming interface for synchronous, cross-system, program-to-program communication.

CTS
Change and Transport System. The Change and Transport System (CTS) provides tools for organizing development projects in Customizing and in the ABAP Workbench and for transporting changes between the SAP systems and their clients. The CTS is made up of the following three blocks: Transport Organizer, Transport Management System, Transport Tools.

Customizing
Adapting an SAP component to meet specific customer requirements by selecting different variants, parameter settings, and so on.

Data archiving
Removing data not currently needed from the relational database and storing it in the archive (see also Archiving object).

Database
A database contains files that are necessary for permanent data storage on the hard disk and one or more database instances. Each R/3 system has just one database.

Database instance
An administrative unit that permits access to a database. A database instance consists of database processes

with a shared set of database buffers in the shared memory. As a rule, there is only one database instance per database. An example of a database system in which the database can have more than one database instance is DB2/390.

In an R/3 system, a database instance can either be on its own on a server, or it can be together with one (or theoretically several) SAP instance(s).

Database server
Server on which (at least) one database instance is located.

DBA
Database administrator.

DCL
Data Control Language. Data control language: a language element for checking and controlling transactions or users.

DDL
Data Definition Language. Language elements used to define relations.

Deadlock
A deadlock of several related transactions waiting for locked objects to be released.

DIAG protocol
A communication protocol between the SAP GUI and dialog work processes on the SAP application level.

Dialog work process
R/3 work process for processing user requests working in dialog mode.

Dispatcher
A process for coordinating the work processes in an instance.

DML
Data Manipulation Language. Language elements for queries on data and for changing data.

Dynpro
DYNamic PROgram, consisting of a screen image and its underlying flow logic.

EDI
Electronic Data Interchange. Cross-company electronic exchange of structured data (for example trade documents) between business partners at home or abroad that may be using different hardware, software, and communication services. For this, the data is structured in accordance with defined standards.

FDDI
Fiber Distributed Data Interchange.

Firewall
Software for protecting a local network against unauthorized access from outside.

Front-end computer
"In general, a computer or processing unit that produces or manipulates data before it is received by another processor." (Computer Dictionary, Microsoft Press).

GUI
Graphical User Interface. Medium via which the user can exchange information with the computer. With the user interface, you can select commands, start programs, display files, or execute other options by pressing function keys or pushbuttons, selecting menu options, or clicking on icons with the mouse.

High availability
Capacity of a service or a system to remain in productive operation for a large part of the time. High availability for an R/3 system means that planned and unplanned downtime can be kept to a minimum. Good system administration is vital to high availability. A reduction in unplanned downtime can be achieved by preventative hardware

and software solutions that aim to reduce the single points of failure in the services supported by the R/3 system. Optimal scheduling of necessary maintenance work can help to reduce planned downtime.

HSM
Hierarchical Storage Management. Software and hardware for archiving data. An HSM system manages data internally in a hierarchical structure based on how often the data is accessed and acts like an infinitely large file system for the application.

HTML
Hypertext Markup Language. Platform-independent language for creating text and graphics pages for the Internet.

HTTP
Hypertext Transfer Protocol. Protocol for transferring data between a Web server and the Web client.

IAC
Internet Application Component. Complete business solutions for linking the SAP system to the Internet. With Internet Application Components (IACs), Internet users can execute transactions, functions and reports via a Web browser interface, and in this way, develop business processes via the Internet or intranet.

IDES
International Demonstration and Education System. IDES included several sample enterprises that serve as models for the relevant business processes in the R/3 system. With simple user instructions and varied master and transaction data, various different scenarios can be enacted. IDES is therefore very useful as training material for the project team.

IDoc
Intermediate Document. An IDoc type filled with specific data.

IDoc type
SAP format in which business process data should be transferred. An IDoc is a specific business process in the form of an IDoc type. An IDoc type is described by the following components:

▶ A control record
Its format is the same for all IDoc types.
▶ One or more data records
A data record consists of a fixed administration part and a data part (segment). The number and format of these segments is different for the different IDoc types.
▶ The status records
They describe the processing stages that an IDoc can pass through. Status records have the same format for all IDoc types.

IMG
Implementation Guide. A tool provided for customer-specific adjustments to the R/3 system. For each application component, the implementation guide contains:

▶ All steps for the implementation of the R/3 system.
▶ All standard settings and all activities for configuring the R/3 system.

The hierarchical structure of the IMG mirrors the structure of the R/3 application components and lists all documentation that is relevant to the implementation of the R/3 system.

Instance
SAP instance. Administrative unit in which the processes of an SAP system that offer one or more services are grouped together.
The following services can be provided by an R/3 instance:

▶ D: Dialog
▶ V: Update

- E: SAP lock management (enqueue)
- B: Background processing (background)
- S: Print formatting (spool)
- G: SAP gateway

An SAP instance consists of a dispatcher and one or more work processes for each of the individual services and a shared set of SAP buffers in the Shared Memory.

The dispatcher manages processing requests. Work processes execute these requests. Each instance provides at least one dialog service and one gateway. Optionally, they can also provide additional services. Only one instance should provide the service of SAP lock management.

IPC
Inter Process Communication.

ITS
Internet Transaction Server. Interface between the SAP system and a Web server for creating dynamic HTML pages.

LAN
Local Area Network. A network within a location that usually has higher transfer rates than in a WAN environment.

LDAP
Lightweight Directory Access Protocol. Protocol for accessing information directories. LDAP enables each application on any platform to access directory information such as e-mail addresses and public keys. LDAP is an open protocol, which means that for the user, the type of server that the directory is located on is irrelevant.

LUW
Logical Unit of Work. From a business logic point of view, there is an intrinsic sequence of database operations that follows the ACID principle (whether executed in its entirety, or not at all). From the database system point of

view, this sequence constitutes a unit that helps to ensure data integrity.

MAPI
Messaging Application Programming Interface. Interface via which SAPoffice mails can also be read from other applications (MAPI clients), such as Microsoft Outlook.

MCOD
Multiple Components in one Database. The combined installation of OLTP and OLAP components of an SAP system infrastructure in a single database, such as an R/3 system and an EBP system in one database. This can help to reduce database administration costs.

OLE
Object Linking and Embedding.

OLTP
Online Transaction Processing. Processing related to data updates.

OMS
Output Management System.

Operation mode
Operation mode. Defines the number and type of work processes in one or more instances during a particular period. Operation modes can be changed automatically.

OS
Operating System.

OSS
Online Service System. The OSS is one of SAP's central service and support systems. The OSS can be used by all SAP customers and partners. New service offers are only made available via the SAP Service Marketplace however.

PAI
Process after input. Technical program flows after data is input into a screen template (in applications developed in ABAP).

PBO
Process before output. Technical program flows before data is output to a screen template (in applications developed in ABAP).

Performance
System performance, operational capacity, measure of the efficiency of a DP system.

Popup
A screen window that is called by and displayed in a primary window.

Port
The name for the channel via which the R/3 system exchanges data with an external system.

Profile
1. Technical grouping of authorizations. Generated automatically by the profile generator as part of role maintenance.
2. Files on operating-system level according to which the R/3 system parameters are set when started (for example, the instance profile).

Profile Generator
A tool for creating profiles in role maintenance with which an authorization profile is automatically generated based on activities in a role.

Pushbutton
An element of the graphical user interface (GUI). By simply clicking on the pushbutton, you can execute the task that is linked to it. Pushbuttons can be activated with the mouse, but also by using the keyboard. To do this, place the keyboard cursor over the corresponding button and press the **ENTER** key. Pushbuttons can contain text and/or graphic symbols.

Q-API
Queue Application Programming Interface for buffered, asynchronous data transfer between decentralized applications and the SAP systems R/2 and R/3, based on CPI-C.

R/3
Realtime System 3.

RAID
Redundant Array of Independent Disks. A hardware-based technology that supports disk redundancy by using disk mirroring and related methods.

RDBMS
Relational Database Management System.

RFC
Remote Function Call. RFC is an SAP interface protocol based on CPI-C. Consequently, the programming of communication flows between systems is made significantly easier. With RFCs, predefined functions can be called and executed on a remote system or within the same system. RFCs monitor communication control, the transfer of parameters, and the handling of errors.

Role
A grouping of activities executed by one person and which contribute to one or more business scenarios in a company. The definition of roles includes authorizations, reports, and user menus.

SAP GUI
SAP Graphical User Interface (see also GUI).

SAP transaction (=SAP LUW)
A logical process in the R/3 system which, from the user's point of view, constitutes a self-contained unit. An SAP transaction guarantees ACID principles over several database transaction steps. The short form for transaction code, with which an ABAP program can be called.

SAProuter
A software module that acts as part of a firewall system and controls network connections between your R/3 network and the outside world (for example SAPNet connection).

Server
The term server has more than one meaning in the SAP environment and should therefore only be used when it is absolutely clear if you are referring to a logical unit such as an SAP instance or a physical unit such as a computer.

Session
A user session in an SAP GUI window.

Shared memory
Main memory area that can be accessed by several operating-system processes, for example, all the work processes in an instance. Sometimes used in the area of RDBMS. Also used to refer to the main memory area shared by the RDBMS processes.

SID
SAP System Identifier. Placeholder for the three-character name of an R/3 system.

SNC
Secure Network Communication. Interface via which the R/3 system can communicate with an external security product to protect the communication connections between the components of an R/3 system.

SQL
Structured Query Language.

SSCR
SAP Software Change Registration. A procedure for registering manual changes to SAP sources and SAP repository objects.

Support package
Collection of corrections provided by SAP for a defined release version of an SAP component (previously: Hot Package).

System infrastructure
Specific system configuration as installed at a customer site. The system infrastructure refers to the necessary systems and clients and their purpose, together with the transport routes for the implementation and maintenance process. The main methods and techniques used are client copy and the transport system. The system infrastructure could, for example, include a development system, a test system, a consolidation system, and a production system.

TCP/IP
Transmission Control Protocol/Internet Protocol.

TDC
Transport domain controller. The application server of an R/3 system in the transport domain, from which transport events between the R/3 systems in that domain are controlled.

TemSe
Temporary sequential objects. Data retention in output management.

TMS
Transport Management System. A tool for managing the transport requests between R/3 systems.

TO
Transport Organizer. Comprehensive tool for managing all change and transport requests.

Transaction
Database transaction: An operational unit on the database that fulfills the ACID principle.

Transaction code
Sequence of alphanumeric characters that identify a transaction in the SAP system.

Transport
A term from R/3 software logistics: The export and import of SAP objects between SAP systems.

Transport domain
A logical group of SAP systems between which transport occurs in accordance with certain rules. The domain is controlled by the Transport Domain Controller.

tRFC
Transactional RFC. RFC for which the ACID principles are applied.

URL
Uniform Resource Locator. Address on the Internet.

WAN
Wide Area Network. A network of computers that covers a relatively large geographical area. WANs are usually made up of at least two LANs (Local Area Networks). Computers connected to this type of network are usually linked via a public network, such as the telephone network. The connection can also be created using rented lines or satellite. The largest WAN is the Internet.

WORM
Write Once, Read Multiple. A memory medium that can be written to only once, but can be read any number of times. WORM guarantees that data written here cannot be changed for several years. The main area of use is in data archiving.

WP: Work process.
The application services of the R/3 system deal with special processes, for example for dialog management, posting change documents, background processing, spooling, lock management. Work processes are assigned to dedicated application servers.

XML
eXtensible Markup Language. A W3C specification. XML is a slimmed down version of SGML that has been specially developed for Web documents. Using XML, you can create tags for providing functions that cannot be implemented with HTML. Thus, for example XML supports links to several documents, whereas HTML links can only reference one document. XML has become the standard for data exchange. In the SAP environment, XML is used both for exchanging data with external systems and also (since Basis release 6.10) as a description language in the configuration files in installation.

F   Bibliography

Kasturi, Rajeev. *SAP R/3 ALE & EDI Technologies*. McGraw Hill 1999.

McFarland Metzger, Sue/Röhrs, Susanne. *SAP R/3 Change and Transport Management: The Official SAP Guide*. Sybex 2000.

SAP AG. *Online documentation Release 4.6C*. http://help.sap.com.

SAP AG. *Online documentation Release 6.20*. http://help.sap.com.

SAP AG. *R/3 Installation Guide Release 4.6C*.

http://service.sap.com/instguides.

SAP AG. *Installation Guide Web Application Server 6.20*. http://service.sap.com/instguides.

SAP AG. *SAPinst Troubleshooting Guide V1.20*. http://service.sap.com/sapinst.

SAP AG. *Language import guide*. http://service.sap.com/instguides.

SAP AG. *Online Help Installation Guide*. http://service.sap.com/instguides.

SAP AG. *Security Guides Bd. I-III*. http://service.sap.com/securityguides.

SAP Labs. *SAP Guide System administration*. SAP PRESS, Bonn 2002.

Schneider, Thomas. *SAP Performance Optimization Guide. Analyzing and Tuning SAP Systems*. 3rd edition. SAP PRESS, Bonn 2003.

Stefani, Helmut: *Archiving Your SAP Data*. SAP PRESS, Bonn 2002.

Index

SAP APO
System Administration

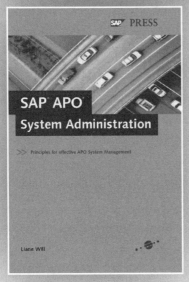

SAP PRESS
240 pages, 2003, hardcover
ISBN 1-59229-012-4

>>> **www.sap-press.com**

Liane Will

SAP APO System Administration
Principles for effective APO
System Management

The administration tasks of an APO
System differ significantly from
those you may be used to with your
R/3 System. This book introduces you
to the architectural innovations of
an APO System and to the distinc-
tive features of APO Administration.
Get up to speed quickly on the
management of liveCache, a central
element of APO. You also learn
about LCApps, which put the application logic into effect, and key
optimization factors. Performance,
a critical element in the successful
use of APO, is a major focus throughout. This book is suitable for use as
preparation for your APO consultant certification, and the included
CD contains detailed roadmaps for
APO introduction and maintenance.

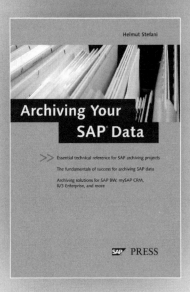

SAP Database
Administration

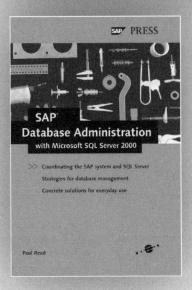

SAP PRESS
328 pages, 2002, hardcover
ISBN 1-59229-005-1

>>> www.sap-press.com

Paul Read
**SAP Database Administration
with Microsoft SQL Server 2000**

This book offers you expert information about SAP database administration using Microsoft SQL Server 2000. The book treats all aspects of SQL Server and the SAP system that play a part in coordinating the two systems productively.

You will learn how to handle routine administration tasks using SAP system tools, with the help of SQL Server tools. Besides providing guidance for practical administration, the author also gives suggestions for developing a database strategy tailored to your specific system landscape. Valuable techniques and indispensable tips for dealing with crises make this book especially useful. The Appendix describes all the parameters that are important for configuring Windows, the SAP instance profiles, and SQL Server.

The book is based on SQL Server 2000. Where the 2000 version differs appreciably from SQL Server 7.0, this release is also considered.

Recommended Reading
by SAP PRESS

Business

N. Egger
SAP BW Professional

IBM Business
Consulting Services
SAP Authorization System

G. Oswald
**SAP Service
and Support**

Rickayzen, Dart,
Brennecke, Schneider
**Practical Workflow
for SAP**

R. Buck-Emden
mySAP CRM

Technical

A. Goebel, D. Ritthaler
SAP Enterprise Portal

S. Hagemann, L. Will
**SAP R/3 System
Administration**

Brochhausen, Kielisch,
Schnerring, Staeck
**SAP HR Technical Principles
and Programming**

T. Schneider
**SAP Performance
Optimization Guide**

F. Heinemann, C. Rau
**Web Programming with the
SAP Web Application Server**

L. Will
**SAP APO System
Administration**

W.Hertleif, C. Wachter
SAP Smart Forms

H. Keller, J. Jacobitz
**ABAP Objects –
The Official Reference**

H. Stefani (Ed.)
Archiving Your SAP Data

www.sap-press.com

Interested in reading more?

Please visit our Web site for all
new book releases from SAP PRESS.

www.sap-press.com